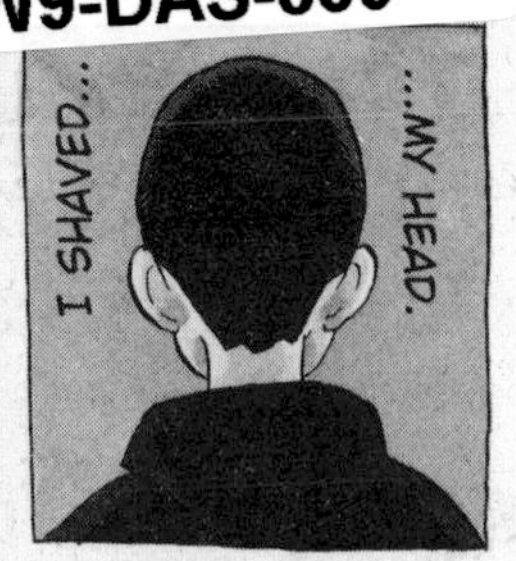
I SHAVED...
...MY HEAD.

村田雄介

Yusuke Murata

It's hard for a manga artist to keep his hair short. And it's getting pretty warm, so I took the plunge and used clippers to shave my head. I'm surprised by how well the bubbles foam up when I use shampoo.

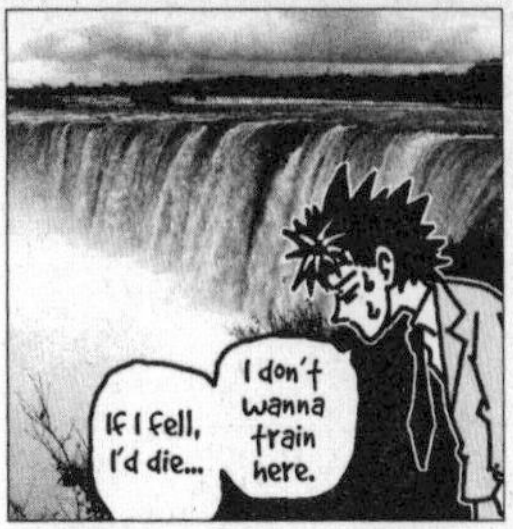
I don't wanna train here.
If I fell, I'd die...

稲垣理一郎

Riichiro Inagaki

In preparation for *Eyeshield* moving on to the world stage, I traveled from New York to Canada and saw all sorts of stuff, but 90 percent of research never gets used. There's no need to force it into the story. Anticipating a silly episode about special training at Niagara Falls, I went there and filmed it, but then never used the footage. That's lucky for Sena!

Eyeshield 21 is the most exciting football manga to hit the scene. A collaborative effort between writer Riichiro Inagaki and artist Yusuke Murata, ***Eyeshield 21*** was originally serialized in Japan's ***Weekly Shonen Jump***. An OAV created for Shueisha's Anime Tour is available in Japan, and the ***Eyeshield 21*** hit animated TV series debuted in spring 2005!

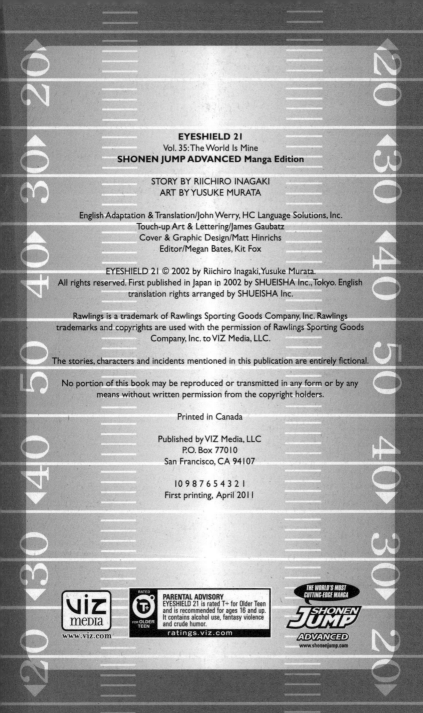

EYESHIELD 21
Vol. 35: The World Is Mine
SHONEN JUMP ADVANCED Manga Edition

STORY BY RIICHIRO INAGAKI
ART BY YUSUKE MURATA

English Adaptation & Translation/John Werry, HC Language Solutions, Inc.
Touch-up Art & Lettering/James Gaubatz
Cover & Graphic Design/Matt Hinrichs
Editor/Megan Bates, Kit Fox

Printed in Canada

Published by VIZ Media, LLC
P.O. Box 77010
San Francisco, CA 94107

10 9 8 7 6 5 4 3 2 1
First printing, April 2011

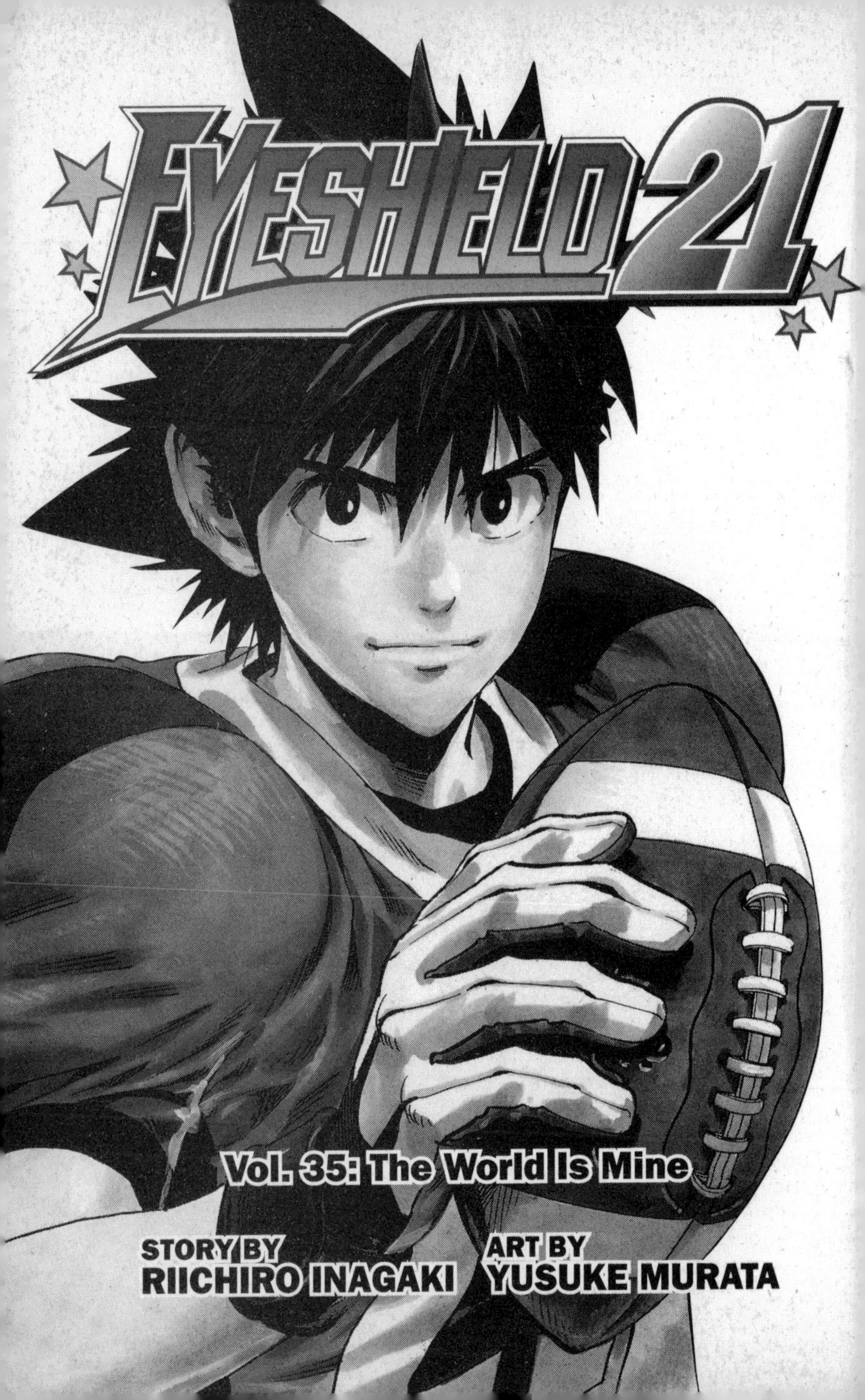

EYESHIELD 21

Vol. 35: The World Is Mine

STORY BY
RIICHIRO INAGAKI

ART BY
YUSUKE MURATA

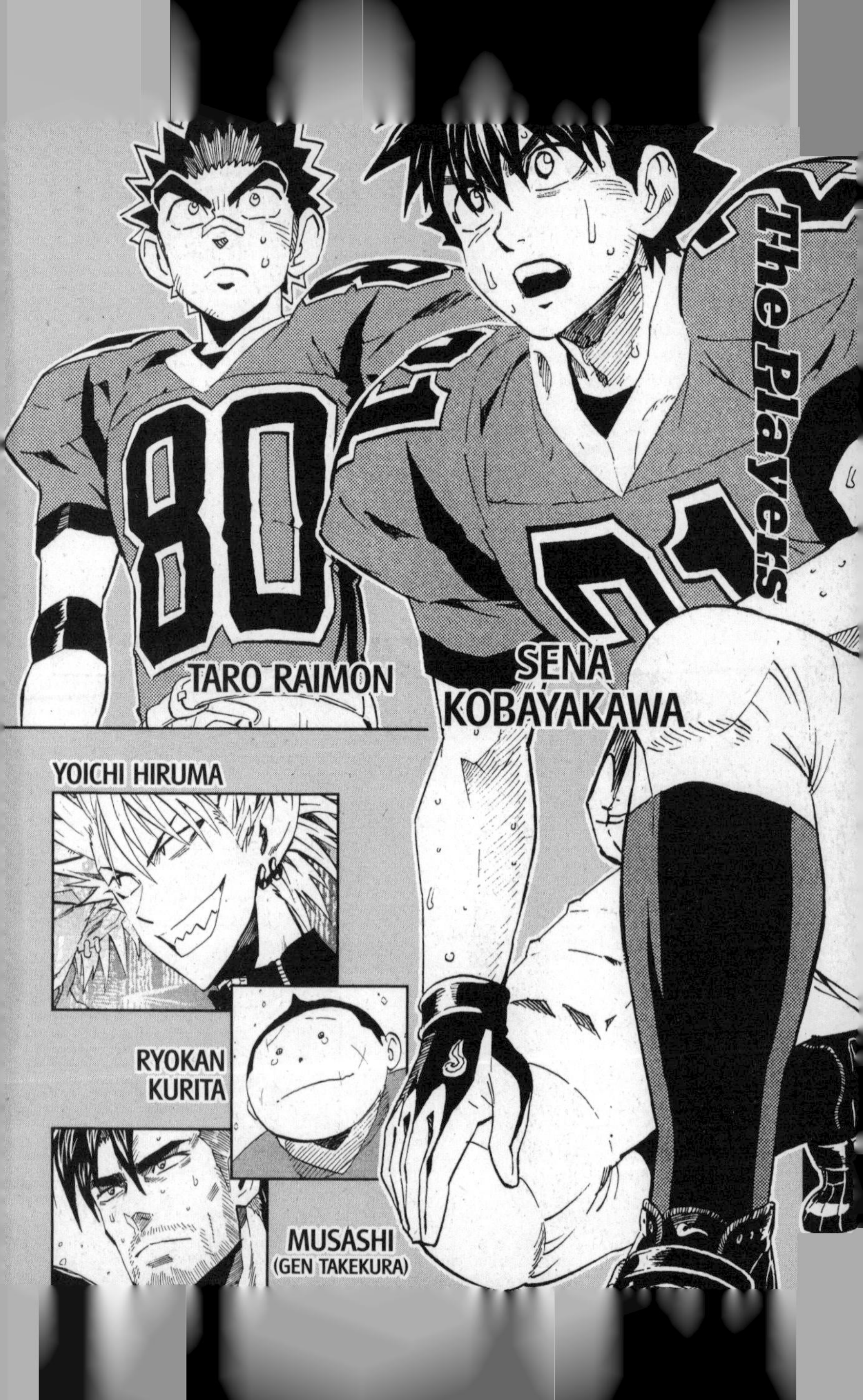
The Players
SENA KOBAYAKAWA
TARO RAIMON
YOICHI HIRUMA
RYOKAN KURITA
MUSASHI (GEN TAKEKURA)

The Story So Far

Shy Sena Kobayakawa joins the Deimon High School football team to reinvent himself. Sena's exceptional running ability comes to light and he competes under a secret identity, Eyeshield 21.

After many trials and tribulations, Deimon reaches the national championship match—the Christmas Bowl! Their opponent is the invincible Teikoku High School. But not a single Devil Bat gives up! Sena runs in a whole new dimension and gets past the unbeatable Yamato!! Deimon wins the championship, and then Sena and Monta hear about an event called the Youth World Cup…

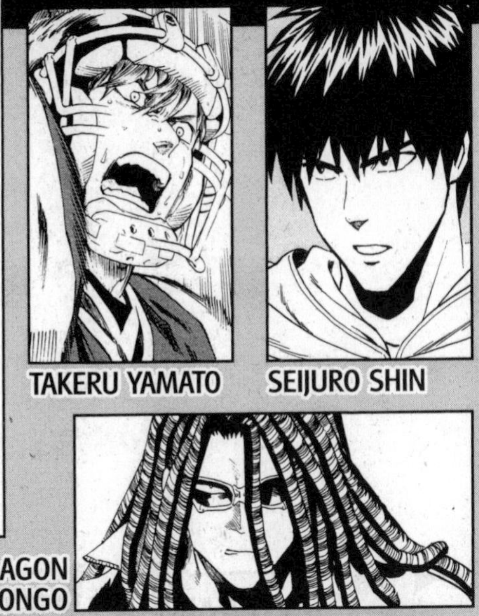
SEIJURO SHIN
TAKERU YAMATO
AGON KONGO

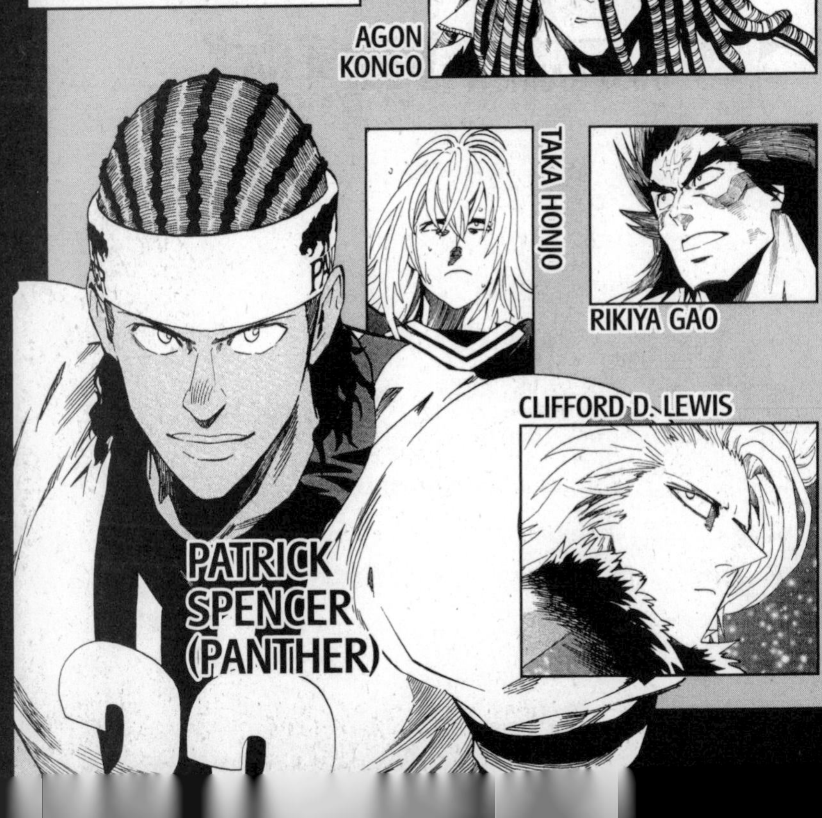
RIKIYA GAO
TAKA HONJO
CLIFFORD D. LEWIS
PATRICK SPENCER (PANTHER)

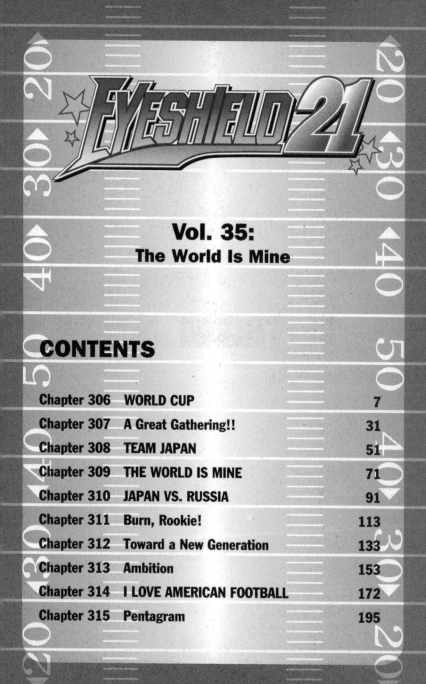

EYESHIELD 21

Vol. 35:
The World Is Mine

CONTENTS

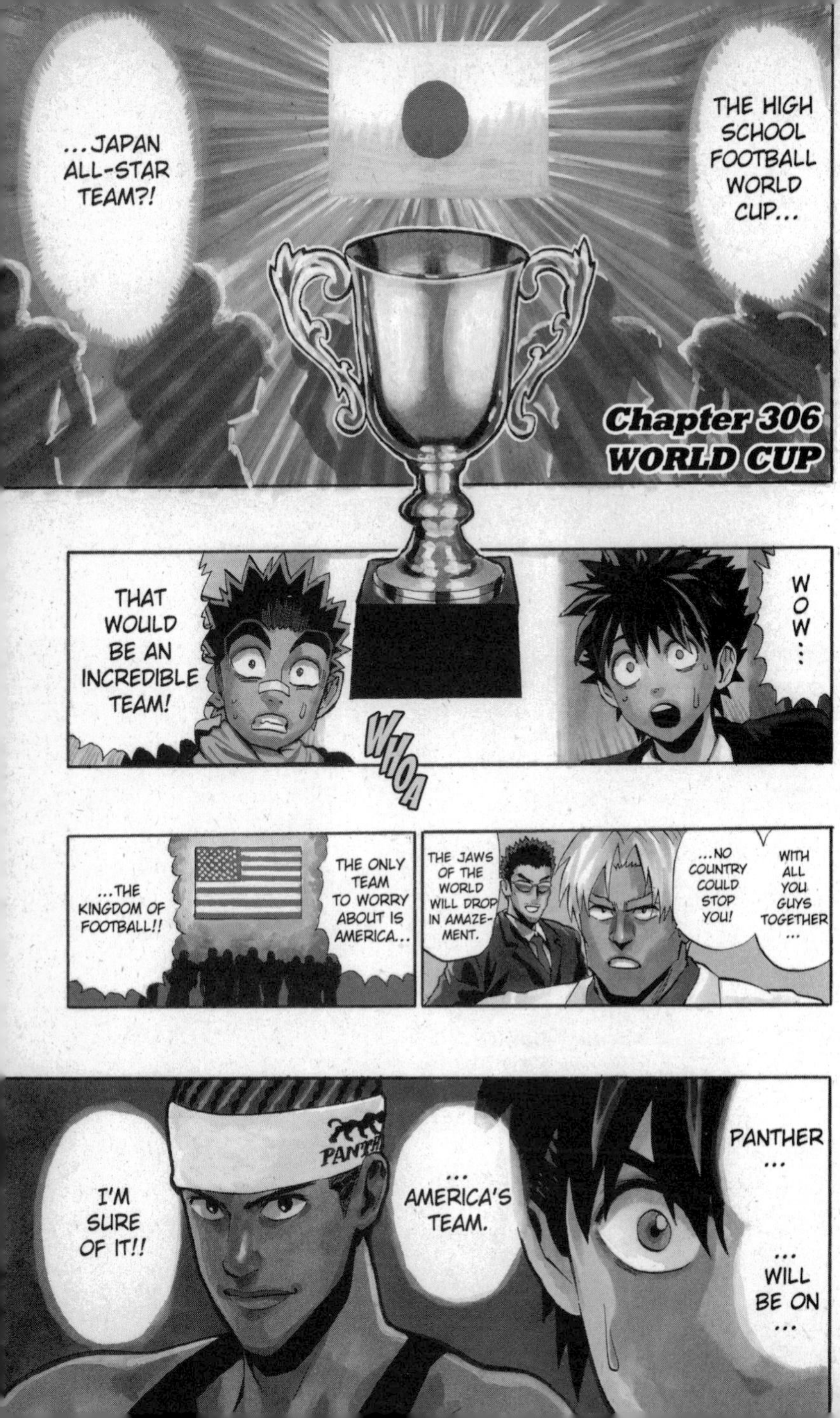

THE HIGH SCHOOL FOOTBALL WORLD CUP...
...JAPAN ALL-STAR TEAM?!
Chapter 306
WORLD CUP
WOW...
THAT WOULD BE AN INCREDIBLE TEAM!
WHOA
WITH ALL YOU GUYS TOGETHER...
...NO COUNTRY COULD STOP YOU!
THE JAWS OF THE WORLD WILL DROP IN AMAZEMENT.
THE ONLY TEAM TO WORRY ABOUT IS AMERICA...
...THE KINGDOM OF FOOTBALL!!
PANTHER...
...WILL BE ON...
...AMERICA'S TEAM.
I'M SURE OF IT!!

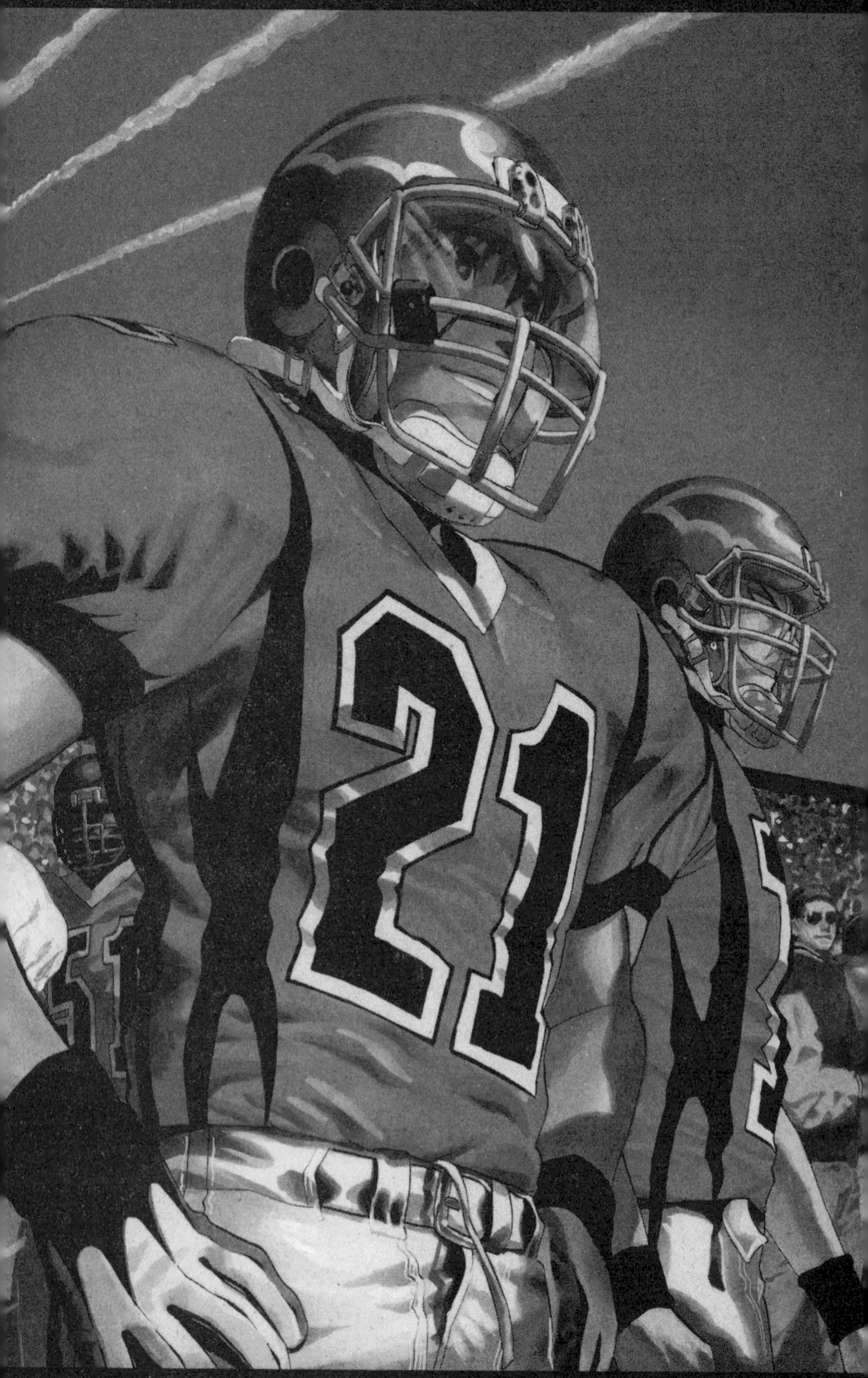

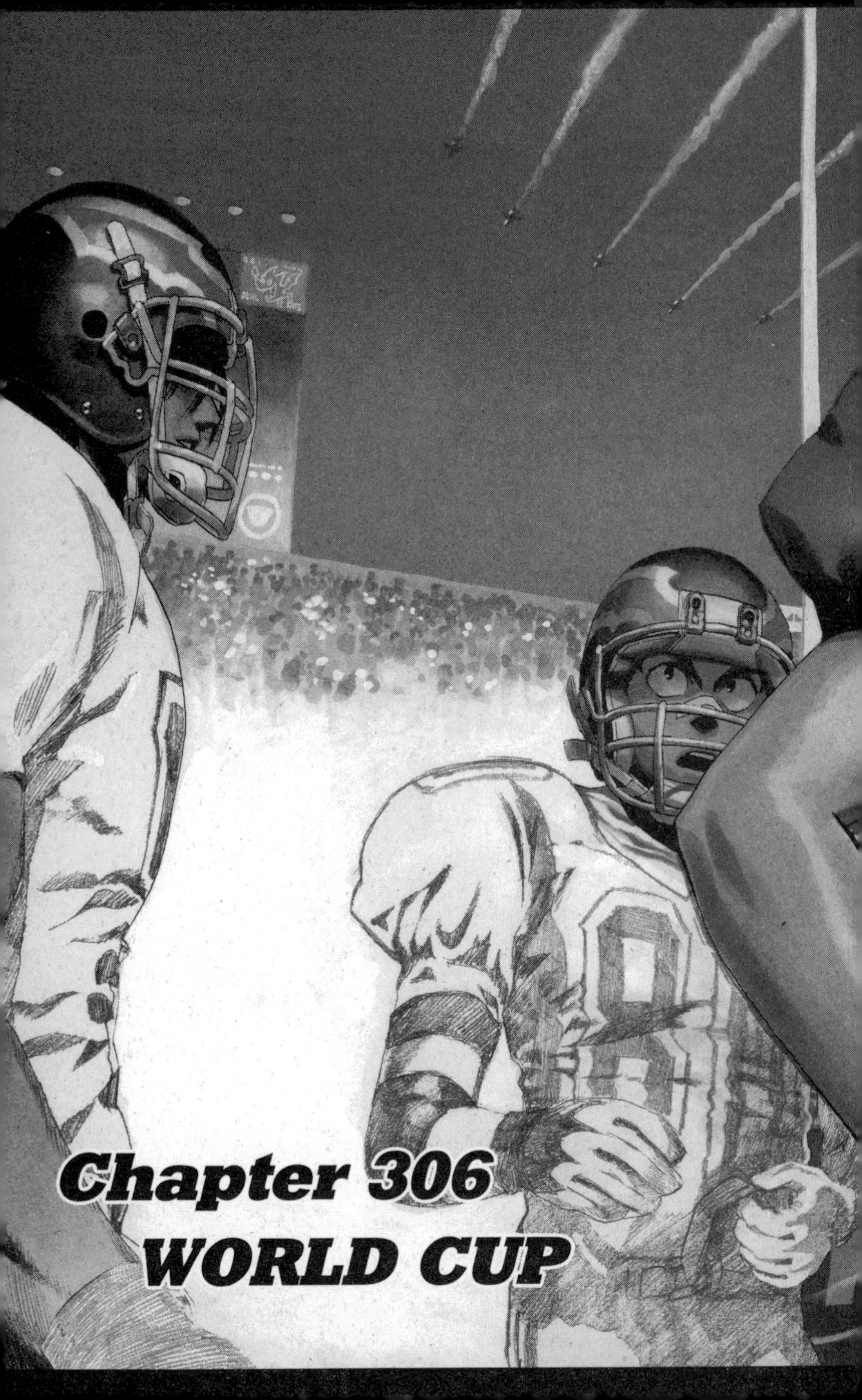
Chapter 306
WORLD CUP

Devil Bat 021

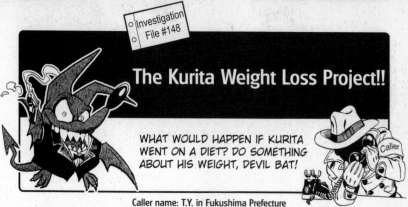

Investigation File #148

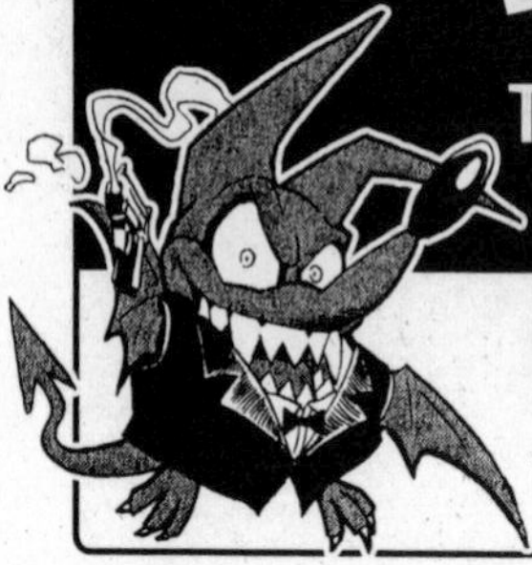

The Kurita Weight Loss Project!!

WHAT WOULD HAPPEN IF KURITA WENT ON A DIET? DO SOMETHING ABOUT HIS WEIGHT, DEVIL BAT!

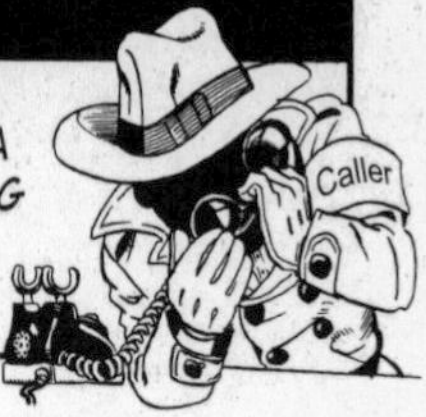
Caller

Caller name: T.Y. in Fukushima Prefecture

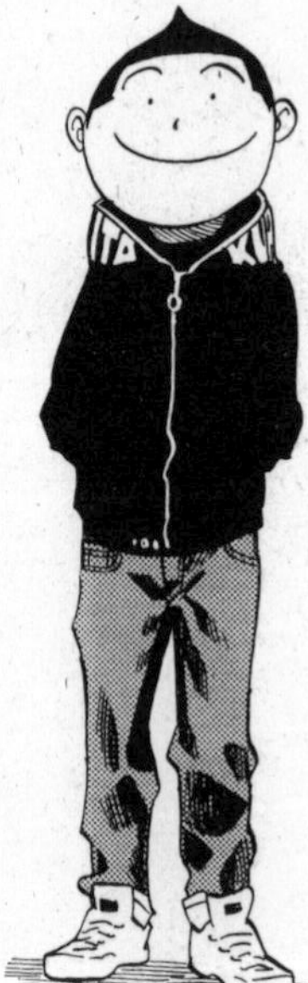
KITA
KU

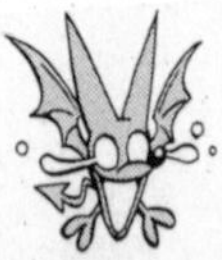

HE DOESN'T HAVE ANY BALANCE!!

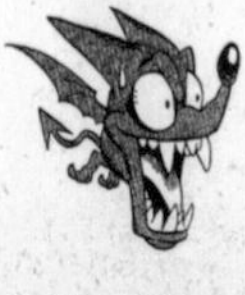

THAT HEAD-SIZE MUST BE GENETIC...

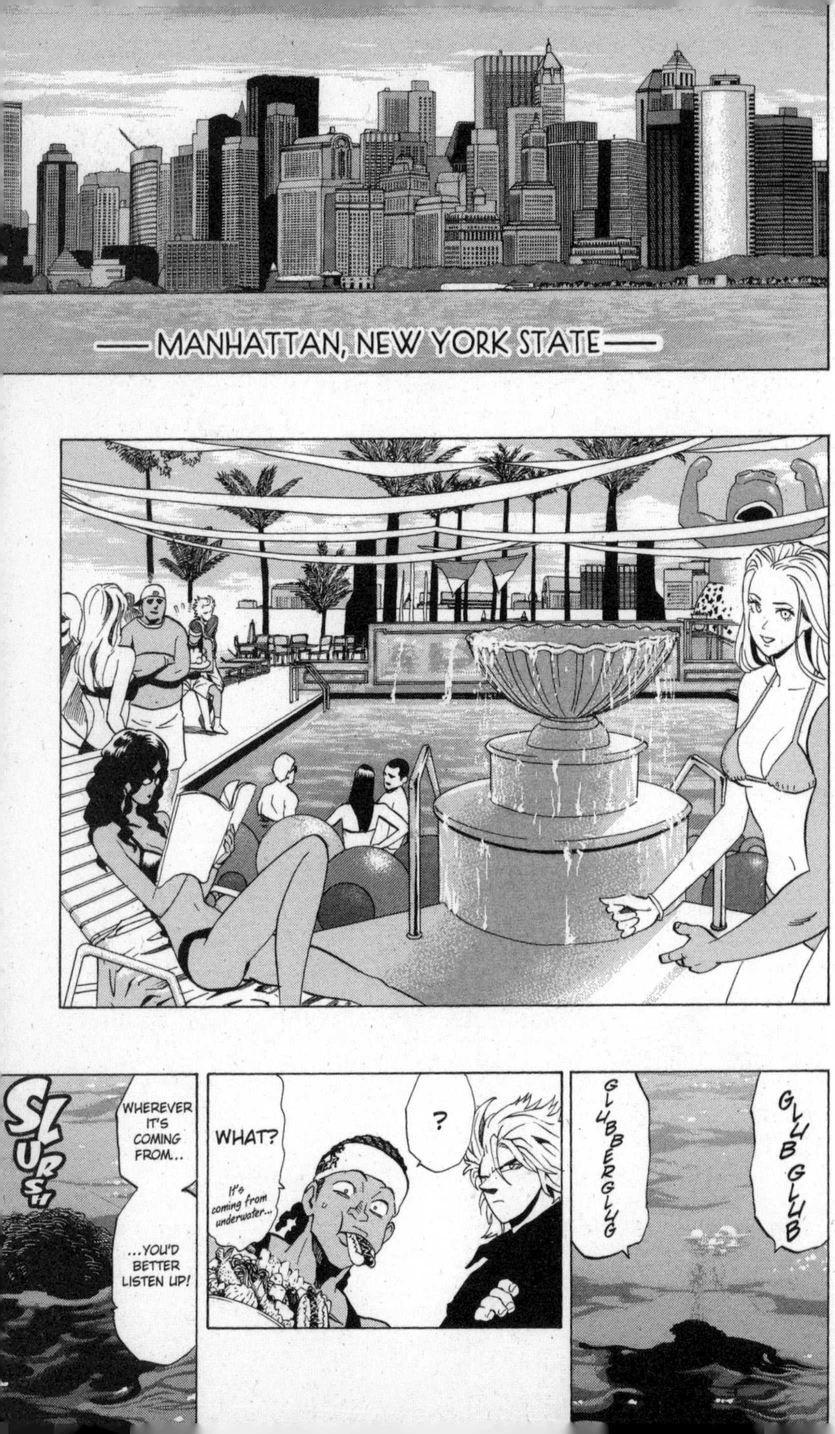
—MANHATTAN, NEW YORK STATE—
GLUB GLUB GLUB
GLUBBERGLUG
?
WHAT?
It's coming from underwater...
WHEREVER IT'S COMING FROM..
SLURSH
...YOU'D BETTER LISTEN UP!

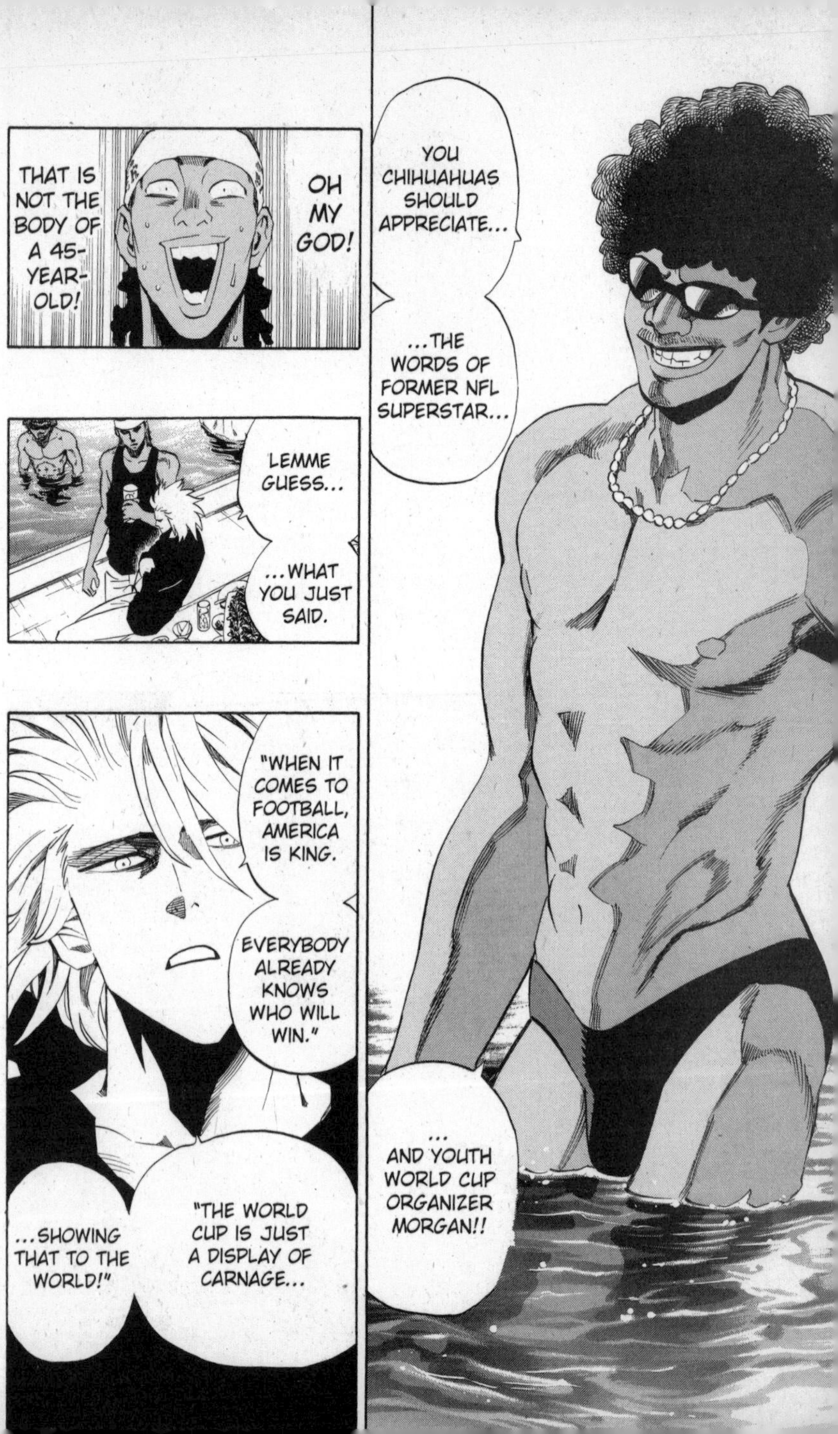
YOU CHIHUAHUAS SHOULD APPRECIATE...
...THE WORDS OF FORMER NFL SUPERSTAR...
...AND YOUTH WORLD CUP ORGANIZER MORGAN!!
OH MY GOD!
THAT IS NOT THE BODY OF A 45-YEAR-OLD!
LEMME GUESS...
...WHAT YOU JUST SAID.
"WHEN IT COMES TO FOOTBALL, AMERICA IS KING.
EVERYBODY ALREADY KNOWS WHO WILL WIN."
"THE WORLD CUP IS JUST A DISPLAY OF CARNAGE...
...SHOWING THAT TO THE WORLD!"

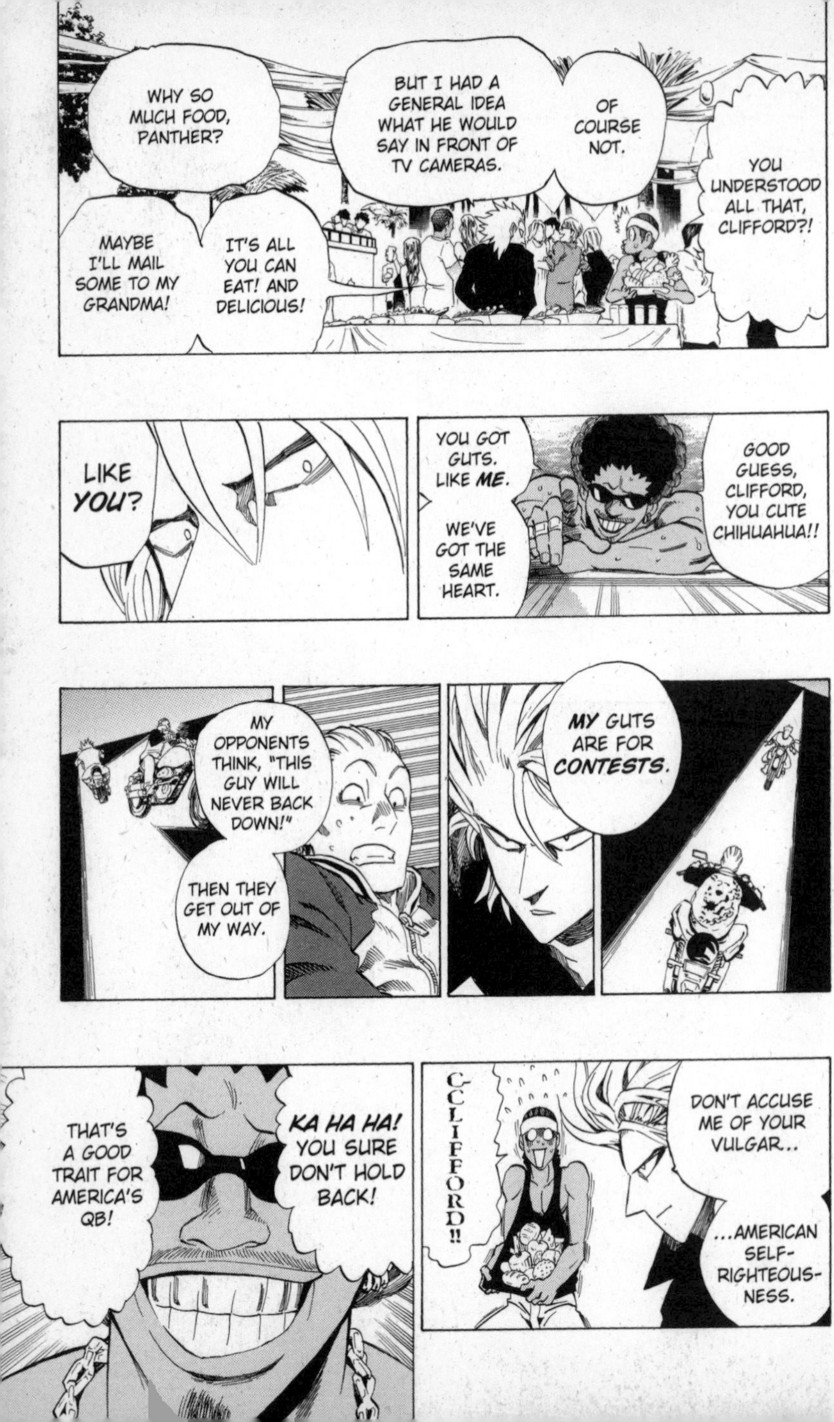
YOU UNDERSTOOD ALL THAT, CLIFFORD?!
OF COURSE NOT.
BUT I HAD A GENERAL IDEA WHAT HE WOULD SAY IN FRONT OF TV CAMERAS.
WHY SO MUCH FOOD, PANTHER?
IT'S ALL YOU CAN EAT! AND DELICIOUS!
MAYBE I'LL MAIL SOME TO MY GRANDMA!
GOOD GUESS, CLIFFORD, YOU CUTE CHIHUAHUA!!
YOU GOT GUTS. LIKE *ME*.
WE'VE GOT THE SAME HEART.
LIKE *YOU*?
MY GUTS ARE FOR *CONTESTS*.
MY OPPONENTS THINK, "THIS GUY WILL NEVER BACK DOWN!"
THEN THEY GET OUT OF MY WAY.
DON'T ACCUSE ME OF YOUR VULGAR...
...AMERICAN SELF-RIGHTEOUSNESS.
C-CLIFFORD!!
KA HA HA! YOU SURE DON'T HOLD BACK!
THAT'S A GOOD TRAIT FOR AMERICA'S QB!

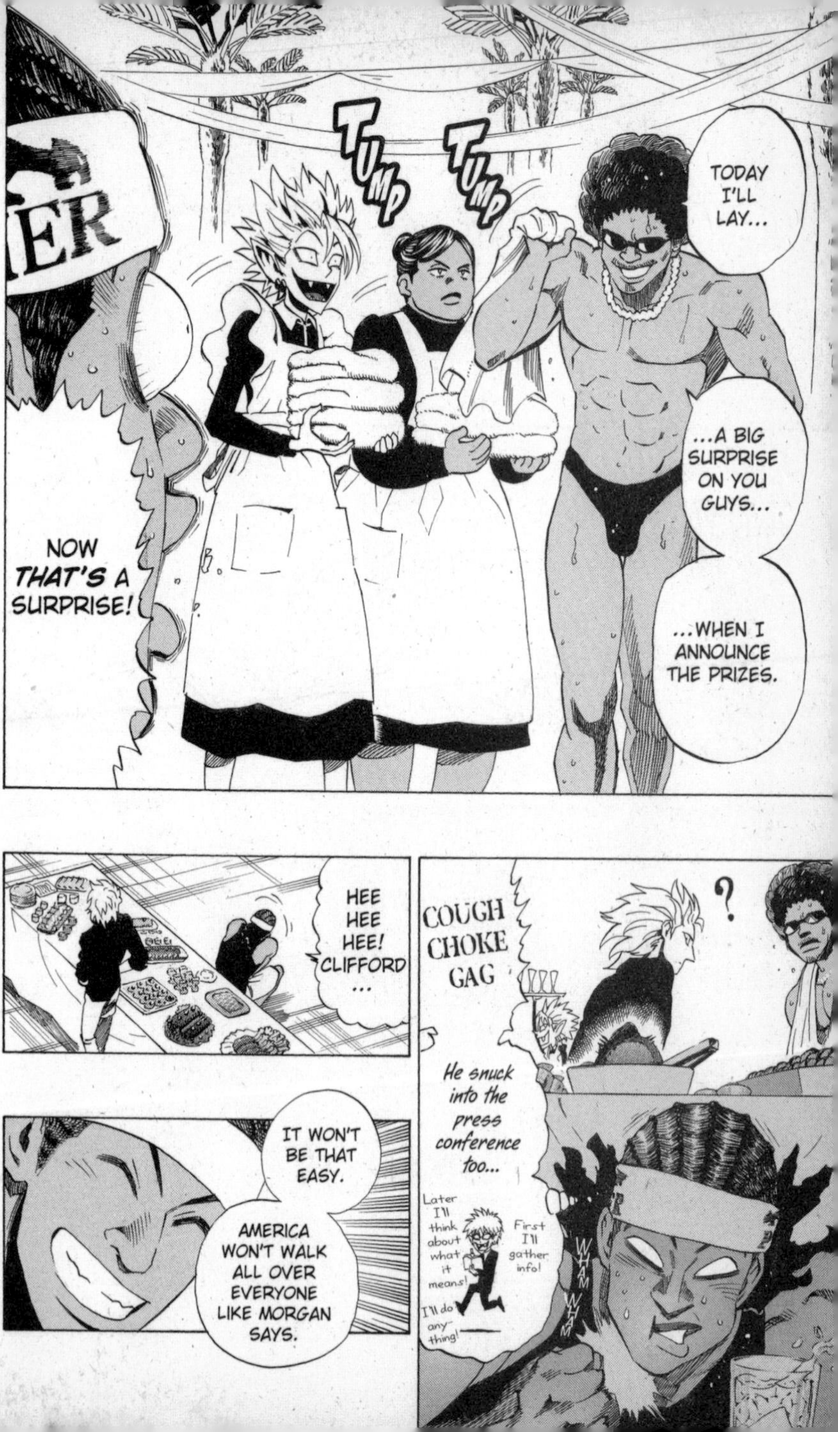
TUMP
TUMP
TODAY I'LL LAY...
...A BIG SURPRISE ON YOU GUYS...
...WHEN I ANNOUNCE THE PRIZES.
NOW THAT'S A SURPRISE!
?
COUGH CHOKE GAG
HEE HEE HEE! CLIFFORD ...
He snuck into the press conference too...
First I'll gather info!
Later I'll think about what it means!
I'll do any-thing!
WHAM WHAM
IT WON'T BE THAT EASY.
AMERICA WON'T WALK ALL OVER EVERYONE LIKE MORGAN SAYS.

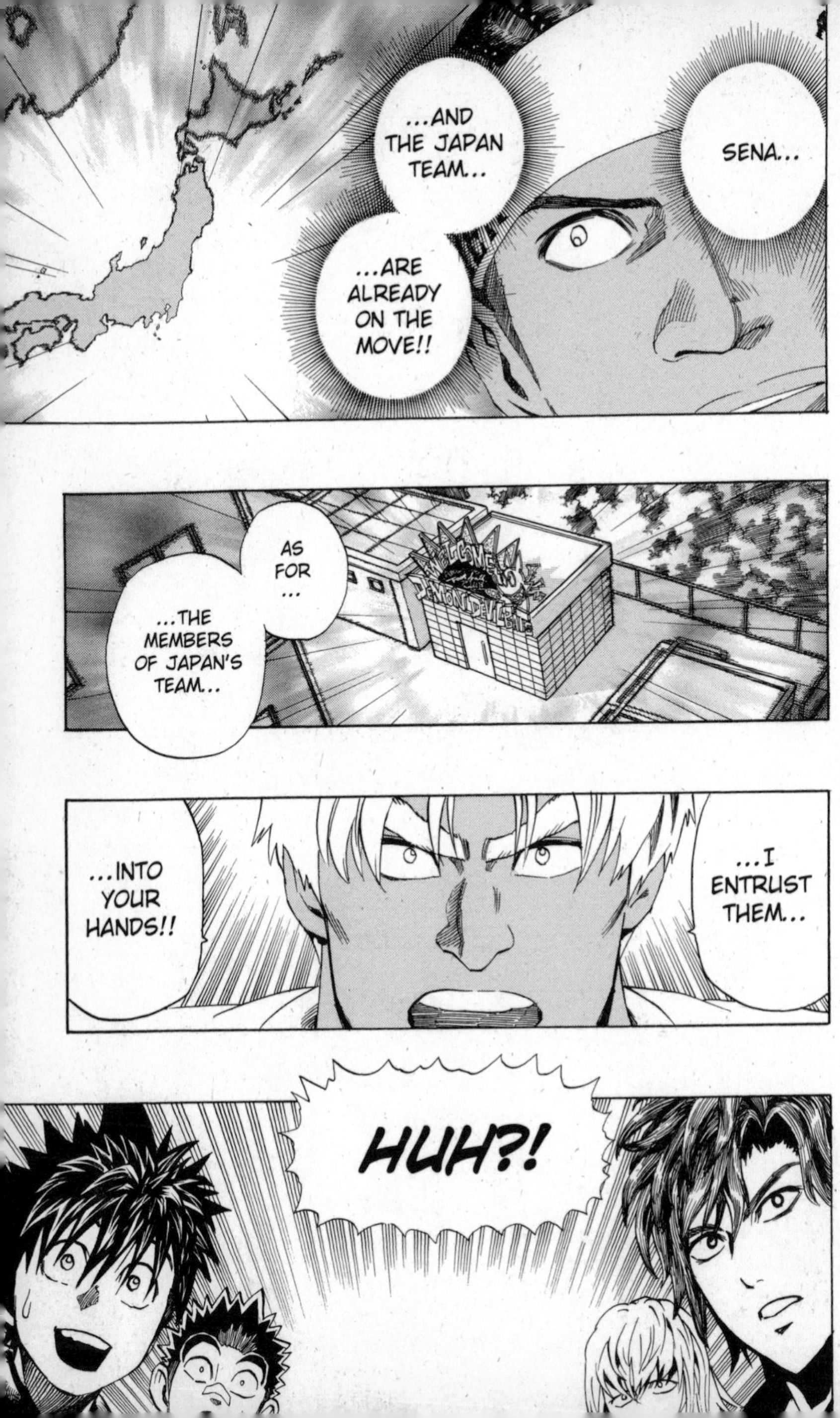
SENA...
...AND THE JAPAN TEAM...
...ARE ALREADY ON THE MOVE!!
AS FOR ...
...THE MEMBERS OF JAPAN'S TEAM...
...I ENTRUST THEM...
...INTO YOUR HANDS!!
HUH?!

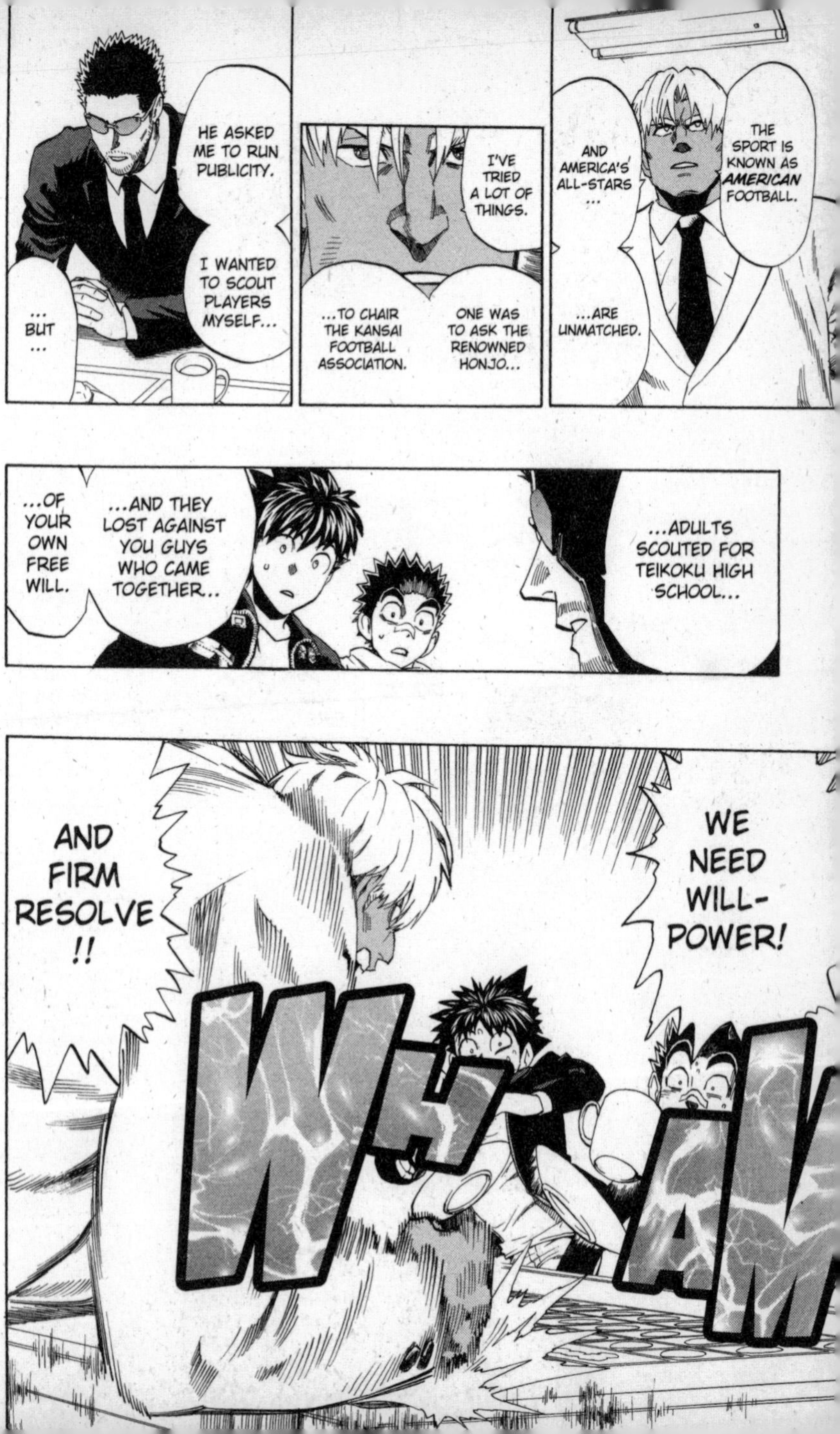
THE SPORT IS KNOWN AS AMERICAN FOOTBALL.
AND AMERICA'S ALL-STARS ...
...ARE UNMATCHED.
I'VE TRIED A LOT OF THINGS.
ONE WAS TO ASK THE RENOWNED HONJO...
...TO CHAIR THE KANSAI FOOTBALL ASSOCIATION.
HE ASKED ME TO RUN PUBLICITY.
I WANTED TO SCOUT PLAYERS MYSELF...
... BUT ...
...ADULTS SCOUTED FOR TEIKOKU HIGH SCHOOL...
...AND THEY LOST AGAINST YOU GUYS WHO CAME TOGETHER...
...OF YOUR OWN FREE WILL.
WE NEED WILL-POWER!
AND FIRM RESOLVE !!
WHAM

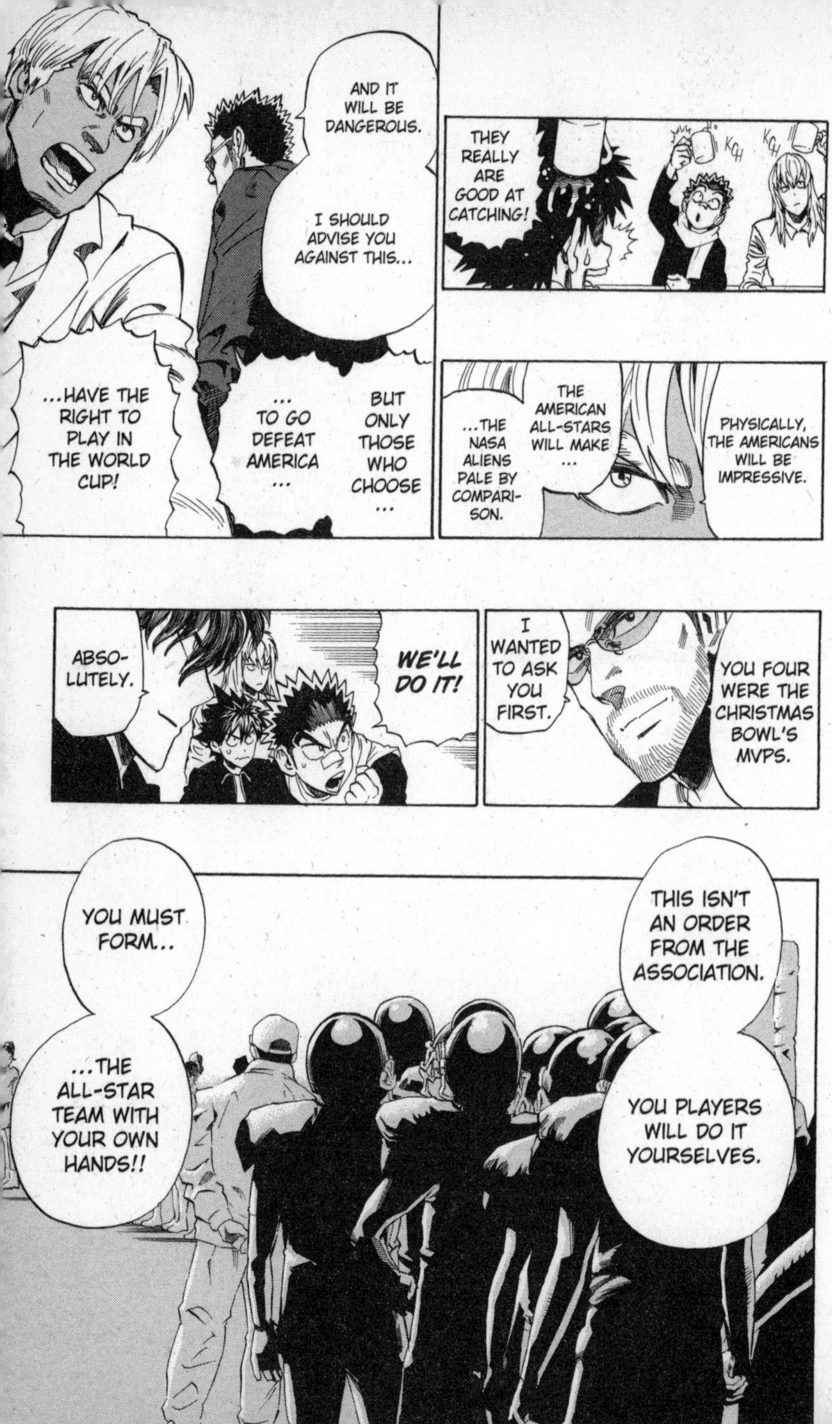

THEY REALLY ARE GOOD AT CATCHING!
KCH
KCH
PHYSICALLY, THE AMERICANS WILL BE IMPRESSIVE.
THE AMERICAN ALL-STARS WILL MAKE...
...THE NASA ALIENS PALE BY COMPARI-SON.
AND IT WILL BE DANGEROUS.
I SHOULD ADVISE YOU AGAINST THIS...
BUT ONLY THOSE WHO CHOOSE...
...TO GO DEFEAT AMERICA...
...HAVE THE RIGHT TO PLAY IN THE WORLD CUP!
YOU FOUR WERE THE CHRISTMAS BOWL'S MVPS.
I WANTED TO ASK YOU FIRST.
WE'LL DO IT!
ABSO-LUTELY.
THIS ISN'T AN ORDER FROM THE ASSOCIATION.
YOU PLAYERS WILL DO IT YOURSELVES.
YOU MUST FORM...
...THE ALL-STAR TEAM WITH YOUR OWN HANDS!!

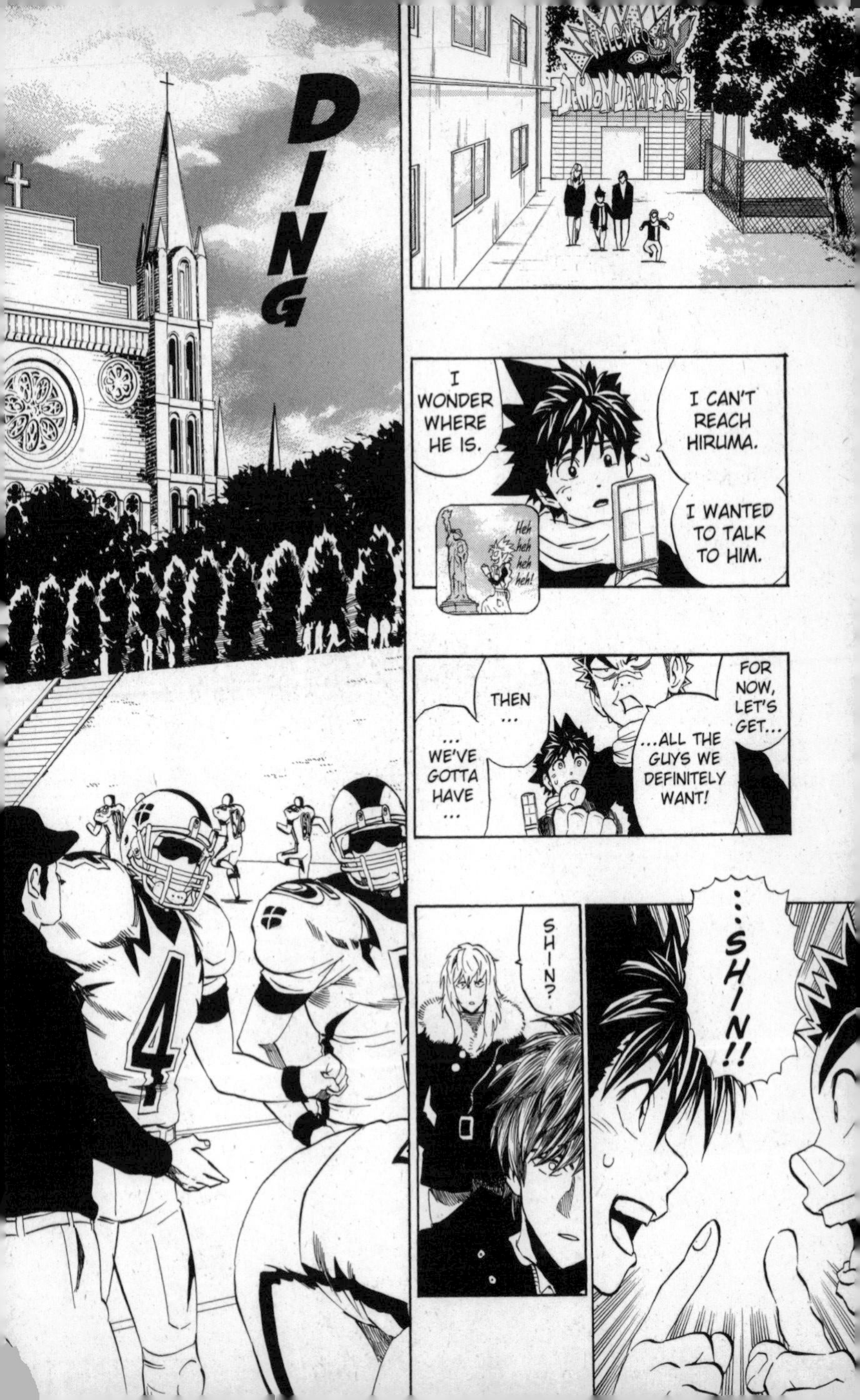
I CAN'T REACH HIRUMA.
I WANTED TO TALK TO HIM.
I WONDER WHERE HE IS.
Heh heh heh heh!
FOR NOW, LET'S GET...
...ALL THE GUYS WE DEFINITELY WANT!
THEN...
...WE'VE GOTTA HAVE...
...SHIN!!
SHIN?
DING

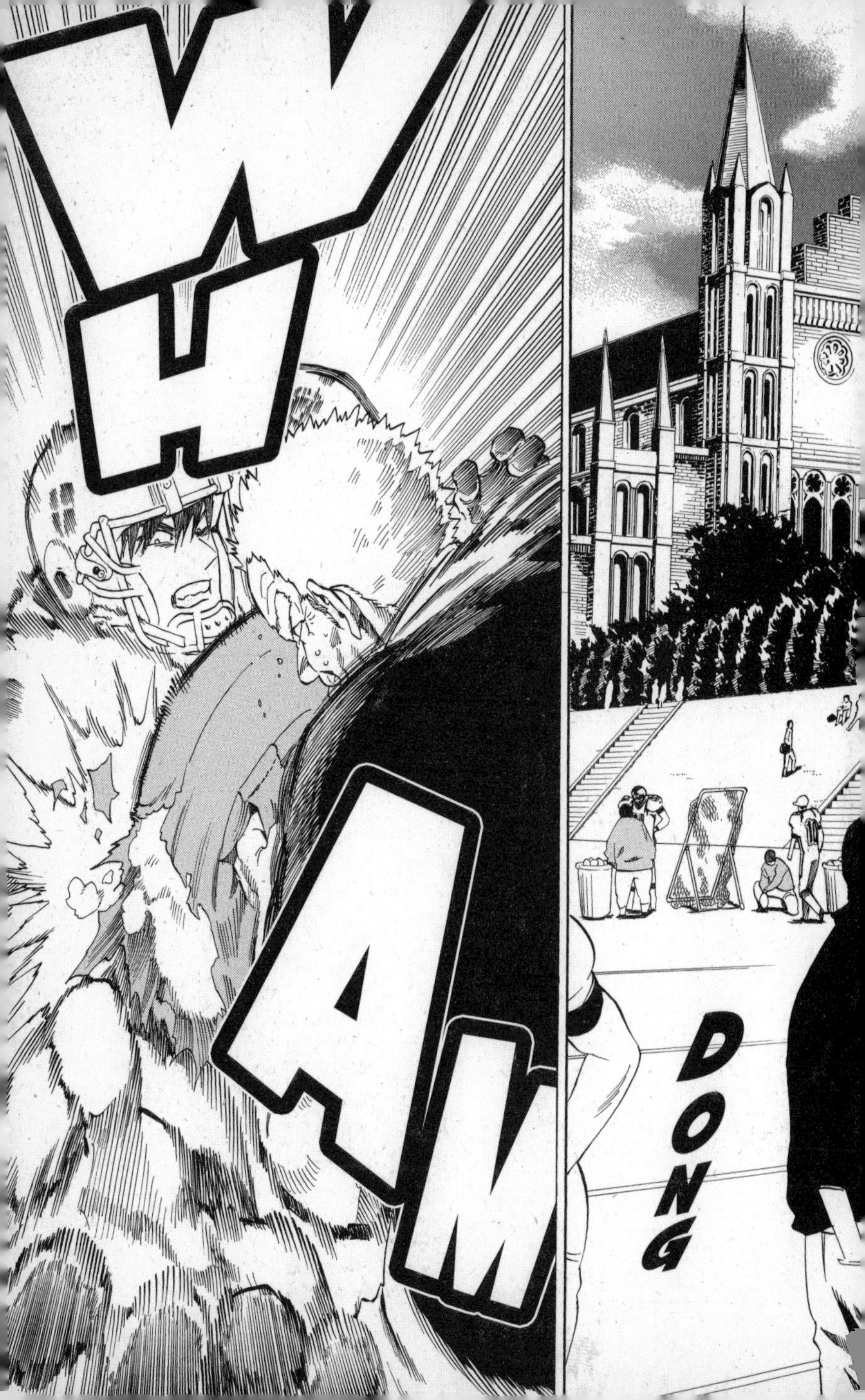
DONG
WHAM

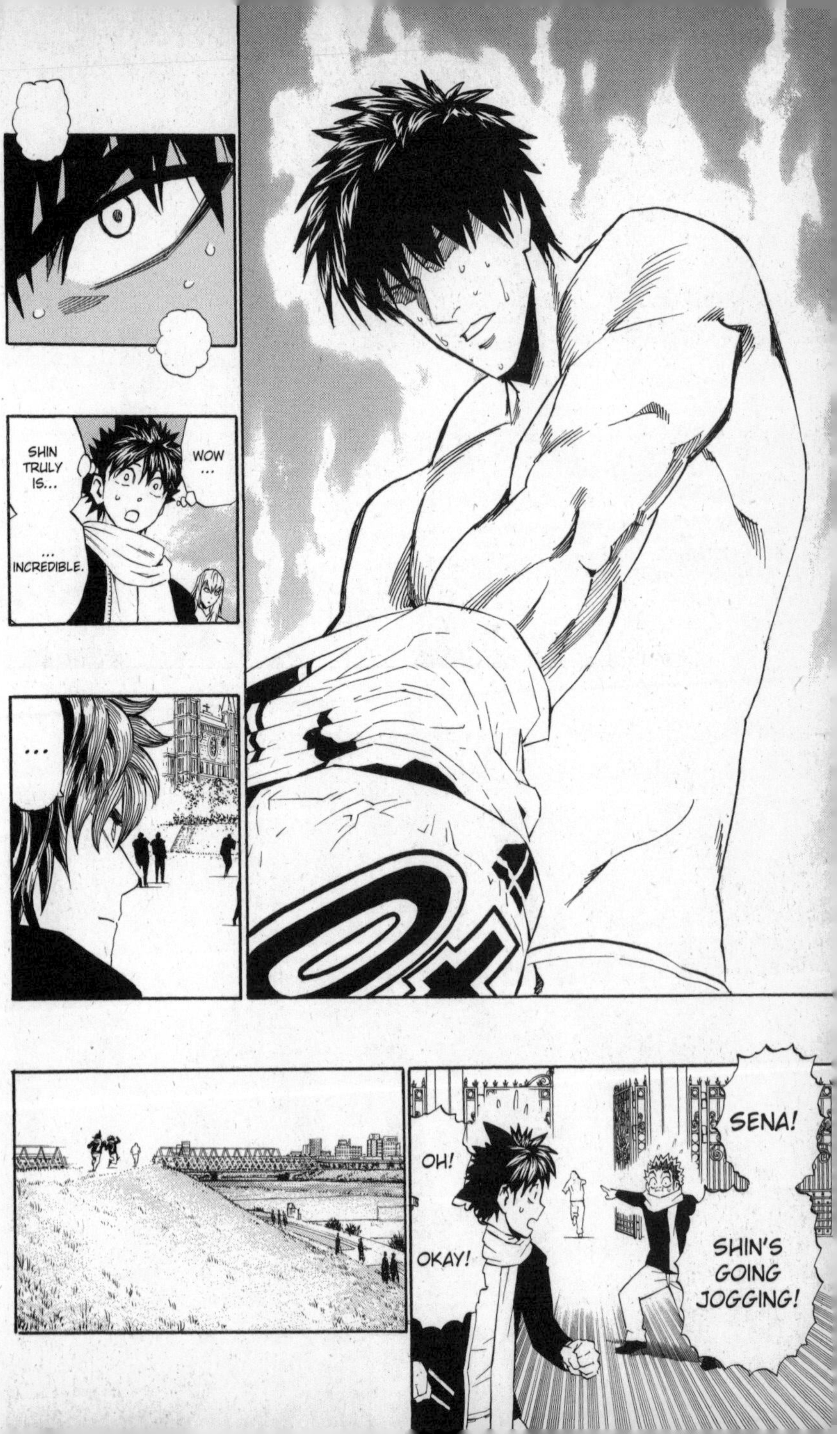
WOW...
SHIN TRULY IS...
...INCREDIBLE.
...
SENA!
SHIN'S GOING JOGGING!
OH!
OKAY!

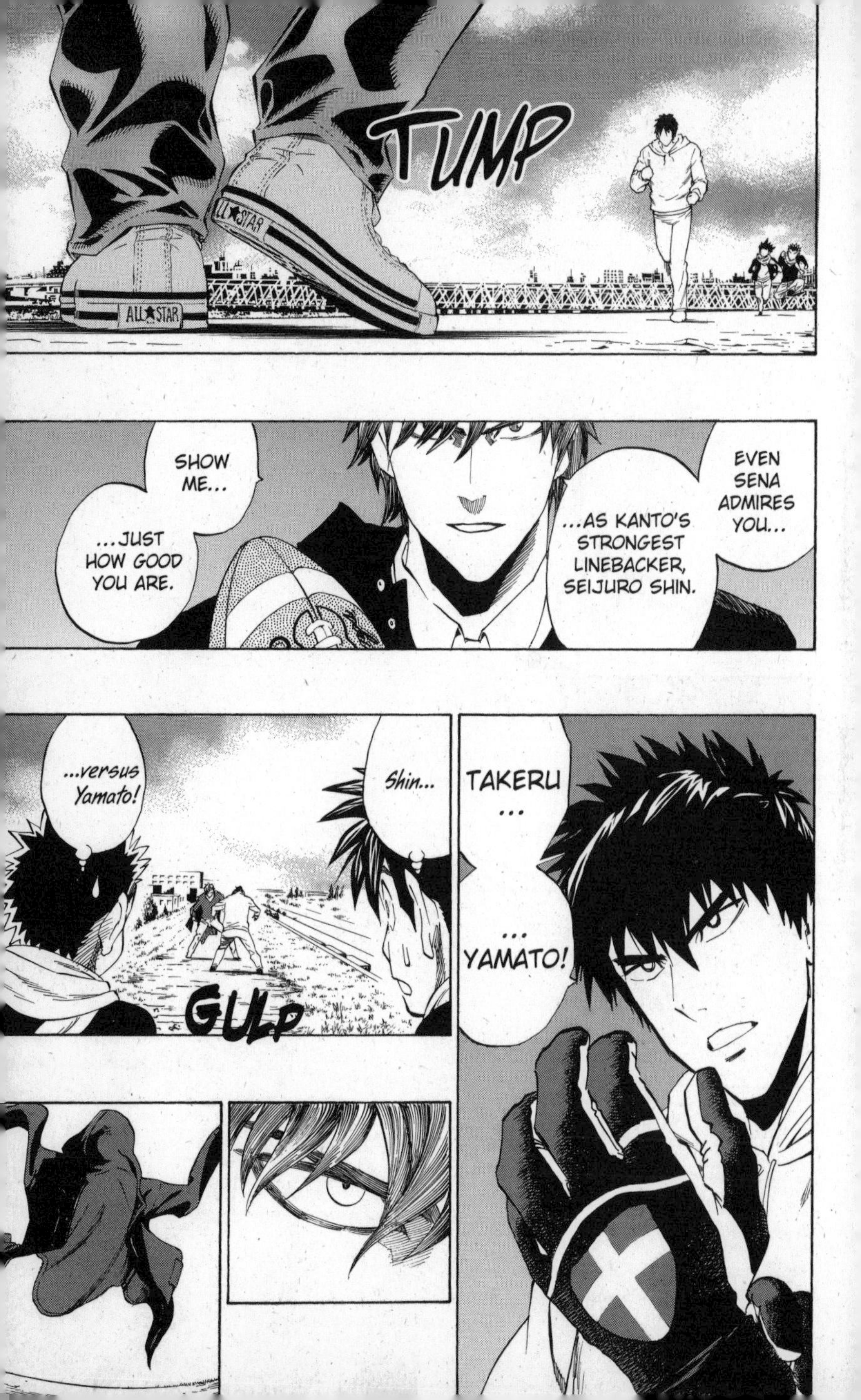
TUMP
ALL★STAR
ALL★STAR
EVEN SENA ADMIRES YOU...
...AS KANTO'S STRONGEST LINEBACKER, SEIJURO SHIN.
SHOW ME...
...JUST HOW GOOD YOU ARE.
TAKERU ...
... YAMATO!
Shin...
...versus Yamato!
GULP

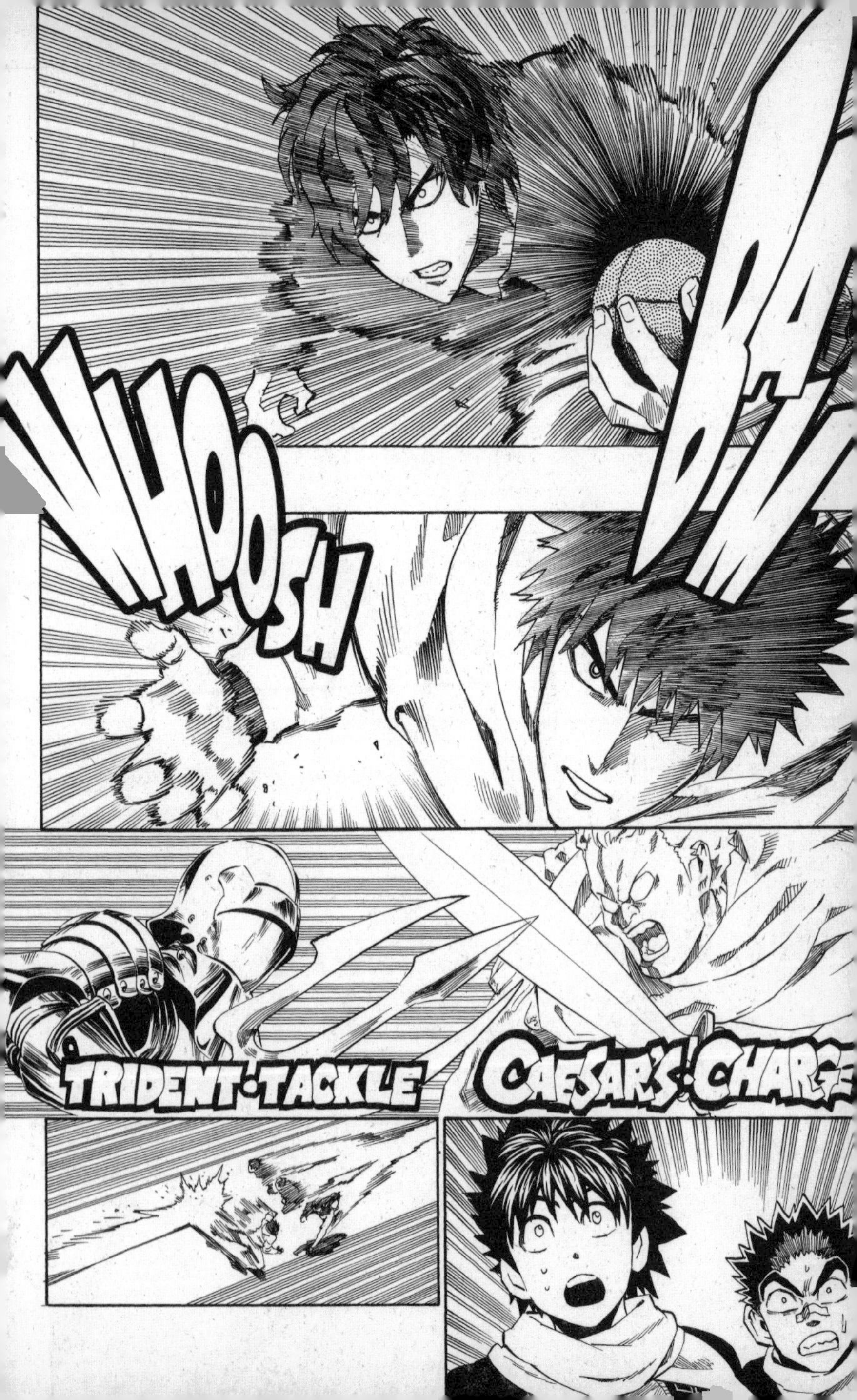
WHOOSH
CAESAR'S CHARGE
TRIDENT TACKLE

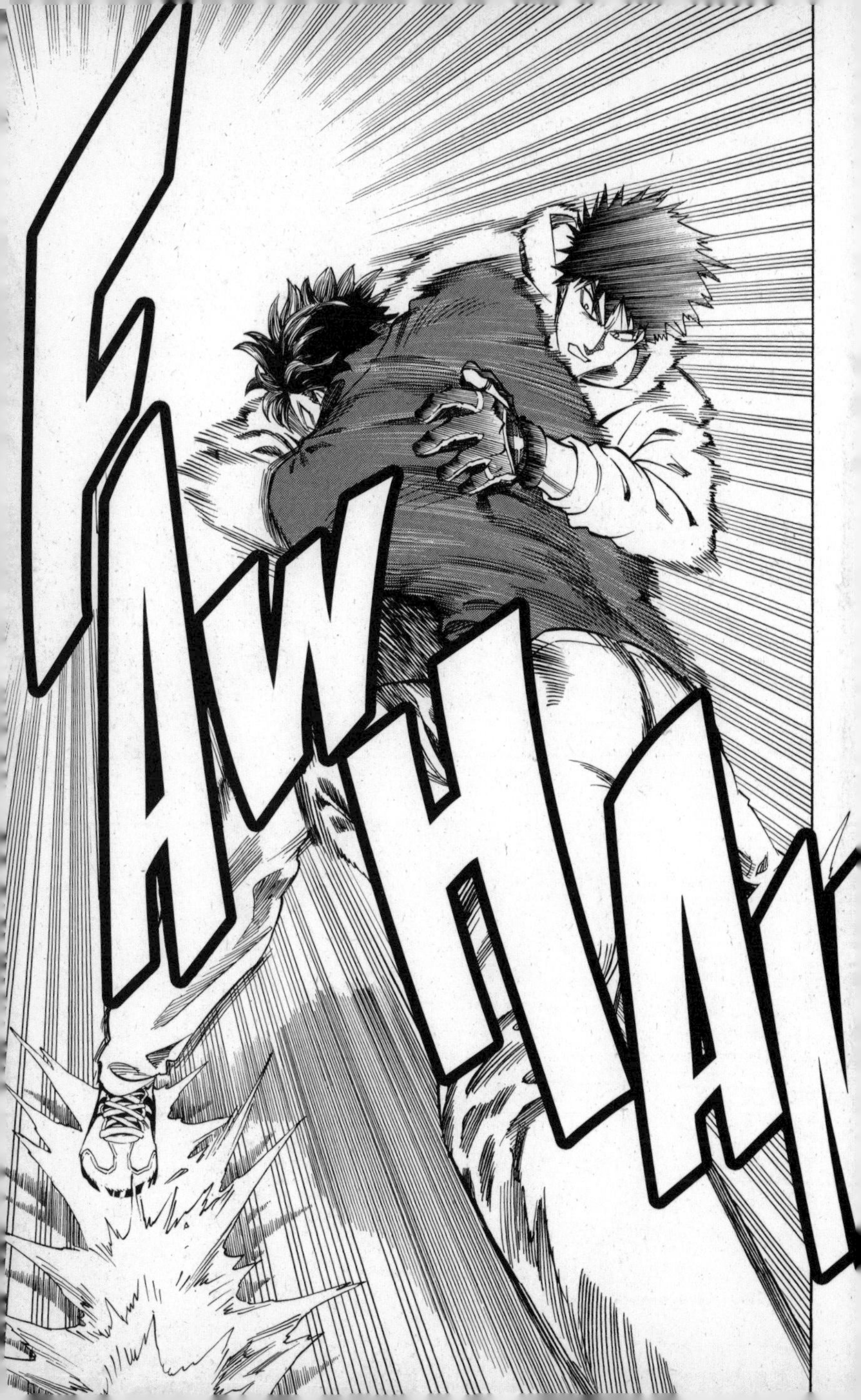

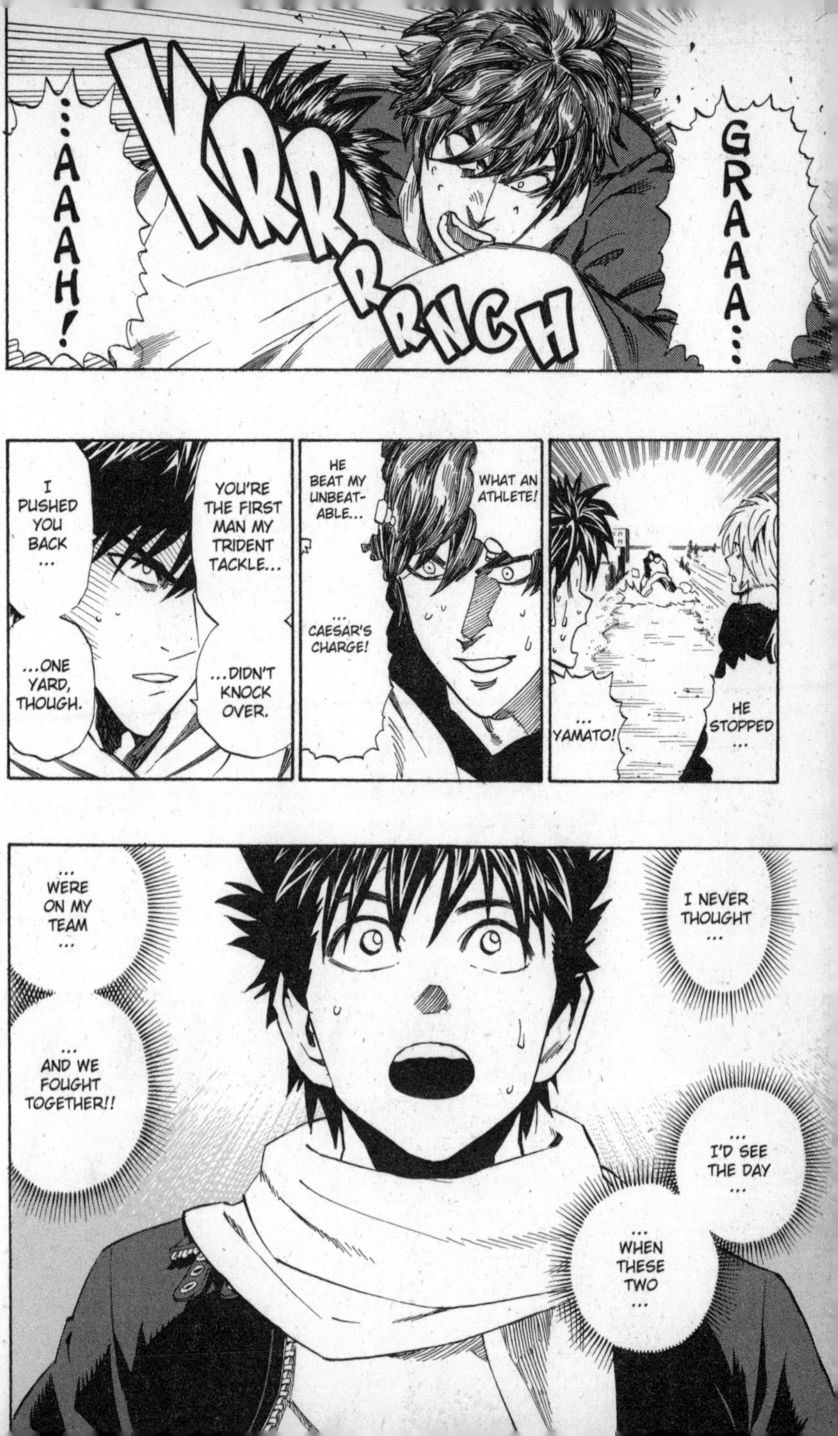
GRAAAA...
KRRRRRNCH
...AAAAH!
HE STOPPED...
...YAMATO!
WHAT AN ATHLETE!
HE BEAT MY UNBEAT-ABLE...
...CAESAR'S CHARGE!
YOU'RE THE FIRST MAN MY TRIDENT TACKLE...
...DIDN'T KNOCK OVER.
I PUSHED YOU BACK...
...ONE YARD, THOUGH.
I NEVER THOUGHT...
...I'D SEE THE DAY...
...WHEN THESE TWO...
...WERE ON MY TEAM...
...AND WE FOUGHT TOGETHER!!

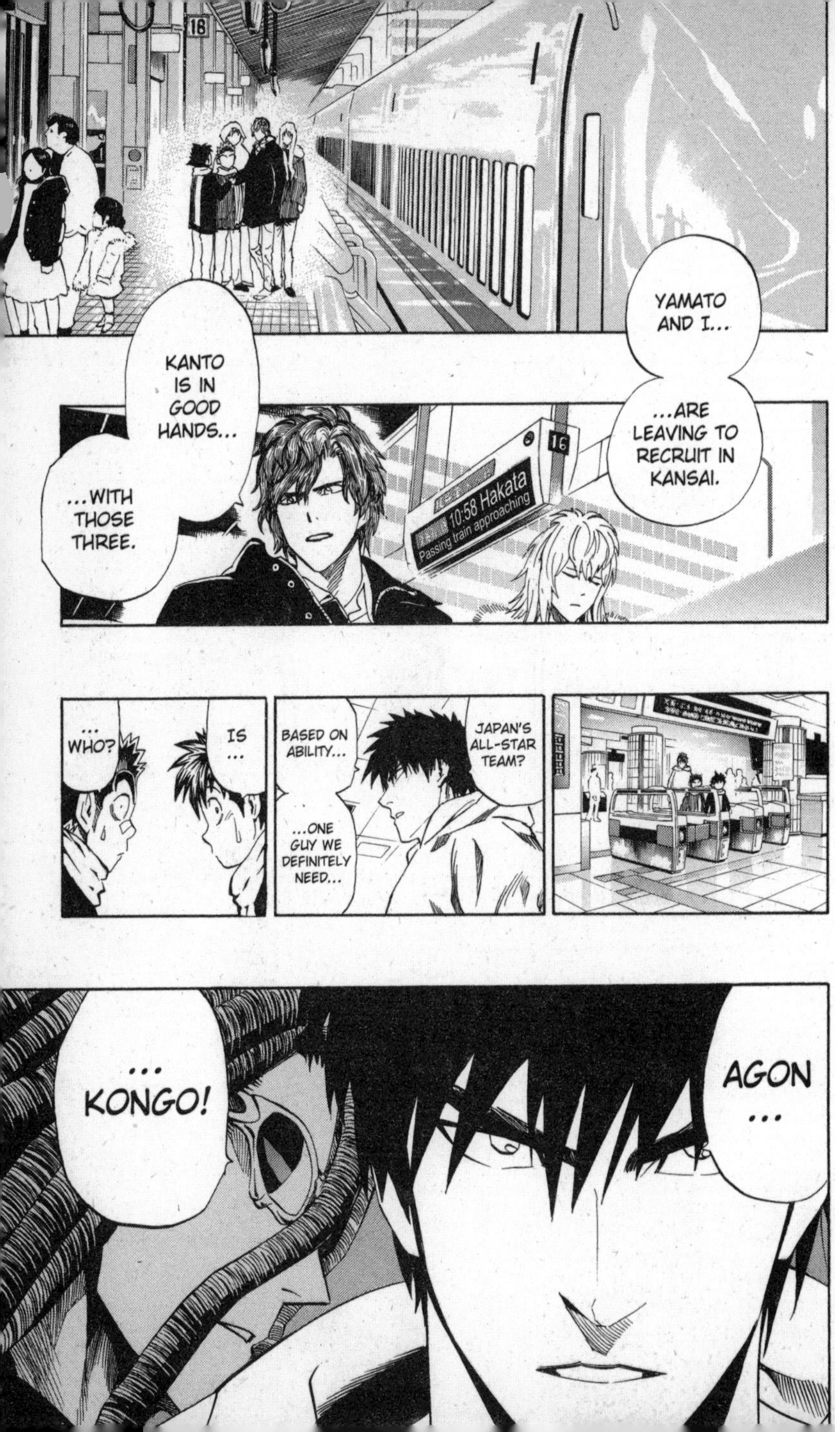

16
YAMATO AND I...
...ARE LEAVING TO RECRUIT IN KANSAI.
KANTO IS IN GOOD HANDS...
...WITH THOSE THREE.
16
10:58 Hakata
Passing train approaching
JAPAN'S ALL-STAR TEAM?
BASED ON ABILITY...
...ONE GUY WE DEFINITELY NEED...
IS...
...WHO?
AGON...
...KONGO!

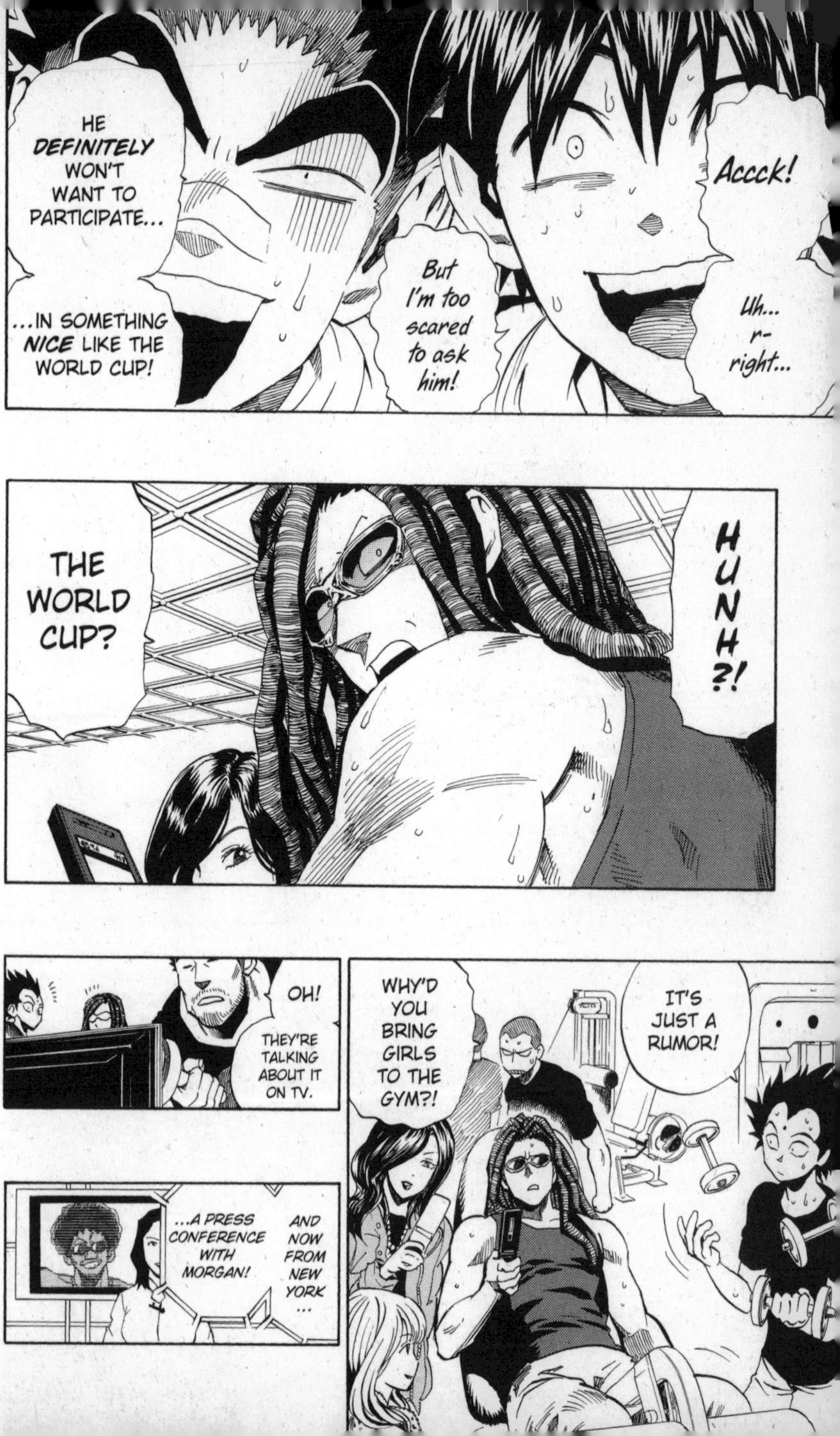
Accck!
Uh... r-right...
But I'm too scared to ask him!
HE *DEFINITELY* WON'T WANT TO PARTICIPATE...
...IN SOMETHING *NICE* LIKE THE WORLD CUP!
HUNH?!
THE WORLD CUP?
IT'S JUST A RUMOR!
WHY'D YOU BRING GIRLS TO THE GYM?!
OH!
THEY'RE TALKING ABOUT IT ON TV.
AND NOW FROM NEW YORK...
...A PRESS CONFERENCE WITH MORGAN!

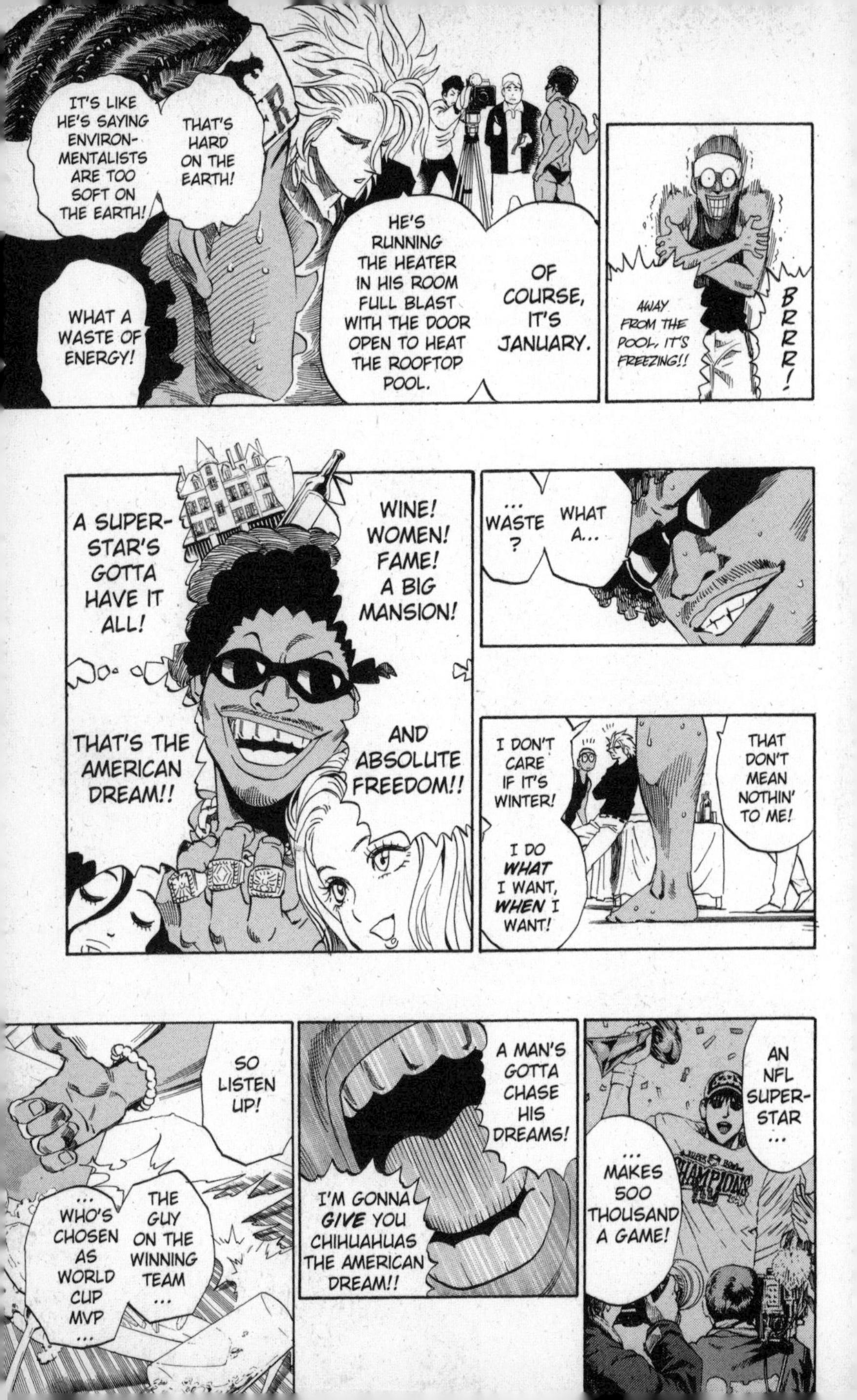
BRRR!
AWAY FROM THE POOL, IT'S FREEZING!!
OF COURSE, IT'S JANUARY.
HE'S RUNNING THE HEATER IN HIS ROOM FULL BLAST WITH THE DOOR OPEN TO HEAT THE ROOFTOP POOL.
THAT'S HARD ON THE EARTH!
IT'S LIKE HE'S SAYING ENVIRONMENTALISTS ARE TOO SOFT ON THE EARTH!
WHAT A WASTE OF ENERGY!
WHAT A...
...WASTE?
THAT DON'T MEAN NOTHIN' TO ME!
I DON'T CARE IF IT'S WINTER!
I DO *WHAT* I WANT, *WHEN* I WANT!
WINE! WOMEN! FAME! A BIG MANSION!
A SUPERSTAR'S GOTTA HAVE IT ALL!
AND ABSOLUTE FREEDOM!!
THAT'S THE AMERICAN DREAM!!
AN NFL SUPERSTAR...
...MAKES 500 THOUSAND A GAME!
A MAN'S GOTTA CHASE HIS DREAMS!
I'M GONNA *GIVE* YOU CHIHUAHUAS THE AMERICAN DREAM!!
SO LISTEN UP!
THE GUY ON THE WINNING TEAM...
...WHO'S CHOSEN AS WORLD CUP MVP...

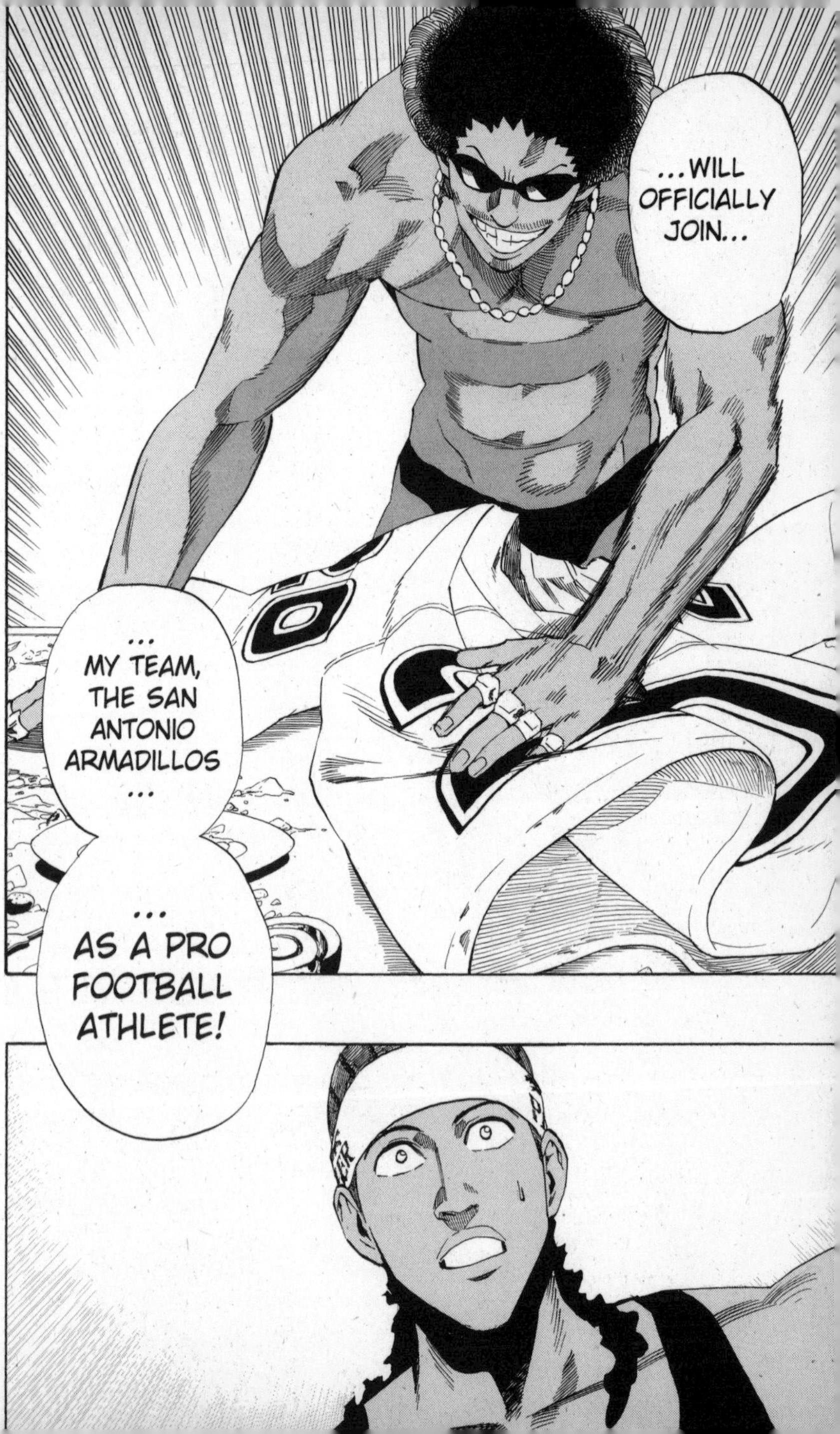
...WILL OFFICIALLY JOIN...
... MY TEAM, THE SAN ANTONIO ARMADILLOS ...
... AS A PRO FOOTBALL ATHLETE!

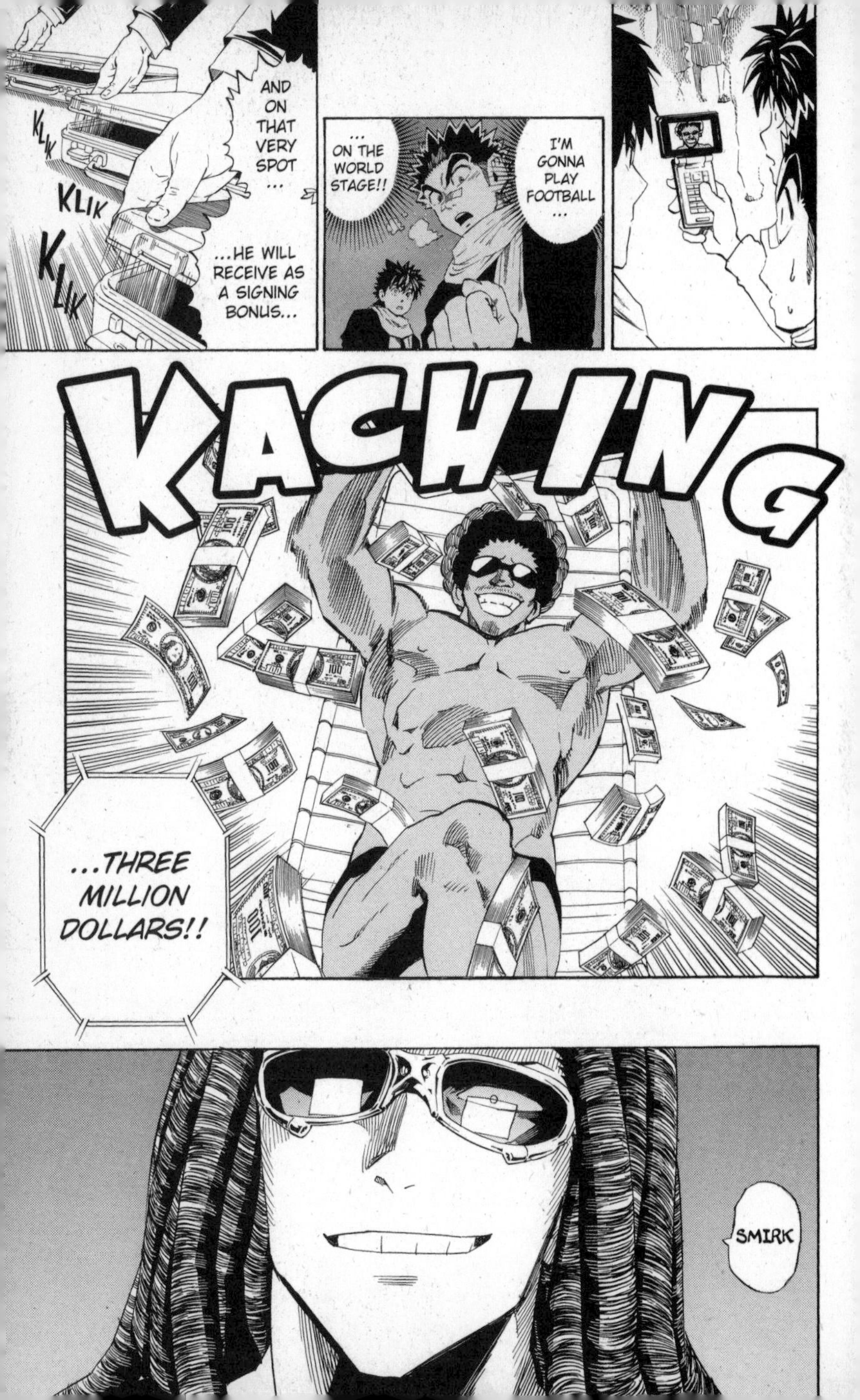
I'M GONNA PLAY FOOTBALL ...
... ON THE WORLD STAGE!!
AND ON THAT VERY SPOT ...
KLIK
KLIK
KLIK
KLIK
...HE WILL RECEIVE AS A SIGNING BONUS...
KACHING
...THREE MILLION DOLLARS!!
SMIRK

Eyeshield 21 Survey Corner **Devil Bat 021**

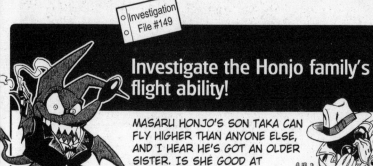

Investigation File #149

Investigate the Honjo family's flight ability!

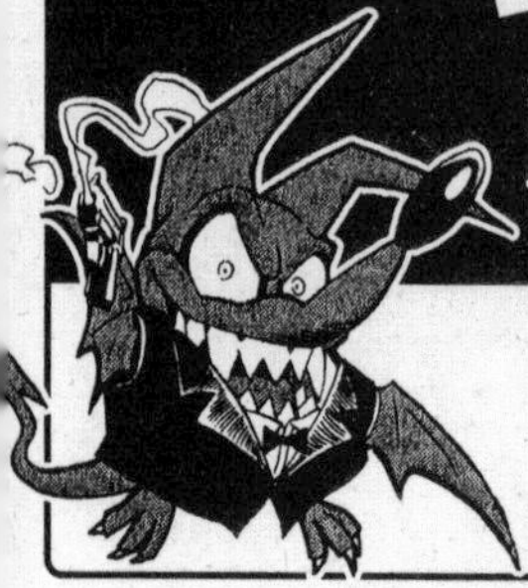

MASARU HONJO'S SON TAKA CAN FLY HIGHER THAN ANYONE ELSE, AND I HEAR HE'S GOT AN OLDER SISTER. IS SHE GOOD AT FLYING, TOO?

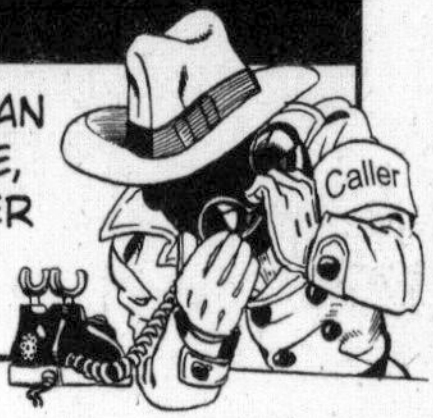
Caller

Caller name: MTNKMK in Aichi Prefecture

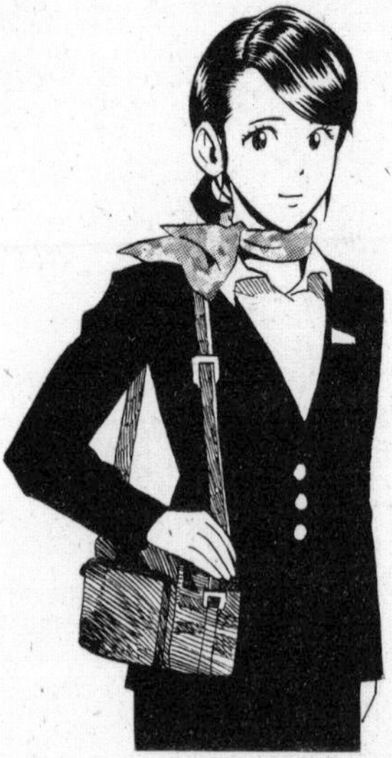

Taka's Older Sister

Name: Hibari Honjo

Age: 20

Occupation: Flight attendant

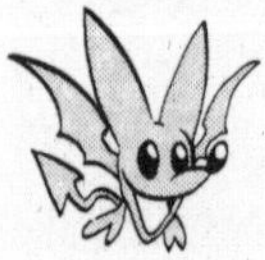

SHE FLIES THE BLUE SKIES EVERY DAY! SHE BABIES TAKA LIKE HE'S HER LITTLE BROTHER!

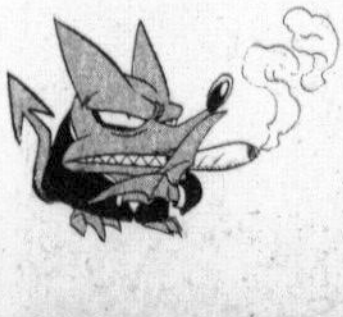

THAT'S BECAUSE HE *IS* HER LITTLE BROTHER.

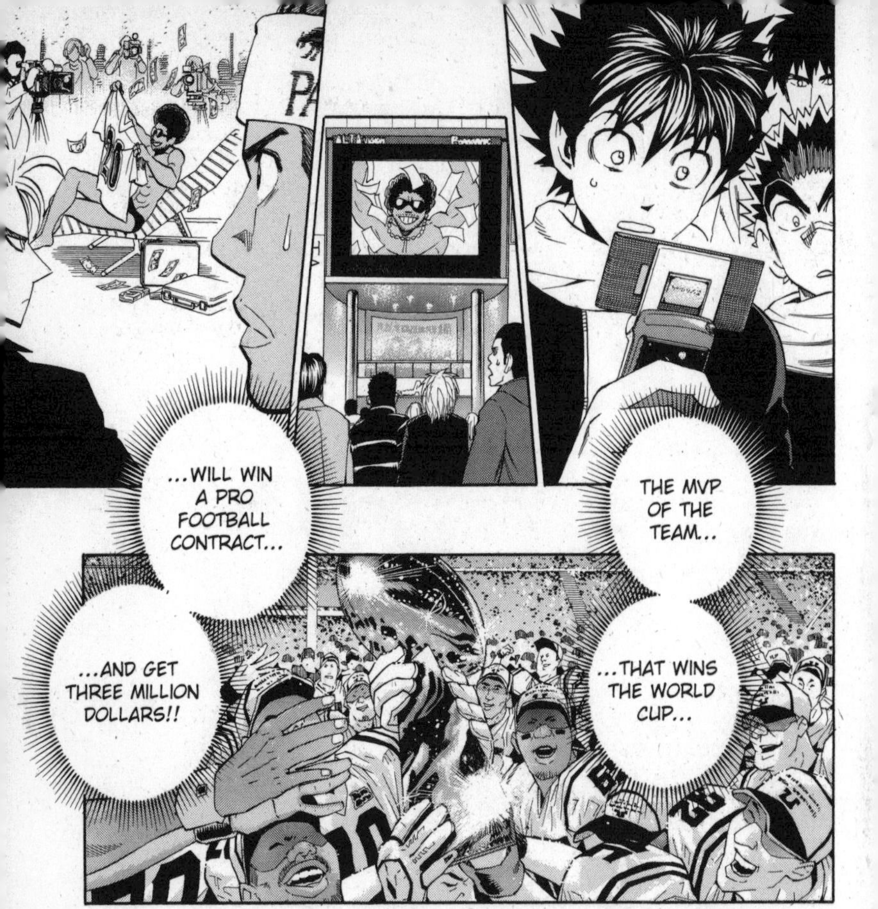
THE MVP OF THE TEAM...
...THAT WINS THE WORLD CUP...
...WILL WIN A PRO FOOTBALL CONTRACT...
...AND GET THREE MILLION DOLLARS!!

Chapter 307 A Great Gathering!!

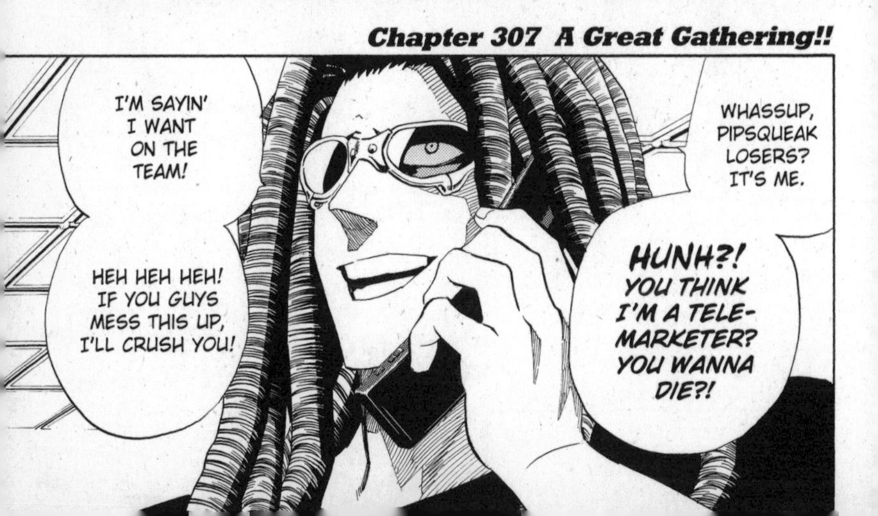
WHASSUP, PIPSQUEAK LOSERS? IT'S ME.
HUNH?! YOU THINK I'M A TELE-MARKETER? YOU WANNA DIE?!
I'M SAYIN' I WANT ON THE TEAM!
HEH HEH HEH! IF YOU GUYS MESS THIS UP, I'LL CRUSH YOU!

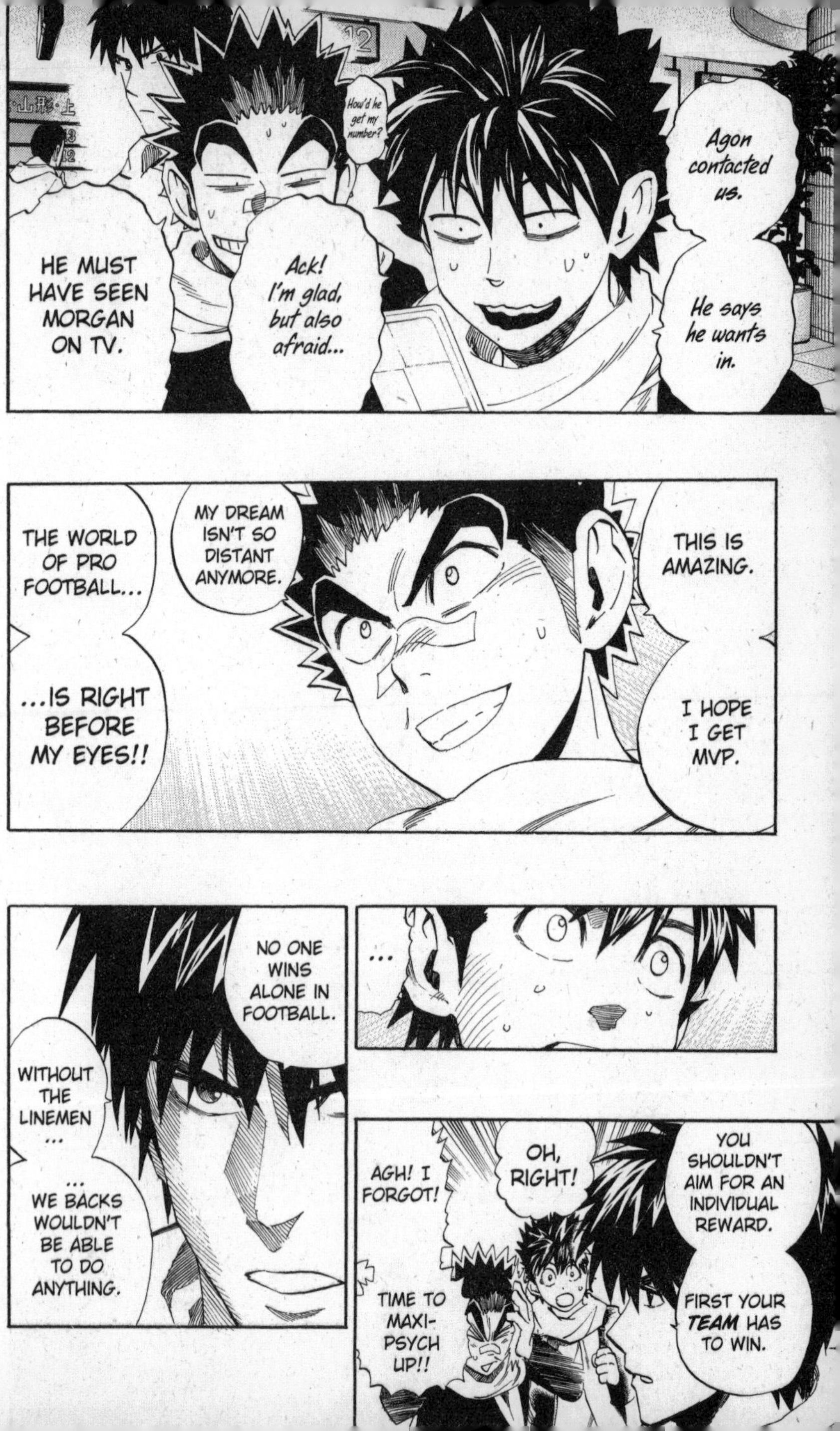
Agon contacted us.
He says he wants in.
How'd he get my number?
Ack! I'm glad, but also afraid...
HE MUST HAVE SEEN MORGAN ON TV.
THIS IS AMAZING.
I HOPE I GET MVP.
MY DREAM ISN'T SO DISTANT ANYMORE.
THE WORLD OF PRO FOOTBALL...
...IS RIGHT BEFORE MY EYES!!
...
YOU SHOULDN'T AIM FOR AN INDIVIDUAL REWARD.
FIRST YOUR *TEAM* HAS TO WIN.
OH, RIGHT!
AGH! I FORGOT!
TIME TO MAXI-PSYCH UP!!
NO ONE WINS ALONE IN FOOTBALL.
WITHOUT THE LINEMEN...
...WE BACKS WOULDN'T BE ABLE TO DO ANYTHING.

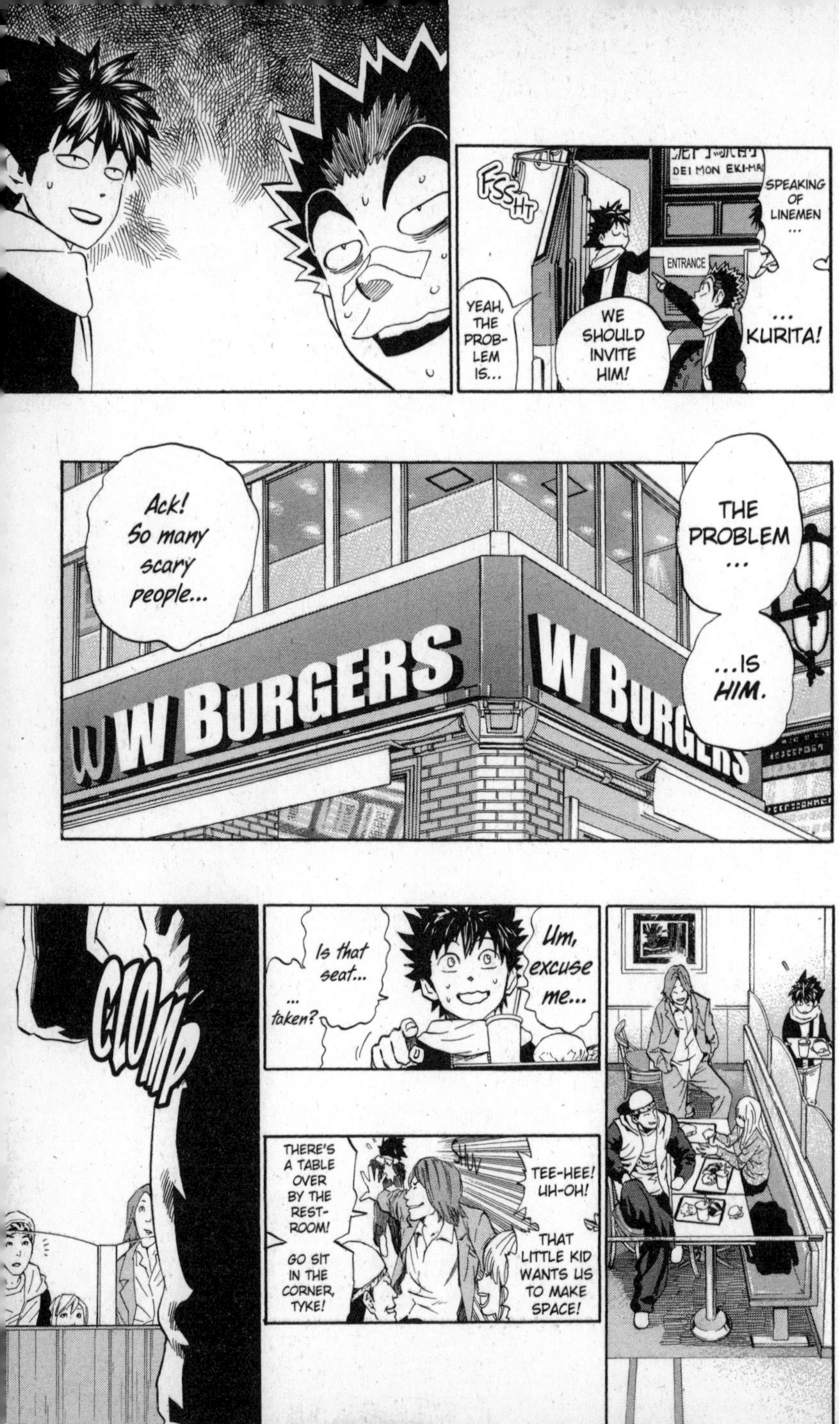
DEIMON EKI-MAE
SPEAKING OF LINEMEN ...
... KURITA!
ENTRANCE
WE SHOULD INVITE HIM!
FSSHT
YEAH, THE PROB-LEM IS...
THE PROBLEM ...
...IS HIM.
W BURGERS
W BURGERS
Ack! So many scary people...
Um, excuse me...
Is that seat... ... taken?
TEE-HEE! UH-OH!
THAT LITTLE KID WANTS US TO MAKE SPACE!
THERE'S A TABLE OVER BY THE REST-ROOM!
GO SIT IN THE CORNER, TYKE!
CLOMP

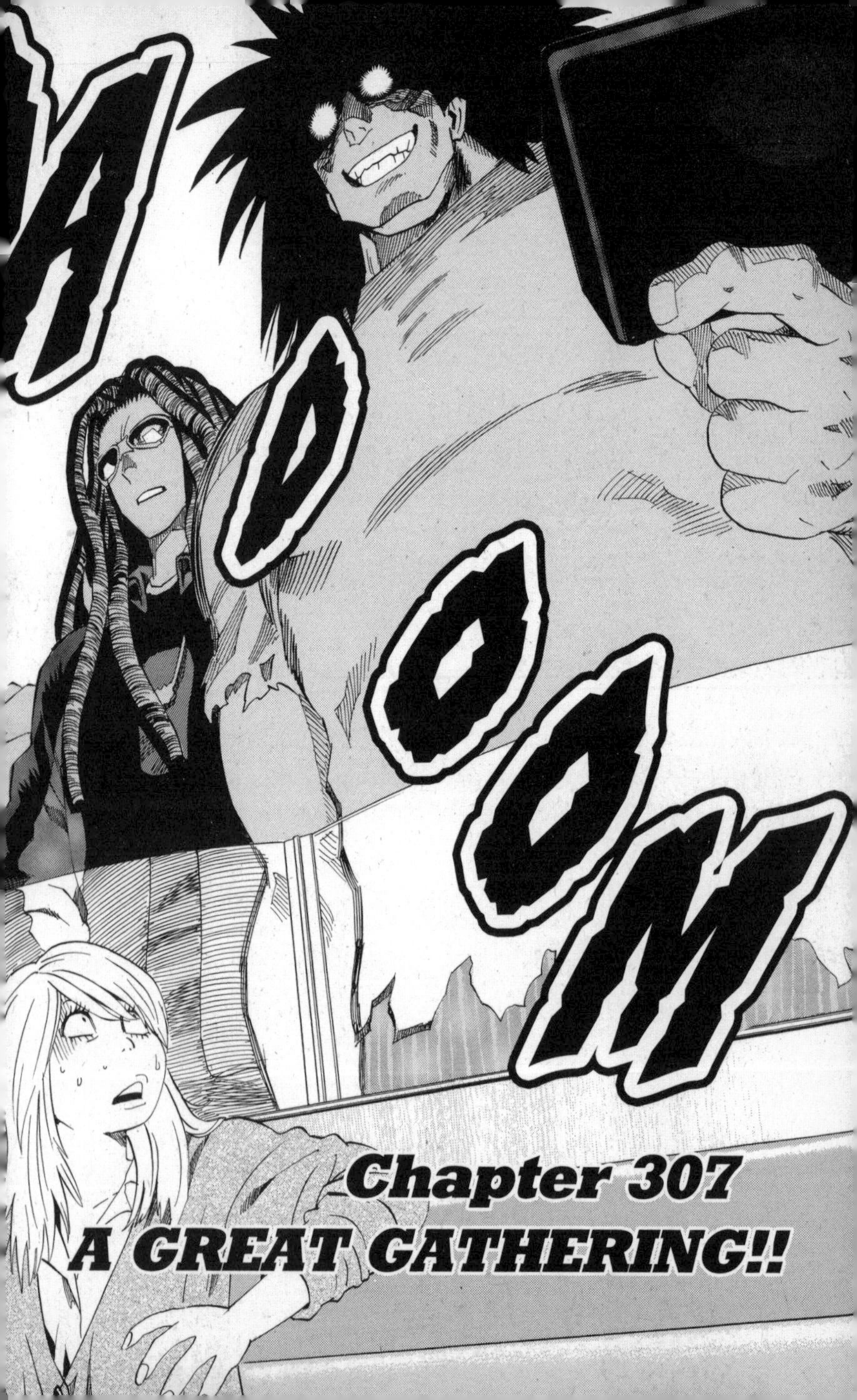
HOOOM

Chapter 307
A GREAT GATHERING!!

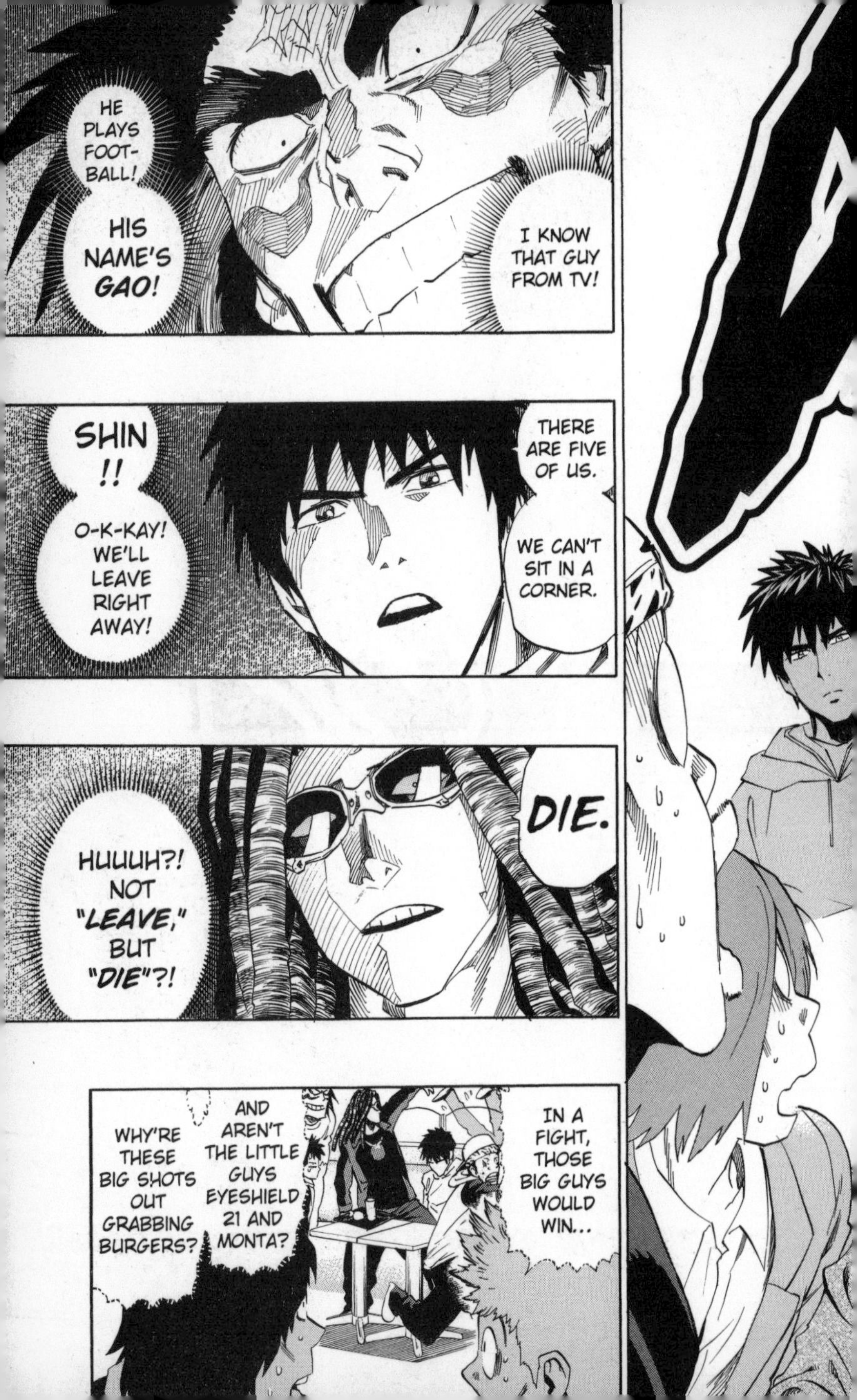
I KNOW THAT GUY FROM TV!
HE PLAYS FOOT-BALL!
HIS NAME'S GAO!
THERE ARE FIVE OF US.
WE CAN'T SIT IN A CORNER.
SHIN!!
O-K-KAY! WE'LL LEAVE RIGHT AWAY!
DIE.
HUUUH?! NOT "LEAVE," BUT "DIE"?!
IN A FIGHT, THOSE BIG GUYS WOULD WIN...
AND AREN'T THE LITTLE GUYS EYESHIELD 21 AND MONTA?
WHY'RE THESE BIG SHOTS OUT GRABBING BURGERS?

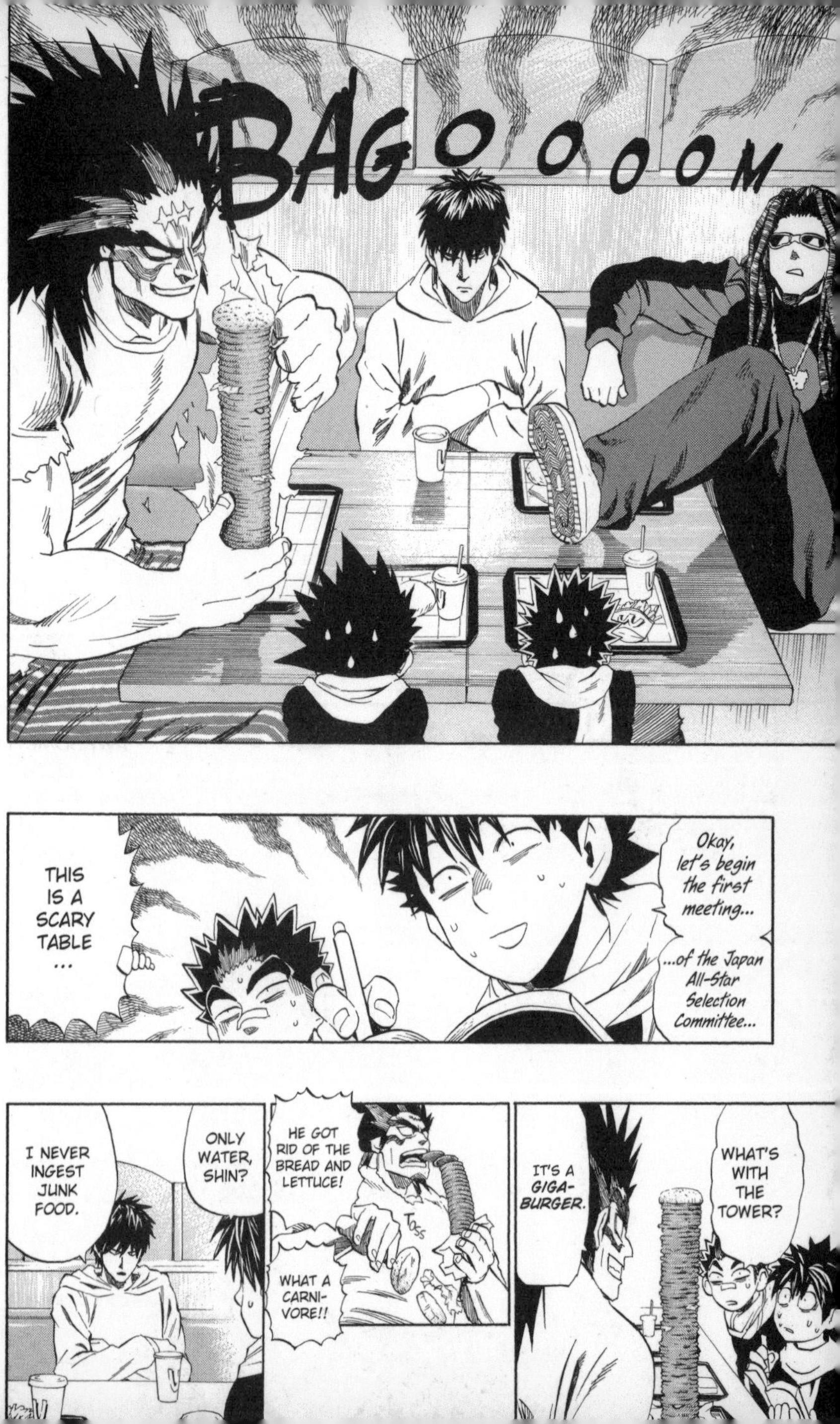
BAGOOOOM
Okay, let's begin the first meeting...
...of the Japan All-Star Selection Committee...
THIS IS A SCARY TABLE ...
WHAT'S WITH THE TOWER?
IT'S A GIGA-BURGER.
HE GOT RID OF THE BREAD AND LETTUCE!
TOSS
WHAT A CARNIVORE!!
ONLY WATER, SHIN?
I NEVER INGEST JUNK FOOD.

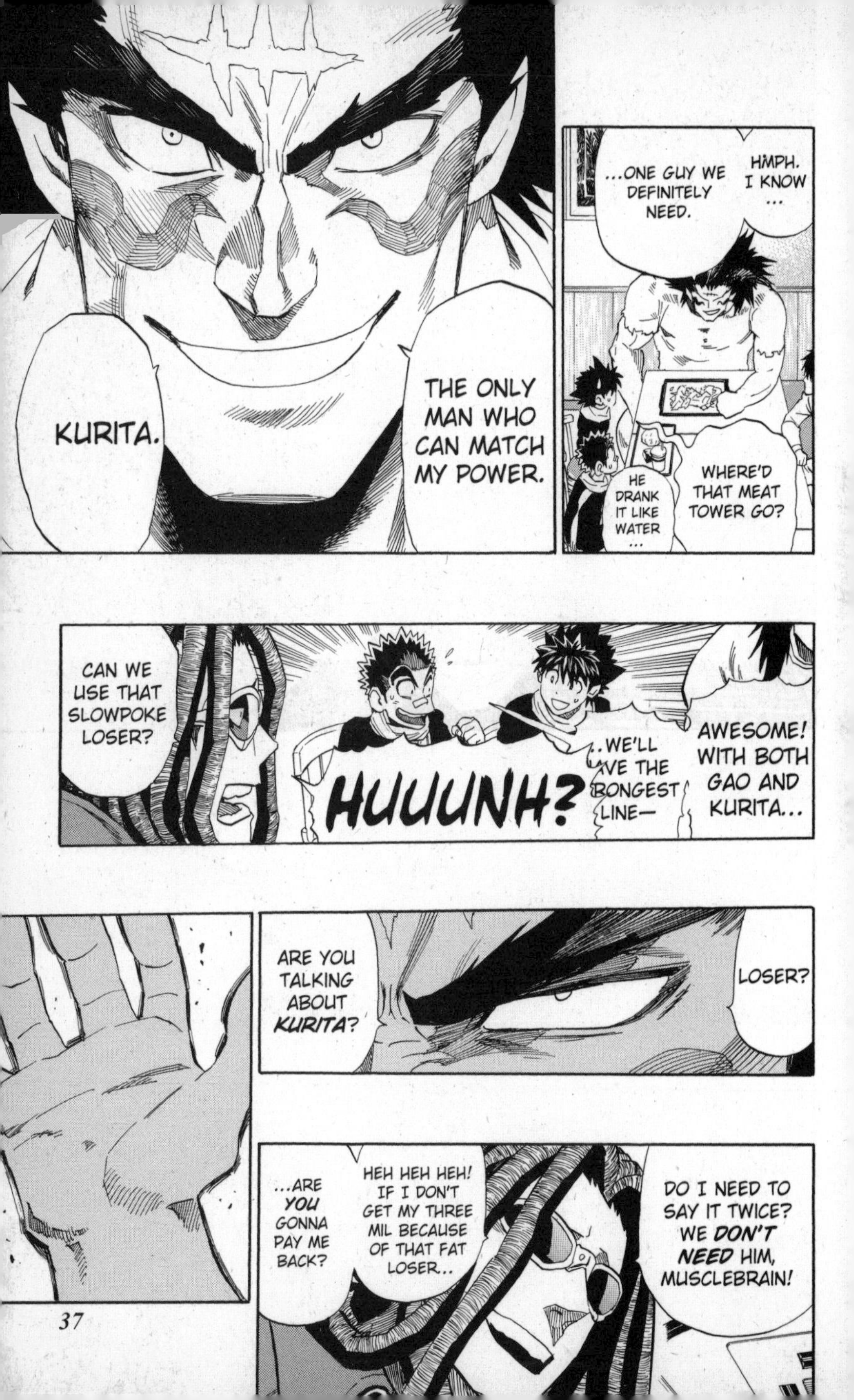
HMPH. I KNOW ...
...ONE GUY WE DEFINITELY NEED.
WHERE'D THAT MEAT TOWER GO?
HE DRANK IT LIKE WATER ...
THE ONLY MAN WHO CAN MATCH MY POWER.
KURITA.
AWESOME! WITH BOTH GAO AND KURITA...
..WE'LL AVE THE RONGEST LINE—
HUUUNH?
CAN WE USE THAT SLOWPOKE LOSER?
LOSER?
ARE YOU TALKING ABOUT KURITA?
DO I NEED TO SAY IT TWICE? WE DON'T NEED HIM, MUSCLEBRAIN!
HEH HEH HEH! IF I DON'T GET MY THREE MIL BECAUSE OF THAT FAT LOSER...
...ARE YOU GONNA PAY ME BACK?

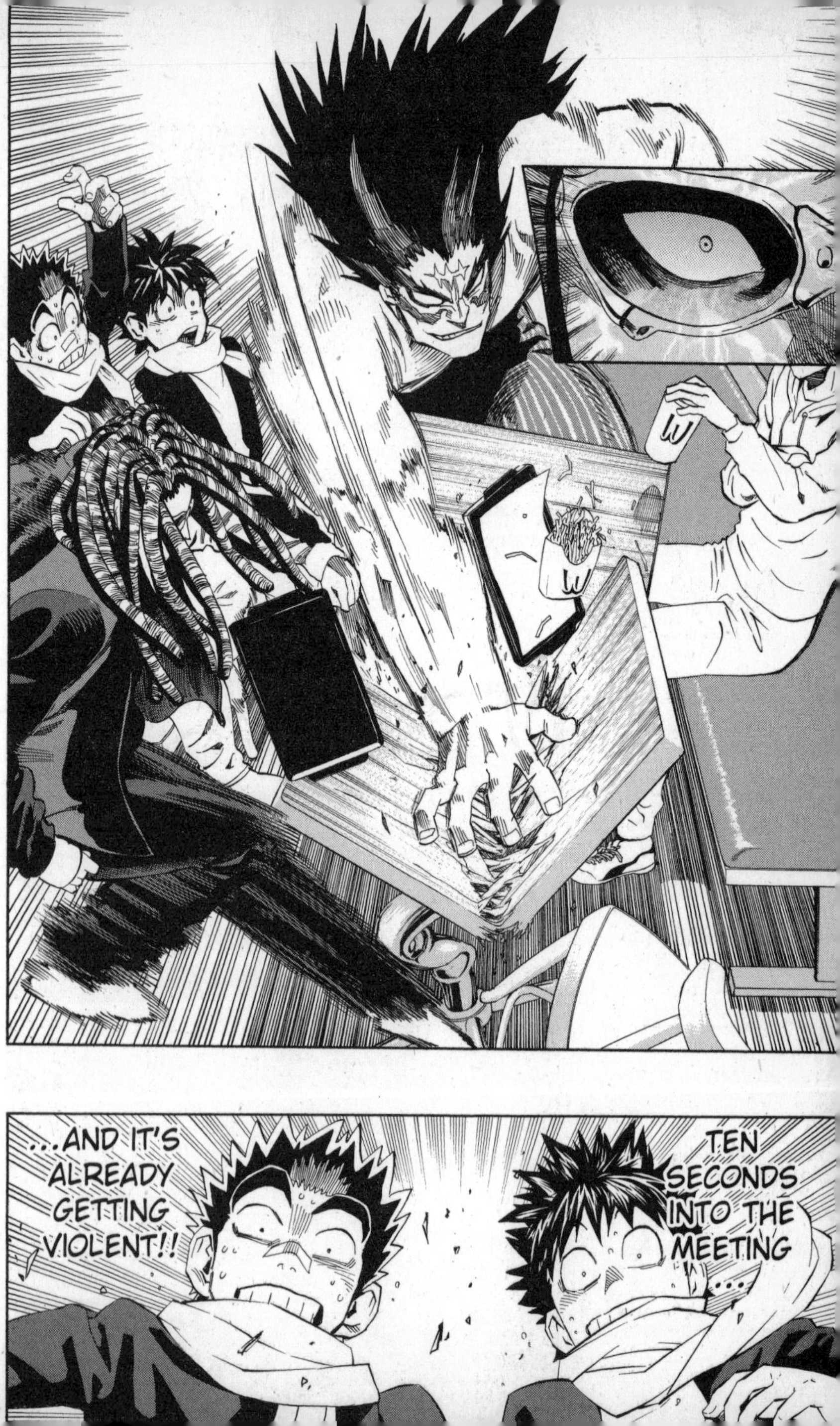
TEN SECONDS INTO THE MEETING...
...AND IT'S ALREADY GETTING VIOLENT!!

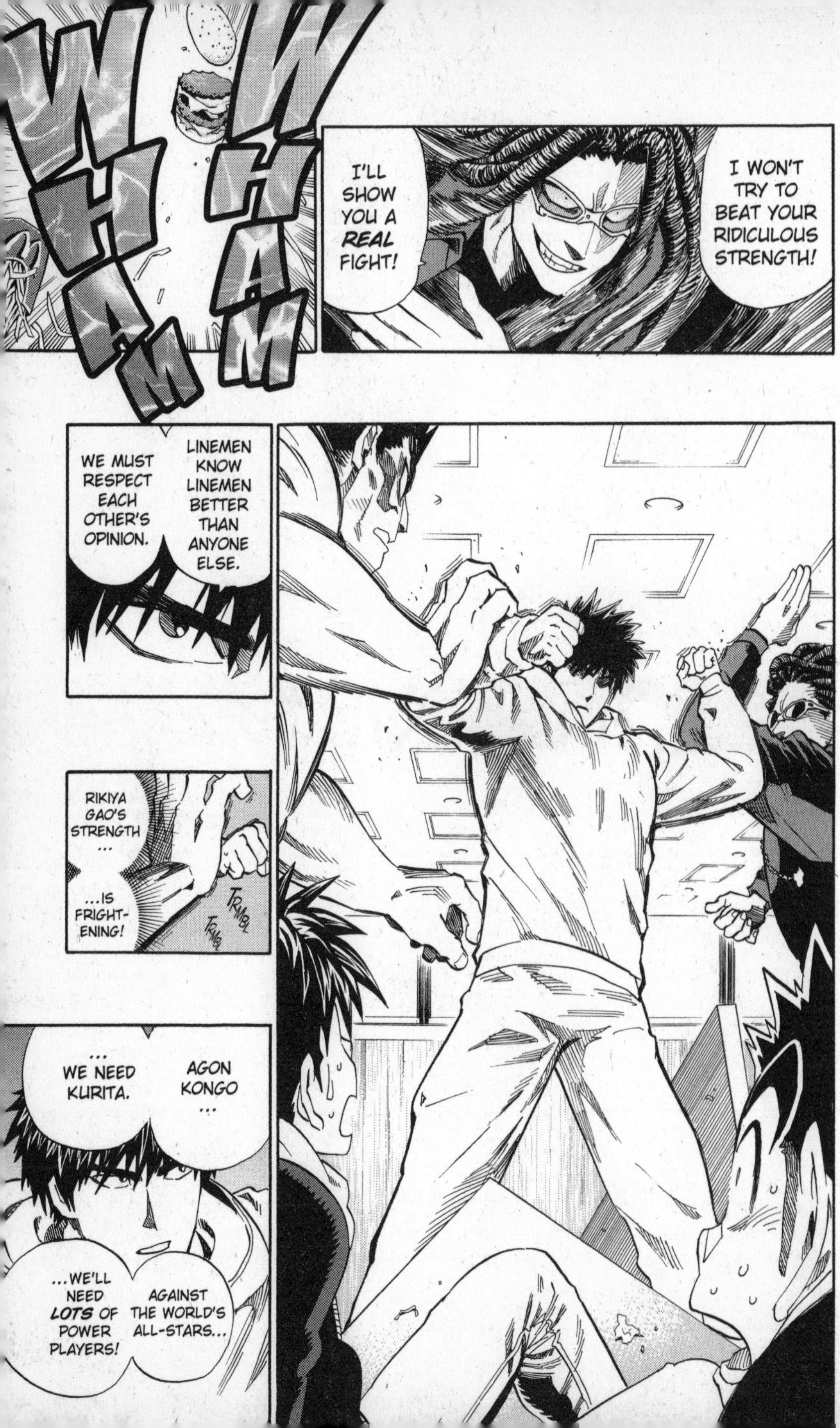
I WON'T TRY TO BEAT YOUR RIDICULOUS STRENGTH!
I'LL SHOW YOU A REAL FIGHT!
WHAM
WHAM
LINEMEN KNOW LINEMEN BETTER THAN ANYONE ELSE.
WE MUST RESPECT EACH OTHER'S OPINION.
RIKIYA GAO'S STRENGTH...
...IS FRIGHTENING!
TRMBL
TRMBL
AGON KONGO...
...WE NEED KURITA.
AGAINST THE WORLD'S ALL-STARS...
...WE'LL NEED LOTS OF POWER PLAYERS!

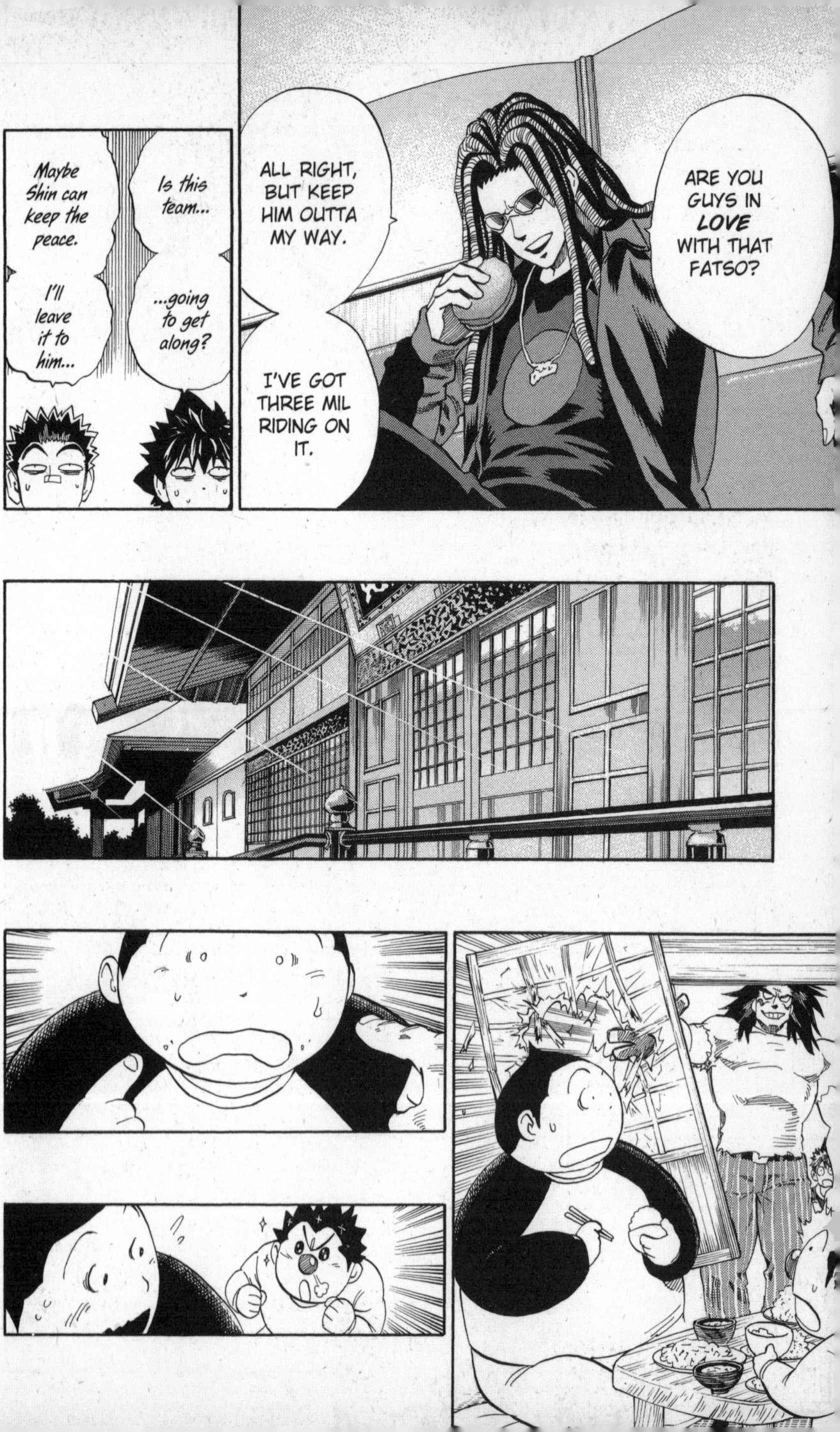
ARE YOU GUYS IN **LOVE** WITH THAT FATSO?
ALL RIGHT, BUT KEEP HIM OUTTA MY WAY.
I'VE GOT THREE MIL RIDING ON IT.
Is this team...
...going to get along?
Maybe Shin can keep the peace.
I'll leave it to him...

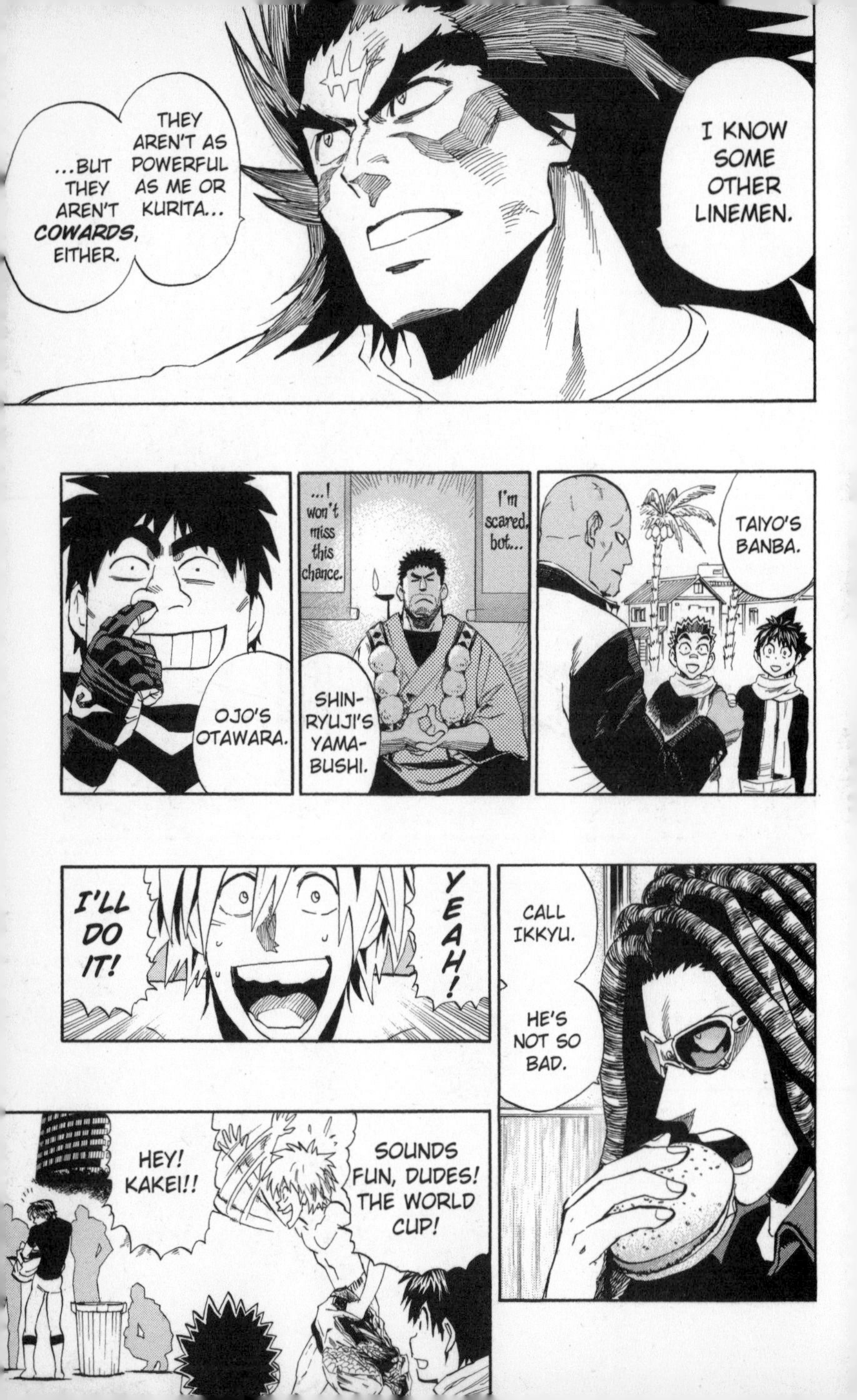
I KNOW SOME OTHER LINEMEN.
THEY AREN'T AS POWERFUL AS ME OR KURITA...
...BUT THEY AREN'T COWARDS, EITHER.
TAIYO'S BANBA.
I'm scared, but...
...I won't miss this chance.
SHINRYUJI'S YAMABUSHI.
OJO'S OTAWARA.
CALL IKKYU.
HE'S NOT SO BAD.
YEAH!
I'LL DO IT!
SOUNDS FUN, DUDES! THE WORLD CUP!
HEY! KAKEI!!

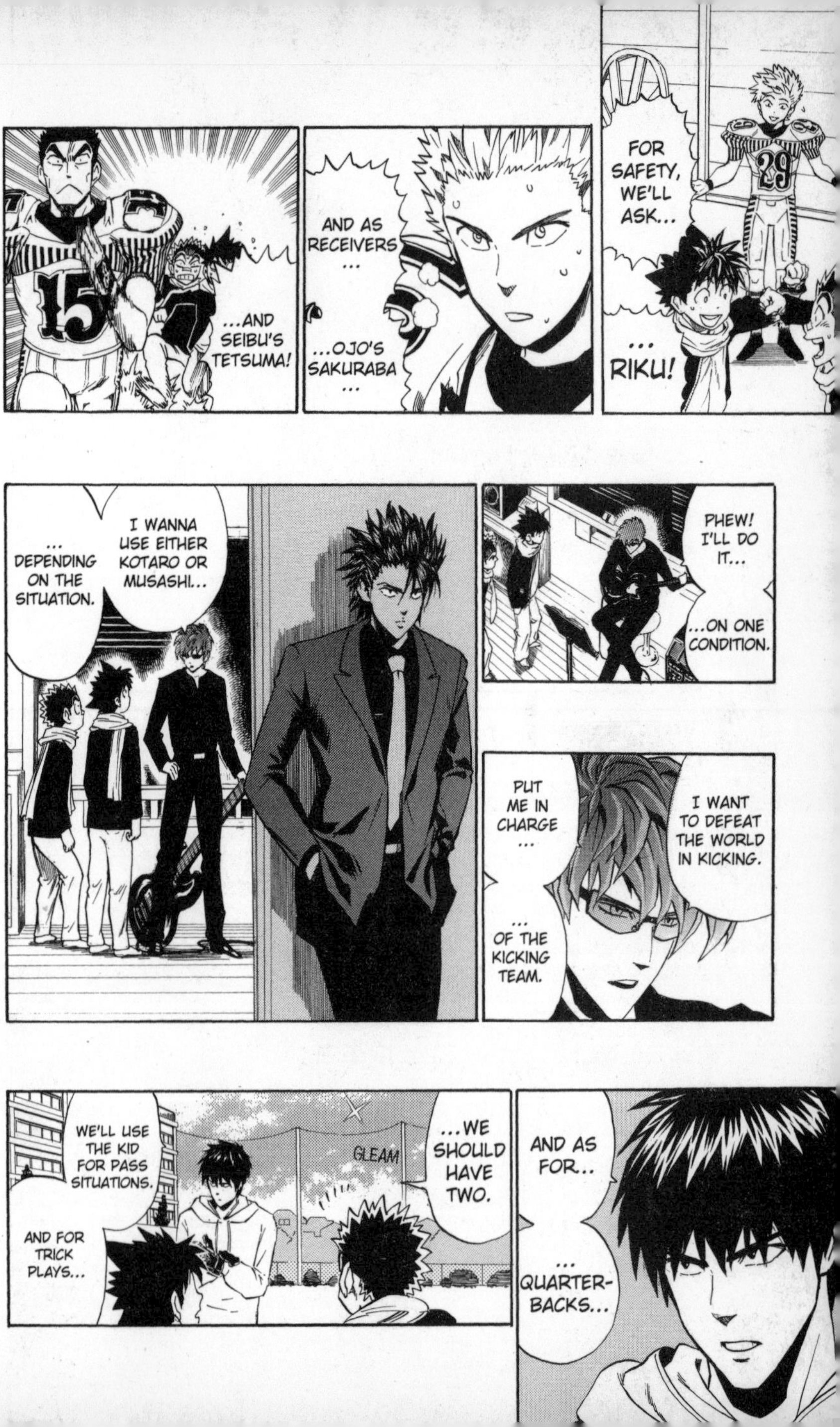
FOR SAFETY, WE'LL ASK...
... RIKU!
AND AS RECEIVERS...
...OJO'S SAKURABA...
...AND SEIBU'S TETSUMA!
PHEW! I'LL DO IT...
...ON ONE CONDITION.
I WANT TO DEFEAT THE WORLD IN KICKING.
PUT ME IN CHARGE...
...OF THE KICKING TEAM.
I WANNA USE EITHER KOTARO OR MUSASHI...
...DEPENDING ON THE SITUATION.
AND AS FOR...
...QUARTER-BACKS...
...WE SHOULD HAVE TWO.
GLEAM
WE'LL USE THE KID FOR PASS SITUATIONS.
AND FOR TRICK PLAYS...

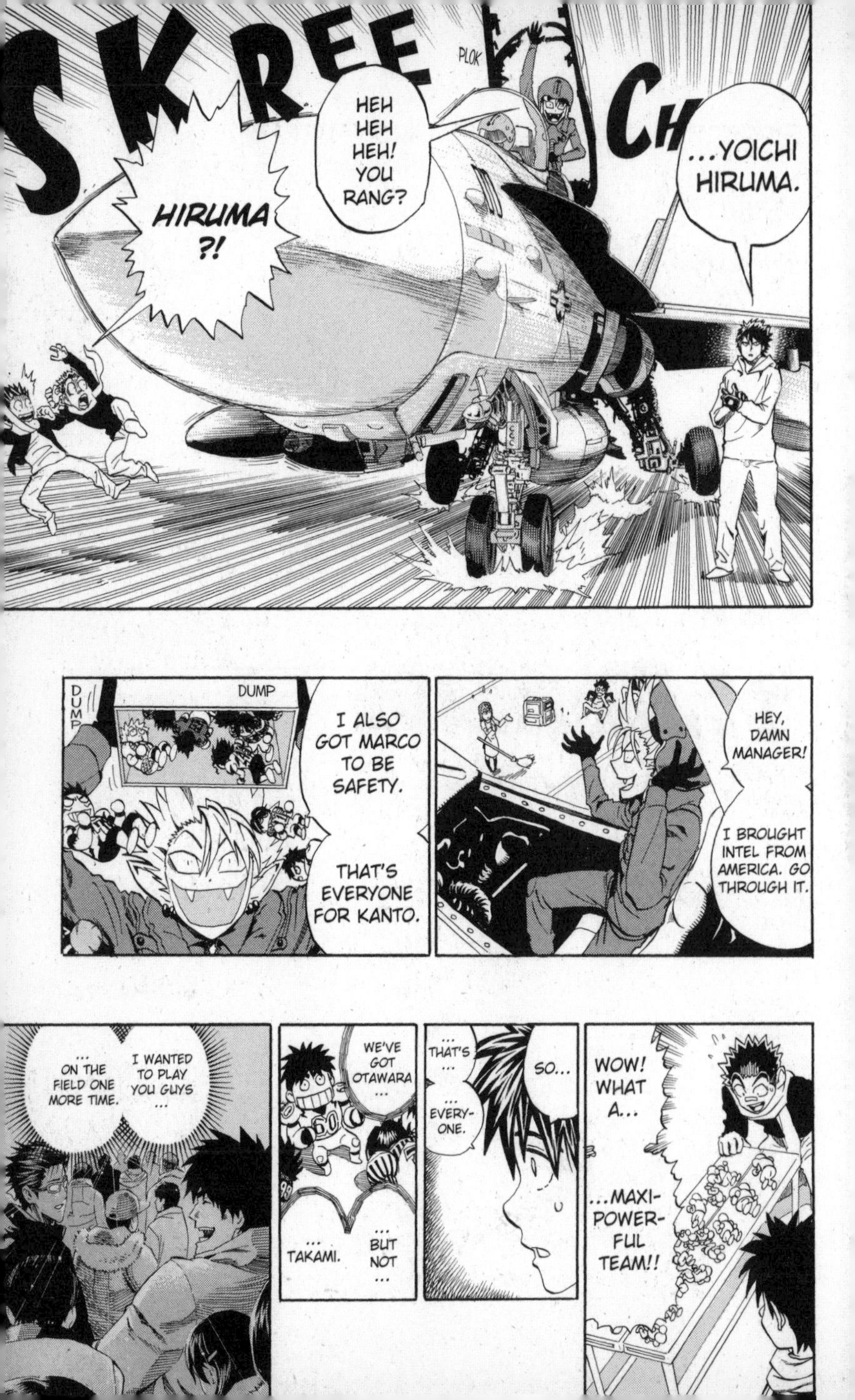
SKREECH
...YOICHI HIRUMA.
PLOK
HEH HEH HEH! YOU RANG?
HIRUMA ?!
HEY, DAMN MANAGER!
I BROUGHT INTEL FROM AMERICA. GO THROUGH IT.
DUMP
I ALSO GOT MARCO TO BE SAFETY.
THAT'S EVERYONE FOR KANTO.
DUMP
WOW! WHAT A...
...MAXI-POWER-FUL TEAM!!
SO...
...THAT'S...
...EVERYONE.
WE'VE GOT OTAWARA...
...BUT NOT...
...TAKAMI.
I WANTED TO PLAY YOU GUYS...
...ON THE FIELD ONE MORE TIME.

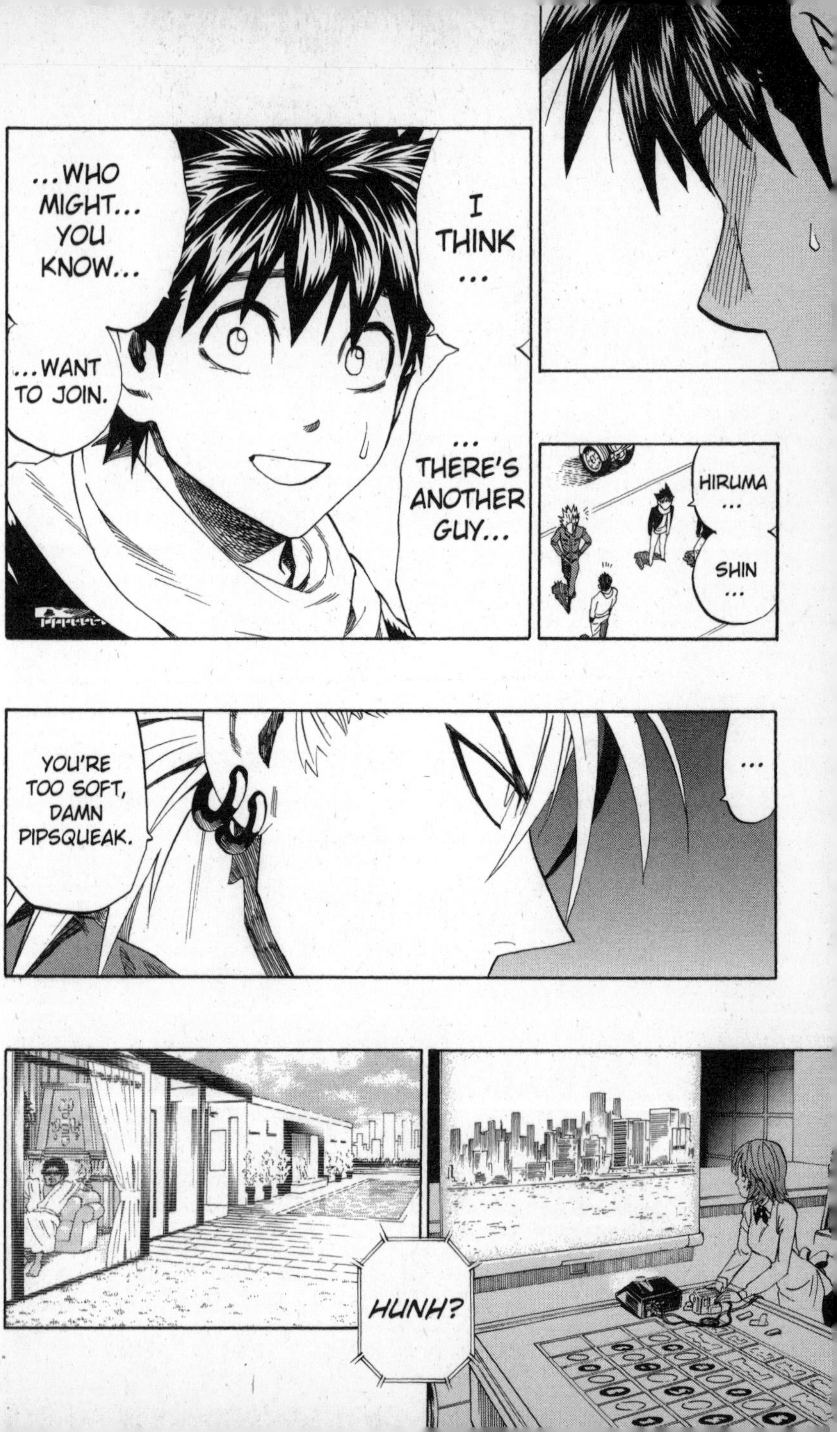
HIRUMA...
SHIN...
I THINK...
...THERE'S ANOTHER GUY...
...WHO MIGHT... YOU KNOW...
...WANT TO JOIN.
...
YOU'RE TOO SOFT, DAMN PIPSQUEAK.
HUNH?

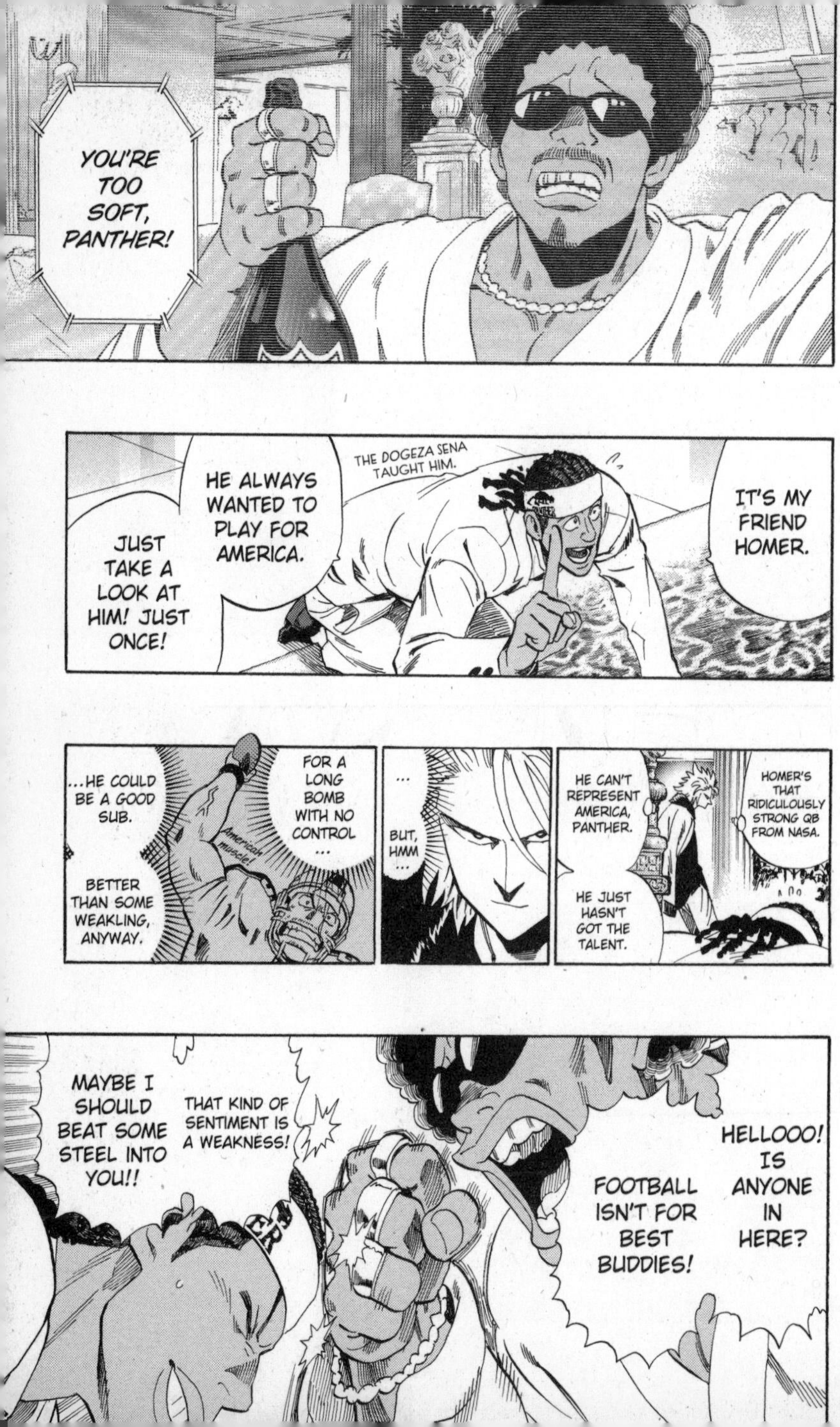
YOU'RE TOO SOFT, PANTHER!
IT'S MY FRIEND HOMER.
THE DOGEZA SENA TAUGHT HIM.
HE ALWAYS WANTED TO PLAY FOR AMERICA.
JUST TAKE A LOOK AT HIM! JUST ONCE!
HOMER'S THAT RIDICULOUSLY STRONG QB FROM NASA.
HE CAN'T REPRESENT AMERICA, PANTHER.
HE JUST HASN'T GOT THE TALENT.
...
BUT, HMM ...
FOR A LONG BOMB WITH NO CONTROL ...
...HE COULD BE A GOOD SUB.
American muscle!
BETTER THAN SOME WEAKLING, ANYWAY.
HELLOOO! IS ANYONE IN HERE?
FOOTBALL ISN'T FOR BEST BUDDIES!
THAT KIND OF SENTIMENT IS A WEAKNESS!
MAYBE I SHOULD BEAT SOME STEEL INTO YOU!!

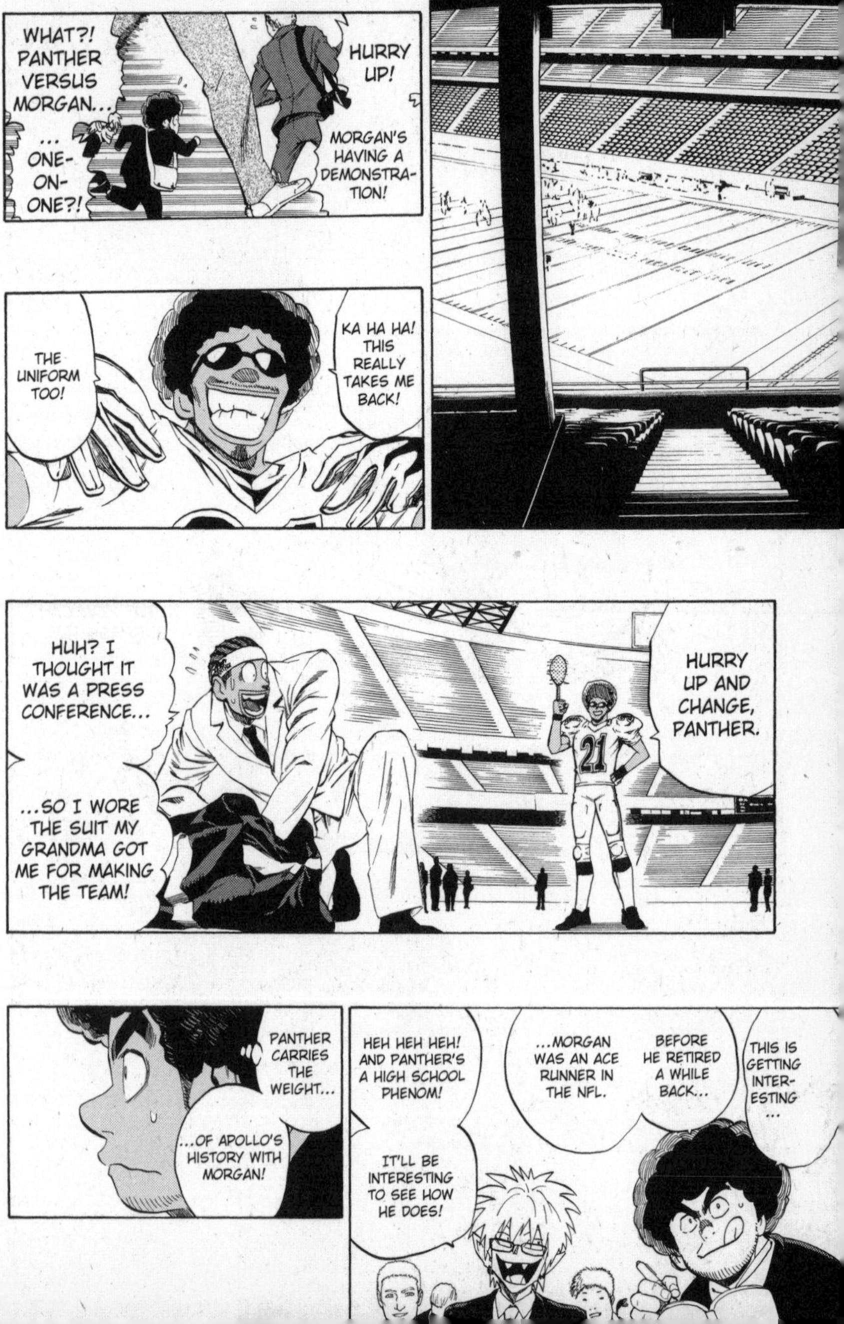
HURRY UP!
MORGAN'S HAVING A DEMONSTRATION!
WHAT?! PANTHER VERSUS MORGAN...
... ONE-ON-ONE?!
KA HA HA! THIS REALLY TAKES ME BACK!
THE UNIFORM TOO!
HURRY UP AND CHANGE, PANTHER.
HUH? I THOUGHT IT WAS A PRESS CONFERENCE...
...SO I WORE THE SUIT MY GRANDMA GOT ME FOR MAKING THE TEAM!
THIS IS GETTING INTERESTING...
BEFORE HE RETIRED A WHILE BACK...
...MORGAN WAS AN ACE RUNNER IN THE NFL.
HEH HEH HEH! AND PANTHER'S A HIGH SCHOOL PHENOM!
IT'LL BE INTERESTING TO SEE HOW HE DOES!
PANTHER CARRIES THE WEIGHT...
...OF APOLLO'S HISTORY WITH MORGAN!

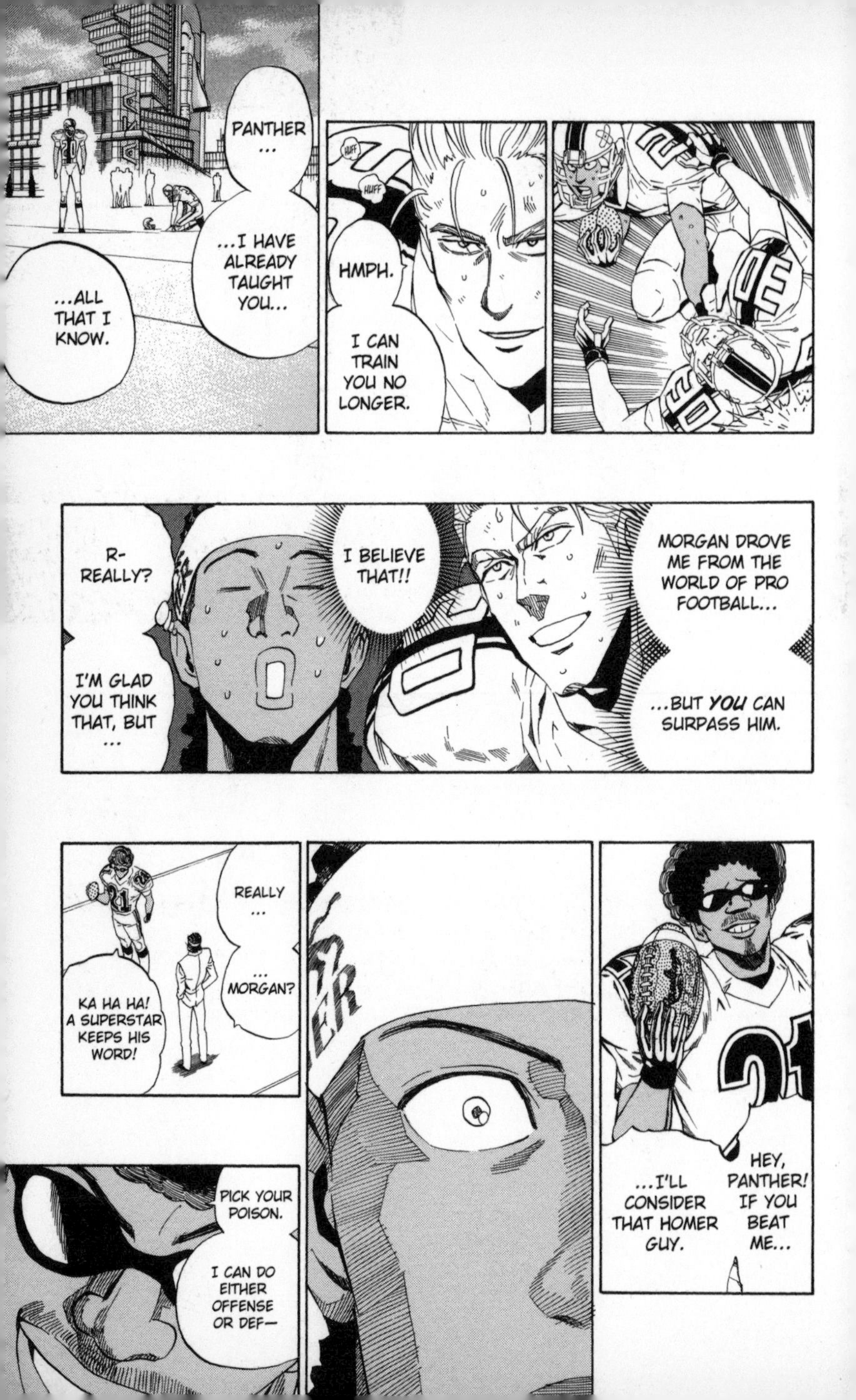
HUFF
HUFF
HMPH.
I CAN TRAIN YOU NO LONGER.
PANTHER...
...I HAVE ALREADY TAUGHT YOU...
...ALL THAT I KNOW.
MORGAN DROVE ME FROM THE WORLD OF PRO FOOTBALL...
...BUT *YOU* CAN SURPASS HIM.
I BELIEVE THAT!!
R-REALLY?
I'M GLAD YOU THINK THAT, BUT...
HEY, PANTHER! IF YOU BEAT ME...
...I'LL CONSIDER THAT HOMER GUY.
REALLY...
...MORGAN?
KA HA HA! A SUPERSTAR KEEPS HIS WORD!
PICK YOUR POISON.
I CAN DO EITHER OFFENSE OR DEF—

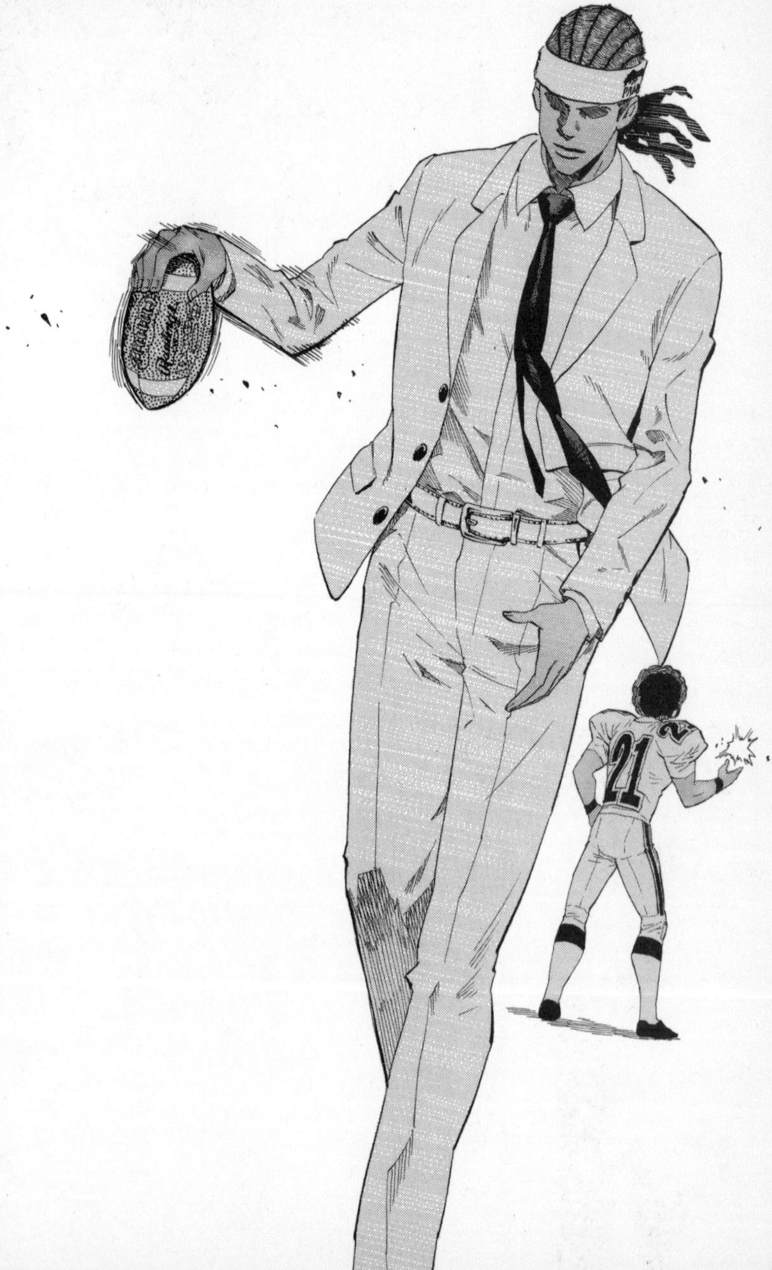
21

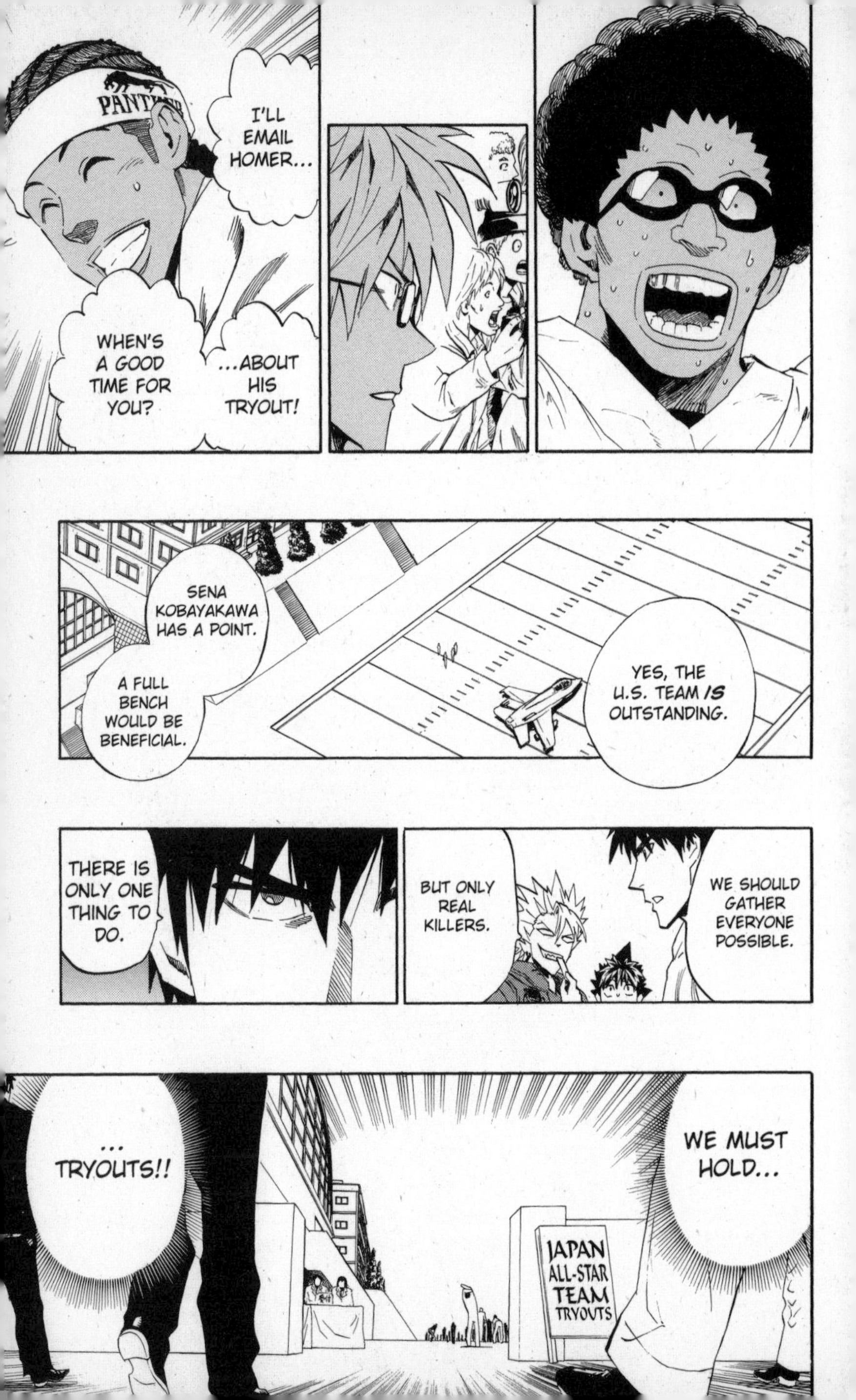
I'LL EMAIL HOMER...
...ABOUT HIS TRYOUT!
WHEN'S A GOOD TIME FOR YOU?
YES, THE U.S. TEAM *IS* OUTSTANDING.
SENA KOBAYAKAWA HAS A POINT.
A FULL BENCH WOULD BE BENEFICIAL.
WE SHOULD GATHER EVERYONE POSSIBLE.
BUT ONLY REAL KILLERS.
THERE IS ONLY ONE THING TO DO.
WE MUST HOLD...
JAPAN ALL-STAR TEAM TRYOUTS
...TRYOUTS!!

Eyeshield 21 Survey Corner Devil Bat 021

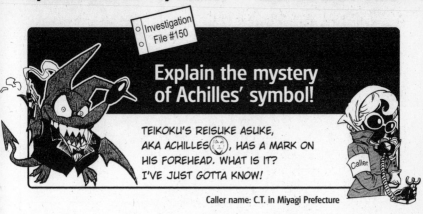

Investigation File #150

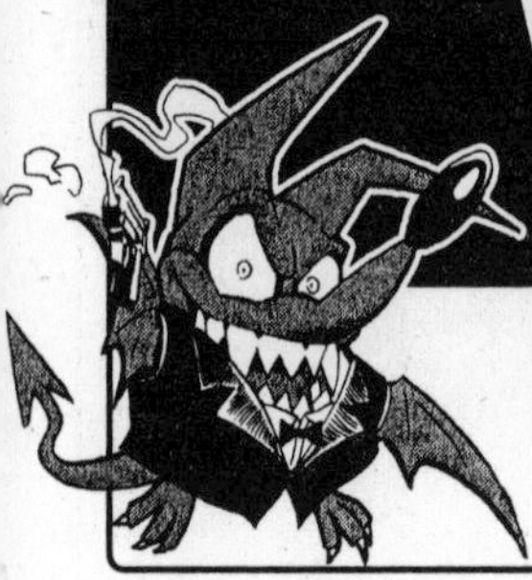

Explain the mystery of Achilles' symbol!

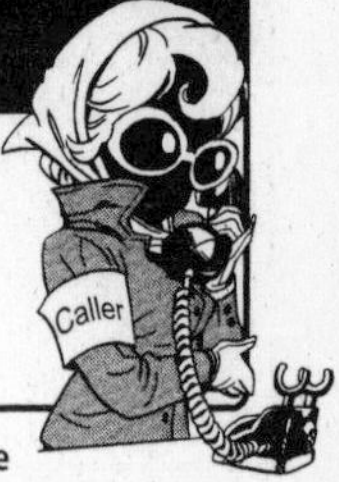
Caller

TEIKOKU'S REISUKE ASUKE, AKA ACHILLES, HAS A MARK ON HIS FOREHEAD. WHAT IS IT? I'VE JUST GOTTA KNOW!

Caller name: C.T. in Miyagi Prefecture

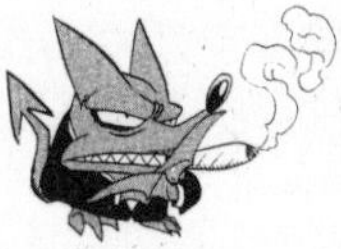

HE USED TO HAVE THE MOST STERLING BALD HEAD YOU EVER SAW, BUT THEN SOMETHING TRAGIC HAPPENED...

ONE DAY, A CERTAIN ***SOMEONE*** MADE THOSE MARKS, AND THEY NEVER WENT AWAY...

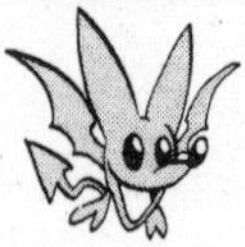

HERE, TAKE A LOOK FOR YOURSELF!

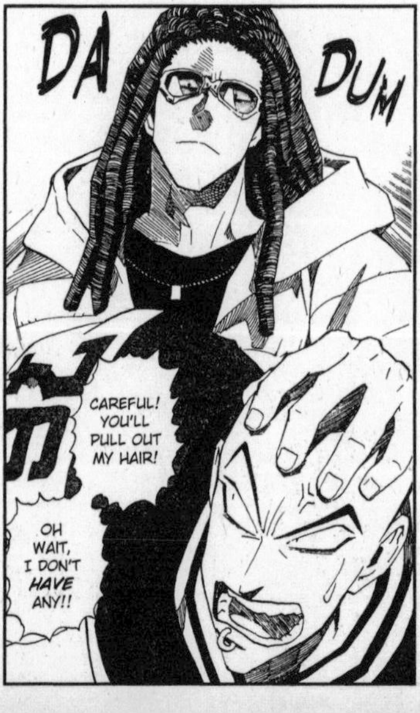
DA
DUM
CAREFUL! YOU'LL PULL OUT MY HAIR!
OH WAIT, I DON'T *HAVE* ANY!!

(from Volume 32, Chapter 280, page 53)

Chapter 308
TEAM JAPAN

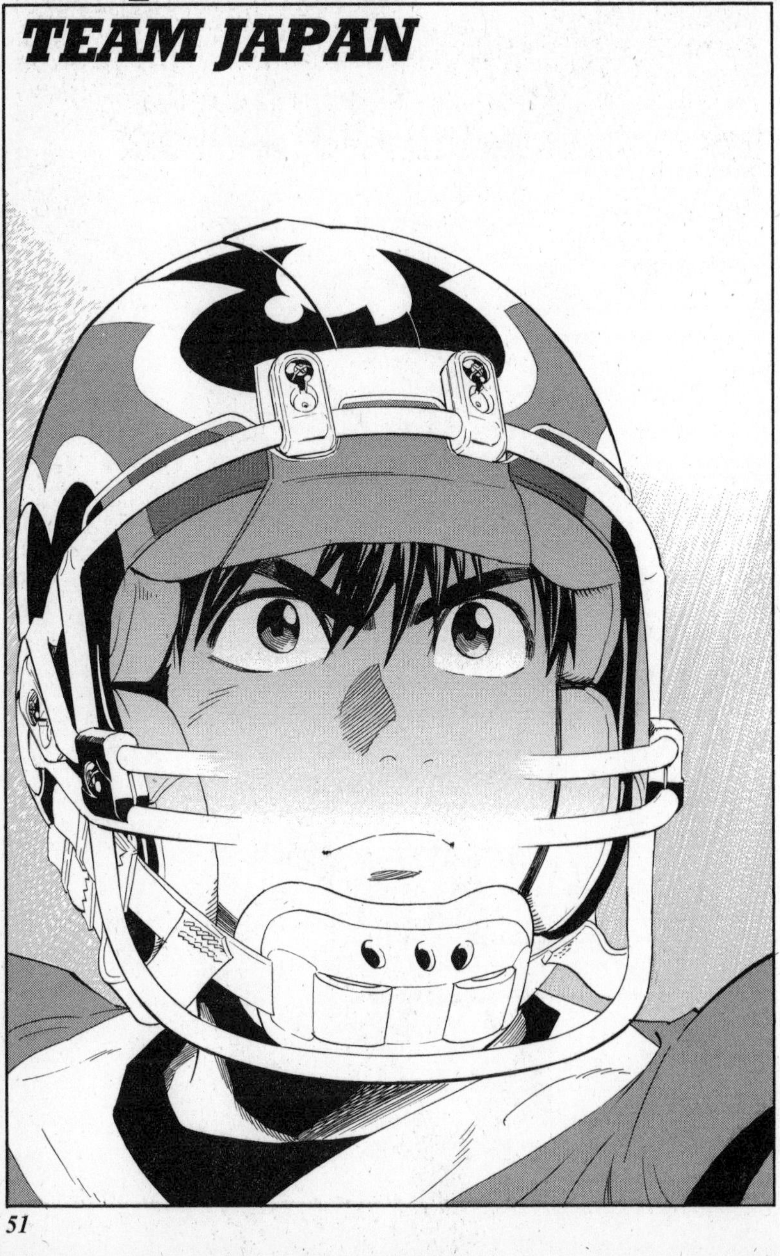

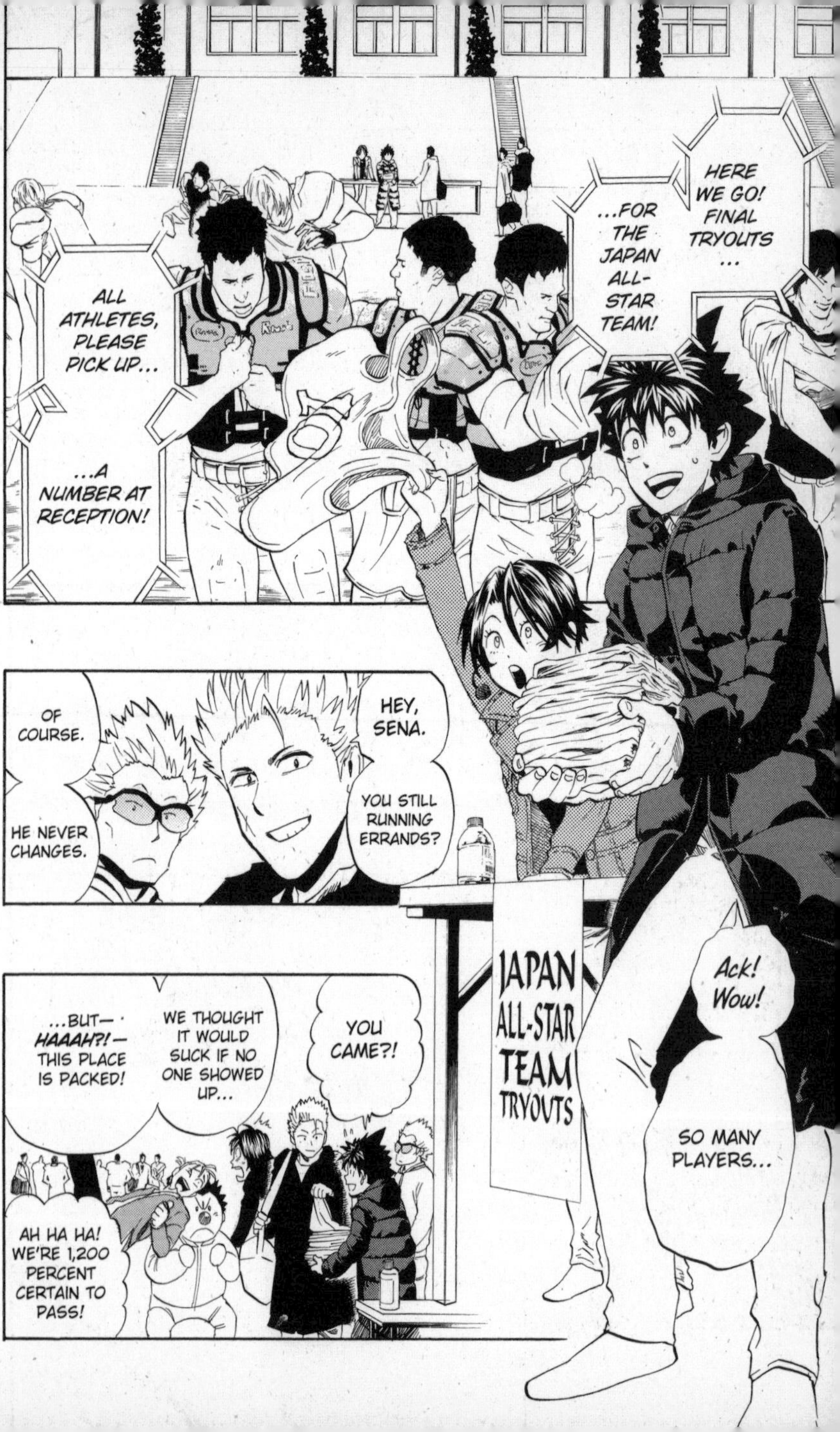
HERE WE GO! FINAL TRYOUTS...
...FOR THE JAPAN ALL-STAR TEAM!
ALL ATHLETES, PLEASE PICK UP...
...A NUMBER AT RECEPTION!
Ack! Wow!
SO MANY PLAYERS...
JAPAN ALL-STAR TEAM TRYOUTS
HEY, SENA.
YOU STILL RUNNING ERRANDS?
OF COURSE.
HE NEVER CHANGES.
YOU CAME?!
WE THOUGHT IT WOULD SUCK IF NO ONE SHOWED UP...
...BUT— HAAAH?! —THIS PLACE IS PACKED!
AH HA HA! WE'RE 1,200 PERCENT CERTAIN TO PASS!

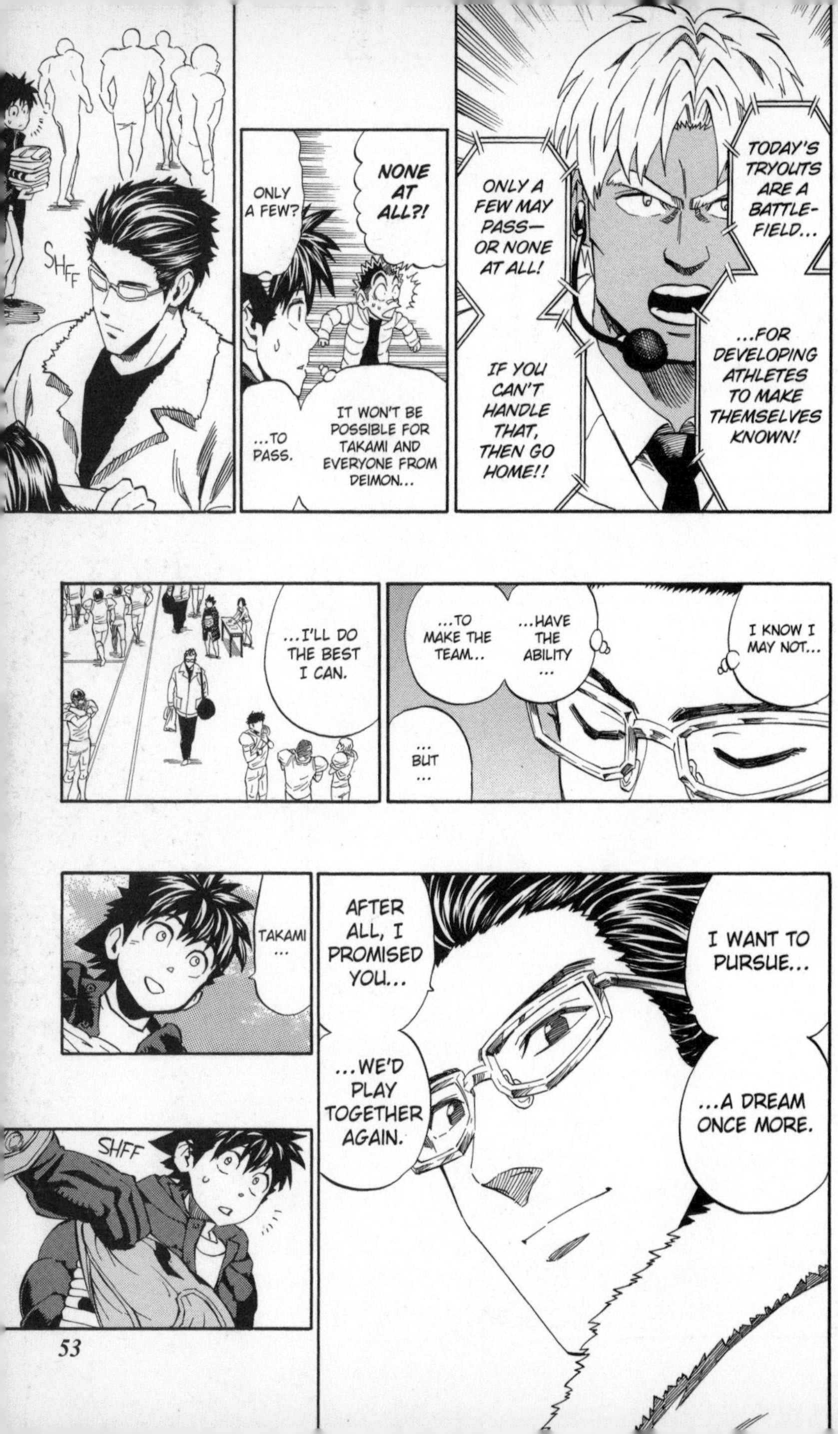
TODAY'S TRYOUTS ARE A BATTLE-FIELD...
...FOR DEVELOPING ATHLETES TO MAKE THEMSELVES KNOWN!
ONLY A FEW MAY PASS— OR NONE AT ALL!
IF YOU CAN'T HANDLE THAT, THEN GO HOME!!
NONE AT ALL?!
ONLY A FEW?
IT WON'T BE POSSIBLE FOR TAKAMI AND EVERYONE FROM DEIMON...
...TO PASS.
SHFF
I KNOW I MAY NOT...
...HAVE THE ABILITY...
...TO MAKE THE TEAM...
...BUT...
...I'LL DO THE BEST I CAN.
I WANT TO PURSUE...
...A DREAM ONCE MORE.
AFTER ALL, I PROMISED YOU...
...WE'D PLAY TOGETHER AGAIN.
TAKAMI...
SHFF

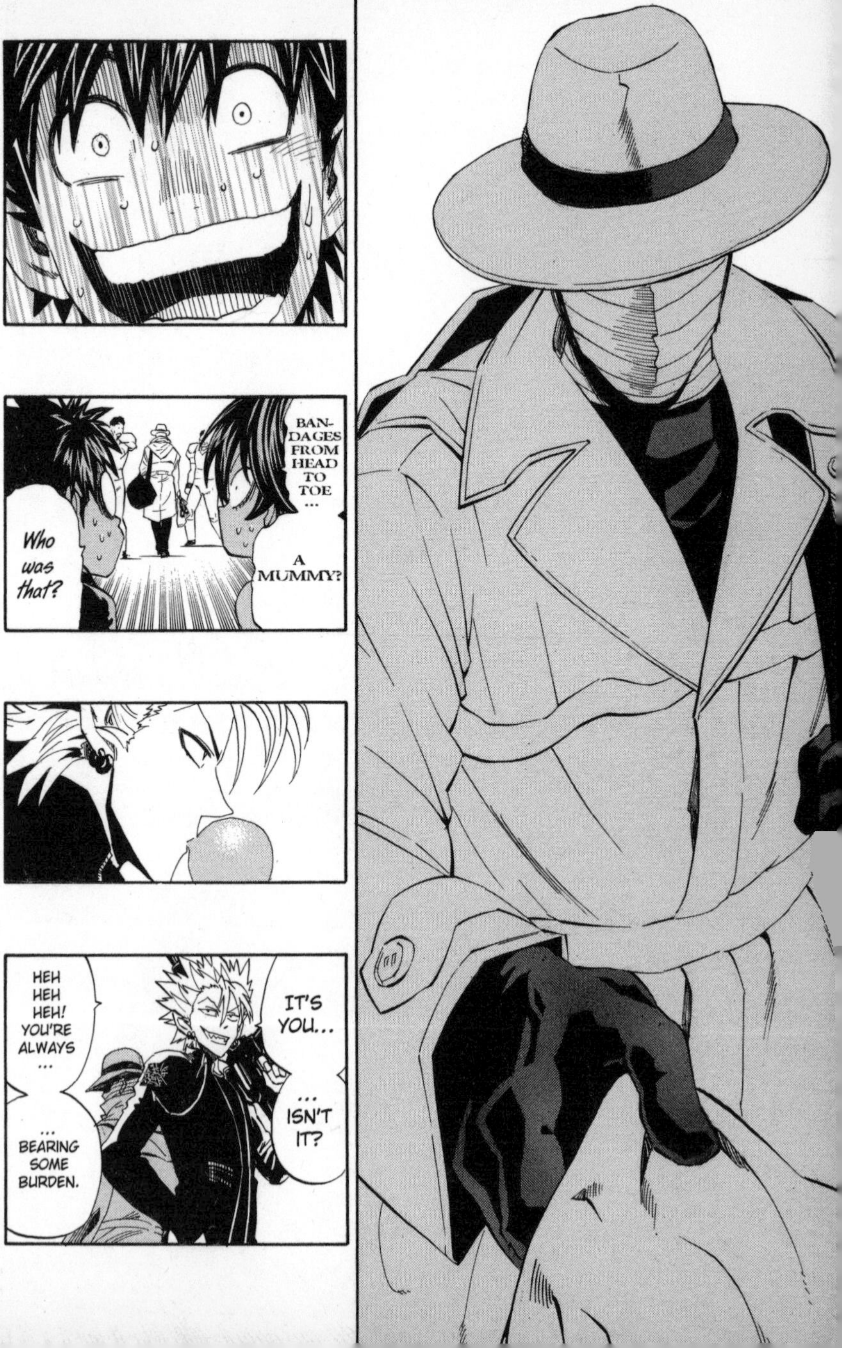
BAN-DAGES FROM HEAD TO TOE...
A MUMMY?
Who was that?
IT'S YOU...
...ISN'T IT?
HEH HEH HEH! YOU'RE ALWAYS...
...BEARING SOME BURDEN.

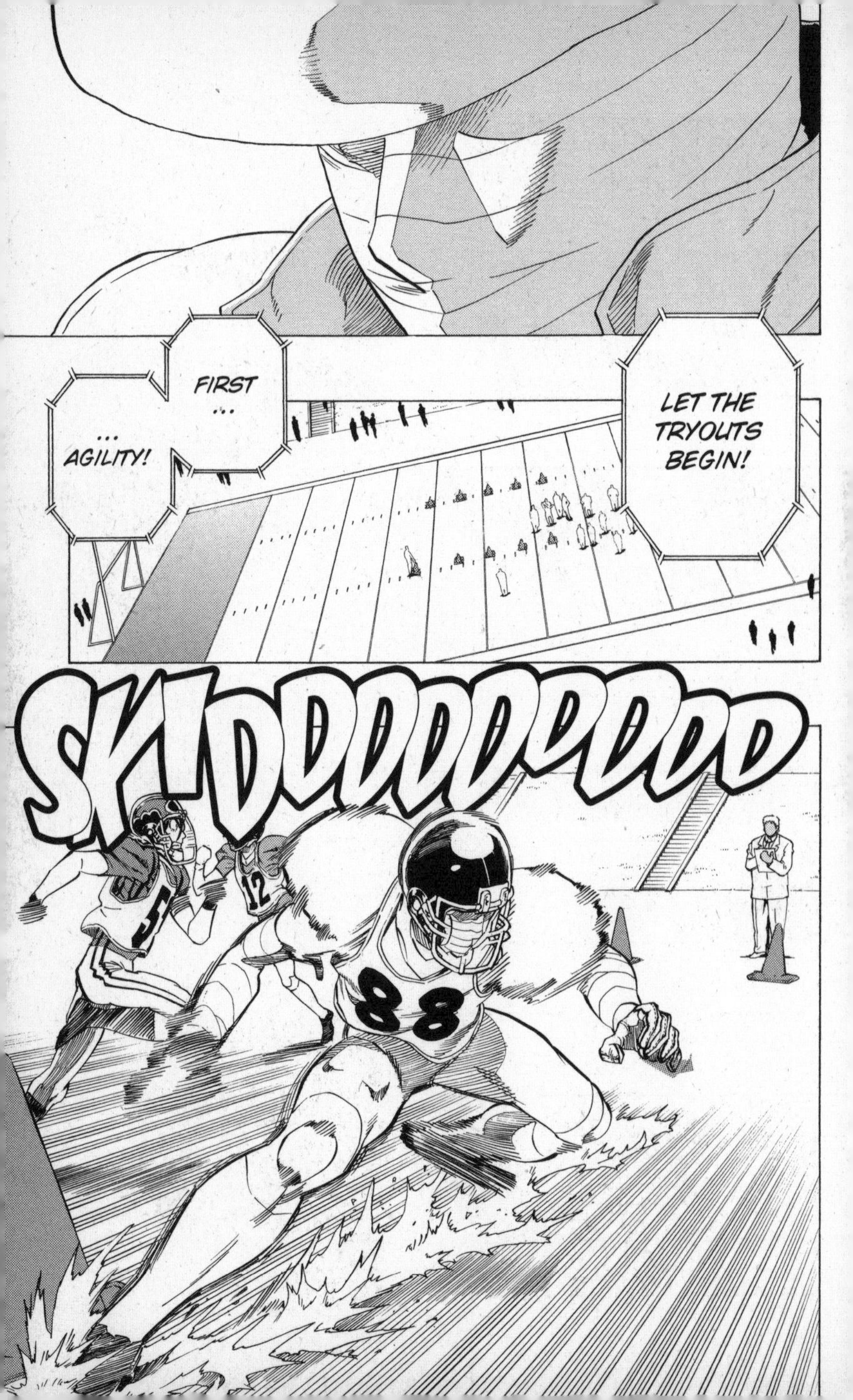
LET THE TRYOUTS BEGIN!
FIRST...
...AGILITY!
SKIDDDDDDDDDD

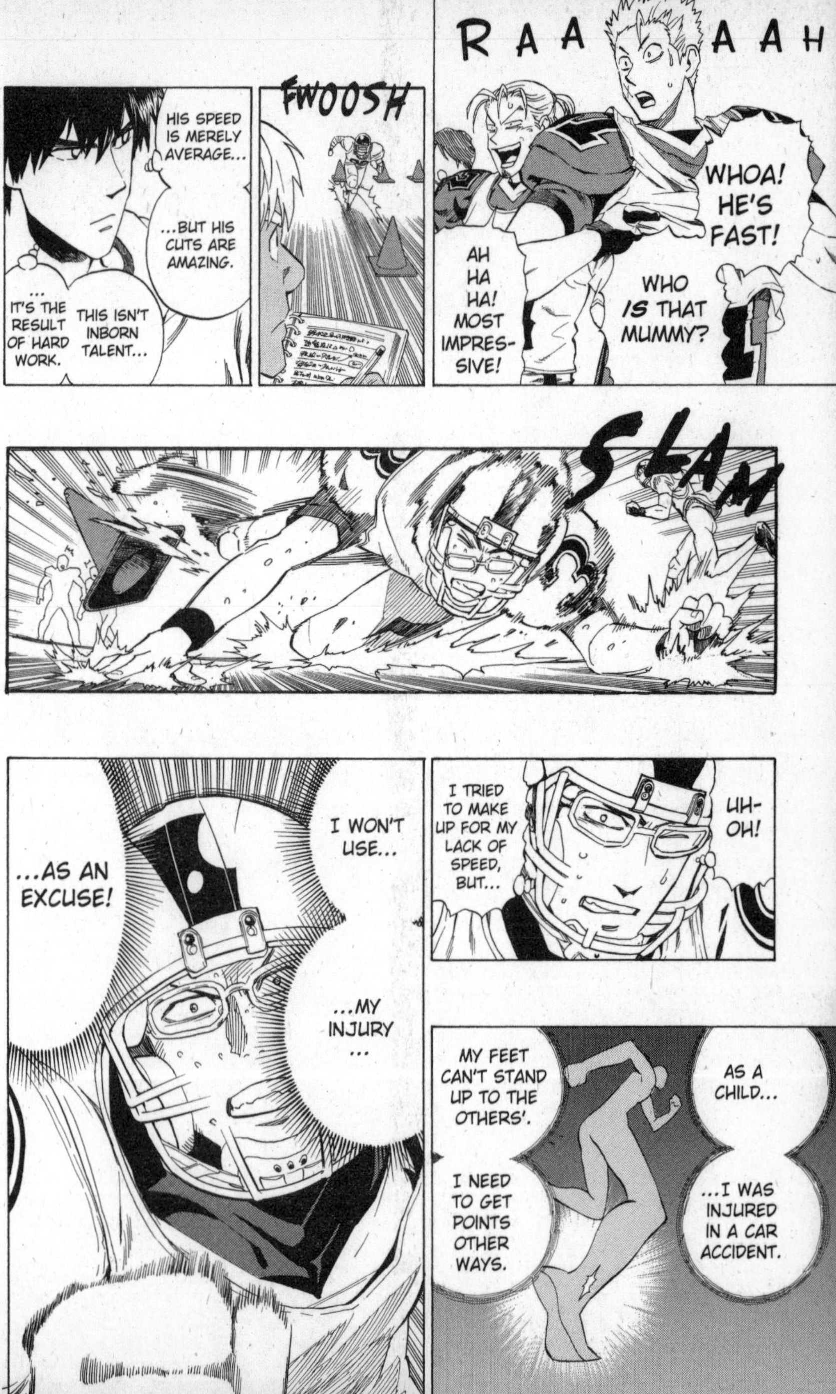
RAAAAH
WHOA! HE'S FAST!
WHO IS THAT MUMMY?
AH HA HA! MOST IMPRES-SIVE!
FWOOSH
HIS SPEED IS MERELY AVERAGE...
...BUT HIS CUTS ARE AMAZING.
THIS ISN'T INBORN TALENT...
...IT'S THE RESULT OF HARD WORK.
SLAM
UH-OH!
I TRIED TO MAKE UP FOR MY LACK OF SPEED, BUT...
AS A CHILD...
...I WAS INJURED IN A CAR ACCIDENT.
MY FEET CAN'T STAND UP TO THE OTHERS'.
I NEED TO GET POINTS OTHER WAYS.
I WON'T USE...
...MY INJURY...
...AS AN EXCUSE!

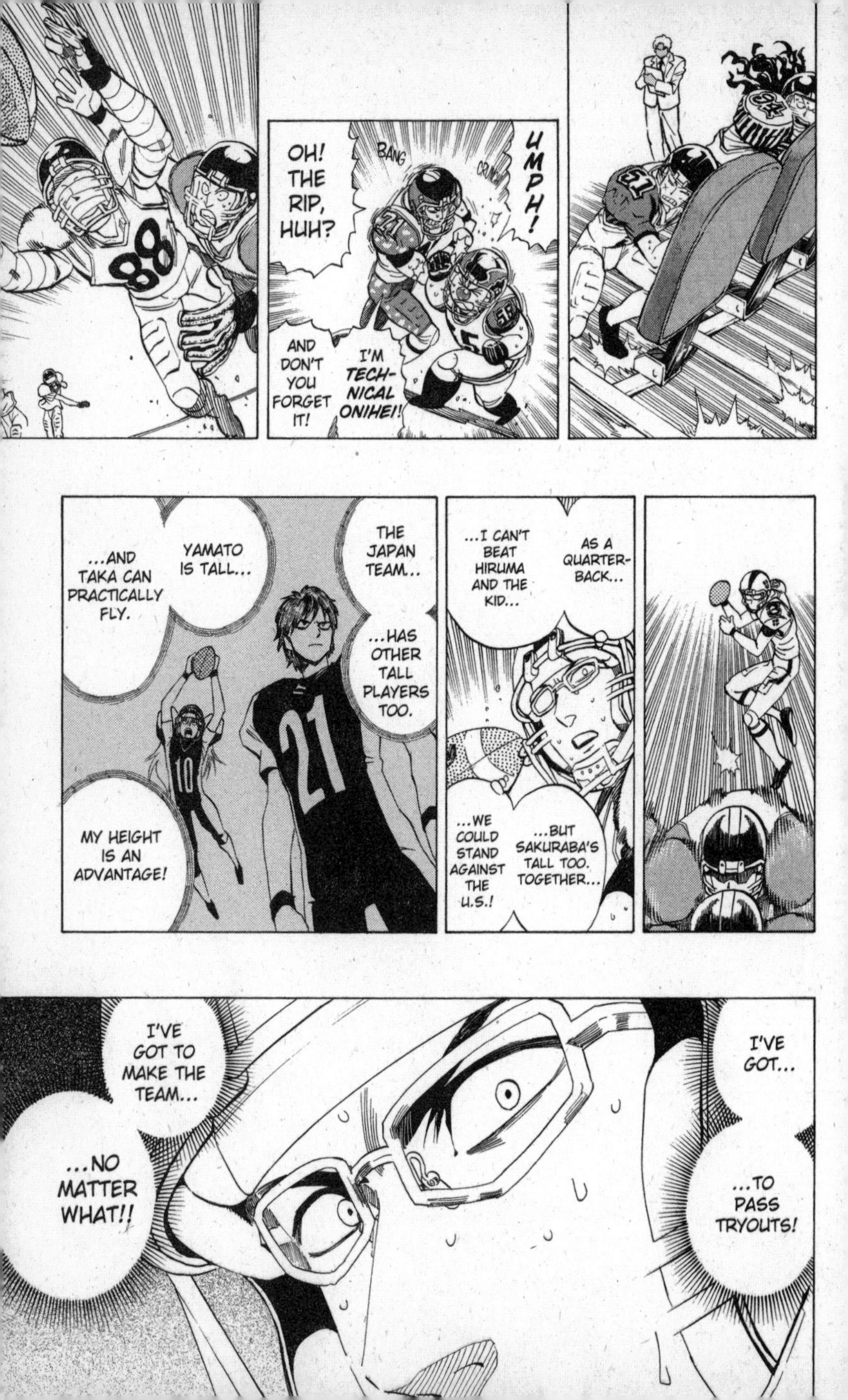
UMPH!
CRUNCH
BANG
OH! THE RIP, HUH?
I'M TECHNICAL ONIHEI!
AND DON'T YOU FORGET IT!
AS A QUARTER-BACK...
...I CAN'T BEAT HIRUMA AND THE KID...
...BUT SAKURABA'S TALL TOO. TOGETHER...
...WE COULD STAND AGAINST THE U.S.!
THE JAPAN TEAM...
YAMATO IS TALL...
...AND TAKA CAN PRACTICALLY FLY.
...HAS OTHER TALL PLAYERS TOO.
MY HEIGHT IS AN ADVANTAGE!
I'VE GOT...
...TO PASS TRYOUTS!
I'VE GOT TO MAKE THE TEAM...
...NO MATTER WHAT!!

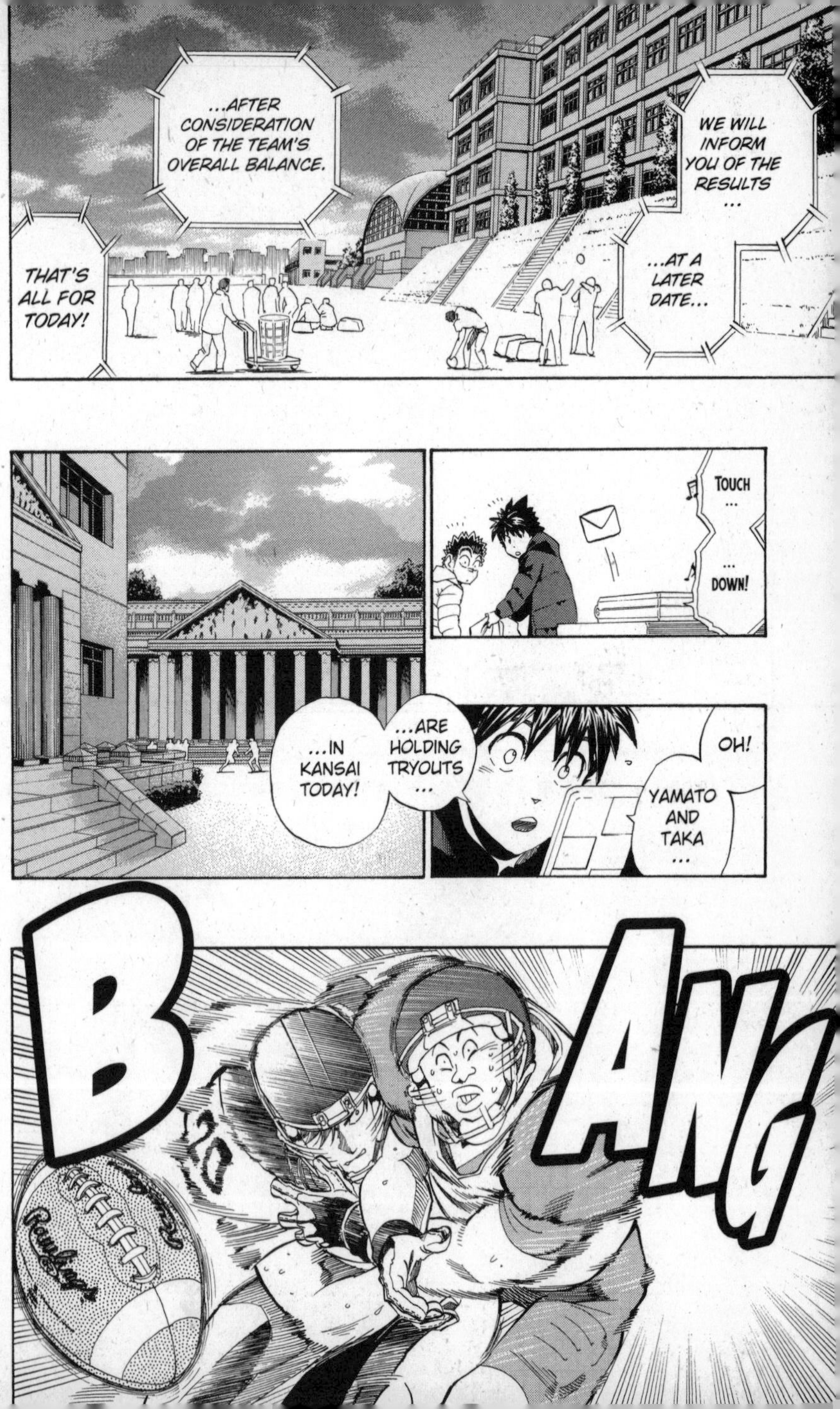
WE WILL INFORM YOU OF THE RESULTS ...
...AFTER CONSIDERATION OF THE TEAM'S OVERALL BALANCE.
...AT A LATER DATE...
THAT'S ALL FOR TODAY!
TOUCH ...
... DOWN!
OH!
YAMATO AND TAKA ...
...ARE HOLDING TRYOUTS ...
...IN KANSAI TODAY!
BANG

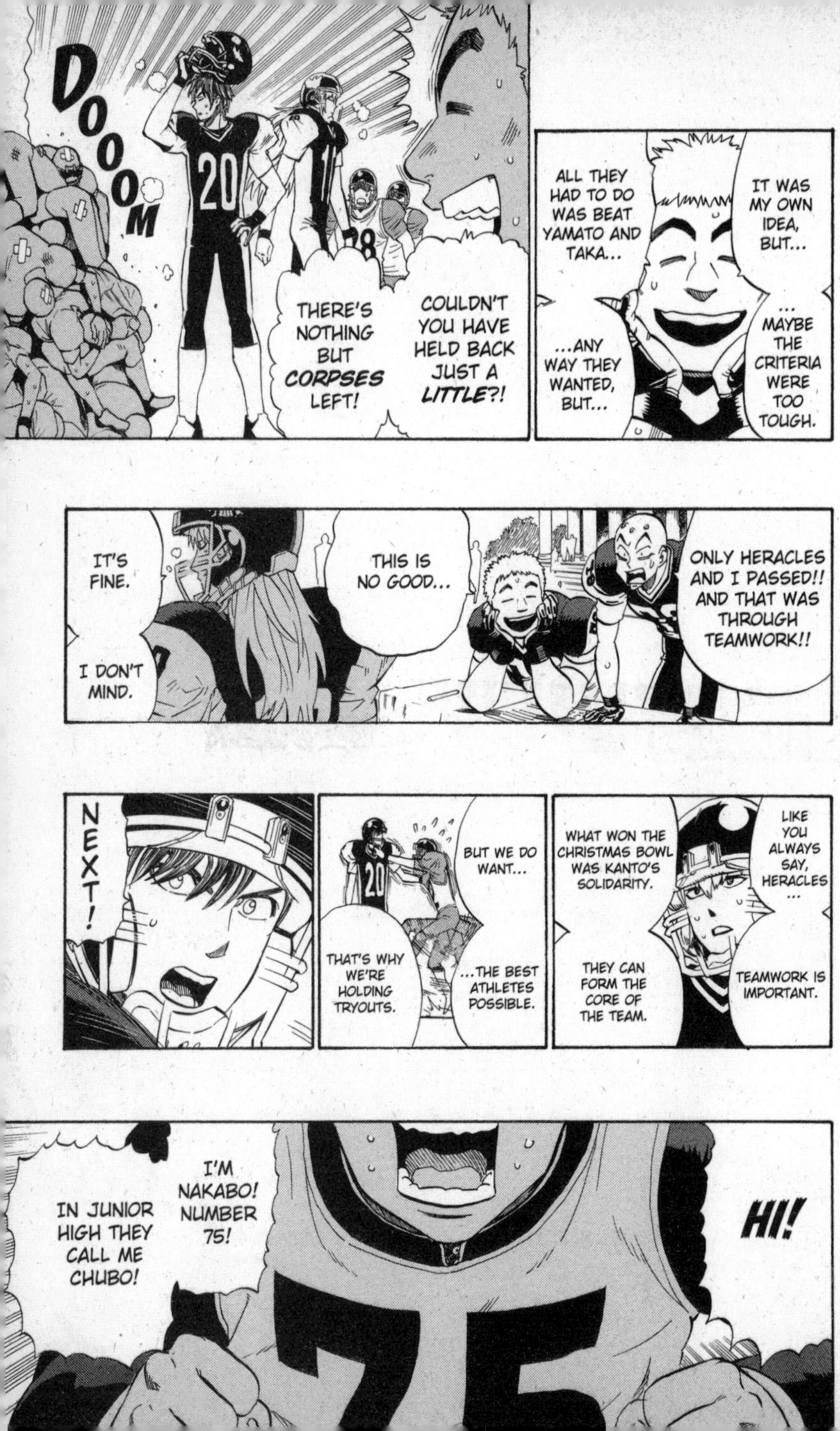
IT WAS MY OWN IDEA, BUT...
ALL THEY HAD TO DO WAS BEAT YAMATO AND TAKA...
...ANY WAY THEY WANTED, BUT...
...MAYBE THE CRITERIA WERE TOO TOUGH.
COULDN'T YOU HAVE HELD BACK JUST A *LITTLE*?!
THERE'S NOTHING BUT **CORPSES** LEFT!
DOOOOM
ONLY HERACLES AND I PASSED!! AND THAT WAS THROUGH TEAMWORK!!
THIS IS NO GOOD...
IT'S FINE.
I DON'T MIND.
LIKE YOU ALWAYS SAY, HERACLES...
TEAMWORK IS IMPORTANT.
WHAT WON THE CHRISTMAS BOWL WAS KANTO'S SOLIDARITY.
THEY CAN FORM THE CORE OF THE TEAM.
BUT WE DO WANT...
...THE BEST ATHLETES POSSIBLE.
THAT'S WHY WE'RE HOLDING TRYOUTS.
NEXT!
HI!
I'M NAKABO! NUMBER 75!
IN JUNIOR HIGH THEY CALL ME CHUBO!

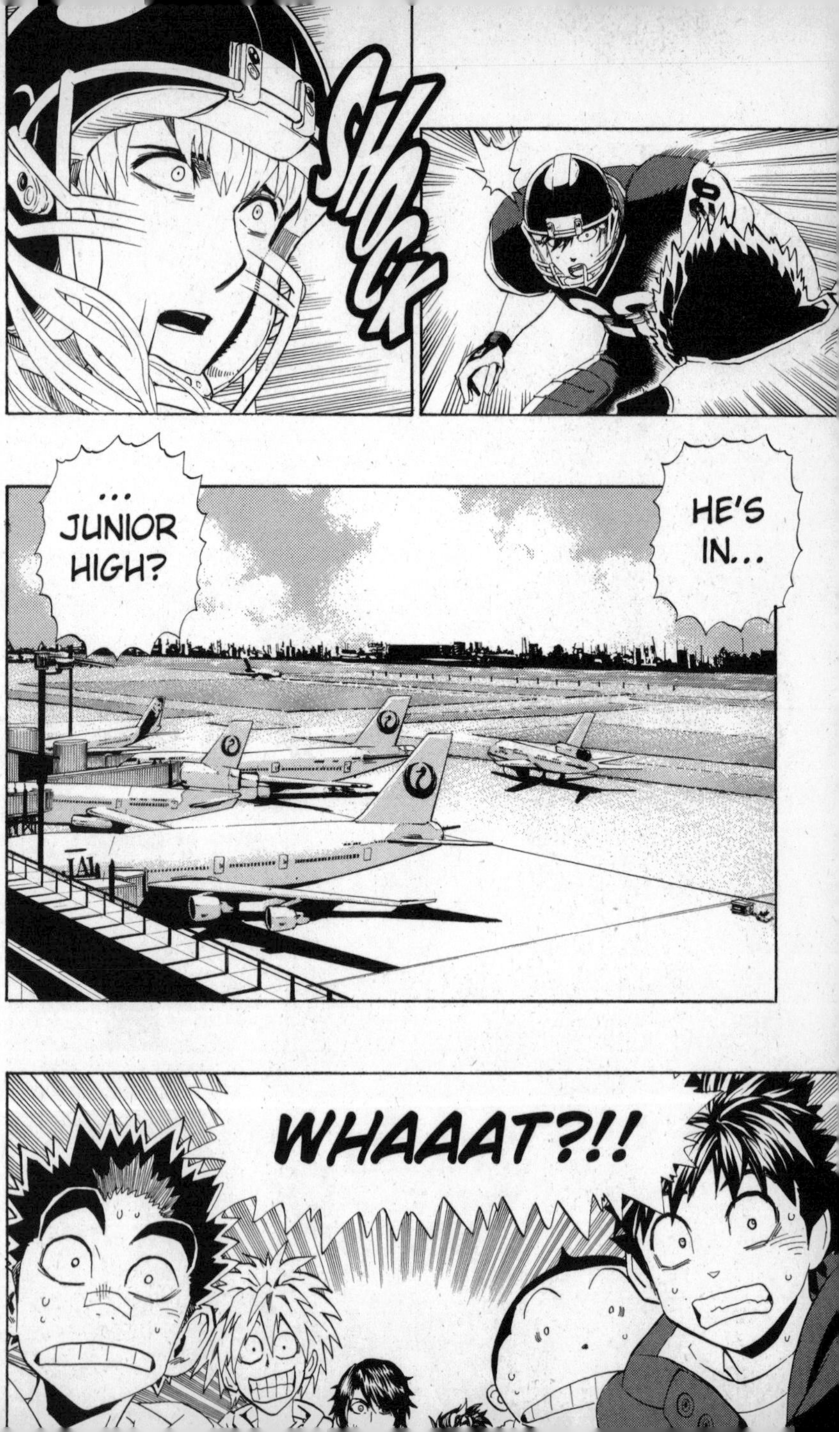
SHOCK
HE'S IN...
...JUNIOR HIGH?
WHAAAT?!!

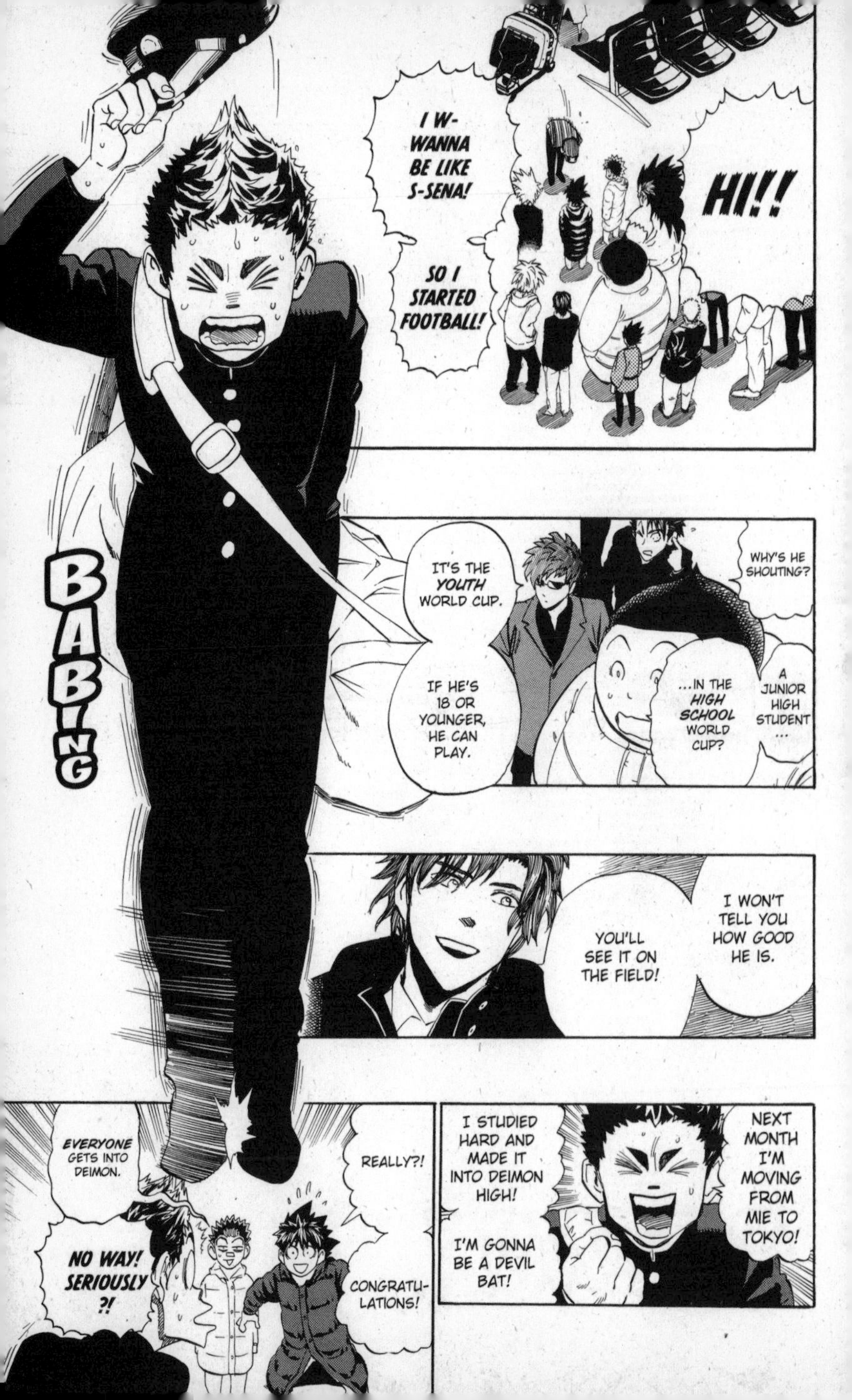
HI!!
I W-WANNA BE LIKE S-SENA!
SO I STARTED FOOTBALL!
WHY'S HE SHOUTING?
A JUNIOR HIGH STUDENT...
...IN THE HIGH SCHOOL WORLD CUP?
IT'S THE YOUTH WORLD CUP.
IF HE'S 18 OR YOUNGER, HE CAN PLAY.
I WON'T TELL YOU HOW GOOD HE IS.
YOU'LL SEE IT ON THE FIELD!
BABING
NEXT MONTH I'M MOVING FROM MIE TO TOKYO!
I STUDIED HARD AND MADE IT INTO DEIMON HIGH!
I'M GONNA BE A DEVIL BAT!
REALLY?!
CONGRATULATIONS!
EVERYONE GETS INTO DEIMON.
NO WAY! SERIOUSLY?!

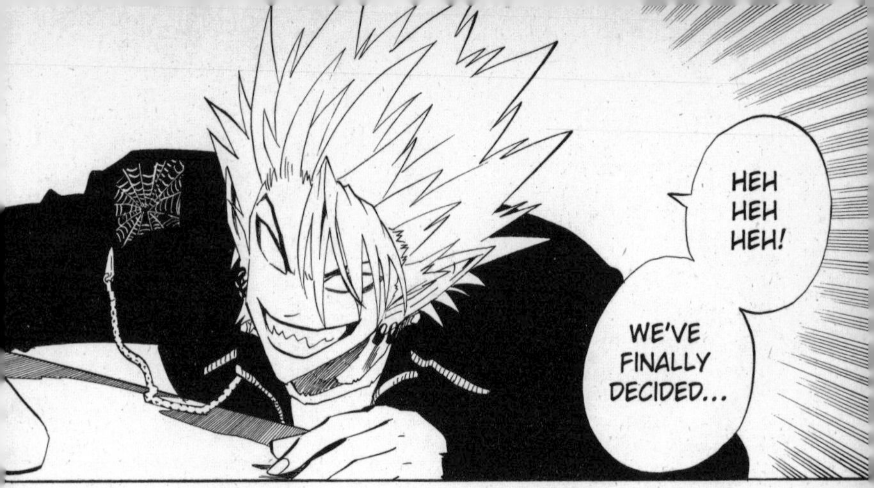
HEH HEH HEH!
WE'VE FINALLY DECIDED...

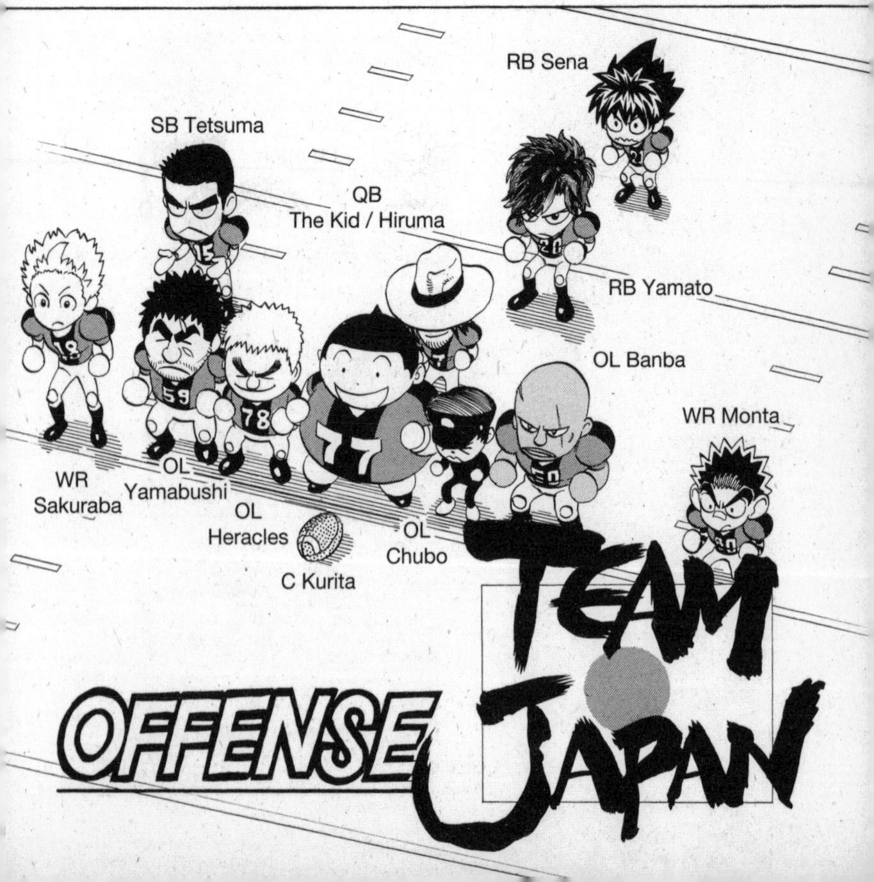
RB Sena
SB Tetsuma
QB The Kid / Hiruma
RB Yamato
OL Banba
WR Monta
OL Yamabushi
WR Sakuraba
OL Chubo
OL Heracles
C Kurita
TEAM JAPAN
OFFENSE

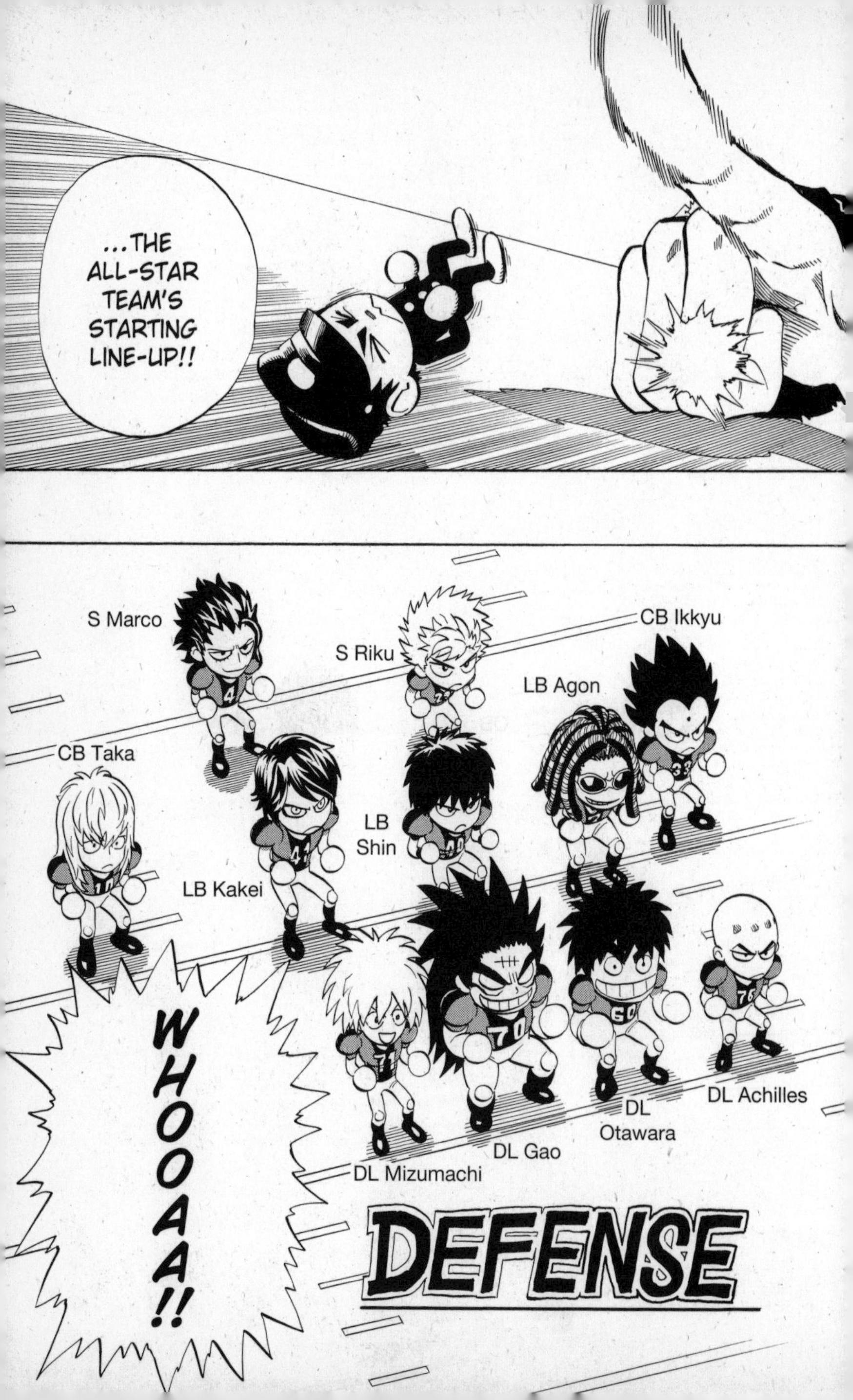
...THE ALL-STAR TEAM'S STARTING LINE-UP!!
CB Ikkyu
S Riku
S Marco
LB Agon
CB Taka
LB Shin
LB Kakei
DL Achilles
DL Otawara
DL Gao
DL Mizumachi
DEFENSE
WHOOAA!!

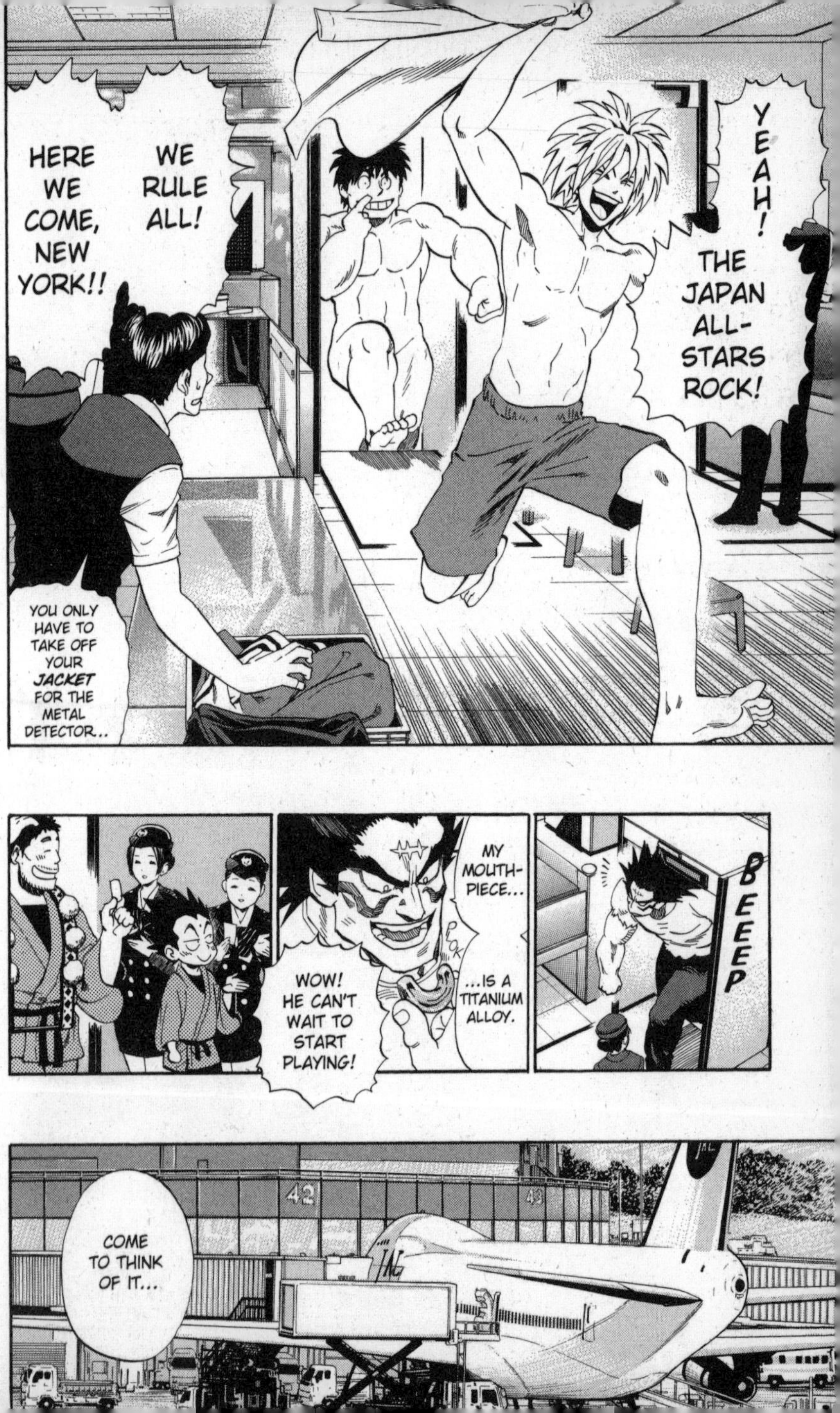
YEAH! THE JAPAN ALL-STARS ROCK!
WE RULE ALL!
HERE WE COME, NEW YORK!!
YOU ONLY HAVE TO TAKE OFF YOUR JACKET FOR THE METAL DETECTOR..
BEEEEP
MY MOUTH-PIECE...
PLOK
...IS A TITANIUM ALLOY.
WOW! HE CAN'T WAIT TO START PLAYING!
COME TO THINK OF IT...

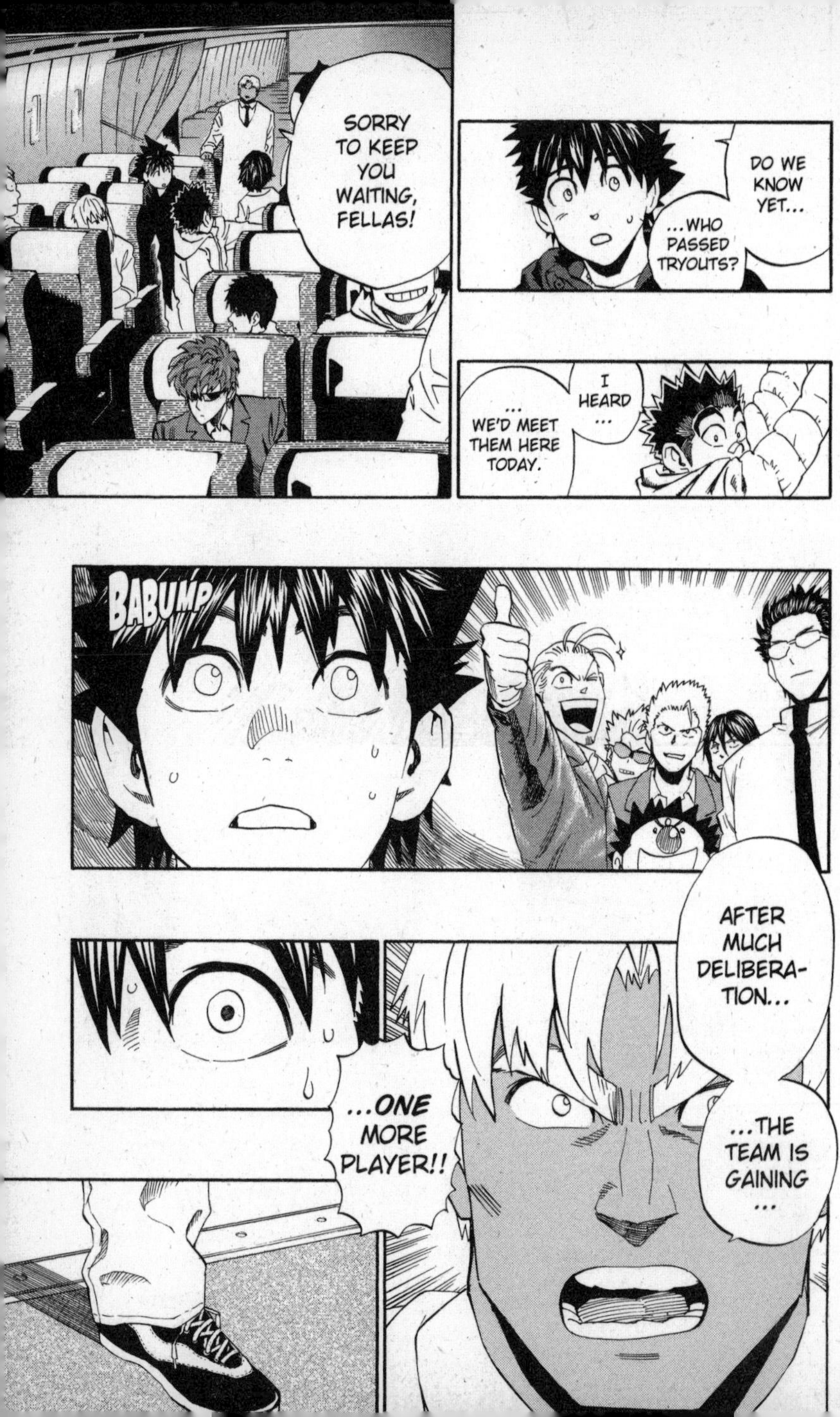
DO WE KNOW YET...
...WHO PASSED TRYOUTS?
I HEARD...
...WE'D MEET THEM HERE TODAY.
SORRY TO KEEP YOU WAITING, FELLAS!
BABUMP
AFTER MUCH DELIBERA-TION...
...THE TEAM IS GAINING...
...ONE MORE PLAYER!!

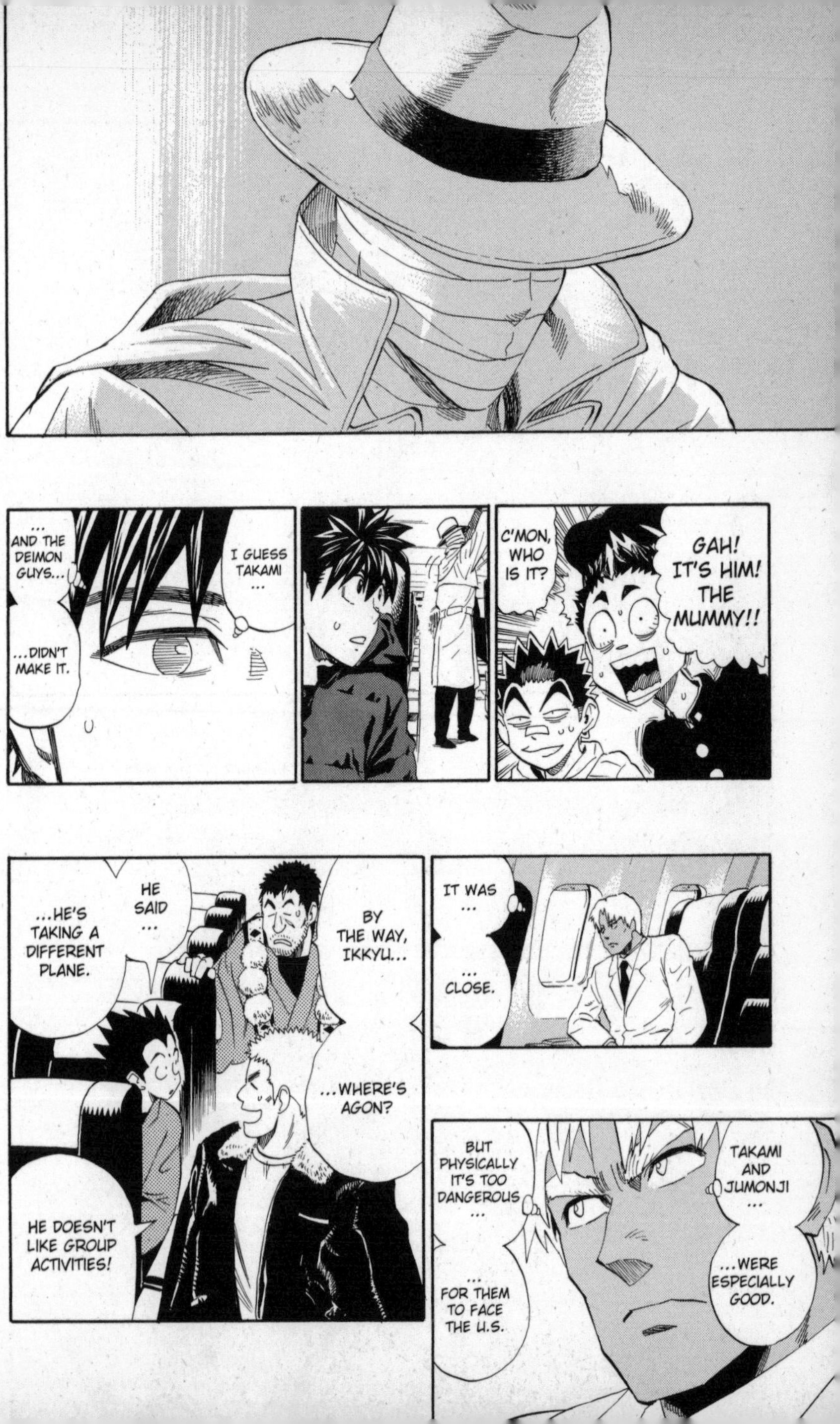
GAH! IT'S HIM! THE MUMMY!!
C'MON, WHO IS IT?
I GUESS TAKAMI...
...AND THE DEIMON GUYS...
...DIDN'T MAKE IT.
IT WAS...
...CLOSE.
TAKAMI AND JUMONJI...
...WERE ESPECIALLY GOOD.
BUT PHYSICALLY IT'S TOO DANGEROUS...
...FOR THEM TO FACE THE U.S.
BY THE WAY, IKKYU...
...WHERE'S AGON?
HE SAID...
...HE'S TAKING A DIFFERENT PLANE.
HE DOESN'T LIKE GROUP ACTIVITIES!

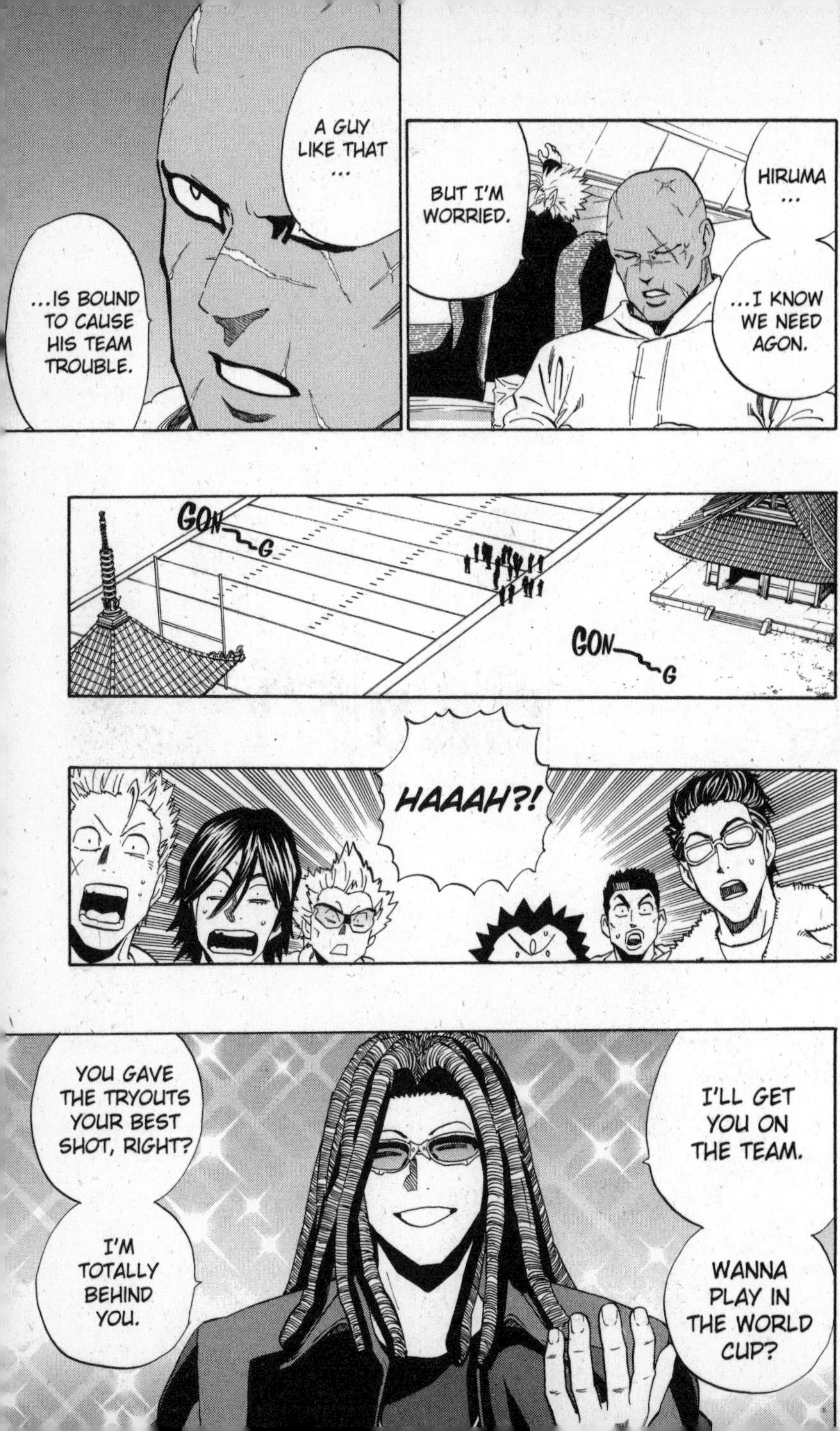
HIRUMA ...
...I KNOW WE NEED AGON.
BUT I'M WORRIED.
A GUY LIKE THAT ...
...IS BOUND TO CAUSE HIS TEAM TROUBLE.
GON—G
GON—G
HAAAH?!
I'LL GET YOU ON THE TEAM.
WANNA PLAY IN THE WORLD CUP?
YOU GAVE THE TRYOUTS YOUR BEST SHOT, RIGHT?
I'M TOTALLY BEHIND YOU.

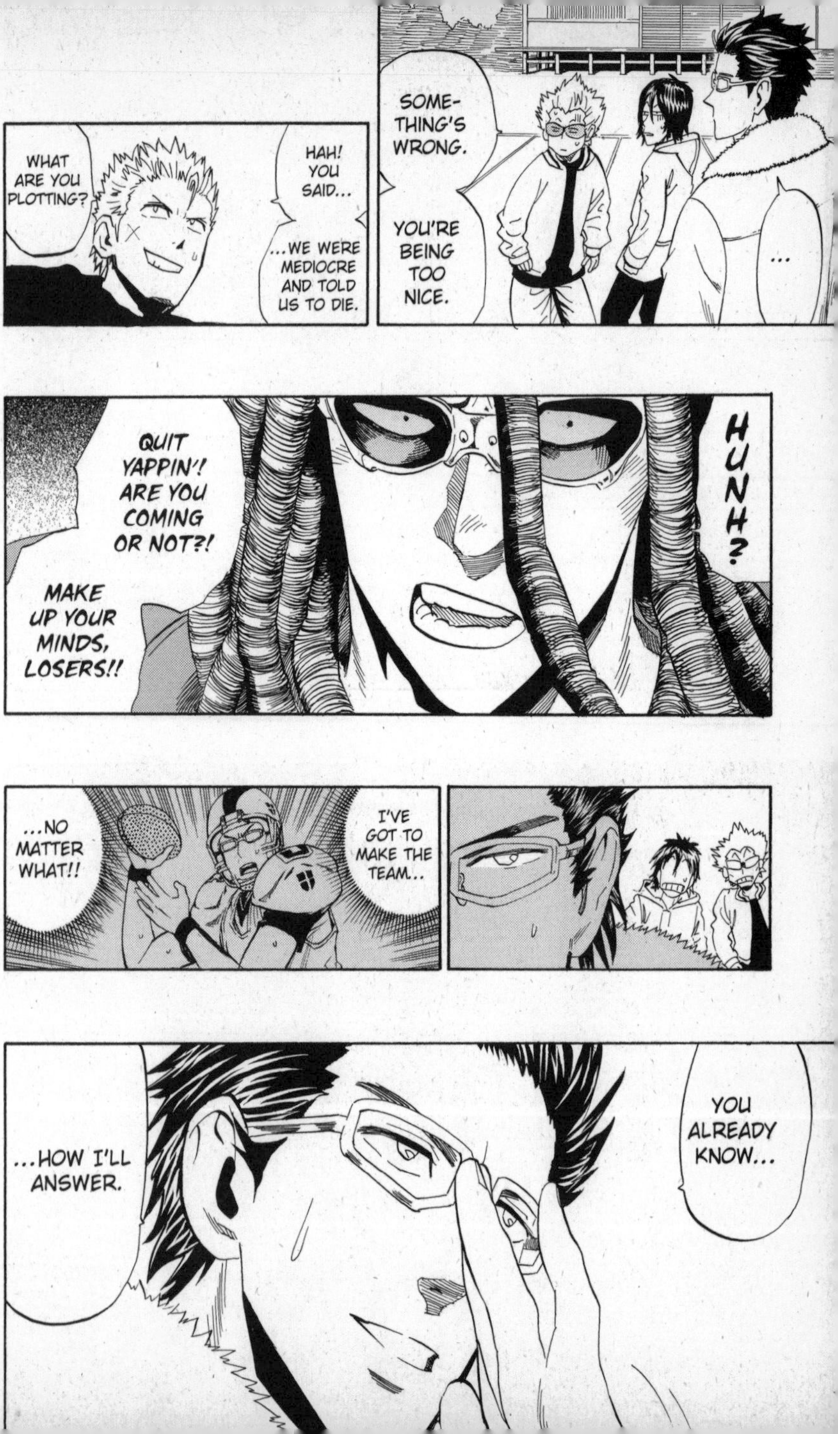
SOME-THING'S WRONG.
YOU'RE BEING TOO NICE.
...
HAH! YOU SAID...
...WE WERE MEDIOCRE AND TOLD US TO DIE.
WHAT ARE YOU PLOTTING?
HUNH?
QUIT YAPPIN'! ARE YOU COMING OR NOT?!
MAKE UP YOUR MINDS, LOSERS!!
I'VE GOT TO MAKE THE TEAM...
...NO MATTER WHAT!!
YOU ALREADY KNOW...
...HOW I'LL ANSWER.

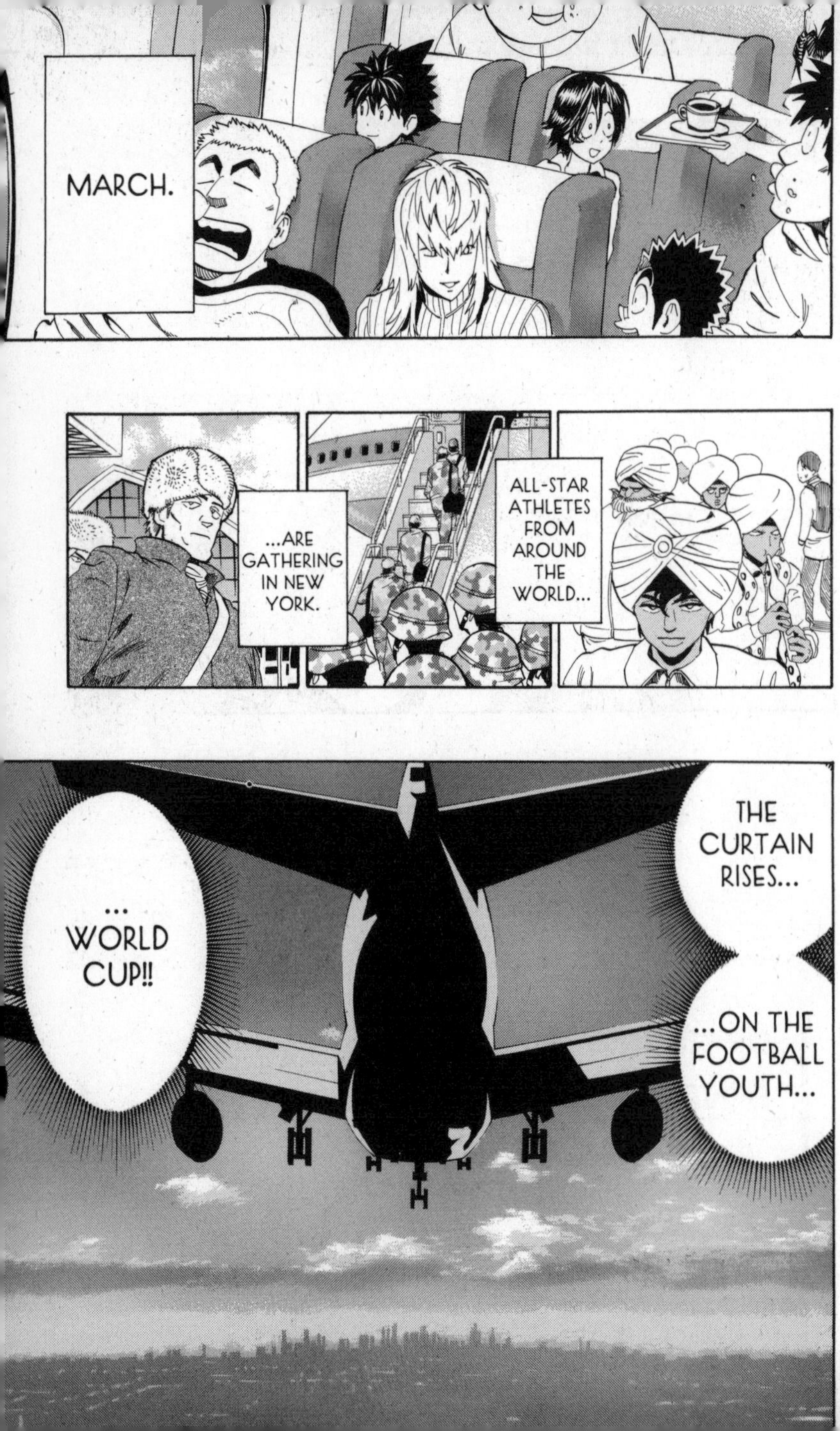
MARCH.
ALL-STAR ATHLETES FROM AROUND THE WORLD...
...ARE GATHERING IN NEW YORK.
THE CURTAIN RISES...
...ON THE FOOTBALL YOUTH...
...WORLD CUP!!

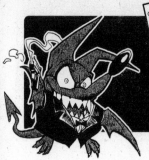

Investigation File #151

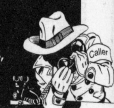

Panther was jumping across building rooftops, but it looked so easy. How does he do that?

Caller

Caller name: S.G. (male) in Tokyo

THERE'S A REAL SPORT CALLED ***PARKOUR***.

IT'S NOTHING BUT YOU AND YOUR BODY JUMPING OVER OBSTACLES AND FLYING AROUND TOWN ACROSS ROOFTOPS AND SUCH.

IT'S DANGEROUS, THOUGH, SO DON'T TAKE IT UP ON A WHIM! YOU SHOULD ONLY DO IT AFTER SERIOUSLY BUILDING YOURSELF UP!

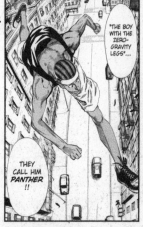

"THE BOY WITH THE ZERO-GRAVITY LEGS"...
THEY CALL HIM ***PANTHER*** !!

(See Volume 7, Chapter 58, page 116.)

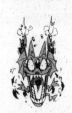

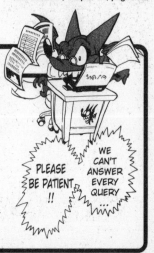

Send your queries for Devil Bat 021 here!!

Devil Bat 021
Shonen Jump Advanced/Eyeshield 21
c/o VIZ Media, LLC
P.O. Box 77010
San Francisco, CA 94107

WE CAN'T ANSWER EVERY QUERY ...
PLEASE BE PATIENT !!

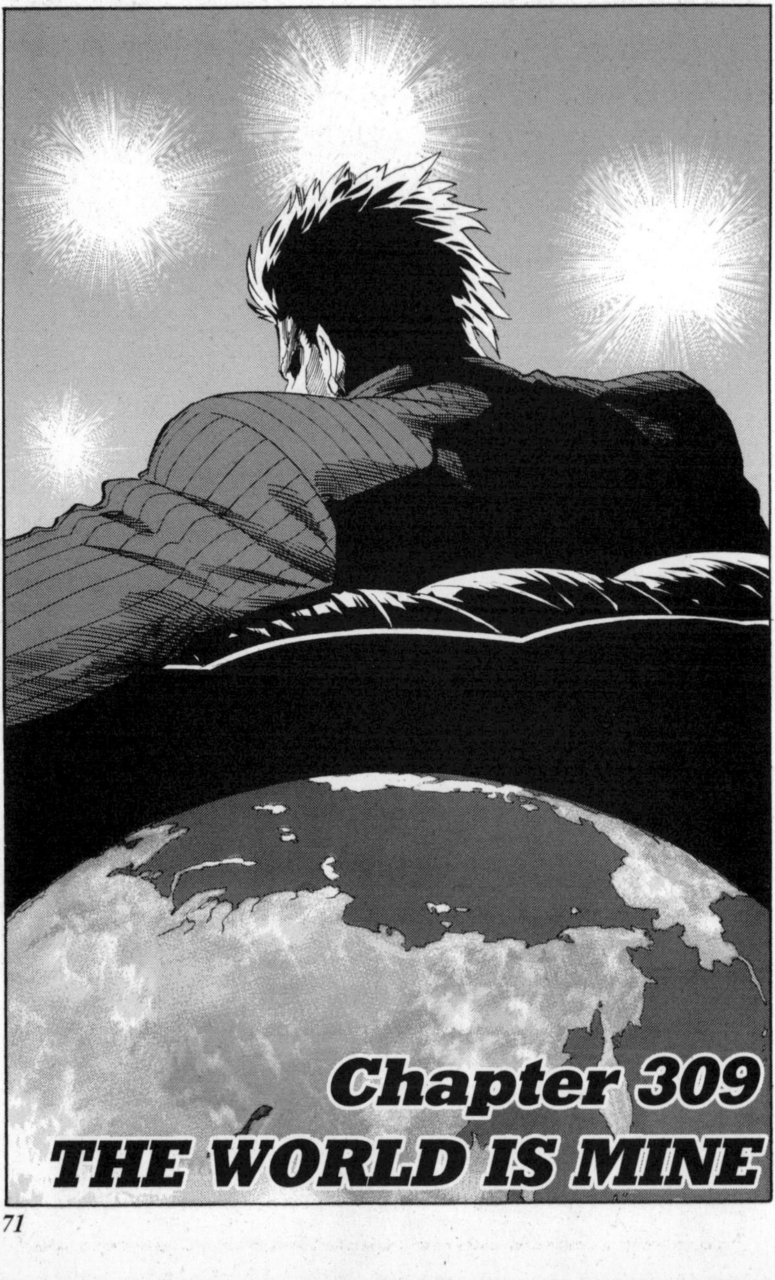
Chapter 309
THE WORLD IS MINE

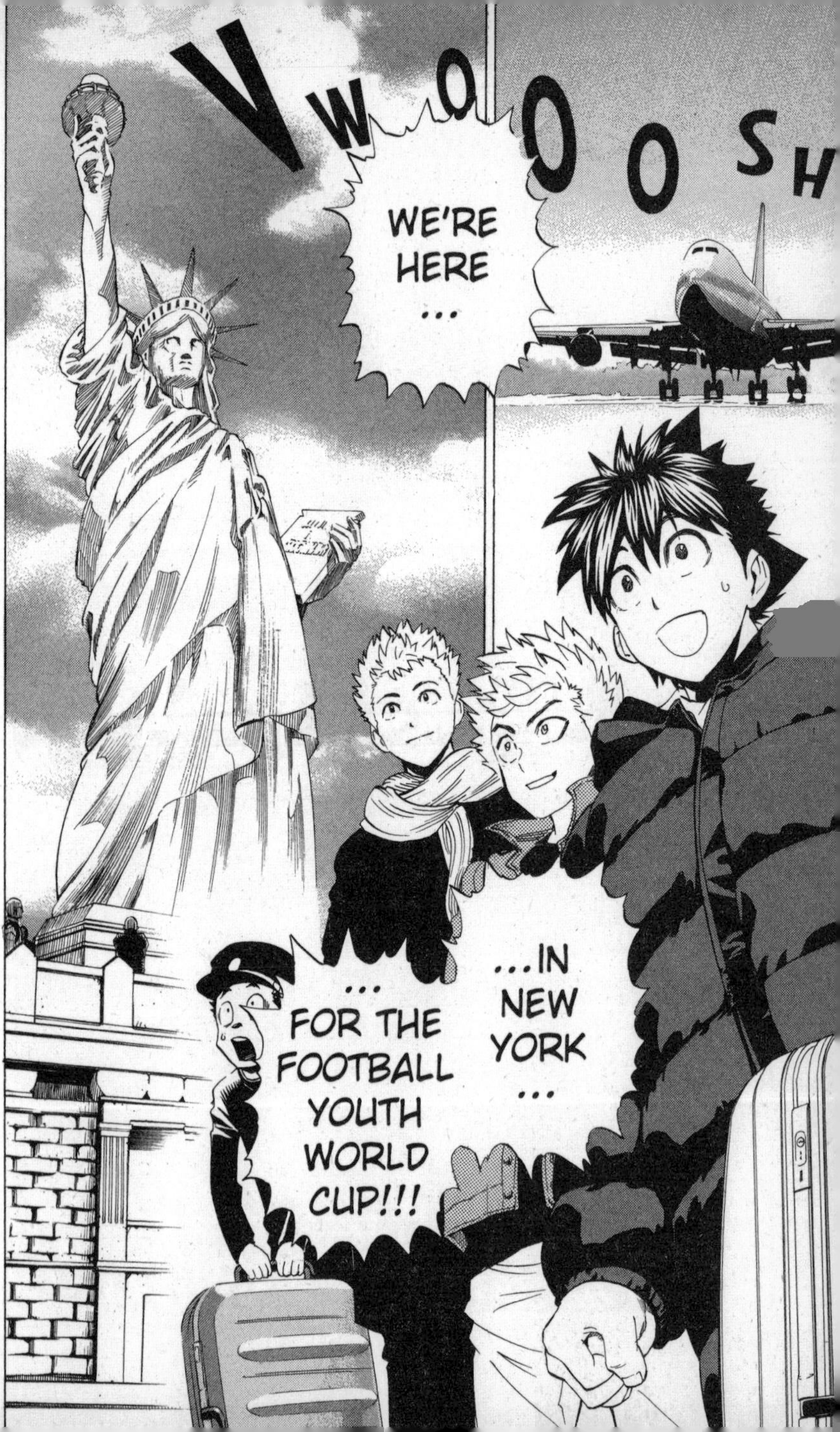
VWOOOSH
WE'RE HERE ...
...IN NEW YORK ...
... FOR THE FOOTBALL YOUTH WORLD CUP!!!

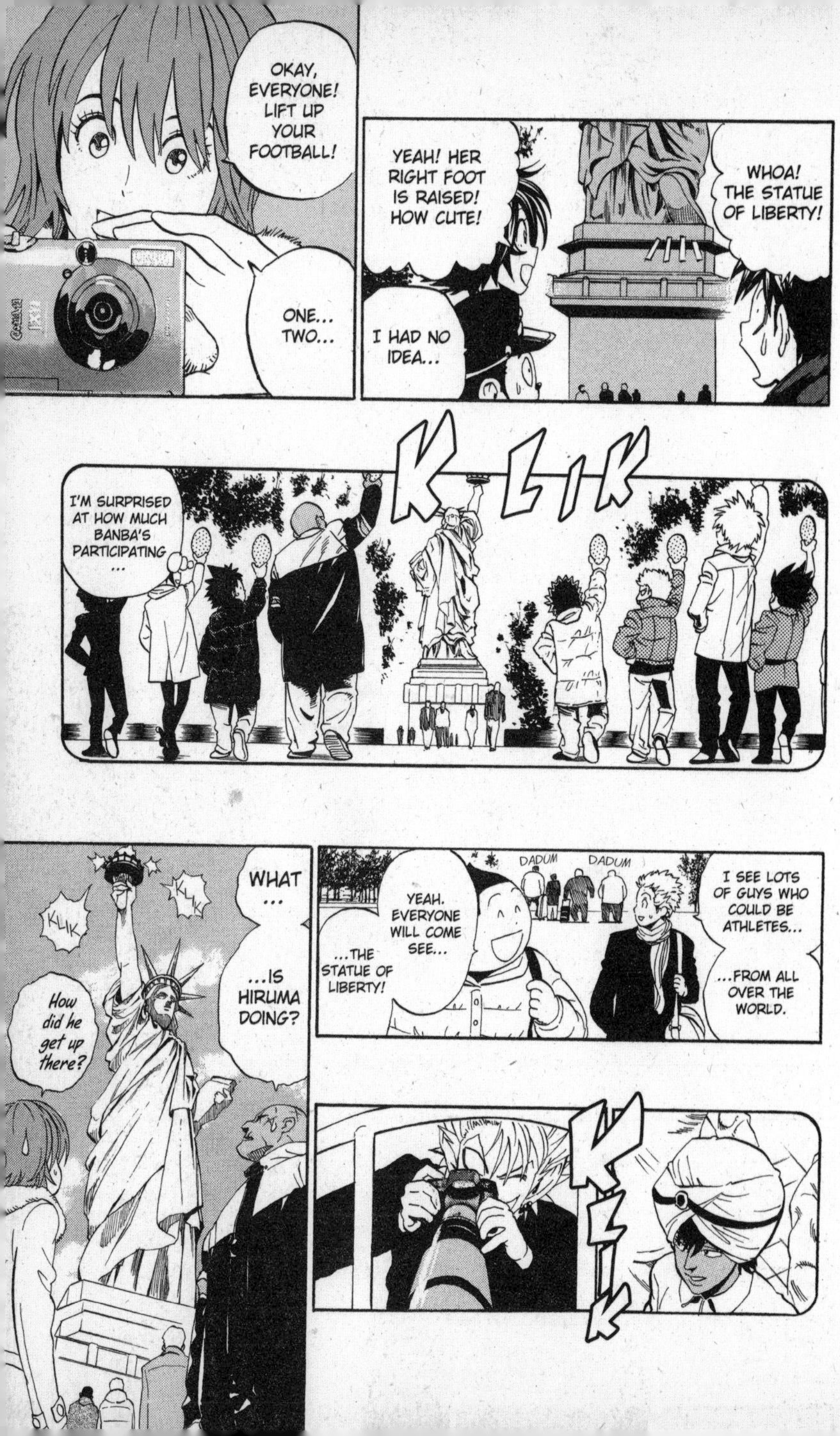
WHOA! THE STATUE OF LIBERTY!
YEAH! HER RIGHT FOOT IS RAISED! HOW CUTE!
I HAD NO IDEA...
OKAY, EVERYONE! LIFT UP YOUR FOOTBALL!
ONE... TWO...
KLIK
I'M SURPRISED AT HOW MUCH BANBA'S PARTICIPATING ...
I SEE LOTS OF GUYS WHO COULD BE ATHLETES...
...FROM ALL OVER THE WORLD.
DADUM
DADUM
YEAH. EVERYONE WILL COME SEE...
...THE STATUE OF LIBERTY!
KLIK
WHAT ...
...IS HIRUMA DOING?
KLIK
KLIK
How did he get up there?

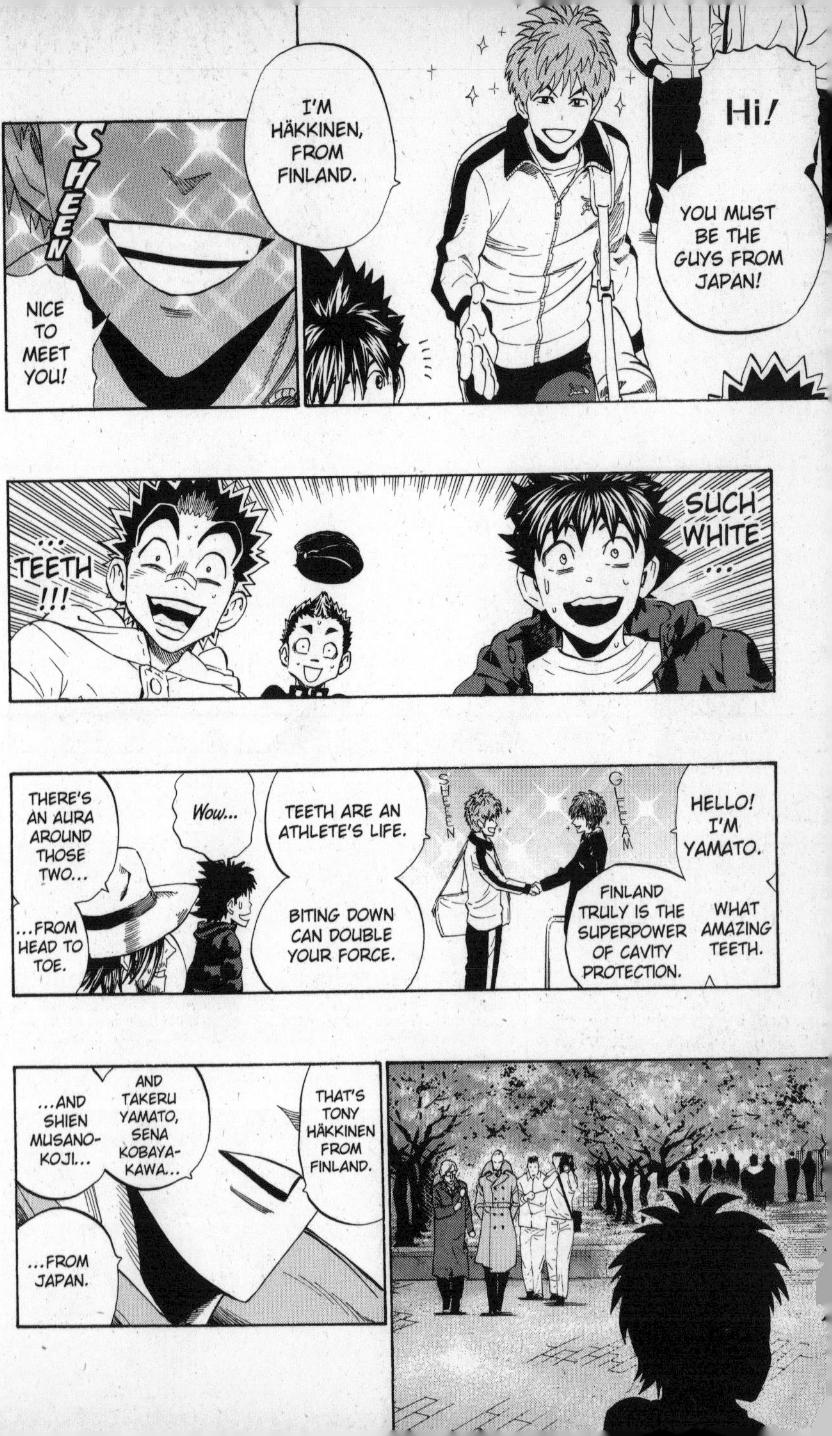
Hi!
YOU MUST BE THE GUYS FROM JAPAN!
I'M HÄKKINEN, FROM FINLAND.
SHEEN
NICE TO MEET YOU!
SUCH WHITE...
...TEETH!!!
HELLO! I'M YAMATO.
WHAT AMAZING TEETH.
FINLAND TRULY IS THE SUPERPOWER OF CAVITY PROTECTION.
GLEAM
SHEEN
TEETH ARE AN ATHLETE'S LIFE.
BITING DOWN CAN DOUBLE YOUR FORCE.
Wow...
THERE'S AN AURA AROUND THOSE TWO...
...FROM HEAD TO TOE.
THAT'S TONY HÄKKINEN FROM FINLAND.
AND TAKERU YAMATO, SENA KOBAYAKAWA...
...AND SHIEN MUSANOKOJI...
...FROM JAPAN.

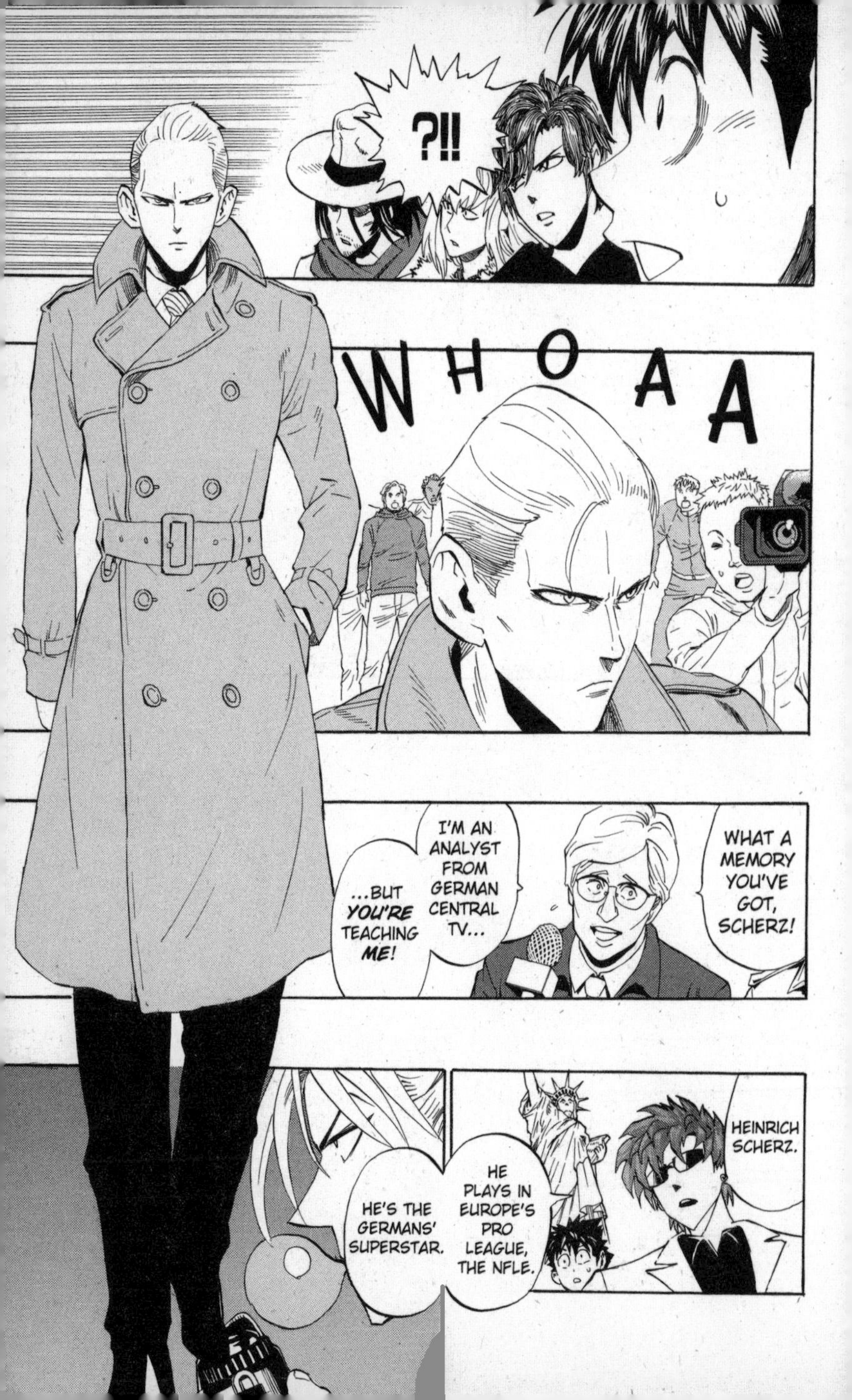
?!!
WHOAA
WHAT A MEMORY YOU'VE GOT, SCHERZ!
I'M AN ANALYST FROM GERMAN CENTRAL TV...
...BUT *YOU'RE* TEACHING *ME*!
HEINRICH SCHERZ.
HE PLAYS IN EUROPE'S PRO LEAGUE, THE NFLE.
HE'S THE GERMANS' SUPERSTAR.

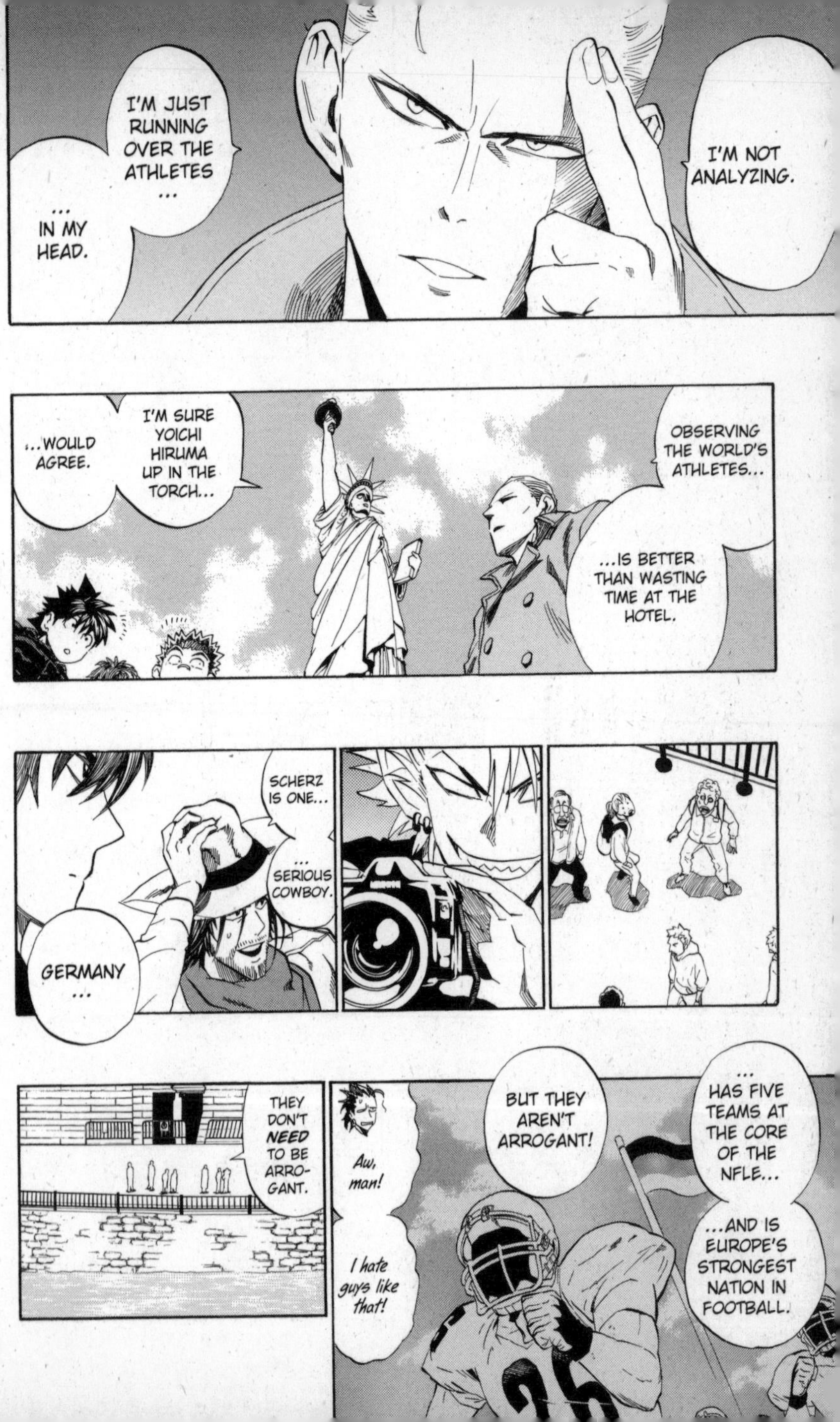
I'M NOT ANALYZING.
I'M JUST RUNNING OVER THE ATHLETES ...
... IN MY HEAD.
OBSERVING THE WORLD'S ATHLETES...
...IS BETTER THAN WASTING TIME AT THE HOTEL.
I'M SURE YOICHI HIRUMA UP IN THE TORCH...
...WOULD AGREE.
SCHERZ IS ONE...
... SERIOUS COWBOY.
GERMANY ...
... HAS FIVE TEAMS AT THE CORE OF THE NFLE...
...AND IS EUROPE'S STRONGEST NATION IN FOOTBALL.
BUT THEY AREN'T ARROGANT!
Aw, man!
I hate guys like that!
THEY DON'T **NEED** TO BE ARRO-GANT.

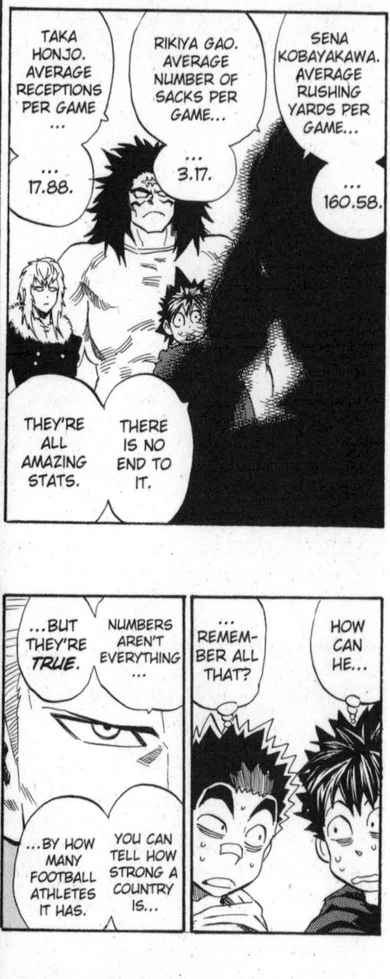
SENA KOBAYAKAWA. AVERAGE RUSHING YARDS PER GAME...
...160.58.
RIKIYA GAO. AVERAGE NUMBER OF SACKS PER GAME...
...3.17.
TAKA HONJO. AVERAGE RECEPTIONS PER GAME...
...17.88.
THERE IS NO END TO IT.
THEY'RE ALL AMAZING STATS.
HOW CAN HE...
...REMEM-BER ALL THAT?
NUMBERS AREN'T EVERYTHING...
...BUT THEY'RE *TRUE*.
YOU CAN TELL HOW STRONG A COUNTRY IS...
...BY HOW MANY FOOTBALL ATHLETES IT HAS.
JAPAN AND A FEW OTHER NATIONS...
...HAVE NUMBERS TO RIVAL GERMANY'S.
IN THE WORLD CUP...
...THE WORLD TAKES ON AMERICA.
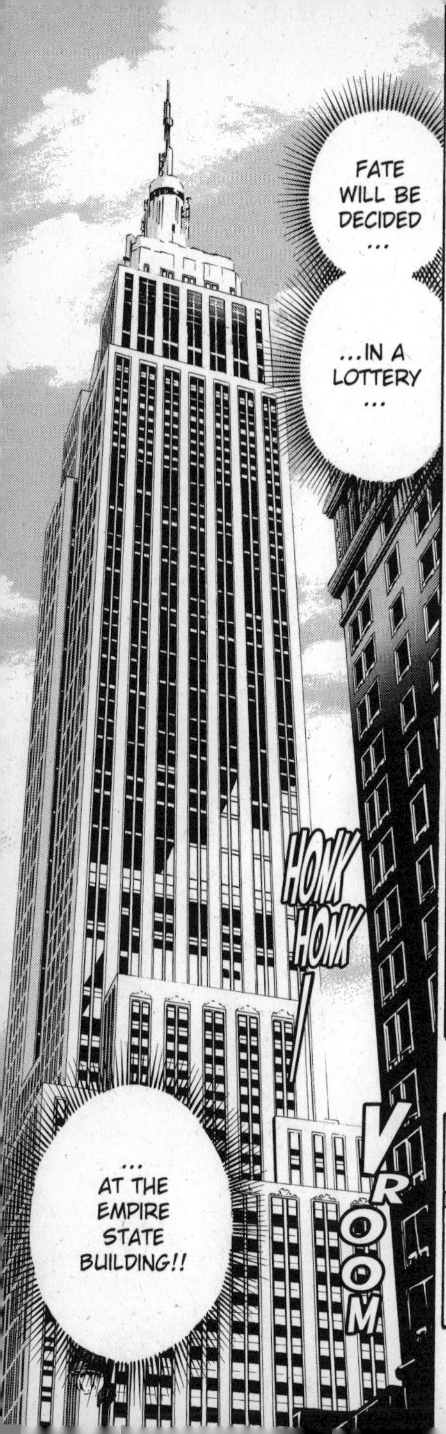
FATE WILL BE DECIDED...
...IN A LOTTERY...
HONK HONK!
VROOM
...AT THE EMPIRE STATE BUILDING!!

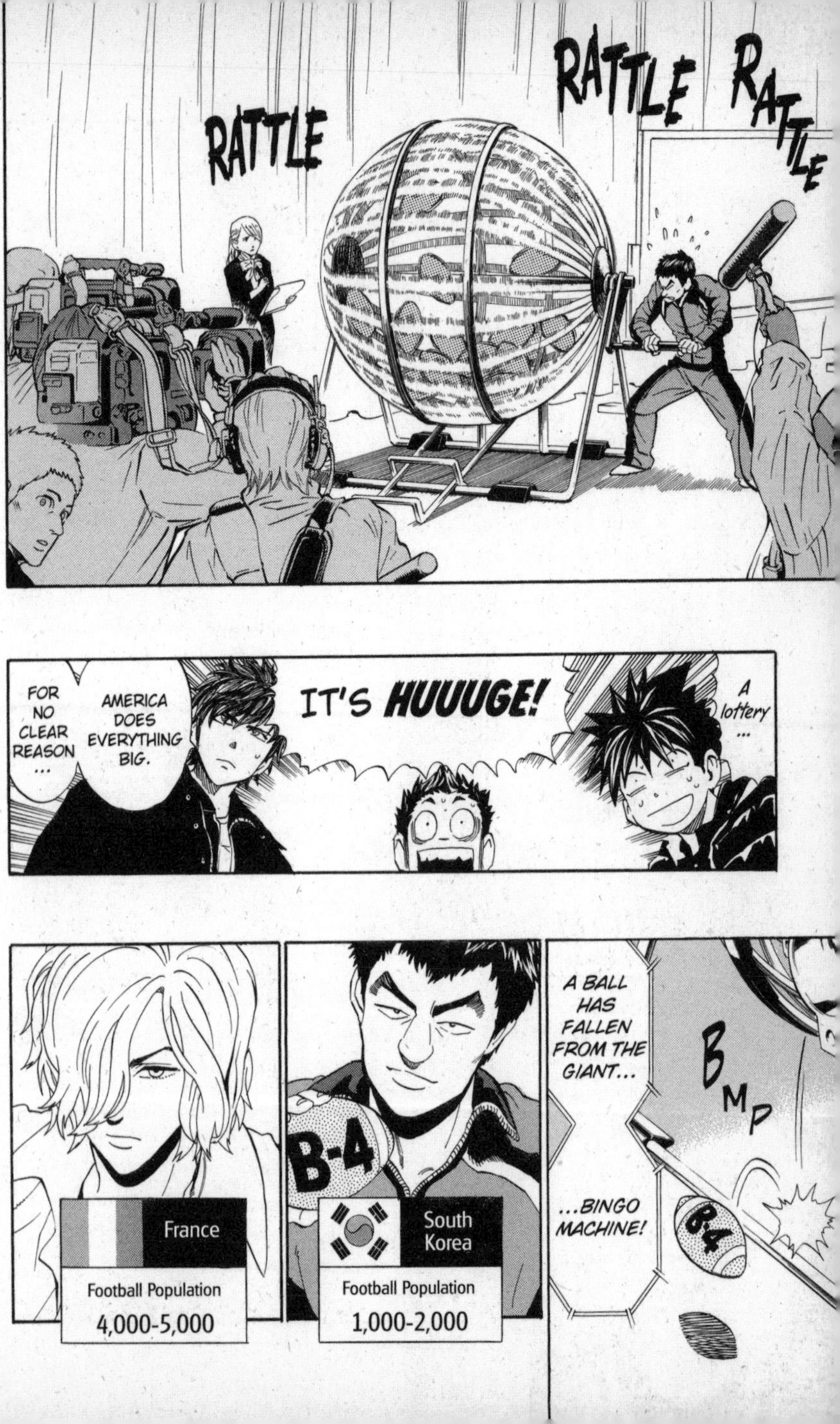
RATTLE RATTLE
RATTLE
A lottery ...
IT'S HUUUGE!
AMERICA DOES EVERYTHING BIG.
FOR NO CLEAR REASON ...
A BALL HAS FALLEN FROM THE GIANT...
BMP
...BINGO MACHINE!
B-4
B-4
South Korea
Football Population
1,000-2,000
France
Football Population
4,000-5,000

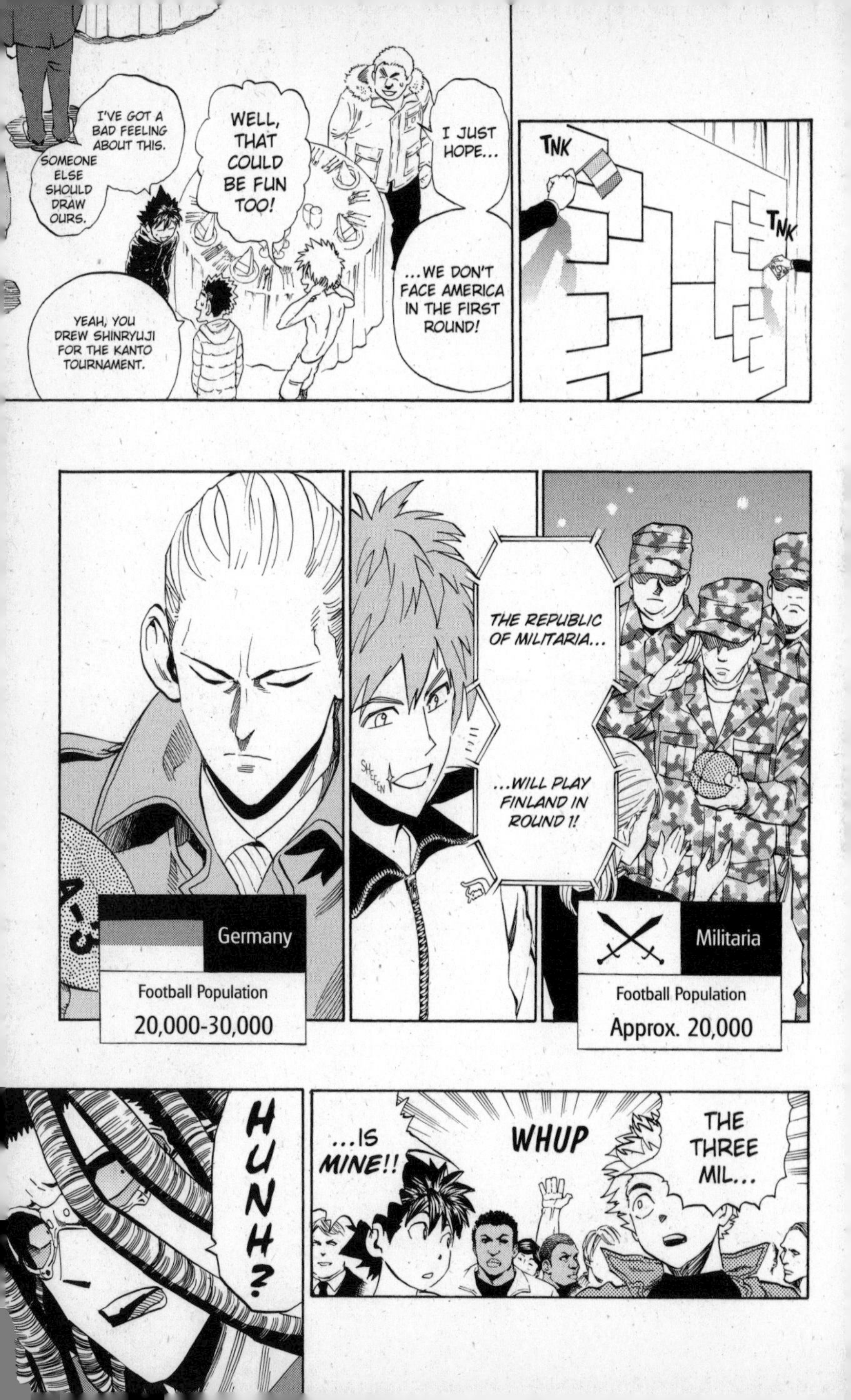
TNK
TNK
I JUST HOPE...
...WE DON'T FACE AMERICA IN THE FIRST ROUND!
WELL, THAT COULD BE FUN TOO!
I'VE GOT A BAD FEELING ABOUT THIS.
SOMEONE ELSE SHOULD DRAW OURS.
YEAH, YOU DREW SHINRYUJI FOR THE KANTO TOURNAMENT.
THE REPUBLIC OF MILITARIA...
...WILL PLAY FINLAND IN ROUND 1!
Militaria
Football Population
Approx. 20,000
SHEEEN
Germany
Football Population
20,000-30,000
THE THREE MIL...
WHUP
...IS MINE!!
HUNH?

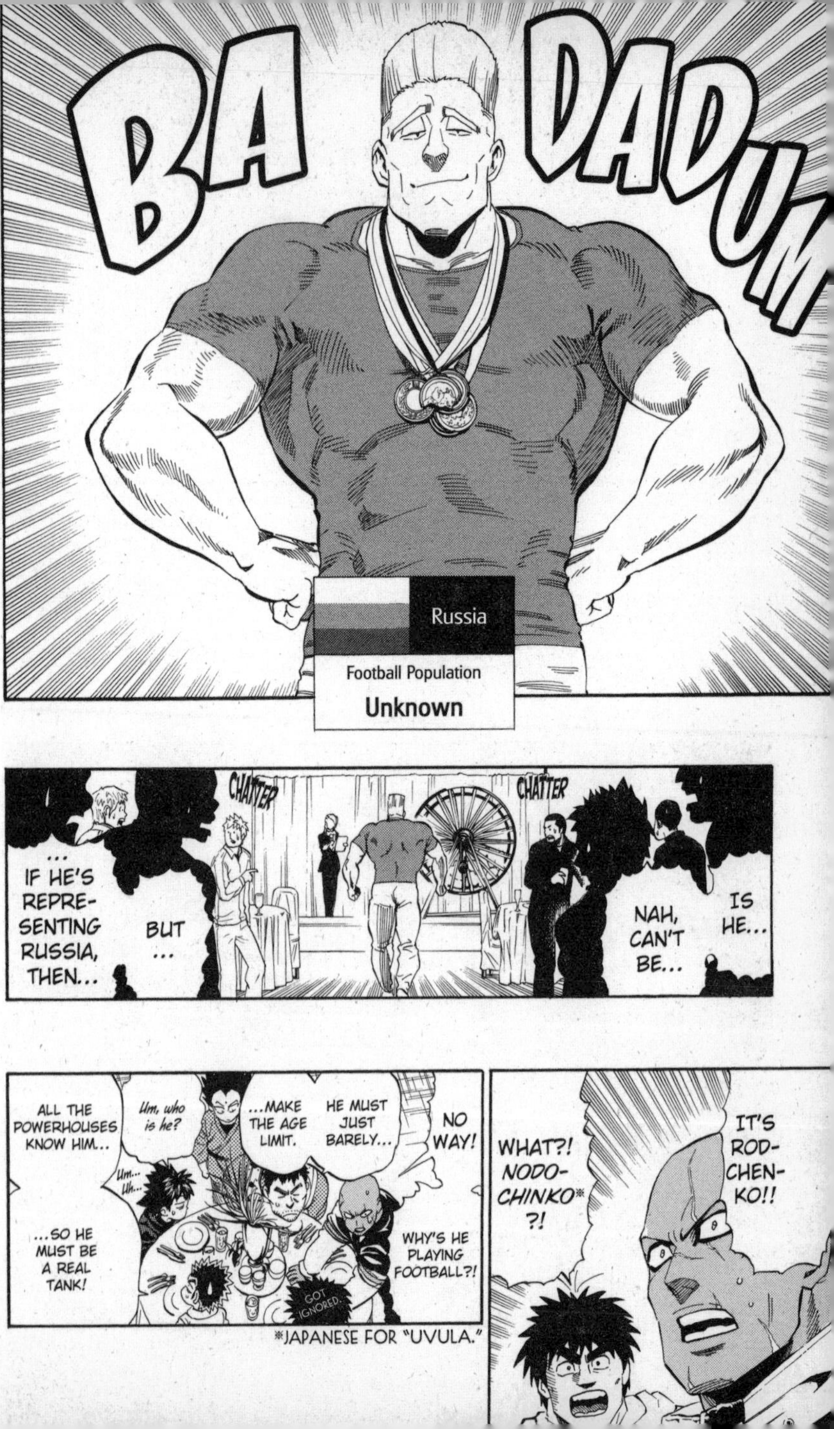
BA DADUM
Russia
Football Population
Unknown
IS HE...
NAH, CAN'T BE...
CHATTER
CHATTER
BUT...
... IF HE'S REPRESENTING RUSSIA, THEN...
IT'S RODCHENKO!!
WHAT?! NODOCHINKO※?!
NO WAY!
HE MUST JUST BARELY...
...MAKE THE AGE LIMIT.
Um, who is he?
ALL THE POWERHOUSES KNOW HIM...
Um... uh...
WHY'S HE PLAYING FOOTBALL?!
...SO HE MUST BE A REAL TANK!
GOT IGNORED.

※JAPANESE FOR "UVULA."

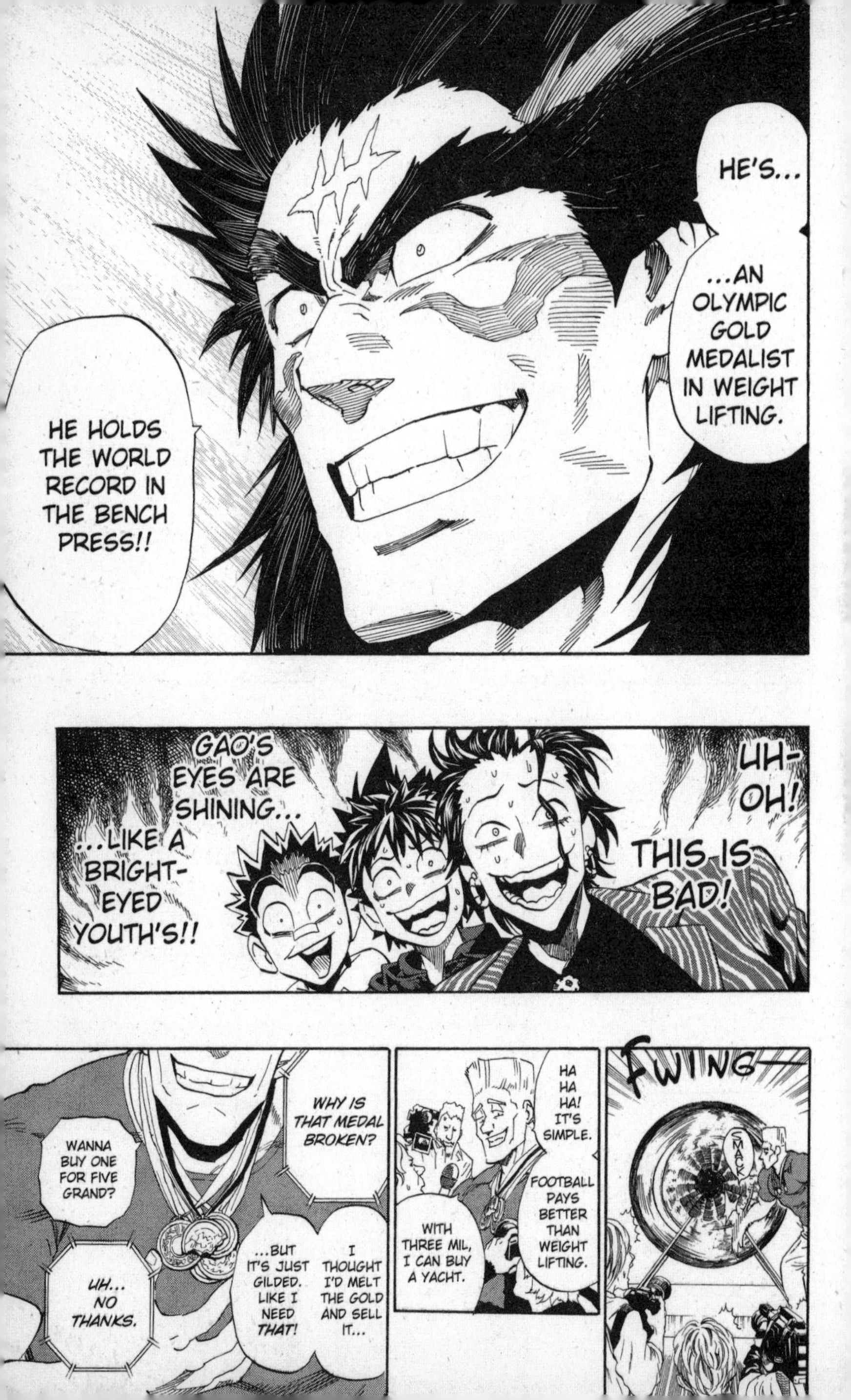
HE'S...
...AN OLYMPIC GOLD MEDALIST IN WEIGHT LIFTING.
HE HOLDS THE WORLD RECORD IN THE BENCH PRESS!!
UH-OH!
THIS IS BAD!
GAO'S EYES ARE SHINING...
...LIKE A BRIGHT-EYED YOUTH'S!!
FWING—
SMACK
HA HA HA! IT'S SIMPLE.
FOOTBALL PAYS BETTER THAN WEIGHT LIFTING.
WITH THREE MIL, I CAN BUY A YACHT.
WHY IS THAT MEDAL BROKEN?
I THOUGHT I'D MELT THE GOLD AND SELL IT...
...BUT IT'S JUST GILDED. LIKE I NEED THAT!
WANNA BUY ONE FOR FIVE GRAND?
UH... NO THANKS.

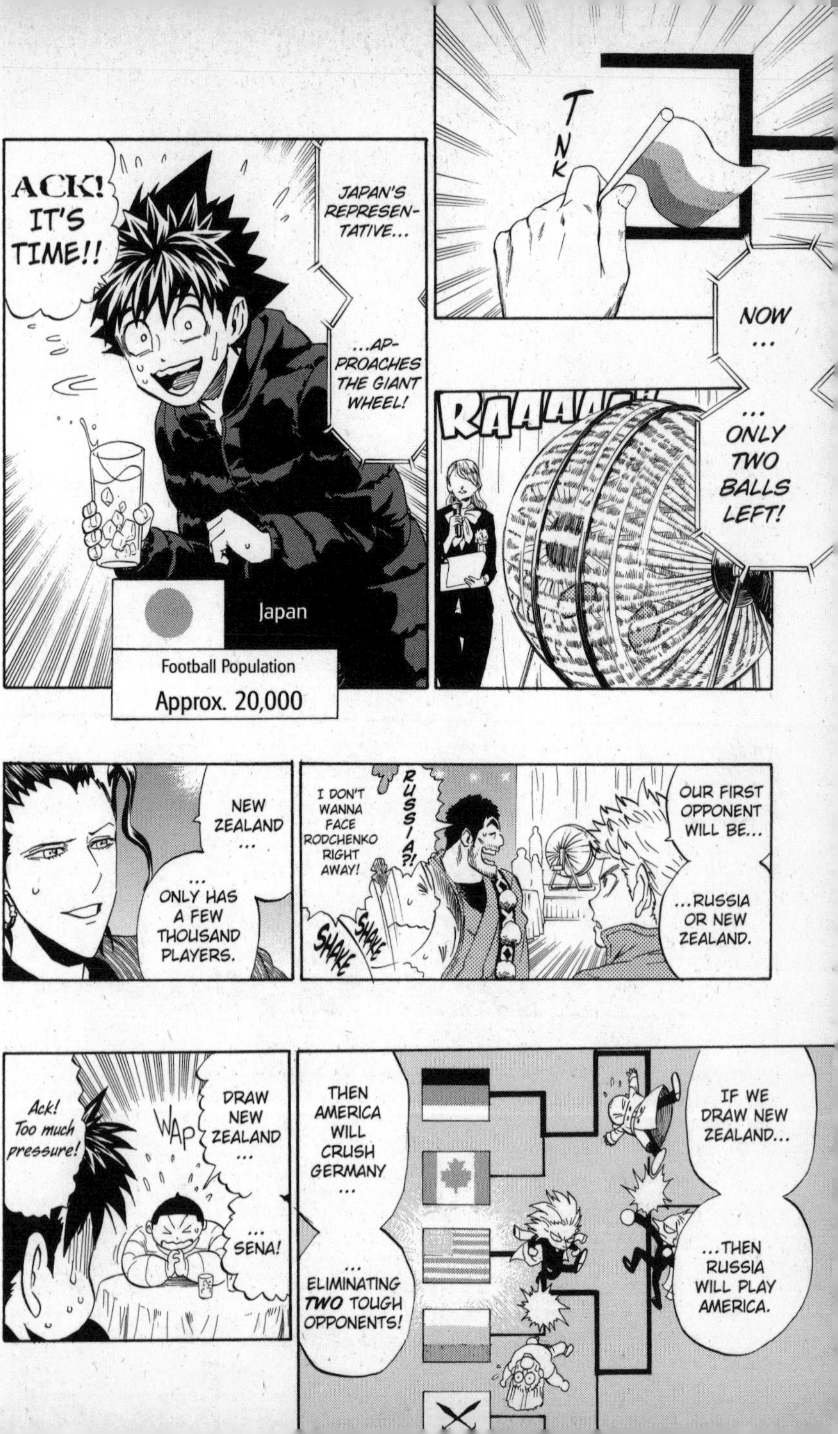
TNK
NOW...
...ONLY TWO BALLS LEFT!
RAAAA
JAPAN'S REPRESENTATIVE...
...APPROACHES THE GIANT WHEEL!
ACK! IT'S TIME!!
Japan
Football Population
Approx. 20,000
OUR FIRST OPPONENT WILL BE...
...RUSSIA OR NEW ZEALAND.
RUSSIA?!
I DON'T WANNA FACE RODCHENKO RIGHT AWAY!
SHAKE
SHAKE
NEW ZEALAND...
...ONLY HAS A FEW THOUSAND PLAYERS.
IF WE DRAW NEW ZEALAND...
...THEN RUSSIA WILL PLAY AMERICA.
THEN AMERICA WILL CRUSH GERMANY...
...ELIMINATING *TWO* TOUGH OPPONENTS!
DRAW NEW ZEALAND...
...SENA!
WAP
Ack! Too much pressure!

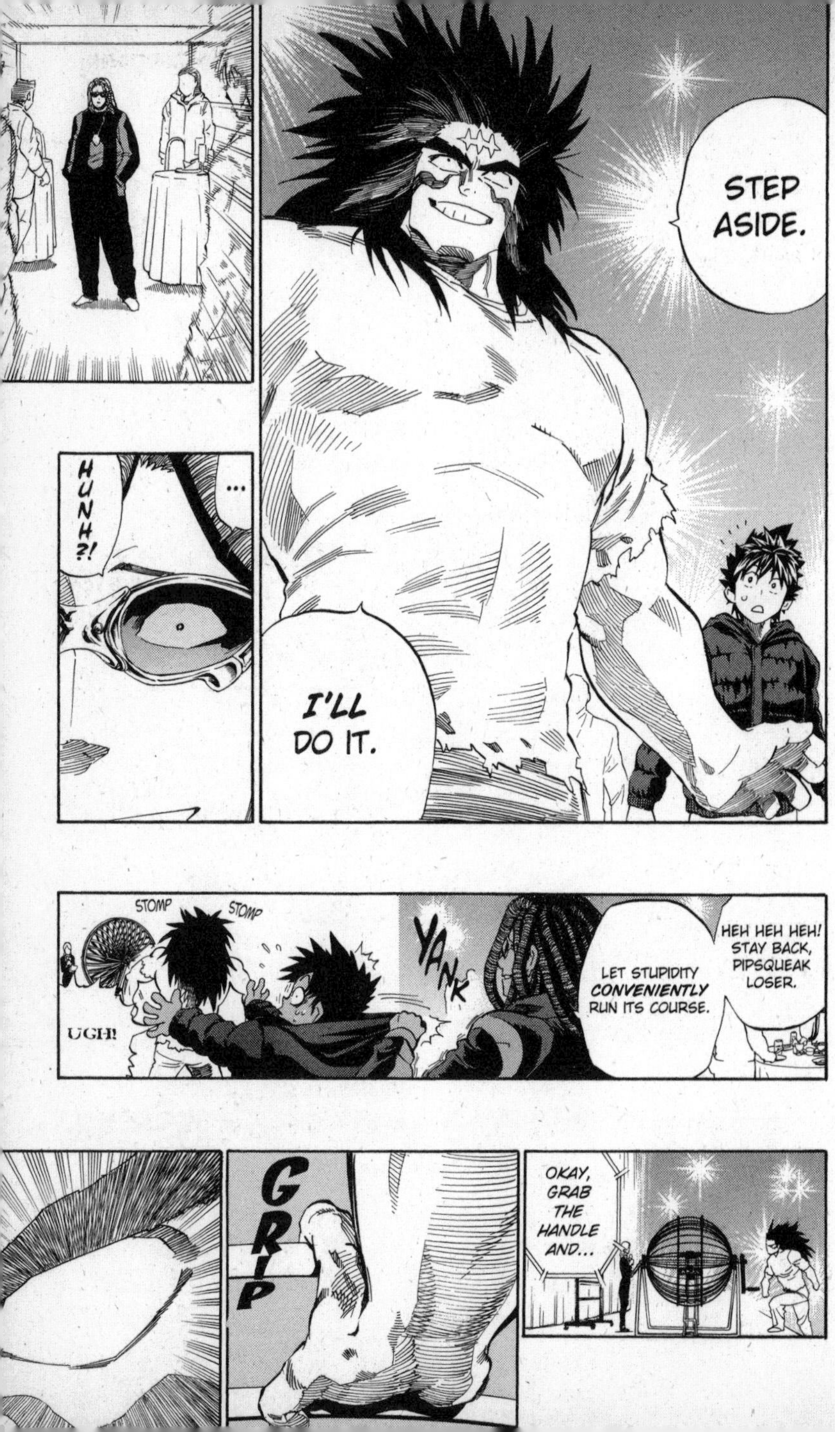
STEP ASIDE.
I'LL DO IT.
...
HUNH?!
HEH HEH HEH! STAY BACK, PIPSQUEAK LOSER.
LET STUPIDITY CONVENIENTLY RUN ITS COURSE.
YANK
STOMP
STOMP
UGH!
OKAY, GRAB THE HANDLE AND...
GRIP

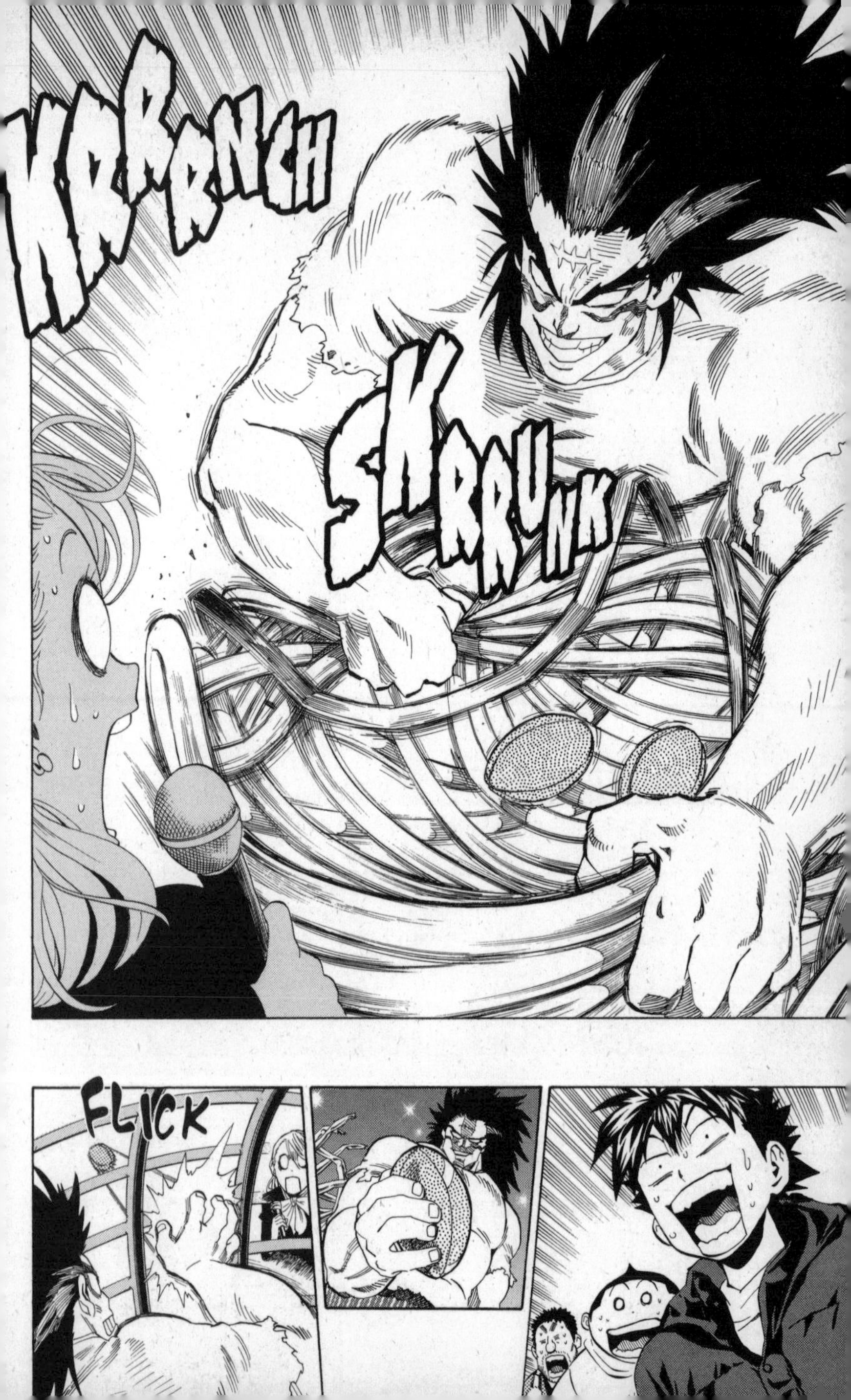
KRRANCH
SKRRUNK
FLICK

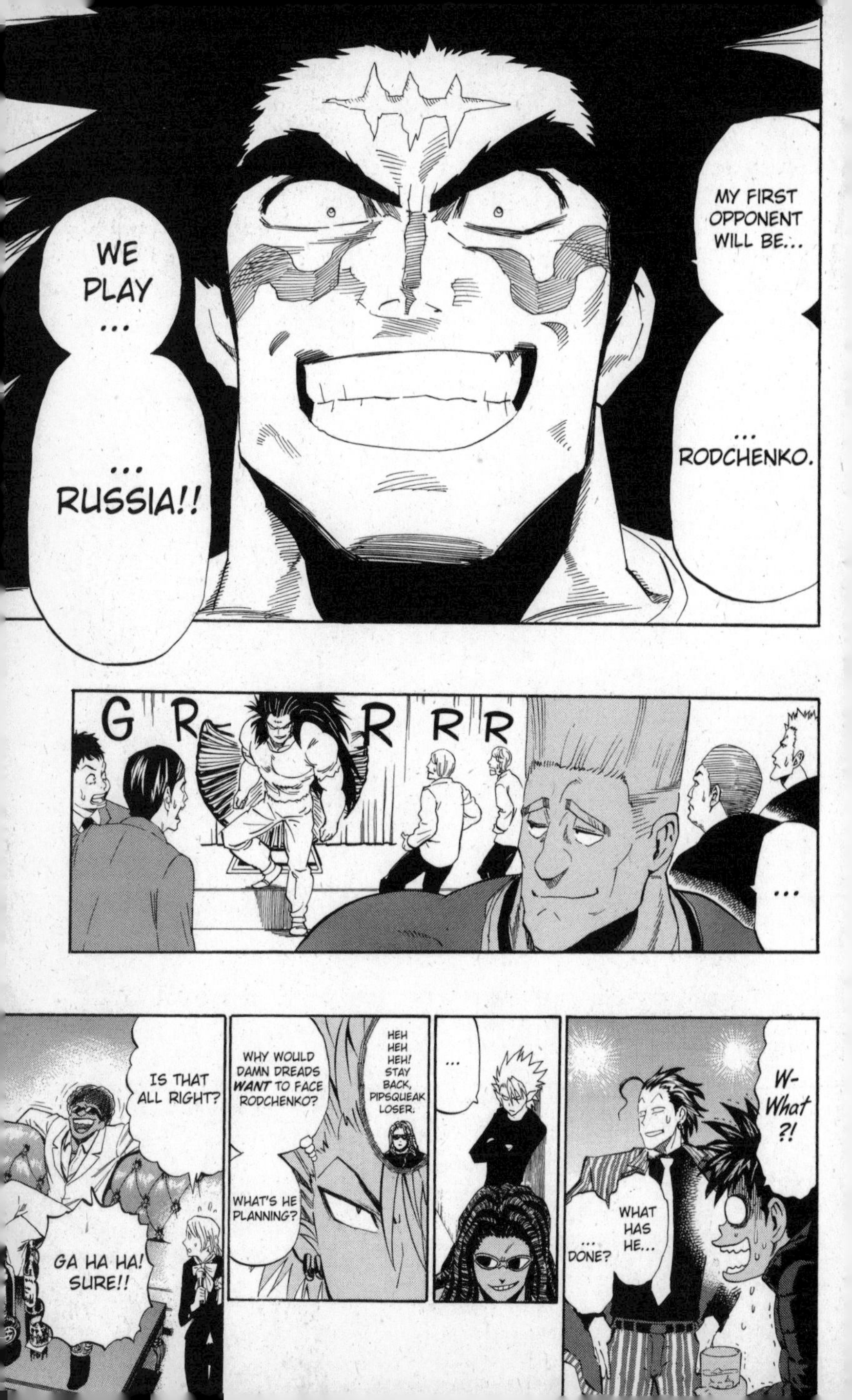

MY FIRST OPPONENT WILL BE... ... RODCHENKO.
WE PLAY ... ... RUSSIA!!
G R R R R R
...
W- What?!
WHAT HAS HE... ... DONE?
...
HEH HEH HEH! STAY BACK, PIPSQUEAK LOSER.
WHY WOULD DAMN DREADS *WANT* TO FACE RODCHENKO?
WHAT'S HE PLANNING?
IS THAT ALL RIGHT?
GA HA HA! SURE!!

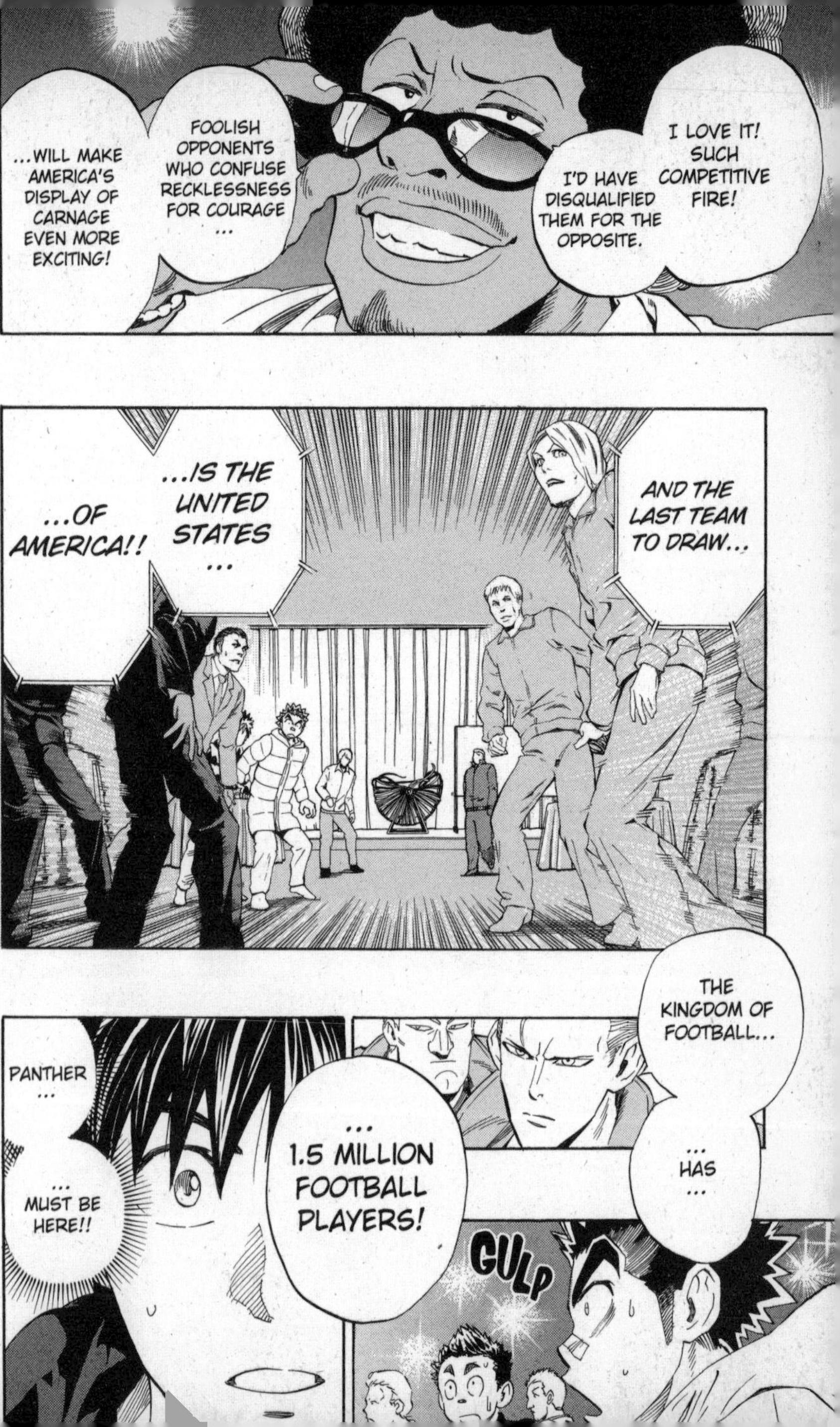
I LOVE IT! SUCH COMPETITIVE FIRE!
I'D HAVE DISQUALIFIED THEM FOR THE OPPOSITE.
FOOLISH OPPONENTS WHO CONFUSE RECKLESSNESS FOR COURAGE ...
...WILL MAKE AMERICA'S DISPLAY OF CARNAGE EVEN MORE EXCITING!
AND THE LAST TEAM TO DRAW...
...IS THE UNITED STATES ...
...OF AMERICA!!
THE KINGDOM OF FOOTBALL...
... HAS ...
... 1.5 MILLION FOOTBALL PLAYERS!
GULP
PANTHER ...
... MUST BE HERE!!

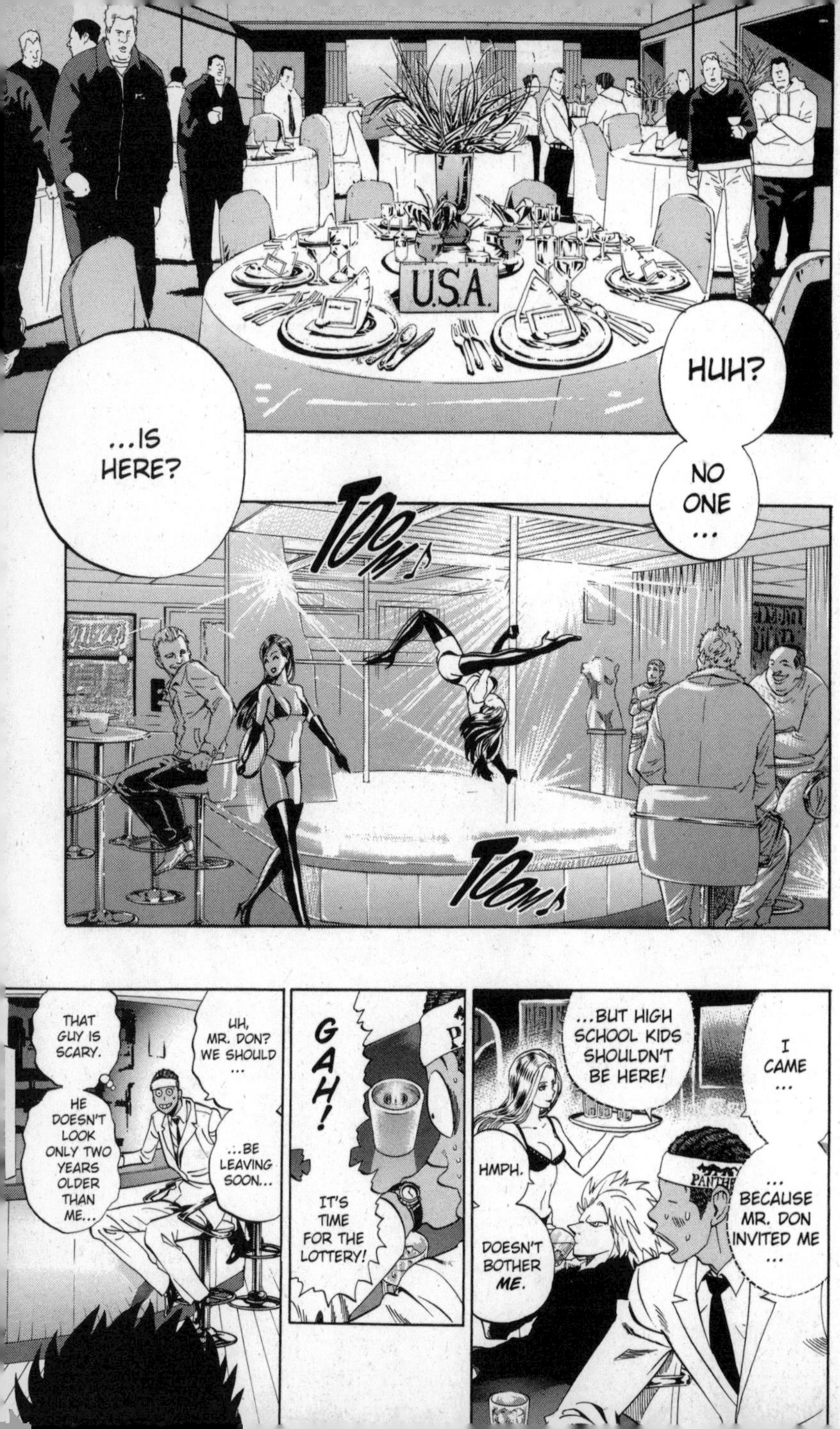
U.S.A.
HUH?
NO ONE ...
...IS HERE?
TOOM♪
TOOM♪
I CAME ...
... BECAUSE MR. DON INVITED ME ...
...BUT HIGH SCHOOL KIDS SHOULDN'T BE HERE!
HMPH.
DOESN'T BOTHER *ME*.
GAH!
IT'S TIME FOR THE LOTTERY!
UH, MR. DON? WE SHOULD ...
...BE LEAVING SOON...
THAT GUY IS SCARY.
HE DOESN'T LOOK ONLY TWO YEARS OLDER THAN ME...

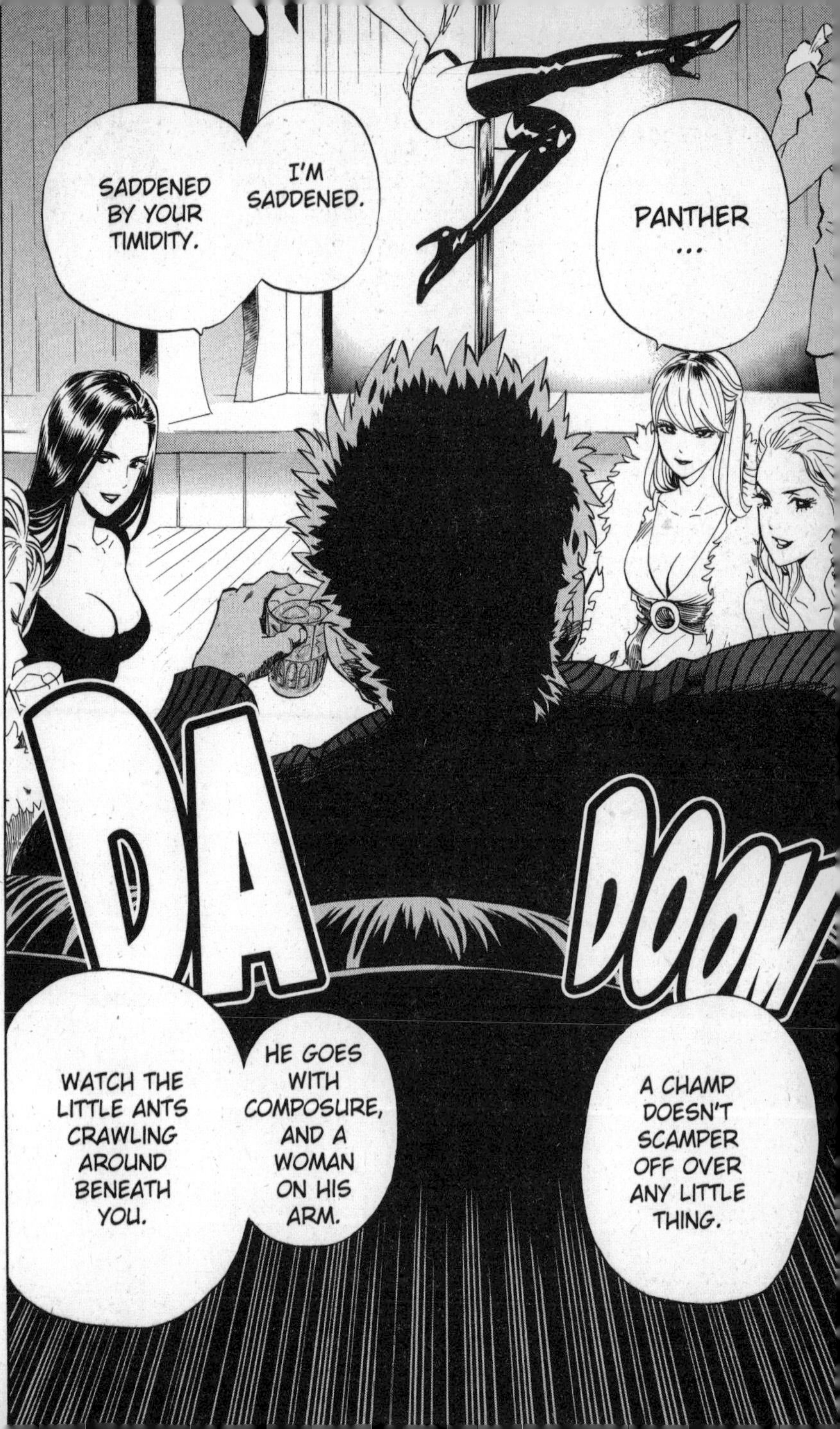
PANTHER...
I'M SADDENED.
SADDENED BY YOUR TIMIDITY.
DA DOOM
A CHAMP DOESN'T SCAMPER OFF OVER ANY LITTLE THING.
HE GOES WITH COMPOSURE, AND A WOMAN ON HIS ARM.
WATCH THE LITTLE ANTS CRAWLING AROUND BENEATH YOU.

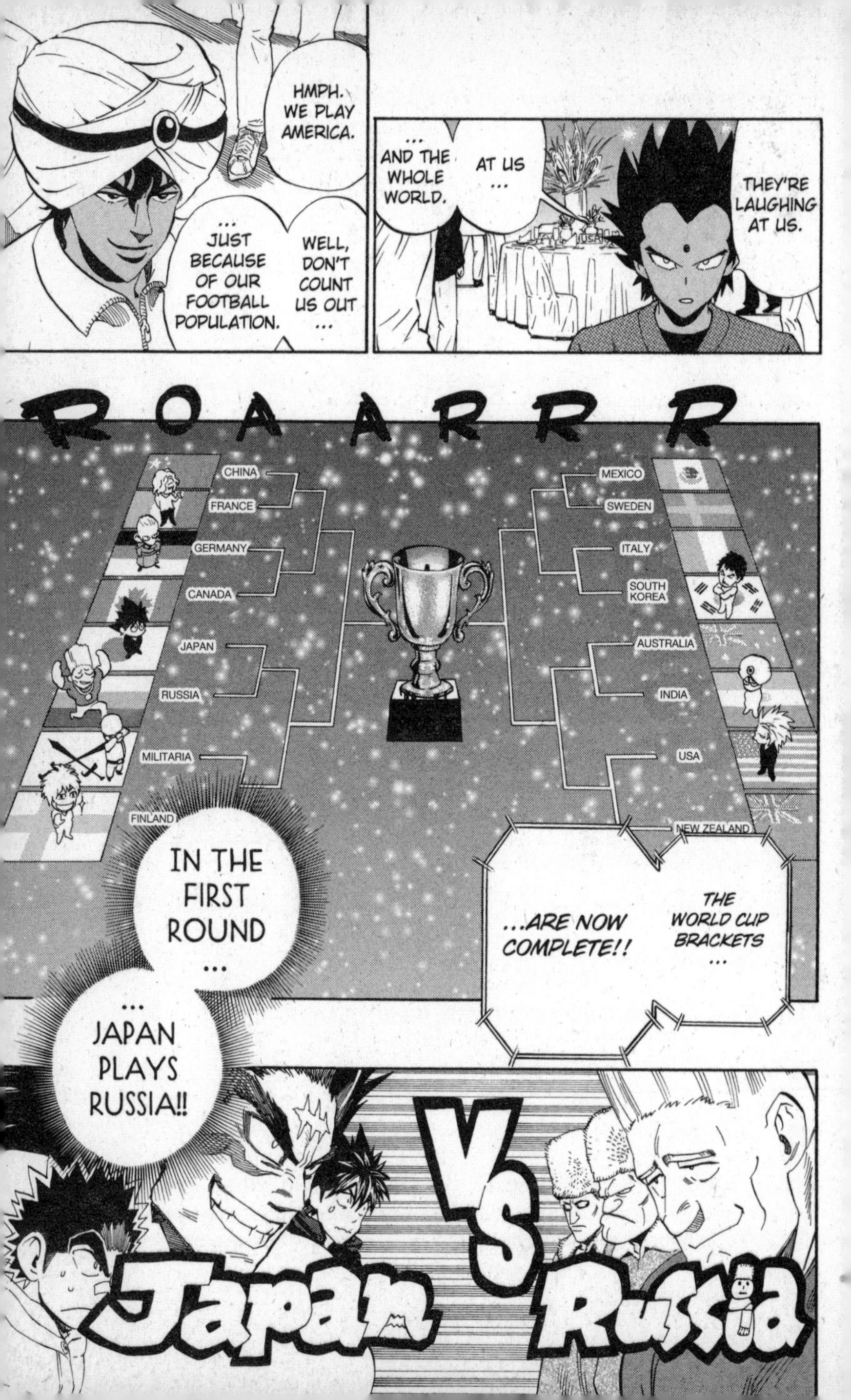
THEY'RE LAUGHING AT US.
AT US ...
... AND THE WHOLE WORLD.
HMPH. WE PLAY AMERICA.
WELL, DON'T COUNT US OUT ...
... JUST BECAUSE OF OUR FOOTBALL POPULATION.
ROAARRR
MEXICO
SWEDEN
ITALY
SOUTH KOREA
AUSTRALIA
INDIA
USA
NEW ZEALAND
CHINA
FRANCE
GERMANY
CANADA
JAPAN
RUSSIA
MILITARIA
FINLAND
THE WORLD CUP BRACKETS ...
...ARE NOW COMPLETE!!
IN THE FIRST ROUND ...
... JAPAN PLAYS RUSSIA!!
Japan VS Russia

Presenting Teams Playing in the World Cup

Football Population
Unknown

Running ··· B
Passing ···· C
Line ········ A
Defense ··· B

Overall Rating	**B**

All the above data is from before Rodchenko joined. Now that the "World's Strongest Man" is playing, their overall rating may be A or S.

Just like the Hakushu Dinosaurs proved with Gao, if you have just one indomitable lineman, you'll destroy your opponents!!

Key Player

IVAN RODCHENKO

Age: 18
Hobbies: wasting
          money

Power ··········· S
Speed ··········· C
Technique ······ C

He has no experience playing football, but he possesses monstrous strength! He can easily bench-press 200-300 kilograms (440-660 lbs.), and he can pull a truck all by himself!

Russia's
Strong Point

Since they train in the freezing cold, they're unbeatable in the snow! Too bad for them it's March now!

Chapter 310

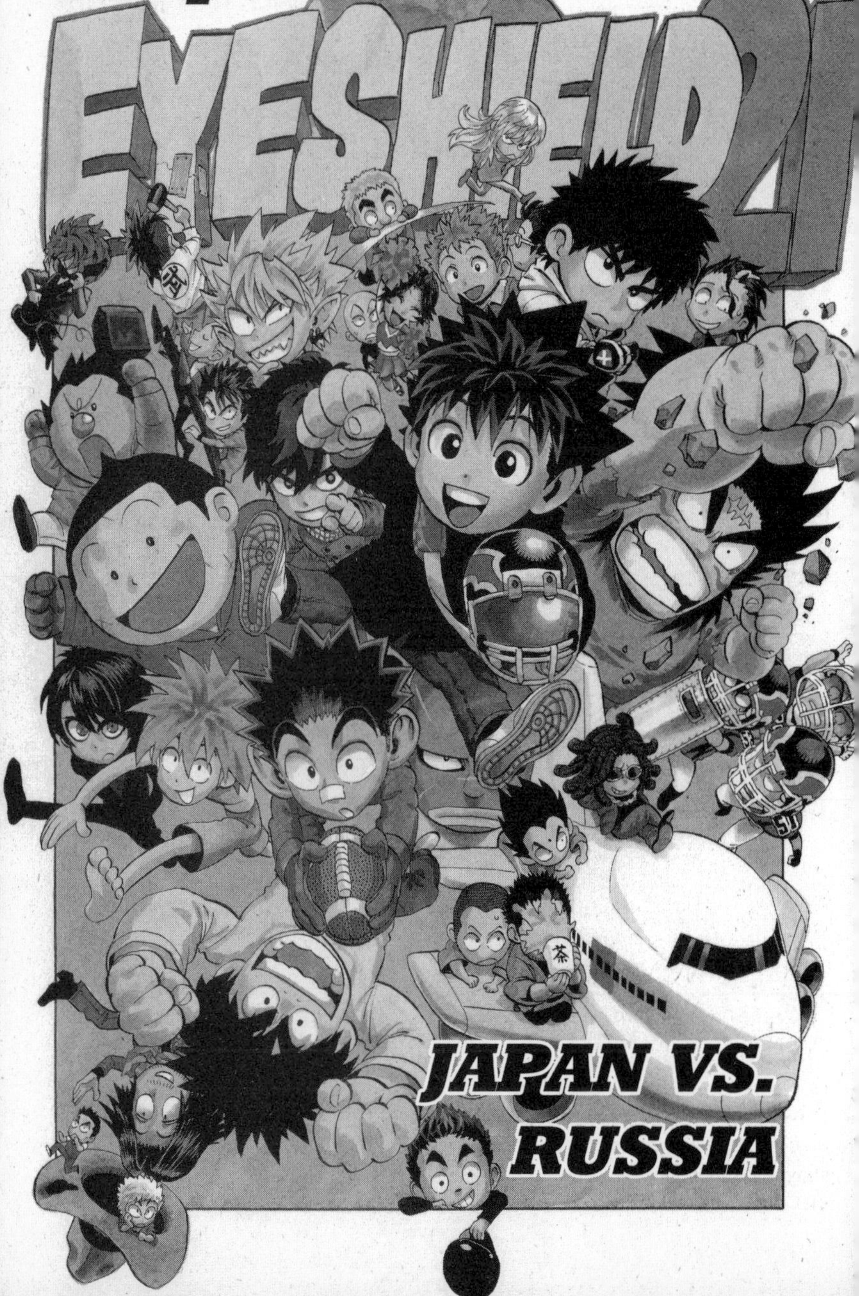
EYESHIELD 21
JAPAN VS.
RUSSIA

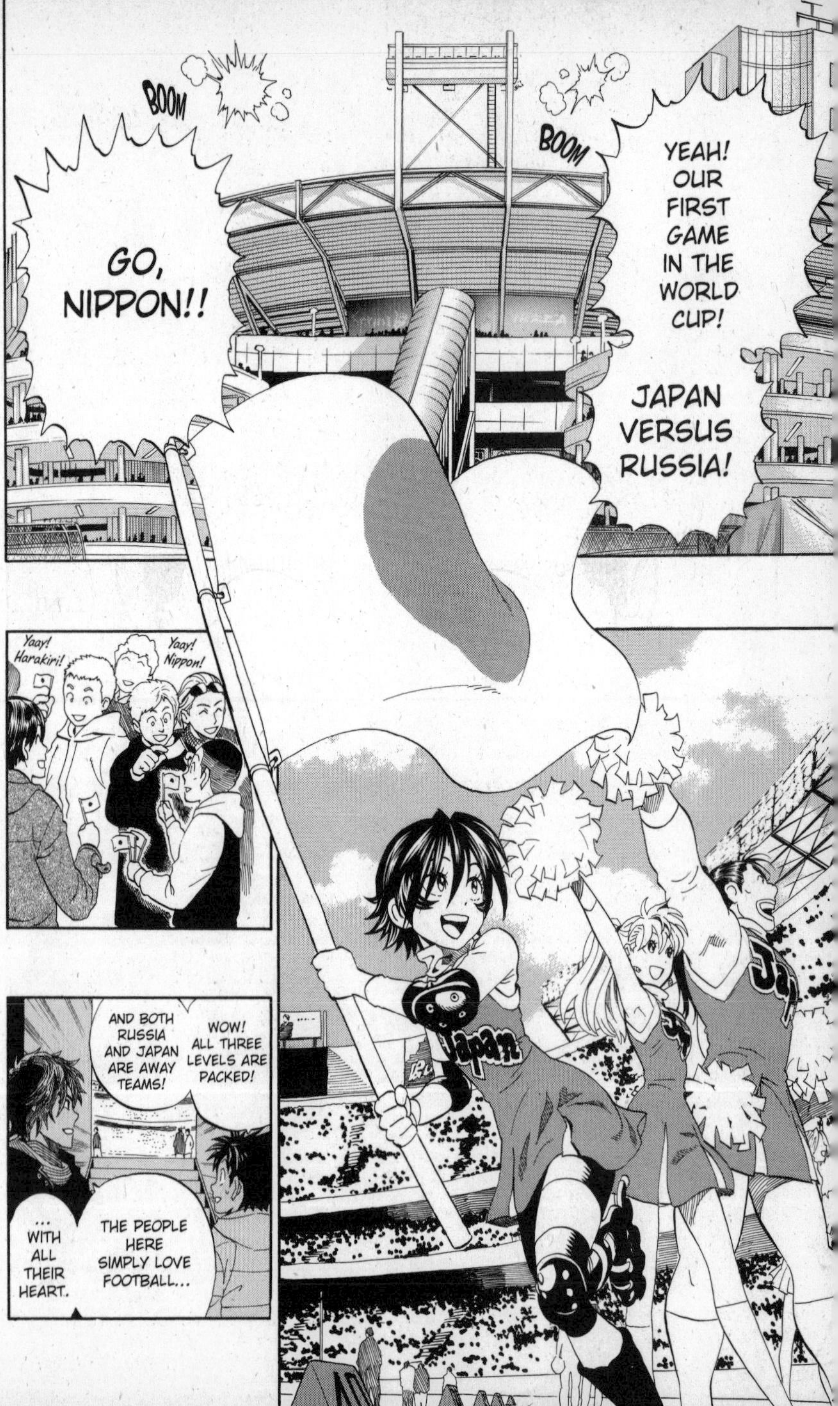
BOOM
BOOM
YEAH! OUR FIRST GAME IN THE WORLD CUP!
JAPAN VERSUS RUSSIA!
GO, NIPPON!!
Yaay! Nippon!
Yaay! Harakiri!
WOW! ALL THREE LEVELS ARE PACKED!
AND BOTH RUSSIA AND JAPAN ARE AWAY TEAMS!
THE PEOPLE HERE SIMPLY LOVE FOOTBALL...
...WITH ALL THEIR HEART.

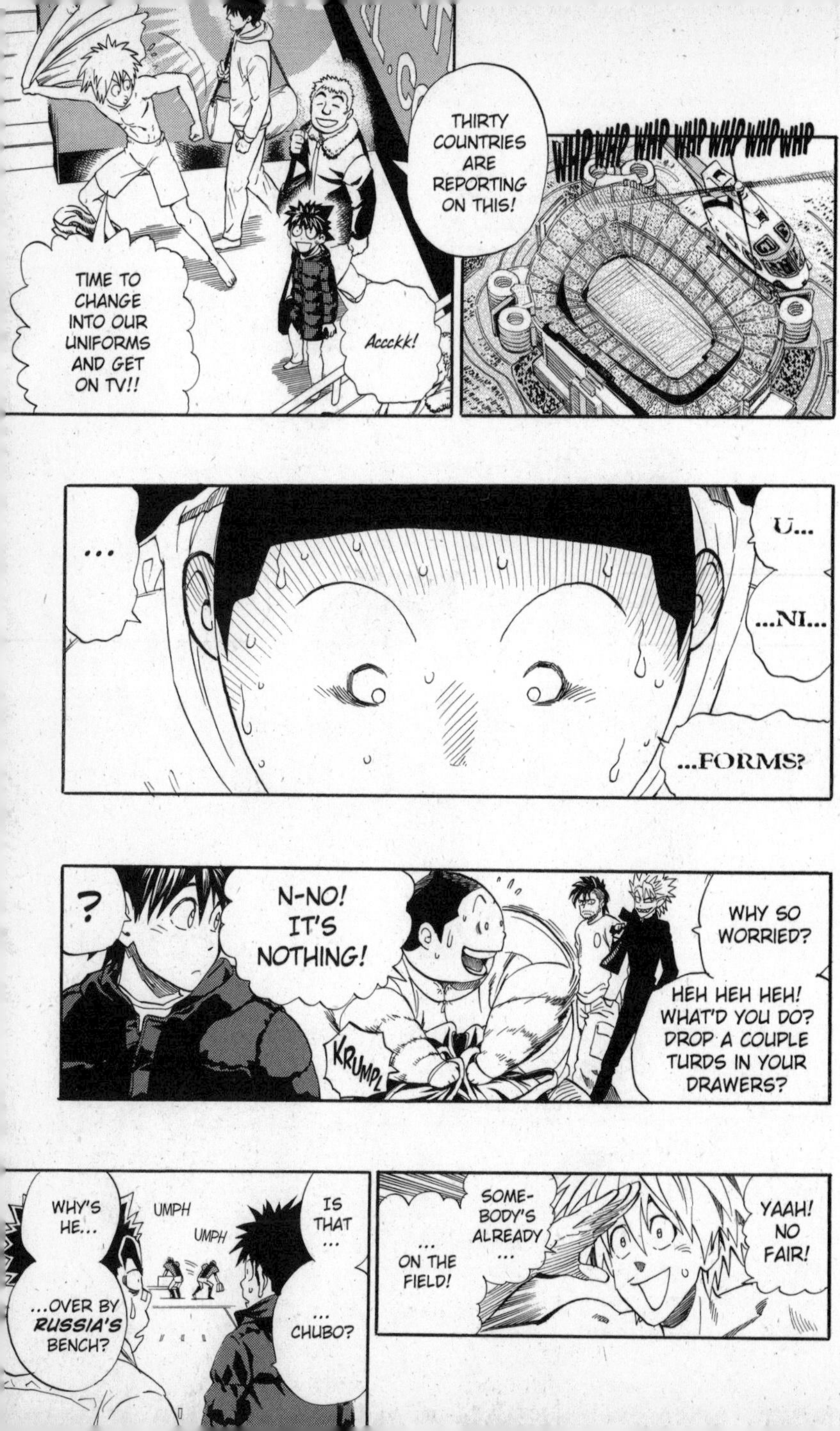
WHP WHP WHP WHP WHP WHP WHP
THIRTY COUNTRIES ARE REPORTING ON THIS!
Accckk!
TIME TO CHANGE INTO OUR UNIFORMS AND GET ON TV!!
U...
...NI...
...FORMS?
...
WHY SO WORRIED?
HEH HEH HEH! WHAT'D YOU DO? DROP A COUPLE TURDS IN YOUR DRAWERS?
N-NO! IT'S NOTHING!
KRUMPL
?
YAAH! NO FAIR!
SOME-BODY'S ALREADY...
...ON THE FIELD!
IS THAT...
...CHUBO?
UMPH
UMPH
WHY'S HE...
...OVER BY RUSSIA'S BENCH?

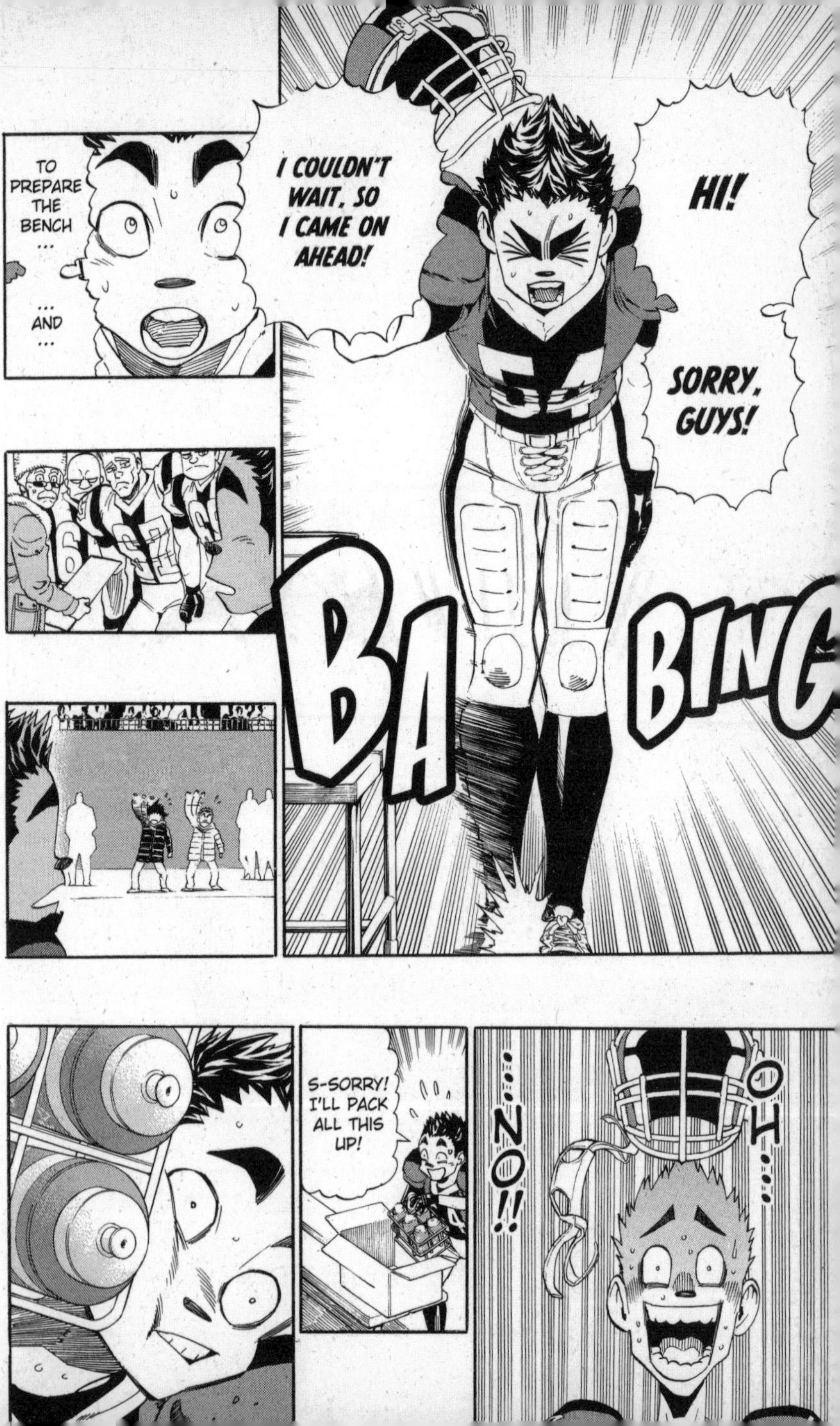
HI!
SORRY, GUYS!
I COULDN'T WAIT, SO I CAME ON AHEAD!
BA BING
TO PREPARE THE BENCH ...
... AND ...
OH...
...NO!!
S-SORRY! I'LL PACK ALL THIS UP!

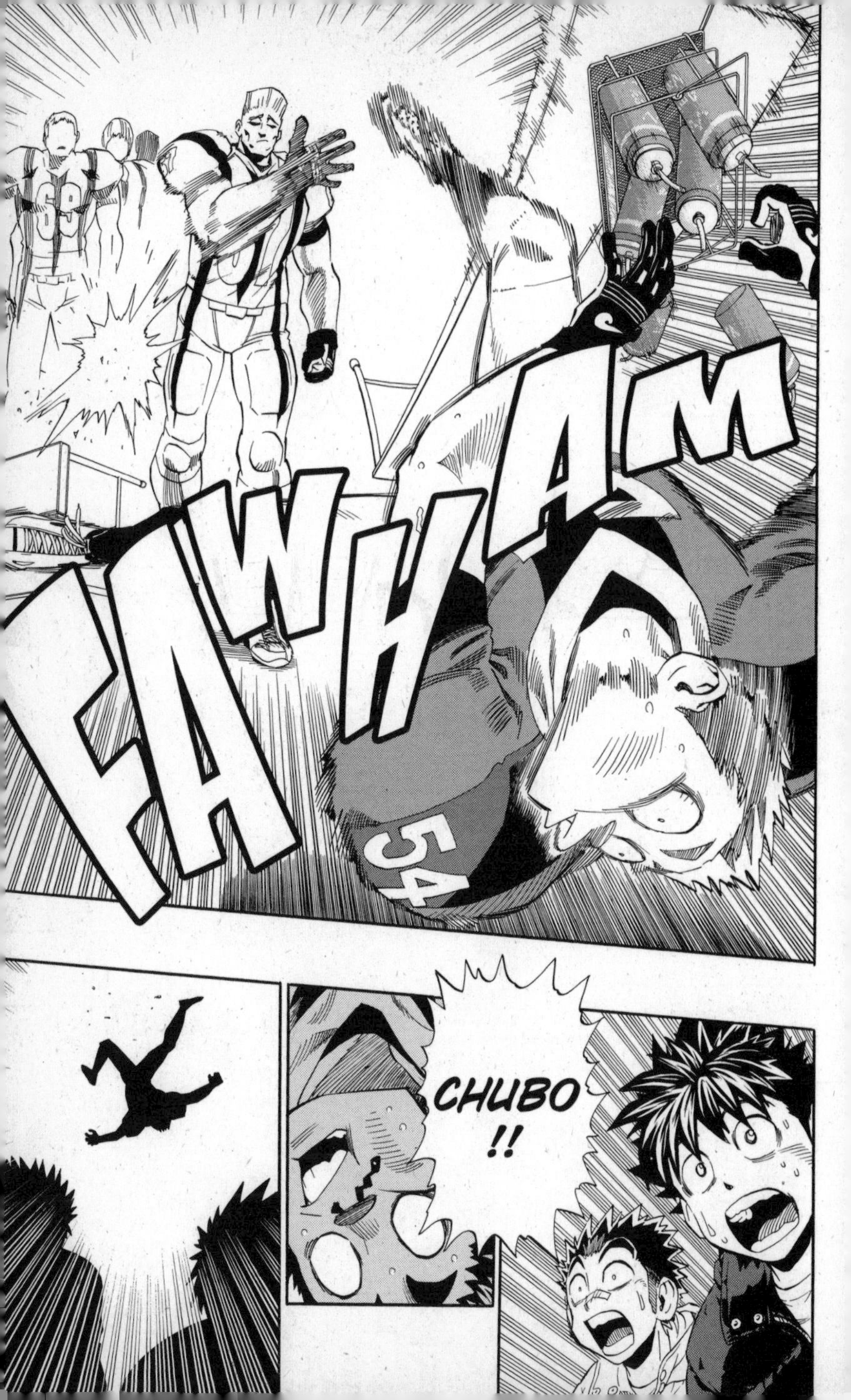
FWHAM
CHUBO !!

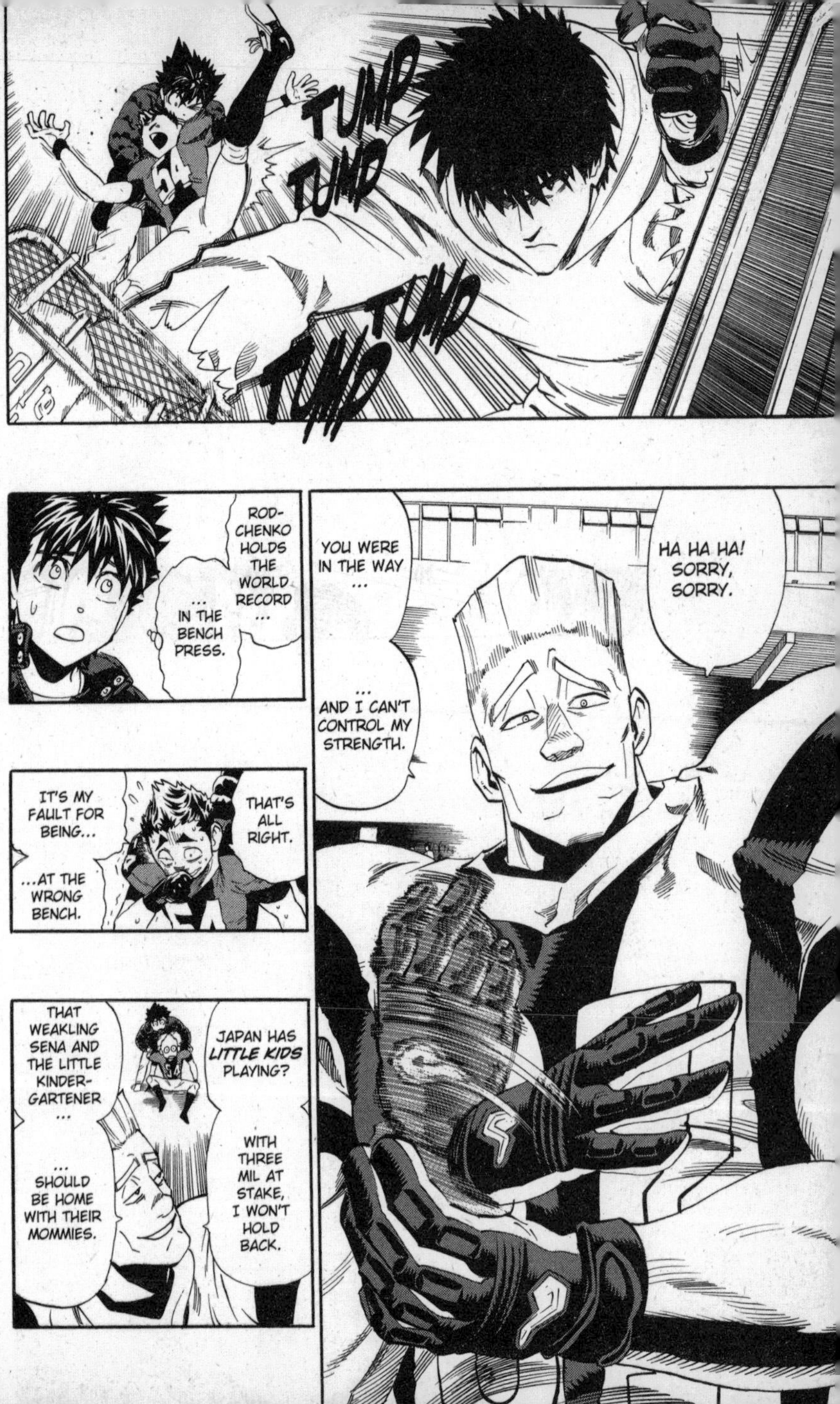
TUMP TUMP
TUMP TUMP
HA HA HA! SORRY, SORRY.
YOU WERE IN THE WAY...
...AND I CAN'T CONTROL MY STRENGTH.
ROD-CHENKO HOLDS THE WORLD RECORD...
...IN THE BENCH PRESS.
THAT'S ALL RIGHT.
IT'S MY FAULT FOR BEING...
...AT THE WRONG BENCH.
JAPAN HAS *LITTLE KIDS* PLAYING?
WITH THREE MIL AT STAKE, I WON'T HOLD BACK.
THAT WEAKLING SENA AND THE LITTLE KINDER-GARTENER...
...SHOULD BE HOME WITH THEIR MOMMIES.

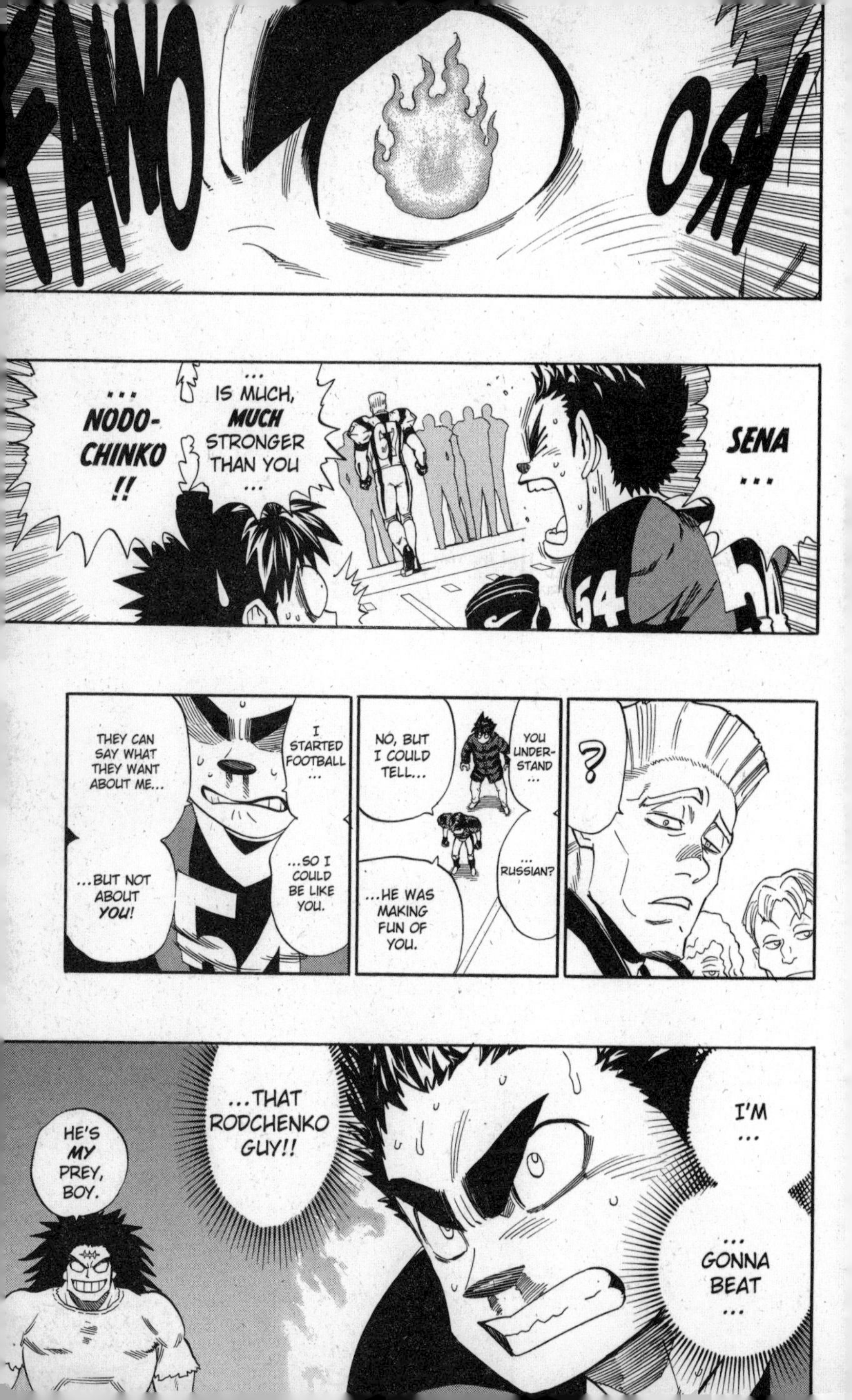
FAWO OSH
SENA ...
... IS MUCH, MUCH STRONGER THAN YOU ...
... NODO-CHINKO !!
?
YOU UNDER-STAND ...
... RUSSIAN?
NO, BUT I COULD TELL...
...HE WAS MAKING FUN OF YOU.
I STARTED FOOTBALL ...
...SO I COULD BE LIKE YOU.
THEY CAN SAY WHAT THEY WANT ABOUT ME...
...BUT NOT ABOUT YOU!
I'M ...
... GONNA BEAT ...
...THAT RODCHENKO GUY!!
HE'S MY PREY, BOY.

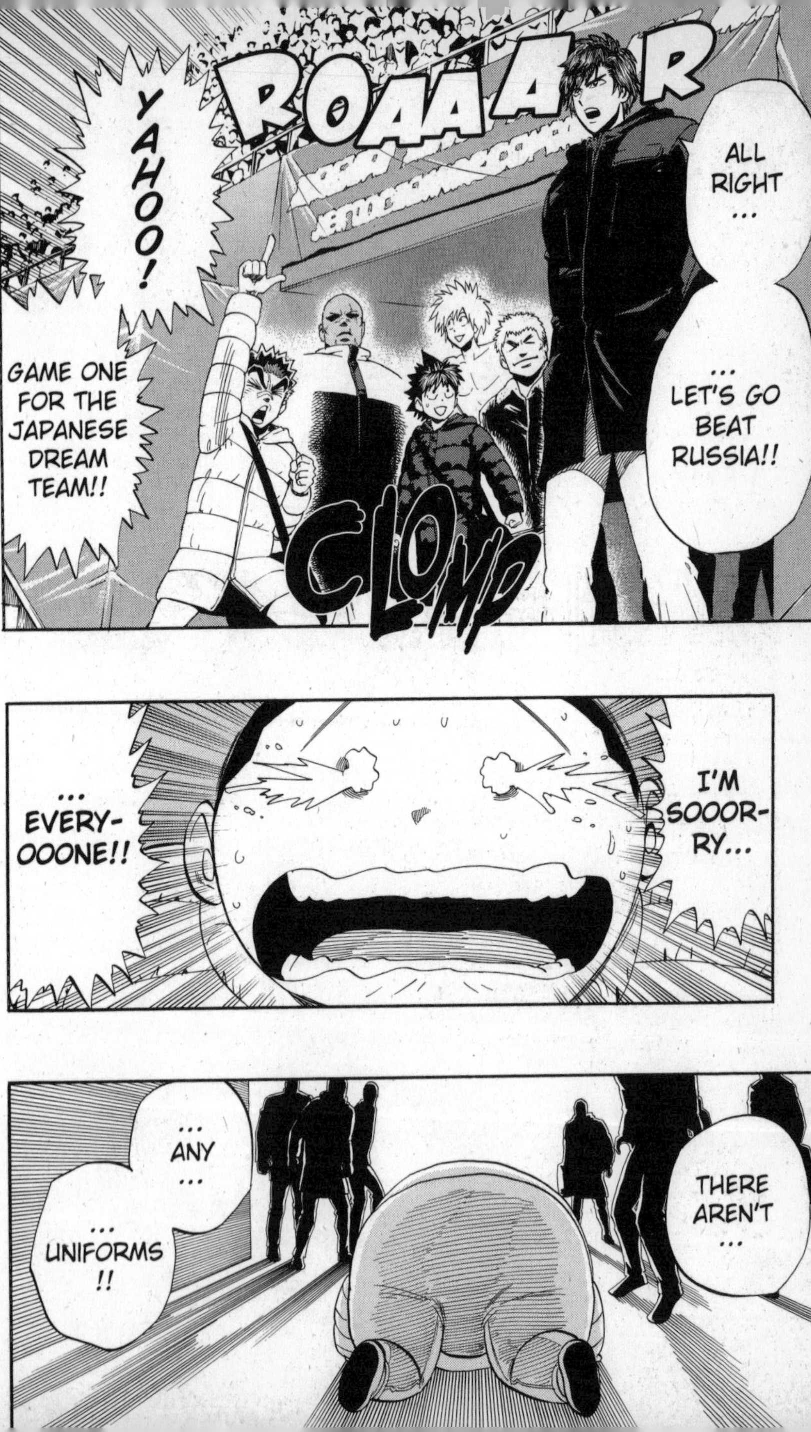
ROAAAR
ALL RIGHT...
...LET'S GO BEAT RUSSIA!!
YAHOO!
GAME ONE FOR THE JAPANESE DREAM TEAM!!
CLOMP
I'M SOOOR-RY...
...EVERY-OOONE!!
THERE AREN'T...
...ANY...
...UNIFORMS!!

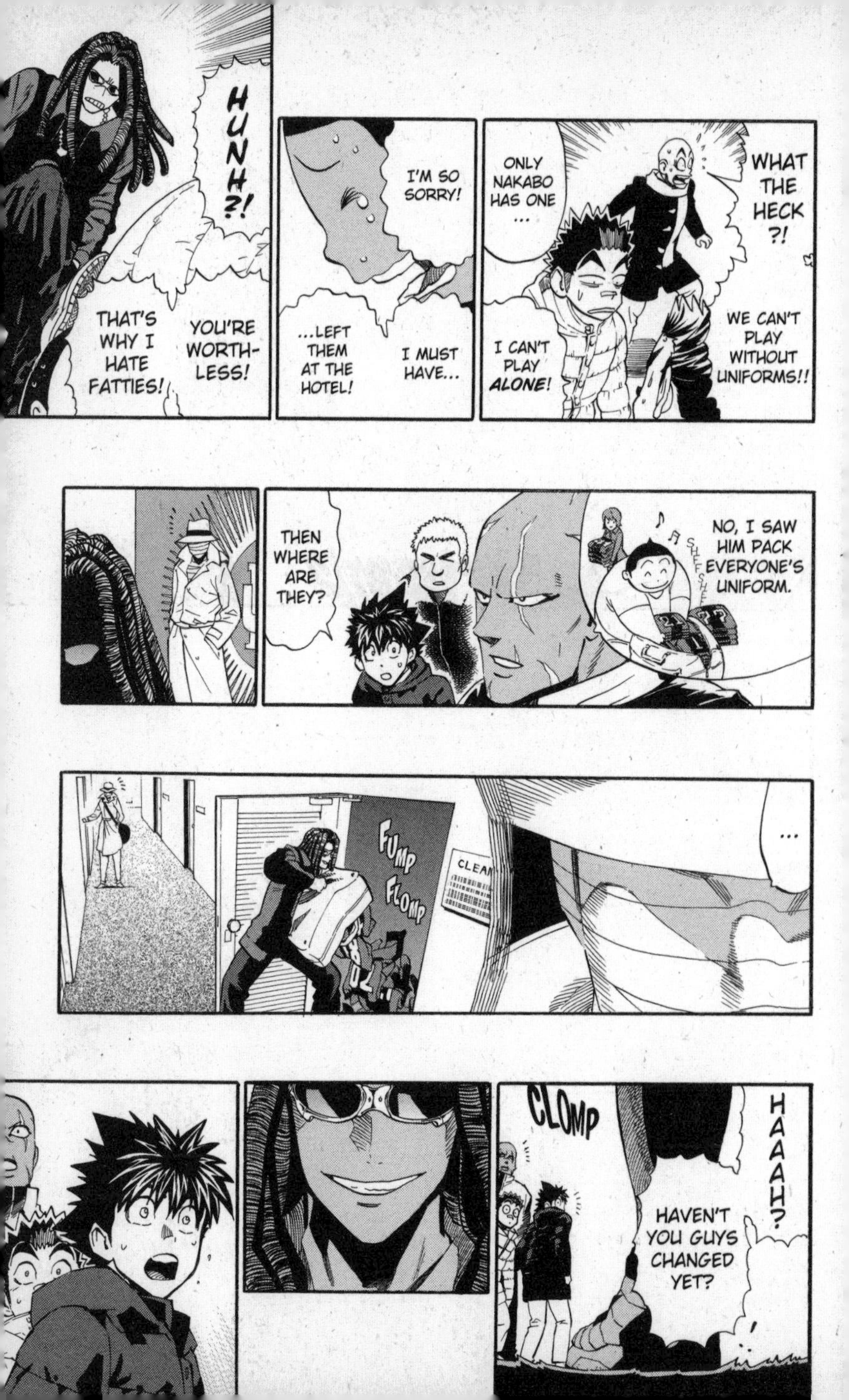
WHAT THE HECK?!
WE CAN'T PLAY WITHOUT UNIFORMS!!
ONLY NAKABO HAS ONE ...
I CAN'T PLAY ALONE!
I'M SO SORRY!
I MUST HAVE...
...LEFT THEM AT THE HOTEL!
HUNH?!
YOU'RE WORTHLESS!
THAT'S WHY I HATE FATTIES!
NO, I SAW HIM PACK EVERYONE'S UNIFORM.
SHFF SHFF
THEN WHERE ARE THEY?
...
CLEAN
FUMP
FLOMP
CLOMP
HAAAAH?
HAVEN'T YOU GUYS CHANGED YET?

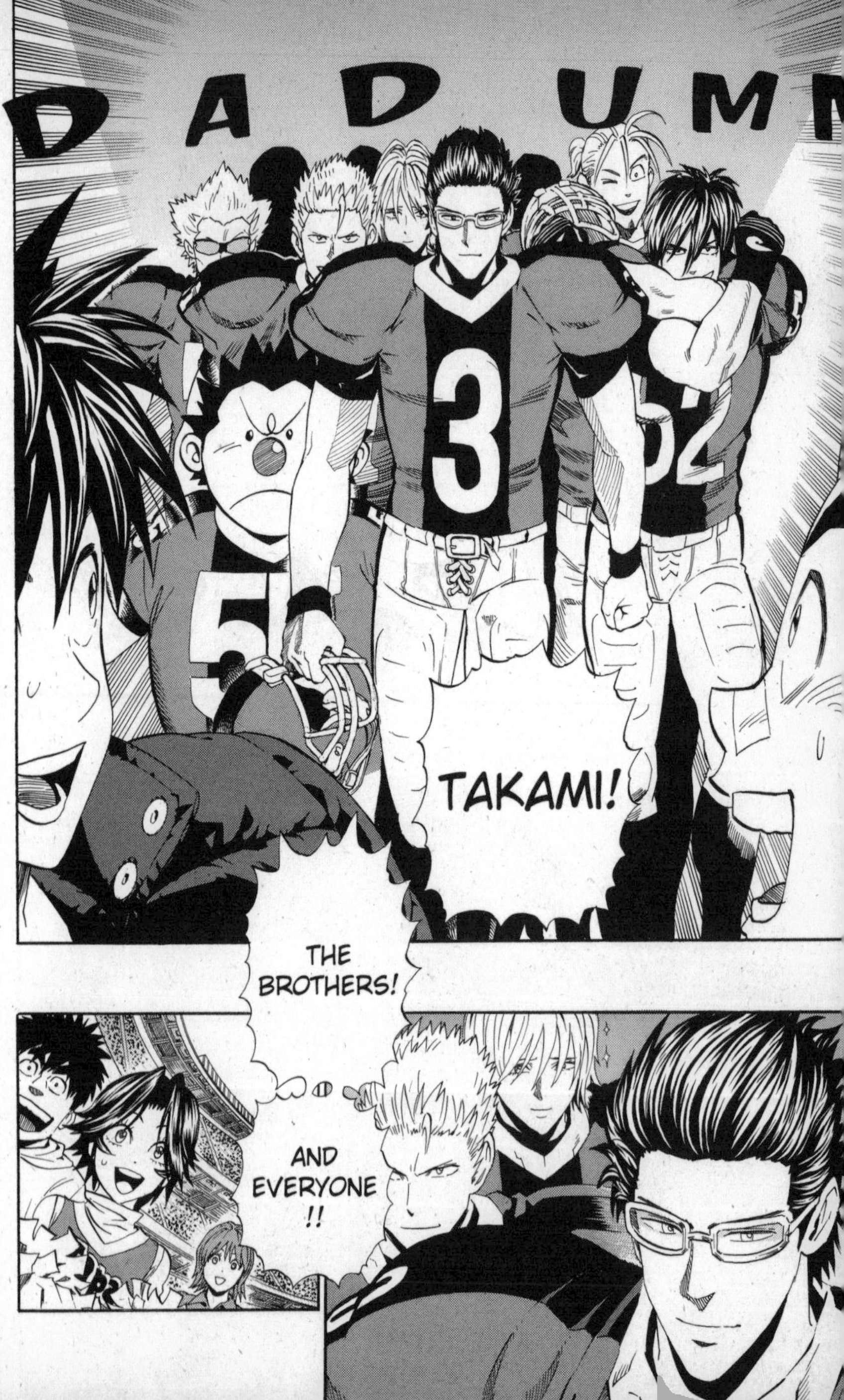
DADUMM
TAKAMI!
THE BROTHERS!
AND EVERYONE !!

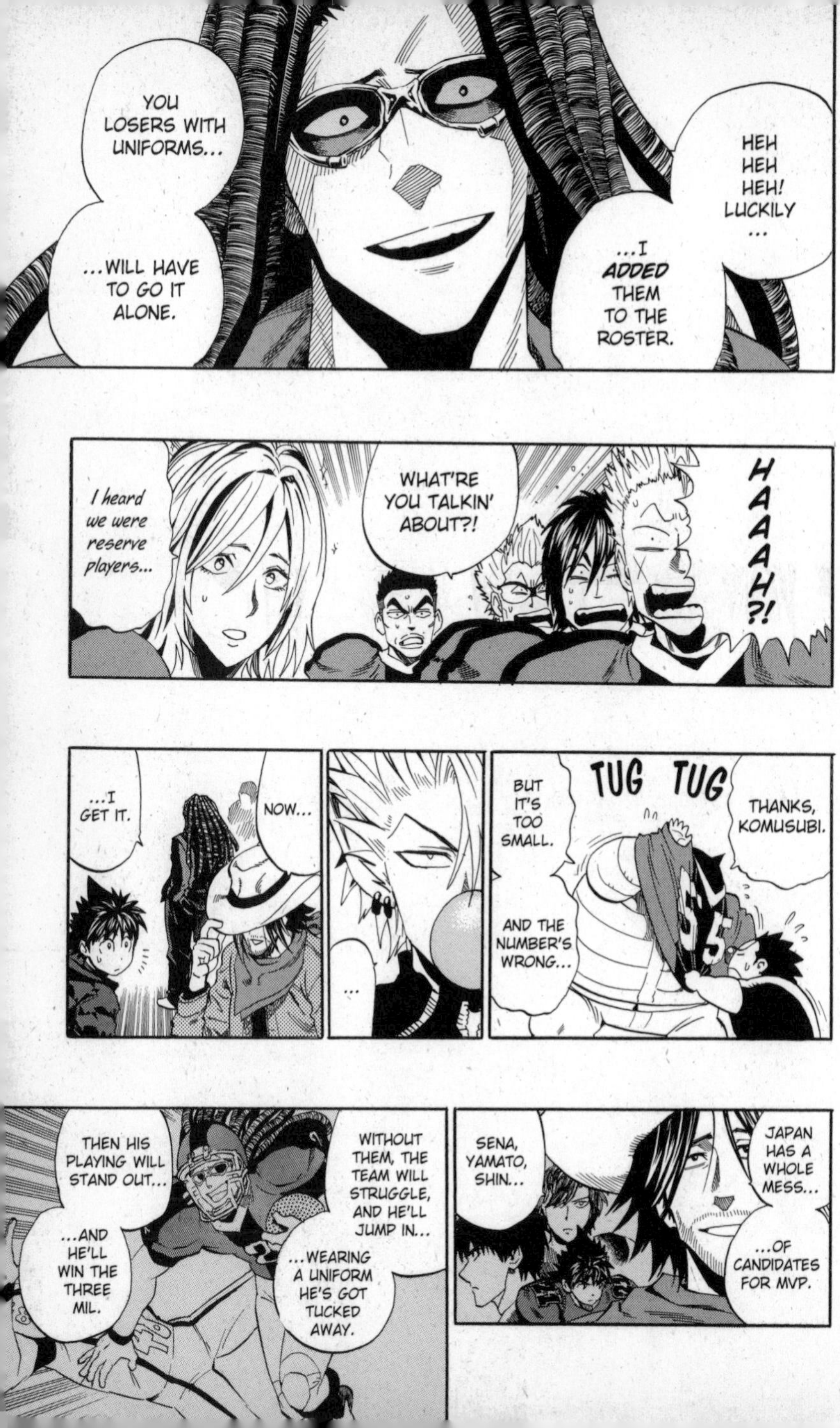
HEH HEH HEH! LUCKILY...
...I *ADDED* THEM TO THE ROSTER.
YOU LOSERS WITH UNIFORMS...
...WILL HAVE TO GO IT ALONE.
HAAAAH?!
WHAT'RE YOU TALKIN' ABOUT?!
I heard we were reserve players...
THANKS, KOMUSUBI.
TUG TUG
BUT IT'S TOO SMALL.
AND THE NUMBER'S WRONG...
...
NOW...
...I GET IT.
JAPAN HAS A WHOLE MESS...
...OF CANDIDATES FOR MVP.
SENA, YAMATO, SHIN...
WITHOUT THEM, THE TEAM WILL STRUGGLE, AND HE'LL JUMP IN...
...WEARING A UNIFORM HE'S GOT TUCKED AWAY.
THEN HIS PLAYING WILL STAND OUT...
...AND HE'LL WIN THE THREE MIL.

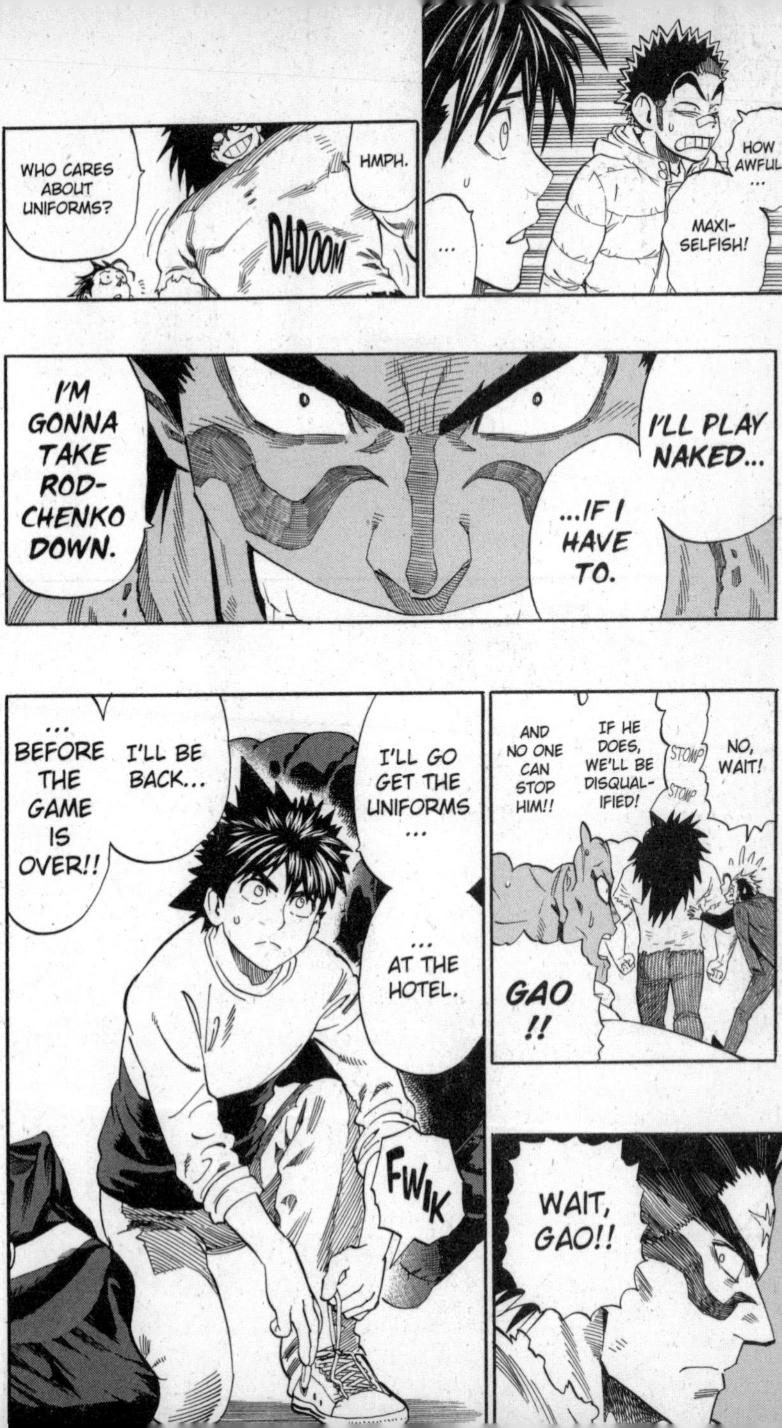
HOW AWFUL ...
MAXI-SELFISH!
...
HMPH.
WHO CARES ABOUT UNIFORMS?
DADOOM
I'LL PLAY NAKED...
...IF I HAVE TO.
I'M GONNA TAKE ROD-CHENKO DOWN.
NO, WAIT!
STOMP
STOMP
IF HE DOES, WE'LL BE DISQUAL-IFIED!
AND NO ONE CAN STOP HIM!!
GAO !!
WAIT, GAO!!
I'LL GO GET THE UNIFORMS ...
... AT THE HOTEL.
I'LL BE BACK...
... BEFORE THE GAME IS OVER!!
FWIK

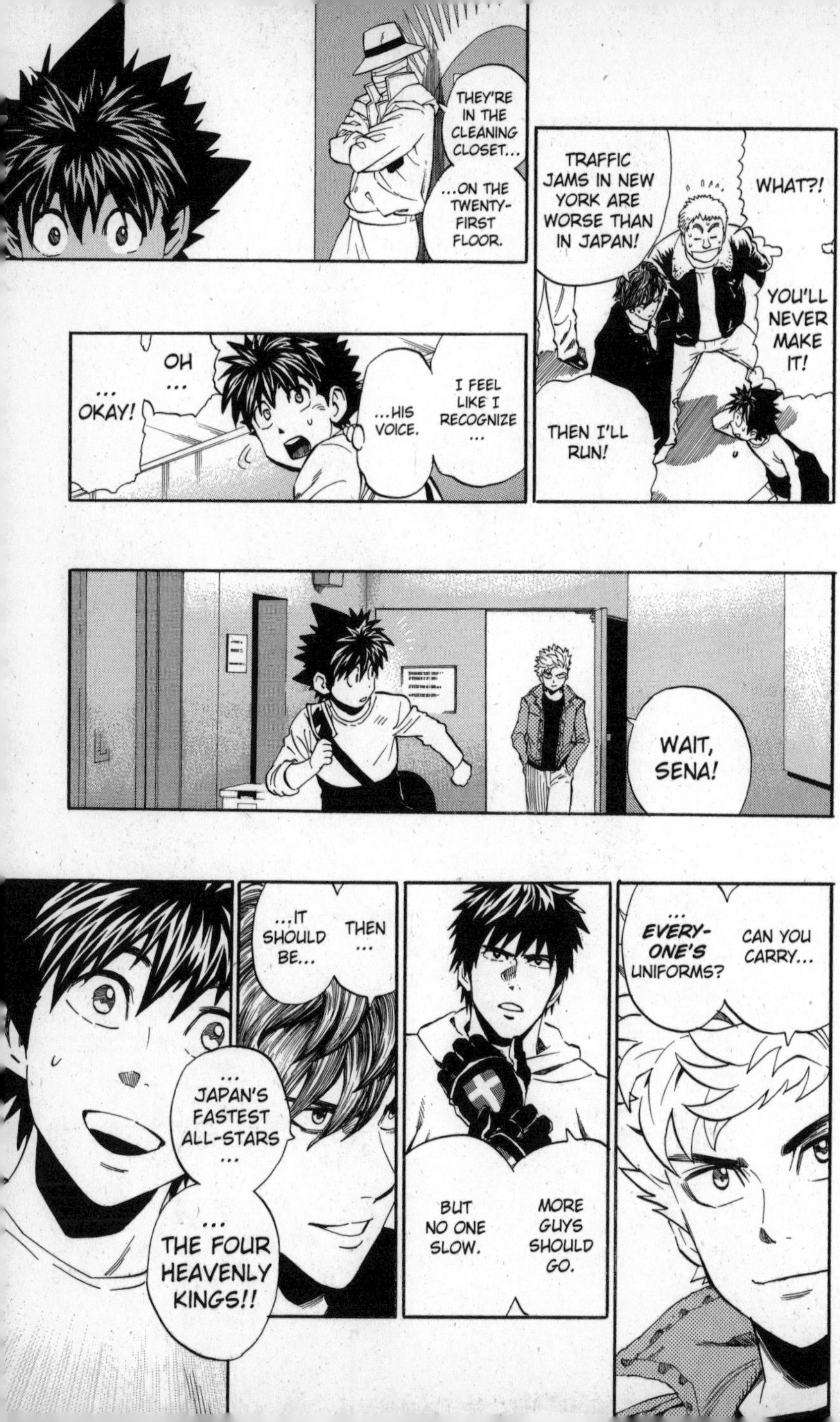
WHAT?!
TRAFFIC JAMS IN NEW YORK ARE WORSE THAN IN JAPAN!
YOU'LL NEVER MAKE IT!
THEN I'LL RUN!
THEY'RE IN THE CLEANING CLOSET...
...ON THE TWENTY-FIRST FLOOR.
I FEEL LIKE I RECOGNIZE...
...HIS VOICE.
OH... ...OKAY!
WAIT, SENA!
CAN YOU CARRY...
...EVERYONE'S UNIFORMS?
MORE GUYS SHOULD GO.
BUT NO ONE SLOW.
THEN...
...IT SHOULD BE...
...JAPAN'S FASTEST ALL-STARS...
...THE FOUR HEAVENLY KINGS!!

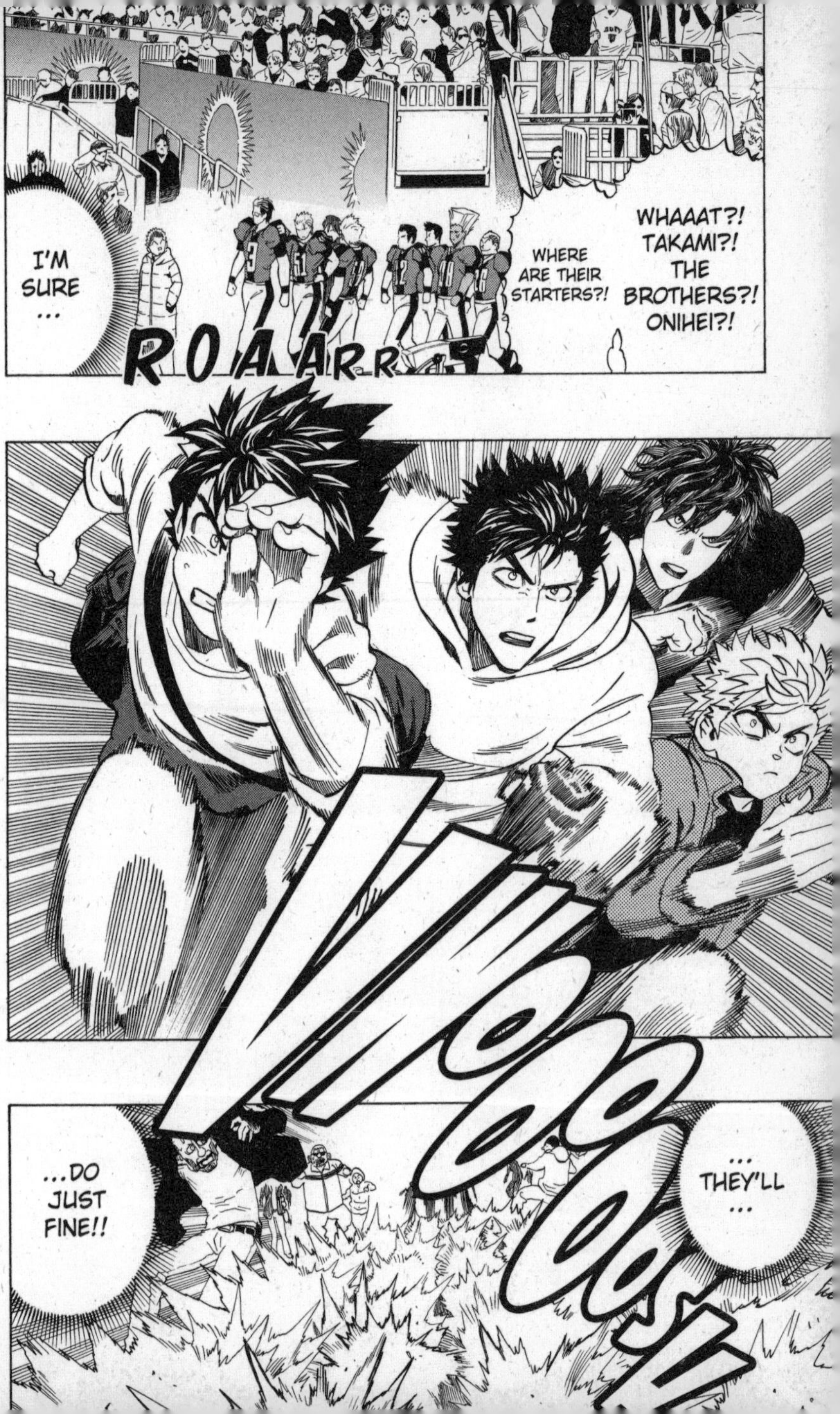
WHAAAT?! TAKAMI?! THE BROTHERS?! ONIHEI?!
WHERE ARE THEIR STARTERS?!
I'M SURE ...
ROAARR
WHOOOOSH!!
... THEY'LL ...
...DO JUST FINE!!

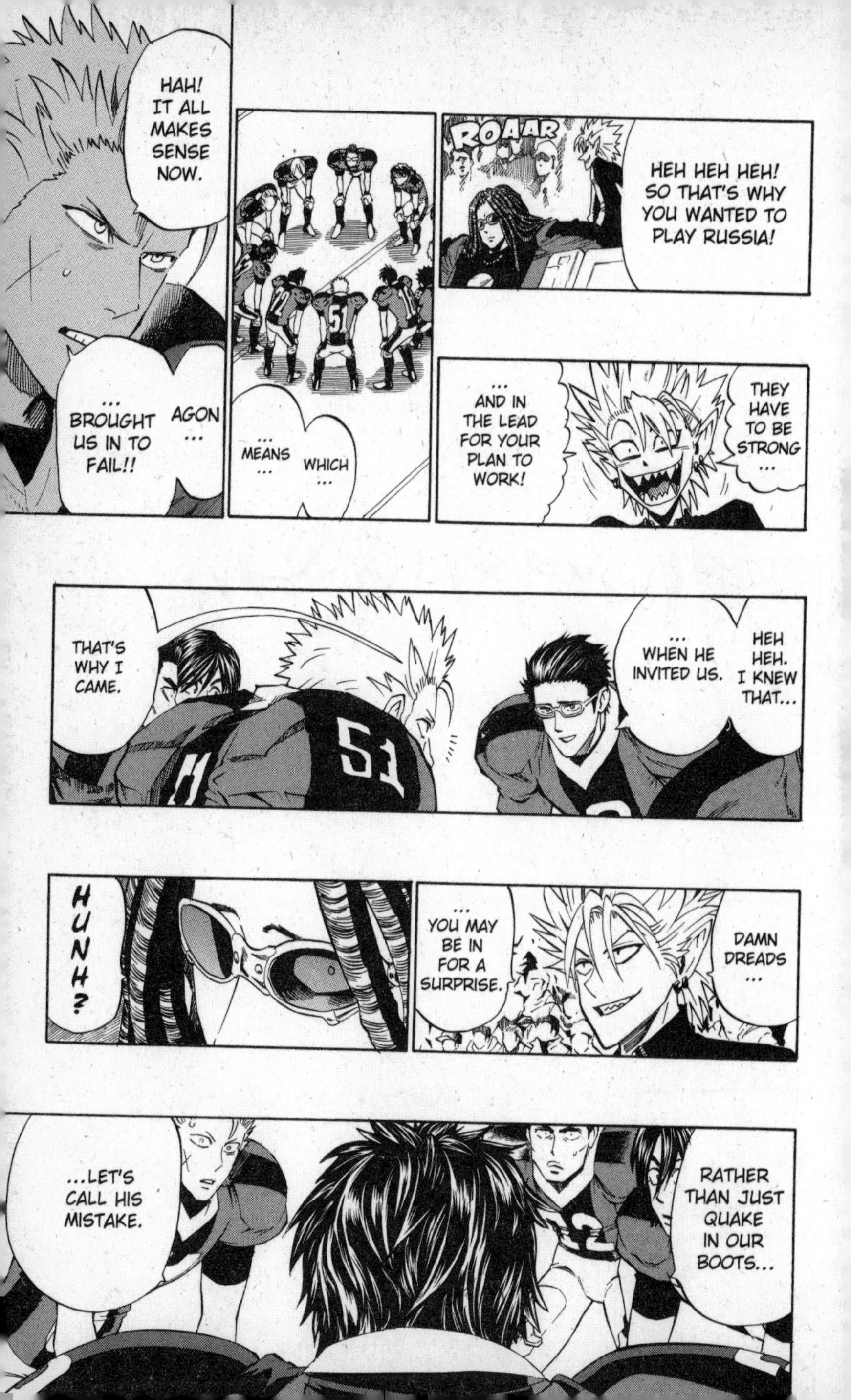
ROAAR
HEH HEH HEH! SO THAT'S WHY YOU WANTED TO PLAY RUSSIA!
THEY HAVE TO BE STRONG ...
... AND IN THE LEAD FOR YOUR PLAN TO WORK!
WHICH ...
... MEANS ...
HAH! IT ALL MAKES SENSE NOW.
AGON ...
... BROUGHT US IN TO FAIL!!
HEH HEH. I KNEW THAT...
... WHEN HE INVITED US.
THAT'S WHY I CAME.
DAMN DREADS ...
... YOU MAY BE IN FOR A SURPRISE.
HUNH?
RATHER THAN JUST QUAKE IN OUR BOOTS...
...LET'S CALL HIS MISTAKE.

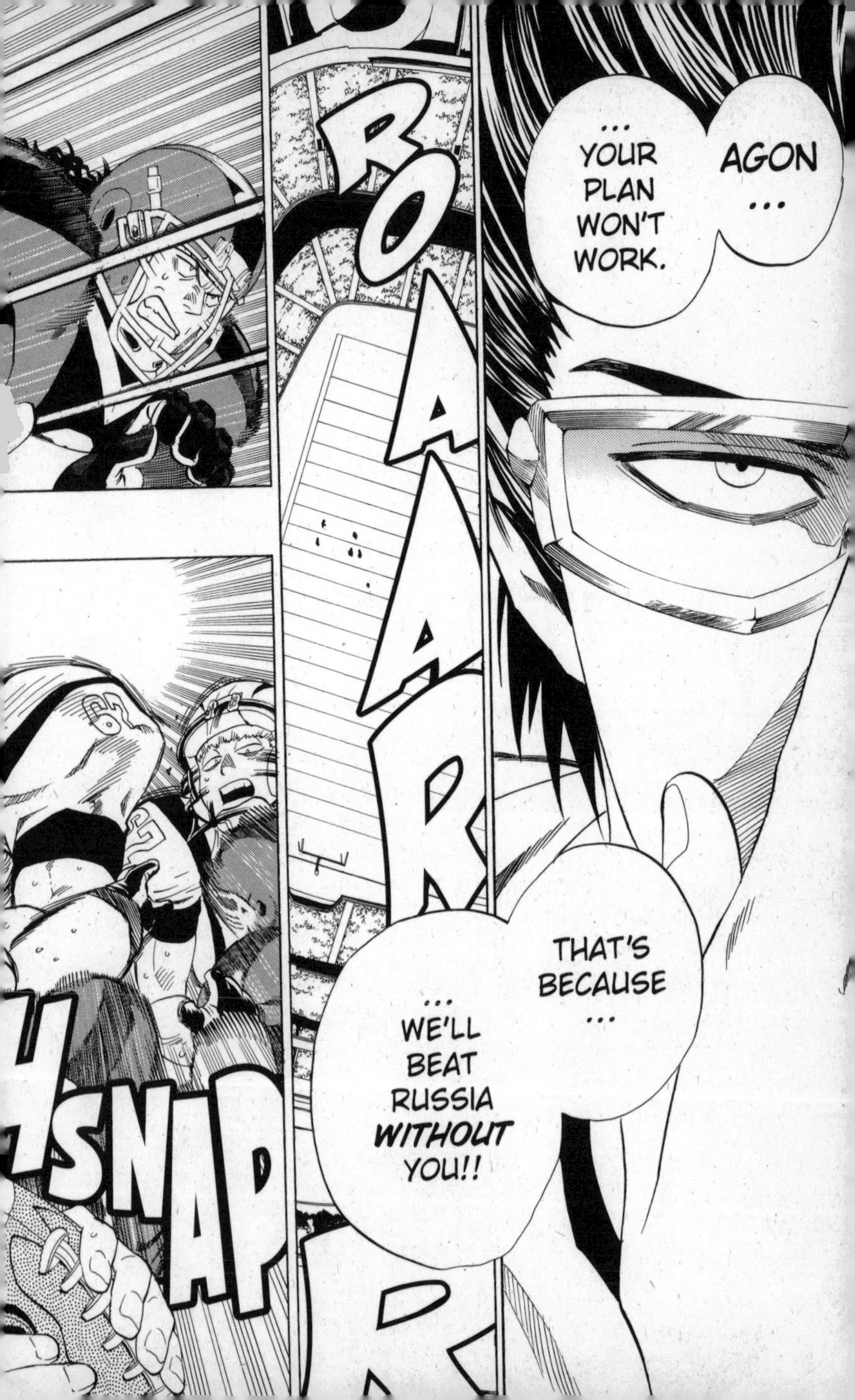

AGON ...
... YOUR PLAN WON'T WORK.
THAT'S BECAUSE ...
... WE'LL BEAT RUSSIA *WITHOUT* YOU!!
ROAAR
SNAP

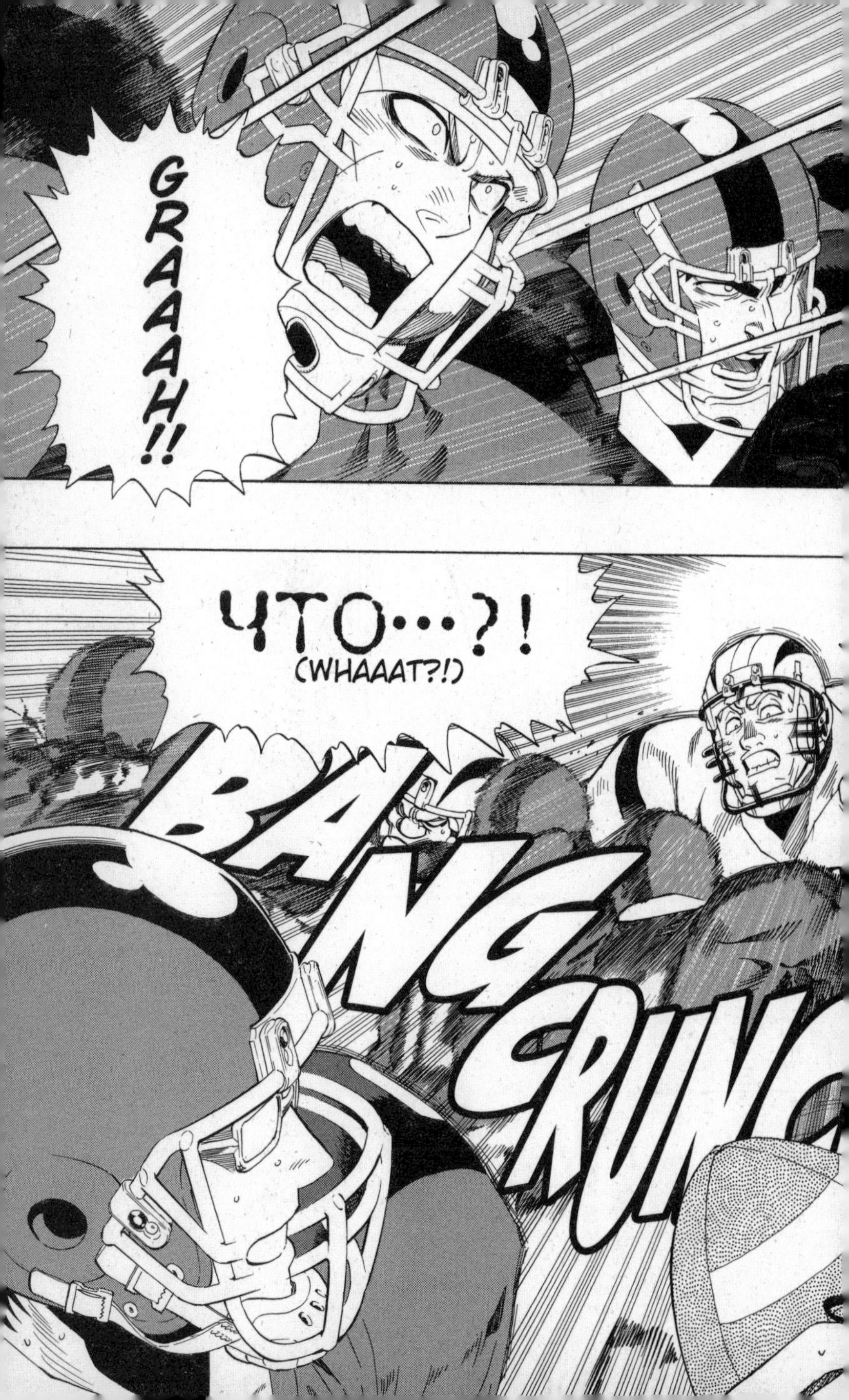
GRAAAAH!!
ЧТО...?!
(WHAAAT?!)
BANG
CRUNC

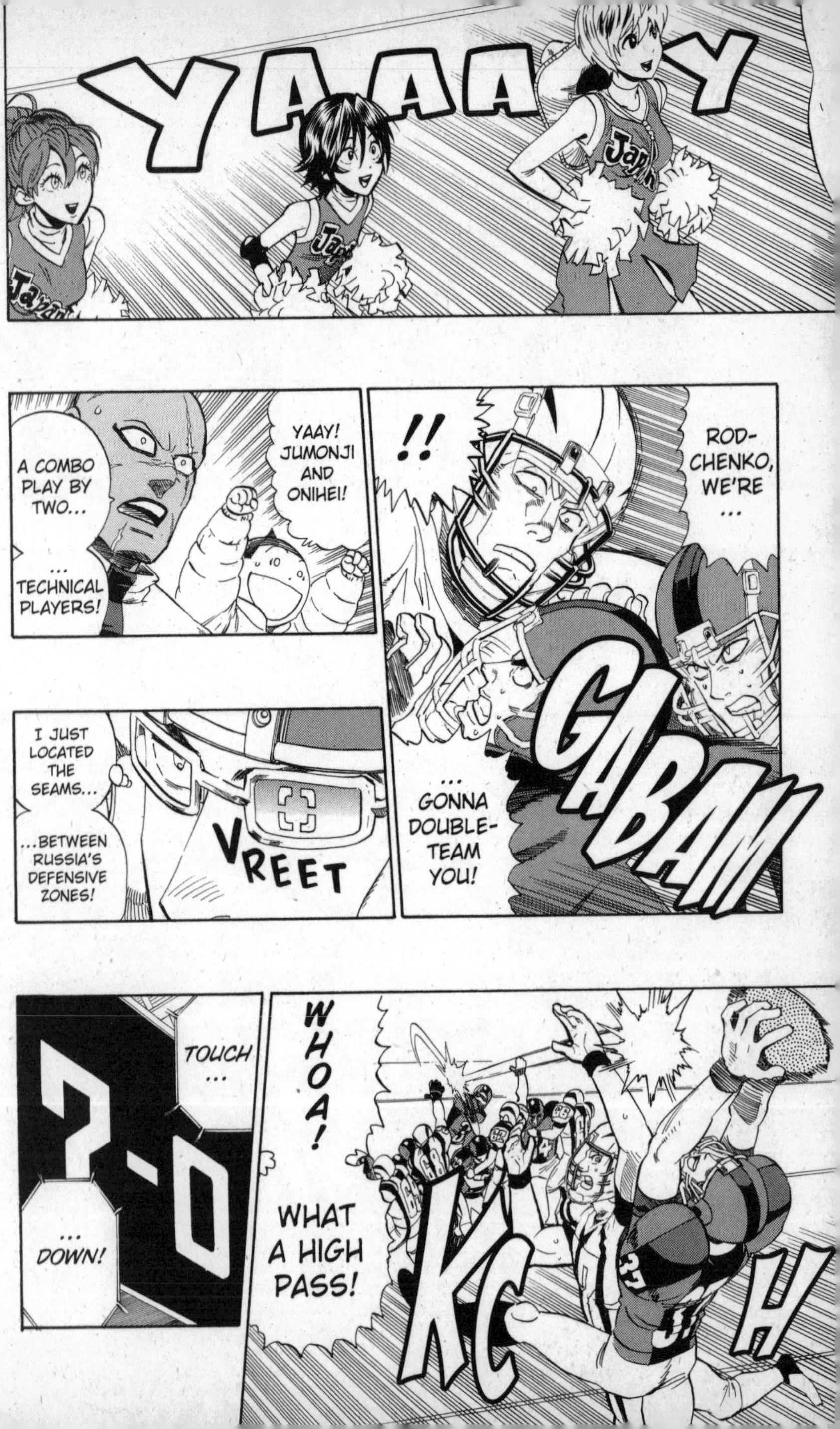
YAAAAY
ROD-CHENKO, WE'RE ...
!!
... GONNA DOUBLE-TEAM YOU!
GABAM
YAAY! JUMONJI AND ONIHEI!
A COMBO PLAY BY TWO...
... TECHNICAL PLAYERS!
I JUST LOCATED THE SEAMS...
...BETWEEN RUSSIA'S DEFENSIVE ZONES!
VREET
WHOA!
WHAT A HIGH PASS!
KCH
TOUCH...
7-0
...DOWN!

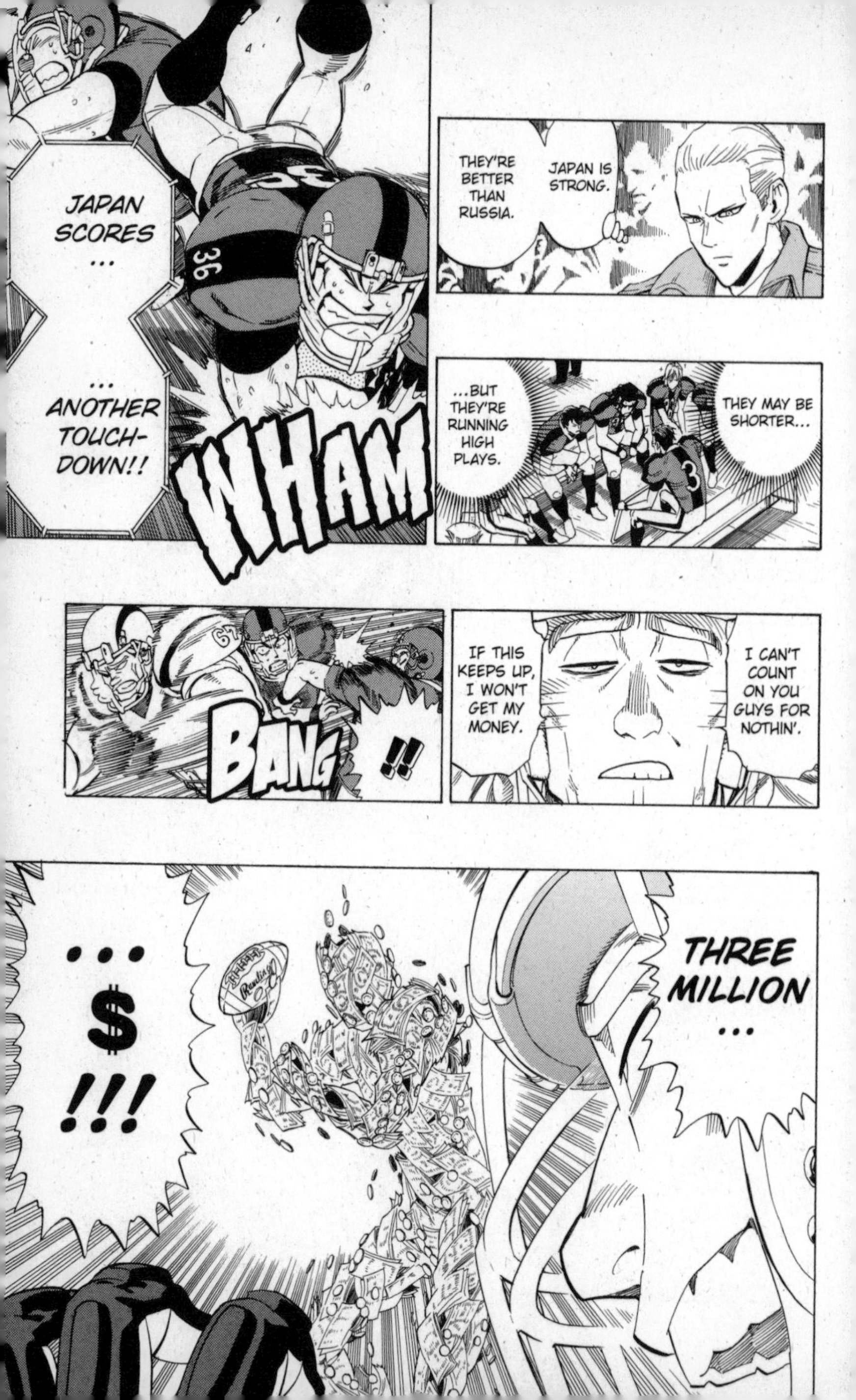
JAPAN IS STRONG.
THEY'RE BETTER THAN RUSSIA.
THEY MAY BE SHORTER...
...BUT THEY'RE RUNNING HIGH PLAYS.
JAPAN SCORES ...
... ANOTHER TOUCH-DOWN!!
WHAM
I CAN'T COUNT ON YOU GUYS FOR NOTHIN'.
IF THIS KEEPS UP, I WON'T GET MY MONEY.
BANG!!
THREE MILLION ...
... $!!!

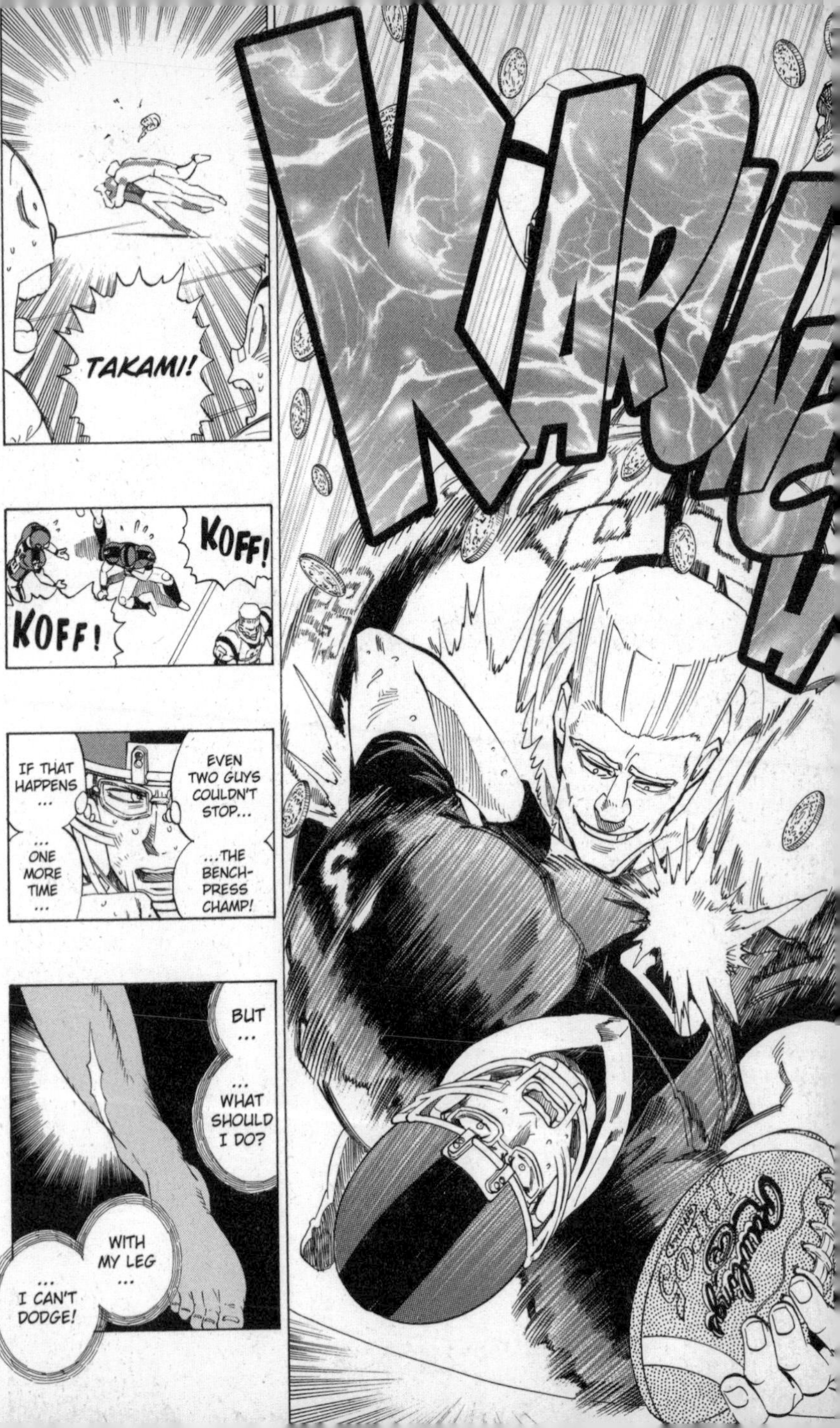
TAKAMI!
KOFF!
KOFF!
EVEN TWO GUYS COULDN'T STOP...
...THE BENCH-PRESS CHAMP!
IF THAT HAPPENS ...
... ONE MORE TIME ...
BUT ...
... WHAT SHOULD I DO?
WITH MY LEG ...
... I CAN'T DODGE!

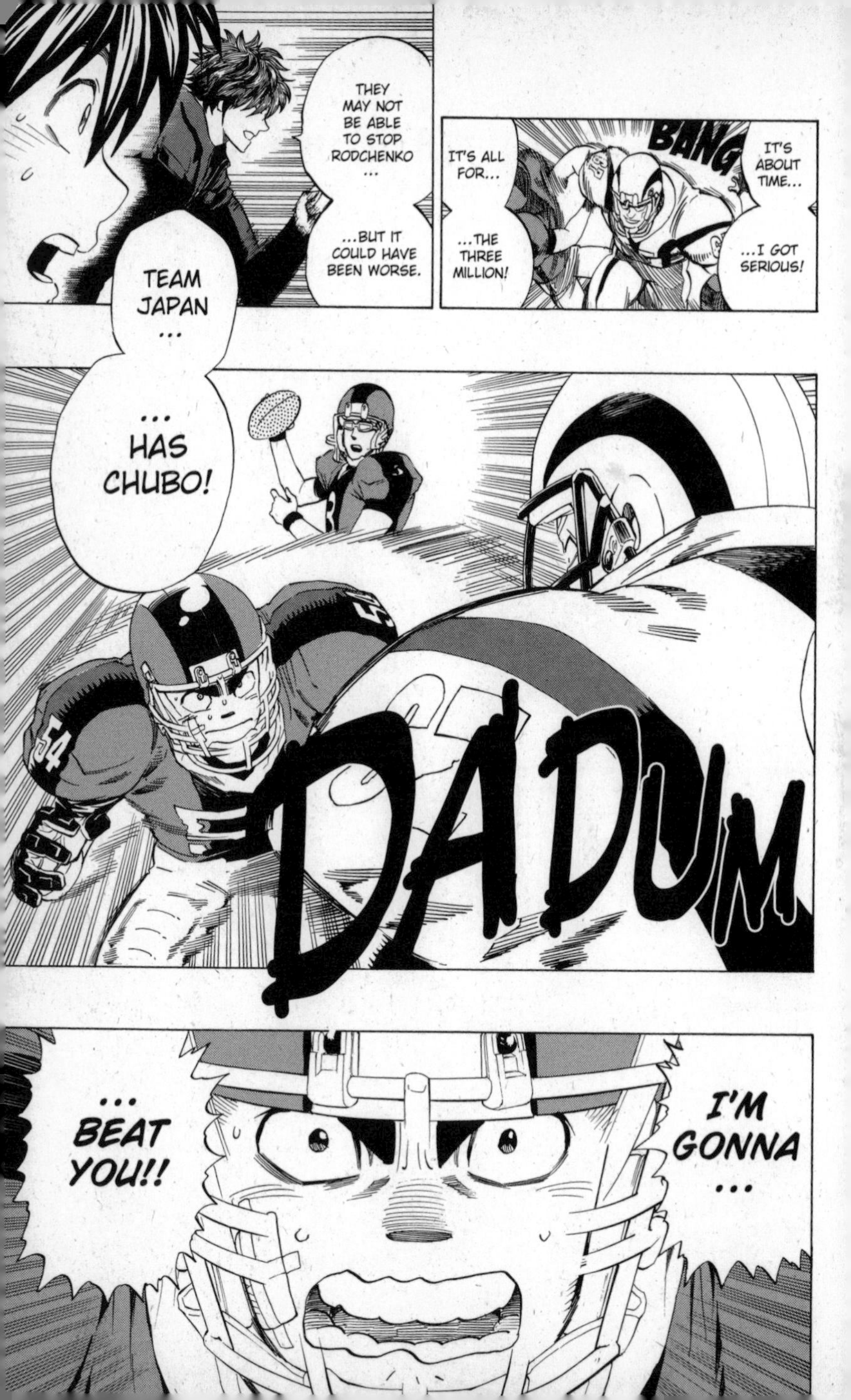
BANG
IT'S ABOUT TIME...
...I GOT SERIOUS!
IT'S ALL FOR...
...THE THREE MILLION!
THEY MAY NOT BE ABLE TO STOP RODCHENKO...
...BUT IT COULD HAVE BEEN WORSE.
TEAM JAPAN...
...HAS CHUBO!
DADUM
I'M GONNA...
...BEAT YOU!!

The Helper All-Stars!!
TEAM JAPAN'S ADDITIONAL MEMBERS

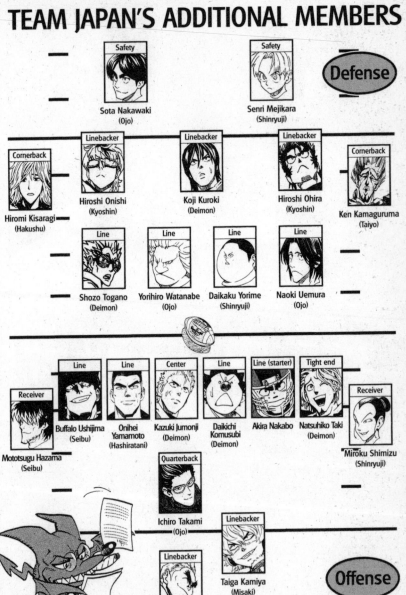

Defense

Safety
Sota Nakawaki
(Ojo)

Safety
Senri Mejikara
(Shinryuji)

Cornerback
Hiromi Kisaragi
(Hakushu)

Linebacker
Hiroshi Onishi
(Kyoshin)

Linebacker
Koji Kuroki
(Deimon)

Linebacker
Hiroshi Ohira
(Kyoshin)

Cornerback
Ken Kamaguruma
(Taiyo)

Line
Shozo Togano
(Deimon)

Line
Yorihiro Watanabe
(Ojo)

Line
Daikaku Yorime
(Shinryuji)

Line
Naoki Uemura
(Ojo)

Receiver
Mototsugu Hazama
(Seibu)

Line
Buffalo Ushijima
(Seibu)

Line
Onihei Yamamoto
(Hashiratani)

Center
Kazuki Jumonji
(Deimon)

Line
Daikichi Komusubi
(Deimon)

Line (starter)
Akira Nakabo

Tight end
Natsuhiko Taki
(Deimon)

Receiver
Miroku Shimizu
(Shinryuji)

Quarterback
Ichiro Takami
(Ojo)

Linebacker
Ganjo Iwashige
(Sado)

Linebacker
Taiga Kamiya
(Misaki)

Offense

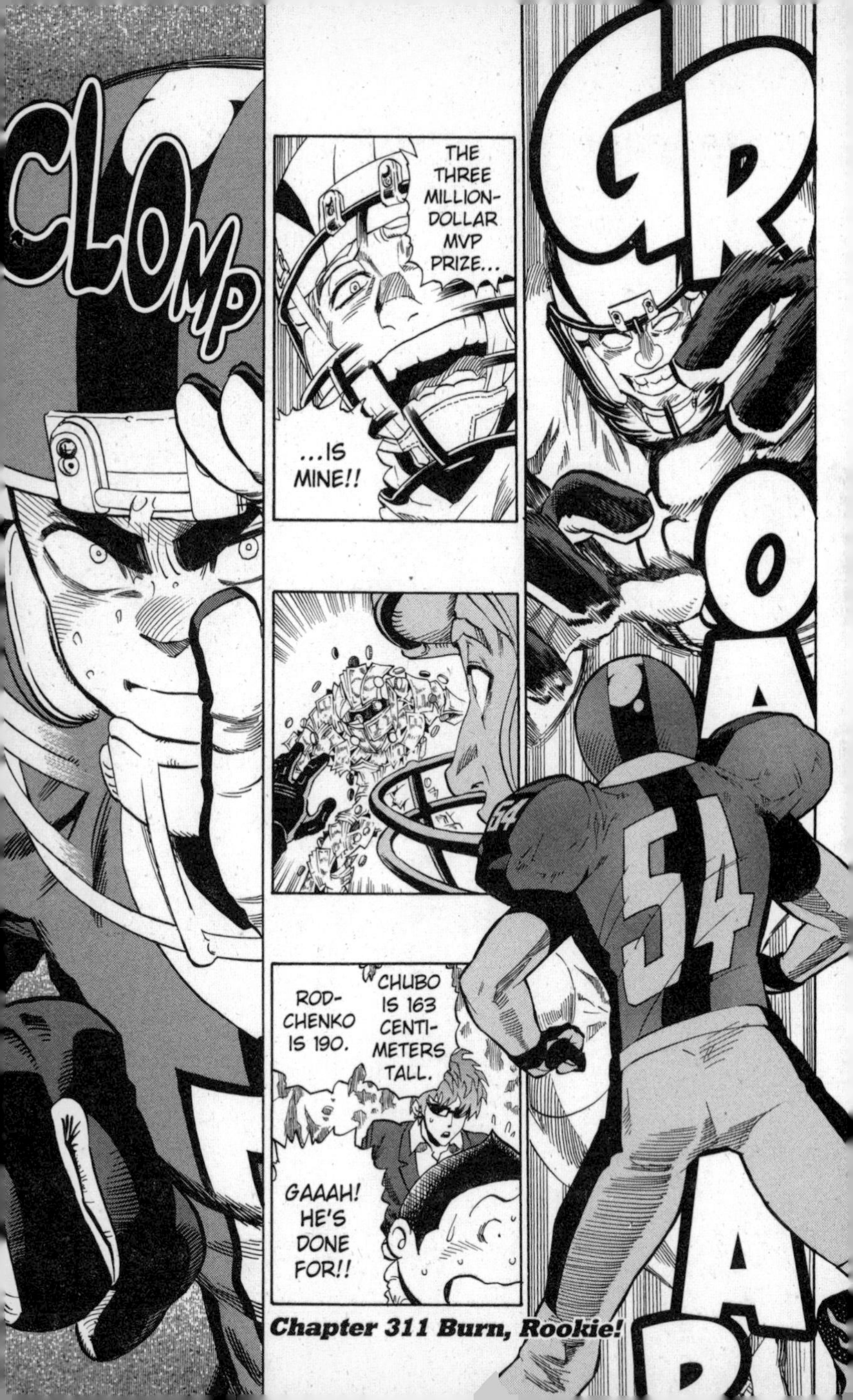
THE THREE MILLION-DOLLAR MVP PRIZE...
...IS MINE!!
CHUBO IS 163 CENTIMETERS TALL.
ROD-CHENKO IS 190.
GAAAH! HE'S DONE FOR!!
CLOMP

Chapter 311 Burn, Rookie!

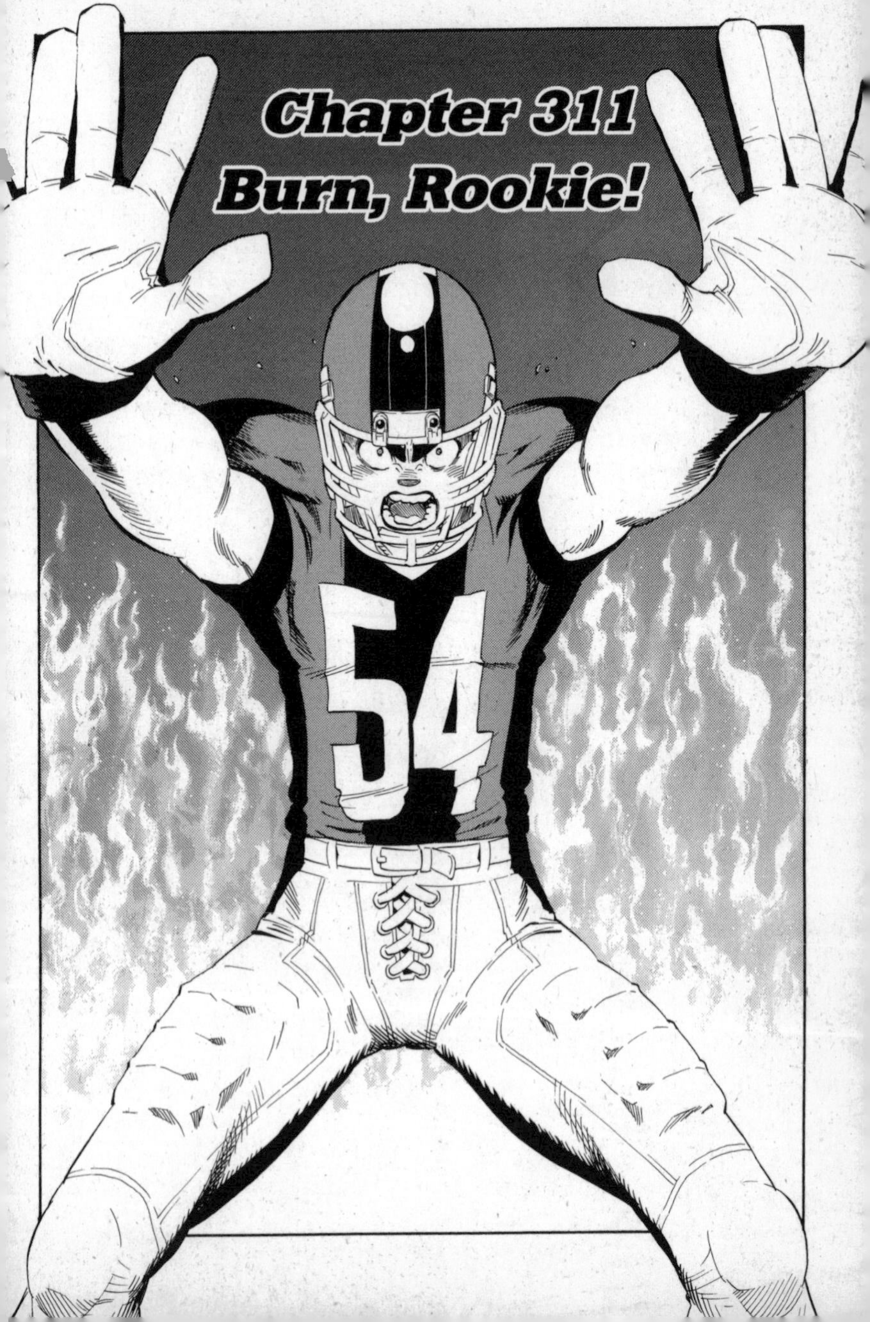
Chapter 311
Burn, Rookie!
54

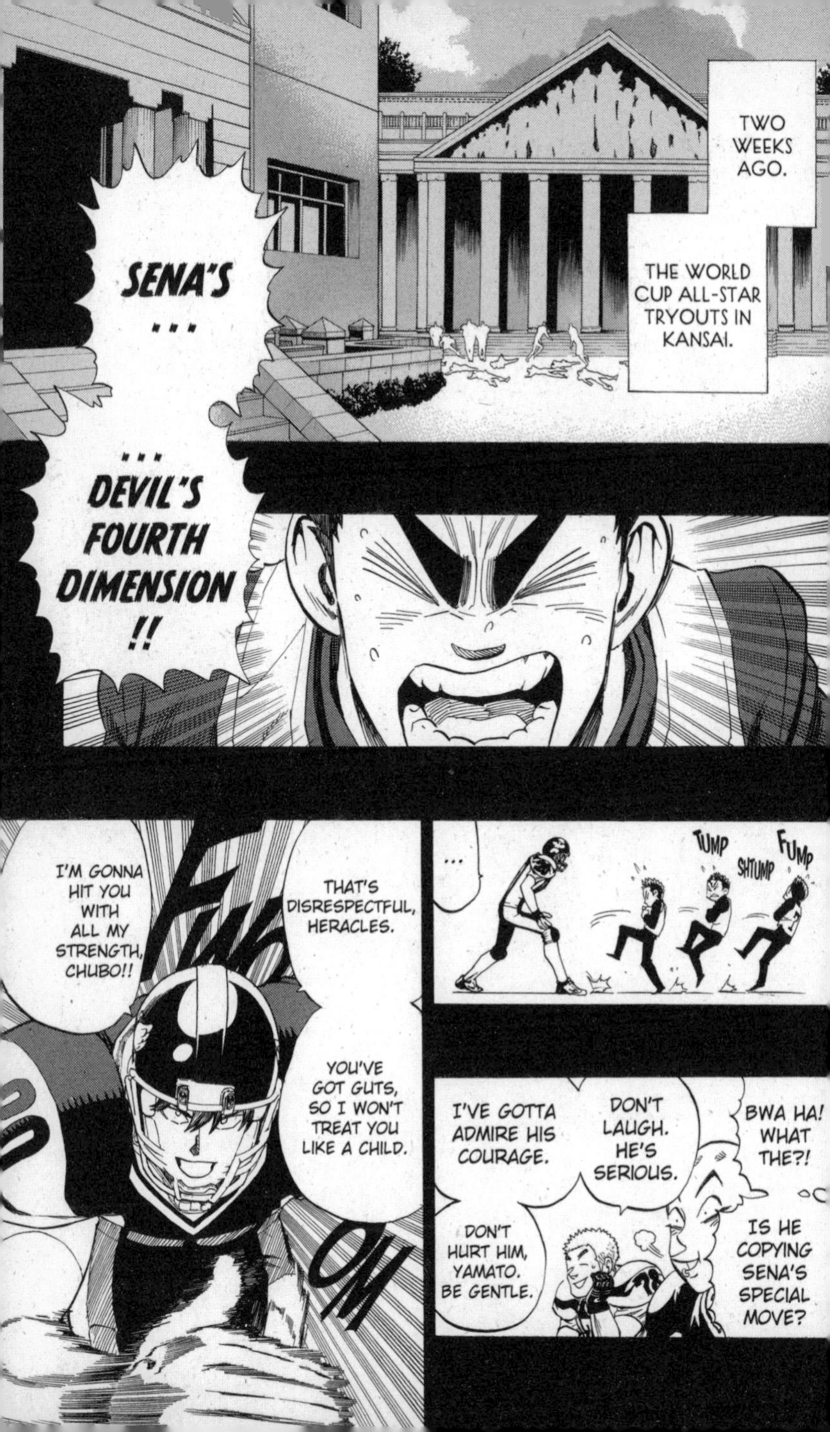
TWO WEEKS AGO.
THE WORLD CUP ALL-STAR TRYOUTS IN KANSAI.
SENA'S ...
... DEVIL'S FOURTH DIMENSION !!
...
TUMP
SHTUMP
FUMP
BWA HA! WHAT THE?!
IS HE COPYING SENA'S SPECIAL MOVE?
DON'T LAUGH. HE'S SERIOUS.
I'VE GOTTA ADMIRE HIS COURAGE.
DON'T HURT HIM, YAMATO. BE GENTLE.
THAT'S DISRESPECTFUL, HERACLES.
YOU'VE GOT GUTS, SO I WON'T TREAT YOU LIKE A CHILD.
I'M GONNA HIT YOU WITH ALL MY STRENGTH, CHUBO!!

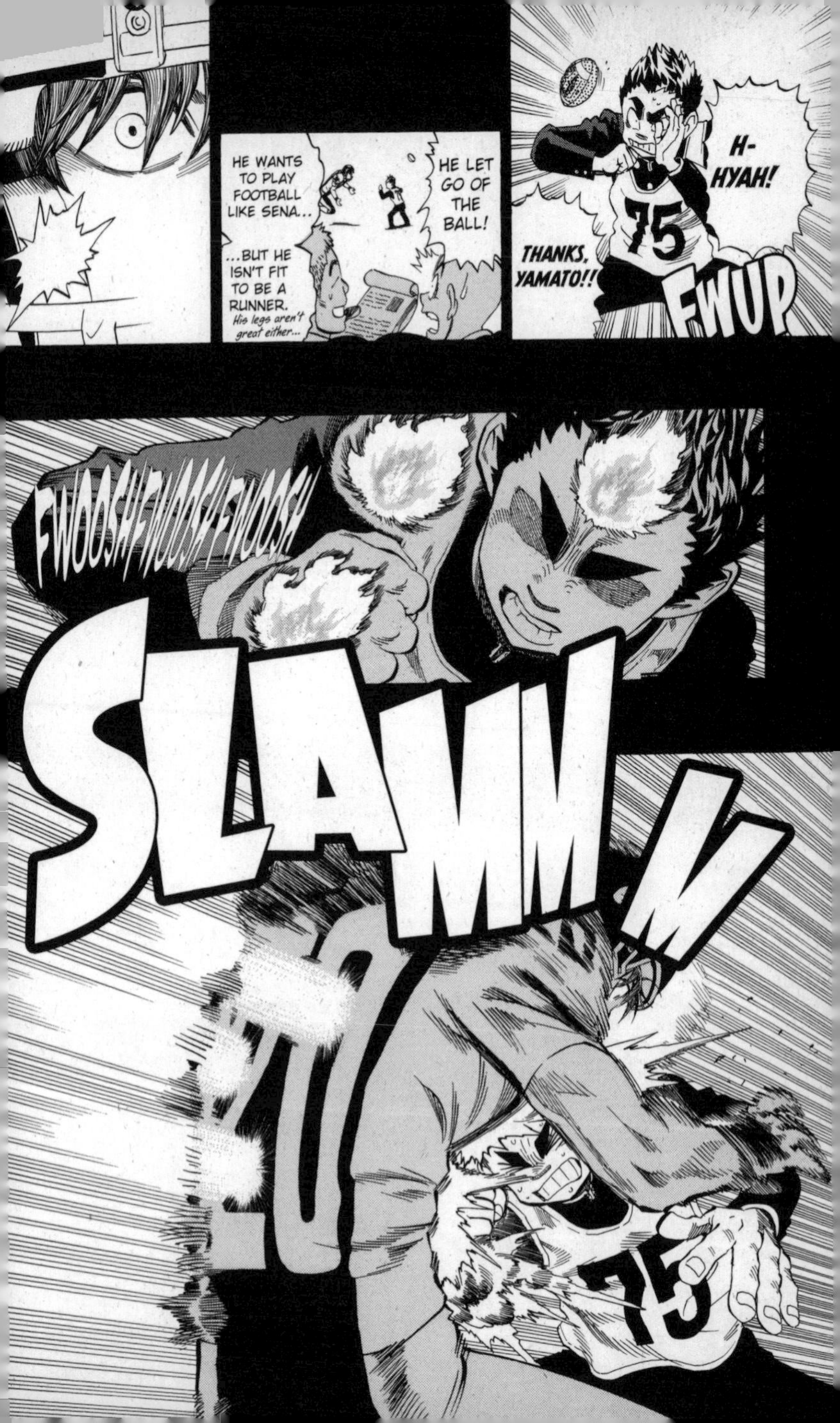
H-HYAH!
THANKS, YAMATO!!
FWUP
HE LET GO OF THE BALL!
HE WANTS TO PLAY FOOTBALL LIKE SENA...
...BUT HE ISN'T FIT TO BE A RUNNER.
His legs aren't great either...
FWOOSH FWOOSH FWOOSH
SLAMM!!

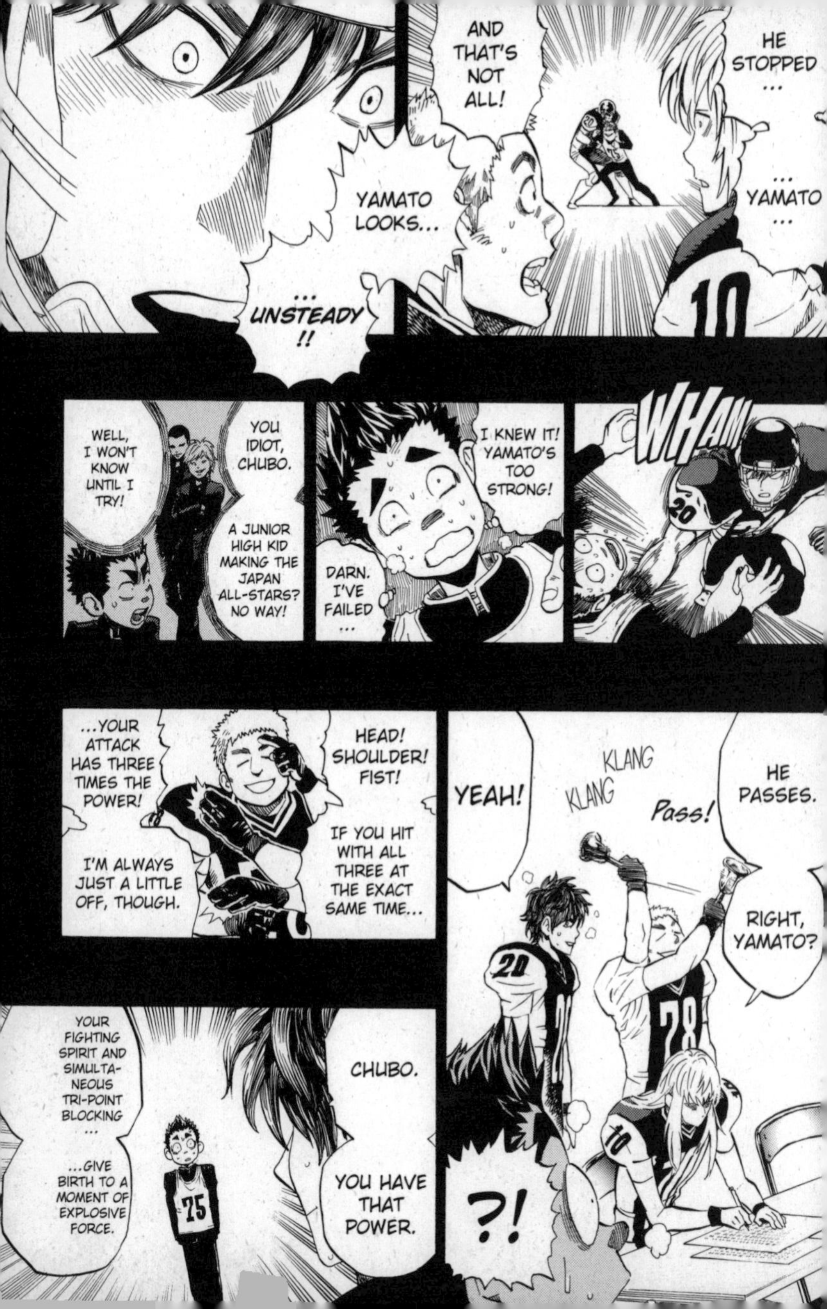
HE STOPPED...
...YAMATO...
AND THAT'S NOT ALL!
YAMATO LOOKS...
...UNSTEADY!!
WHAM
I KNEW IT! YAMATO'S TOO STRONG!
DARN. I'VE FAILED...
YOU IDIOT, CHUBO.
A JUNIOR HIGH KID MAKING THE JAPAN ALL-STARS? NO WAY!
WELL, I WON'T KNOW UNTIL I TRY!
HE PASSES.
RIGHT, YAMATO?
Pass!
KLANG
KLANG
YEAH!
?!
HEAD! SHOULDER! FIST!
IF YOU HIT WITH ALL THREE AT THE EXACT SAME TIME...
...YOUR ATTACK HAS THREE TIMES THE POWER!
I'M ALWAYS JUST A LITTLE OFF, THOUGH.
CHUBO.
YOU HAVE THAT POWER.
YOUR FIGHTING SPIRIT AND SIMULTA-NEOUS TRI-POINT BLOCKING...
...GIVE BIRTH TO A MOMENT OF EXPLOSIVE FORCE.

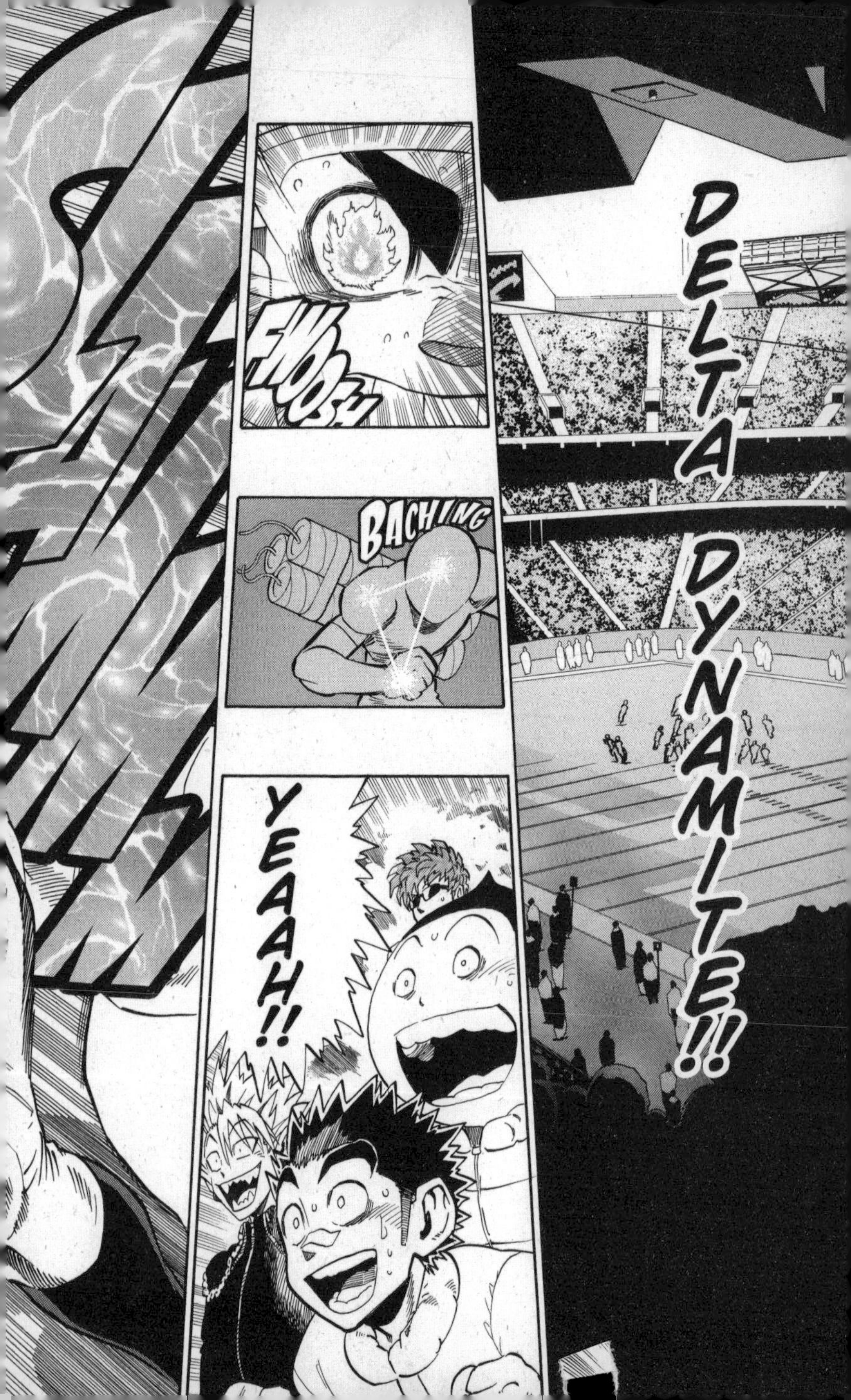
DELTA DYNAMITE!!
FWOOSH
BACHING
YEAAAH!!

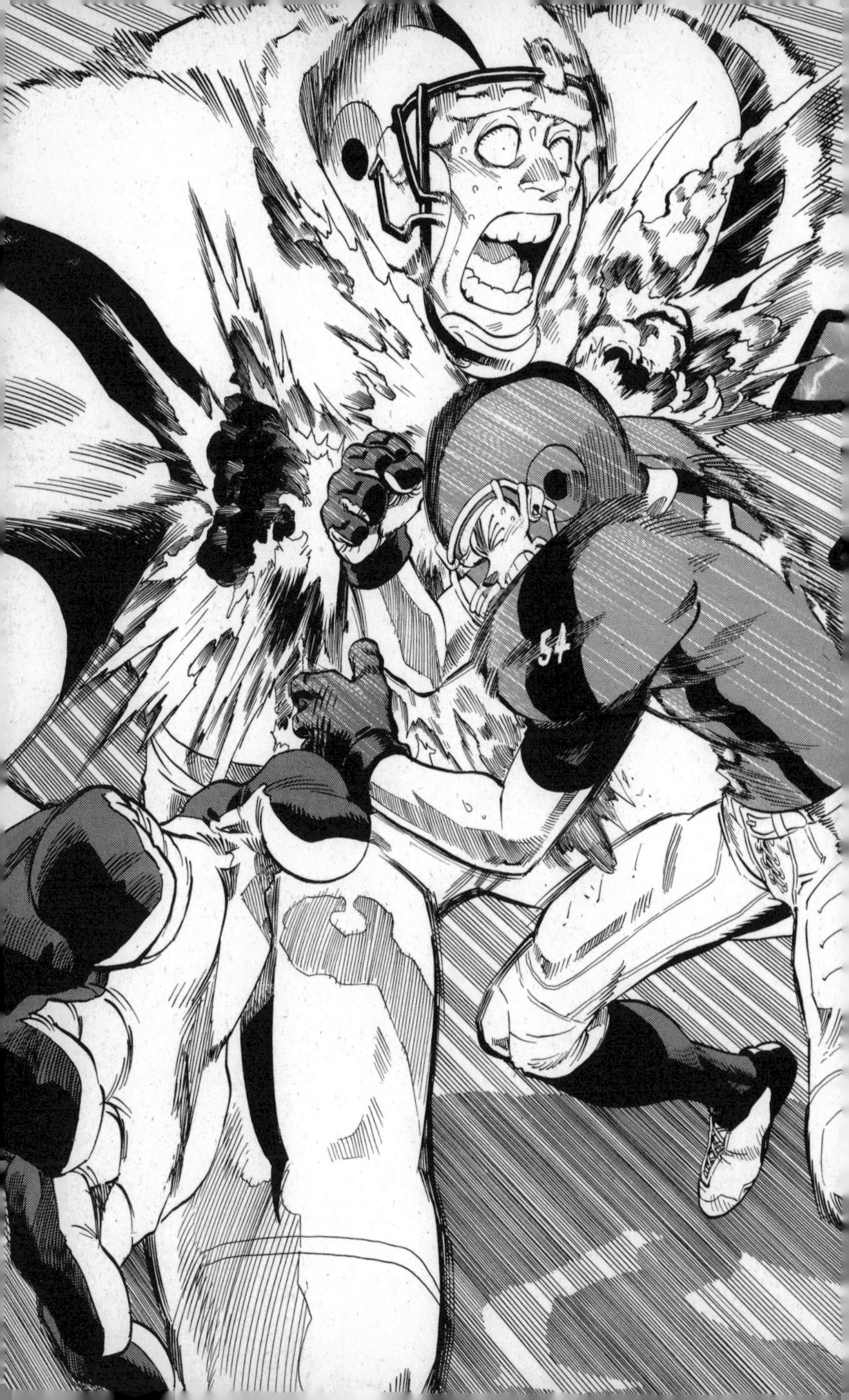

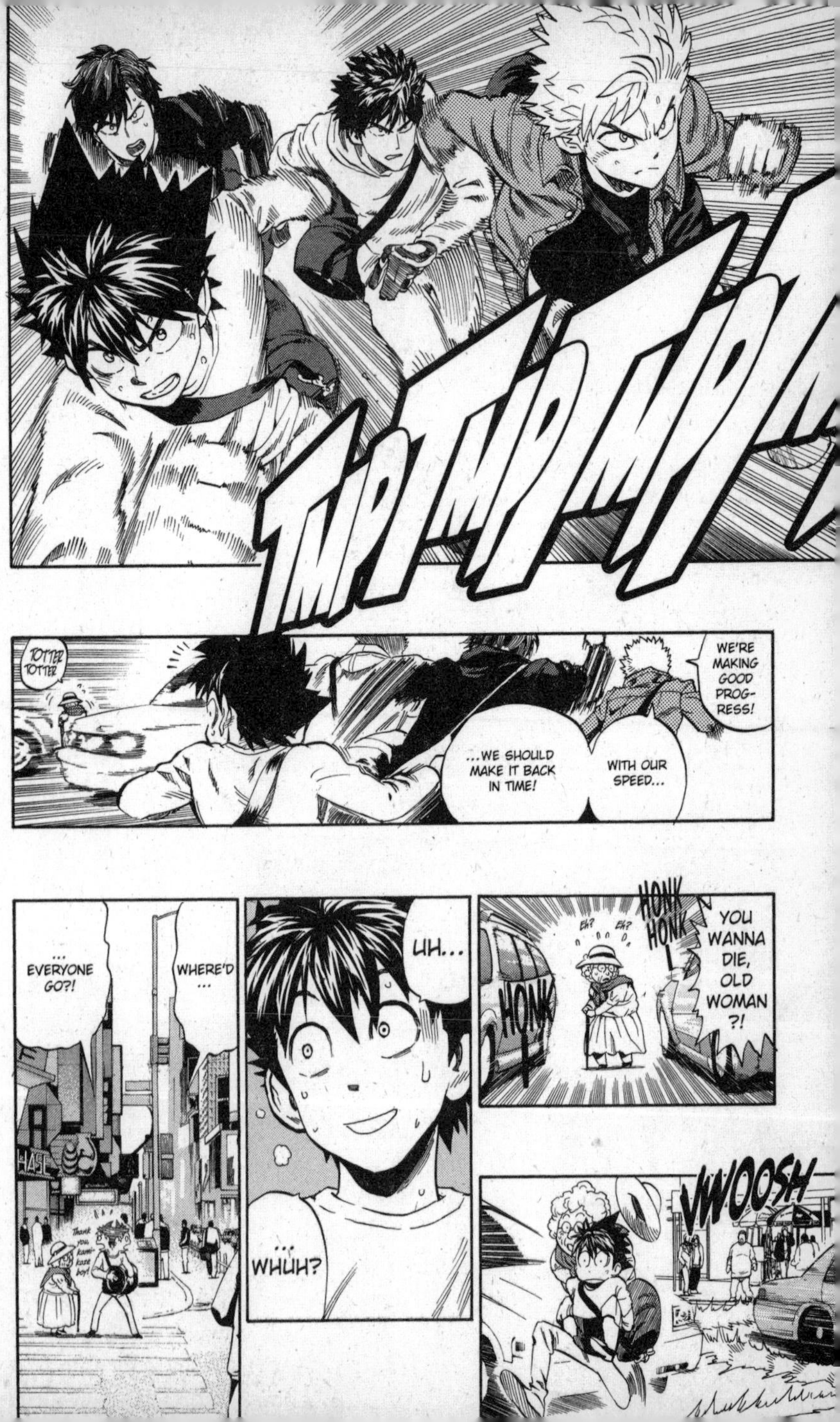
TMP-TMP-TMP-
WE'RE MAKING GOOD PROG-RESS!
WITH OUR SPEED...
...WE SHOULD MAKE IT BACK IN TIME!
TOTTER TOTTER
HONK HONK
YOU WANNA DIE, OLD WOMAN?!
Eh? Eh?
HONK
VWOOSH
UH...
...WHUH?
WHERE'D ...
... EVERYONE GO?!
Thank you, kamikaze boy!

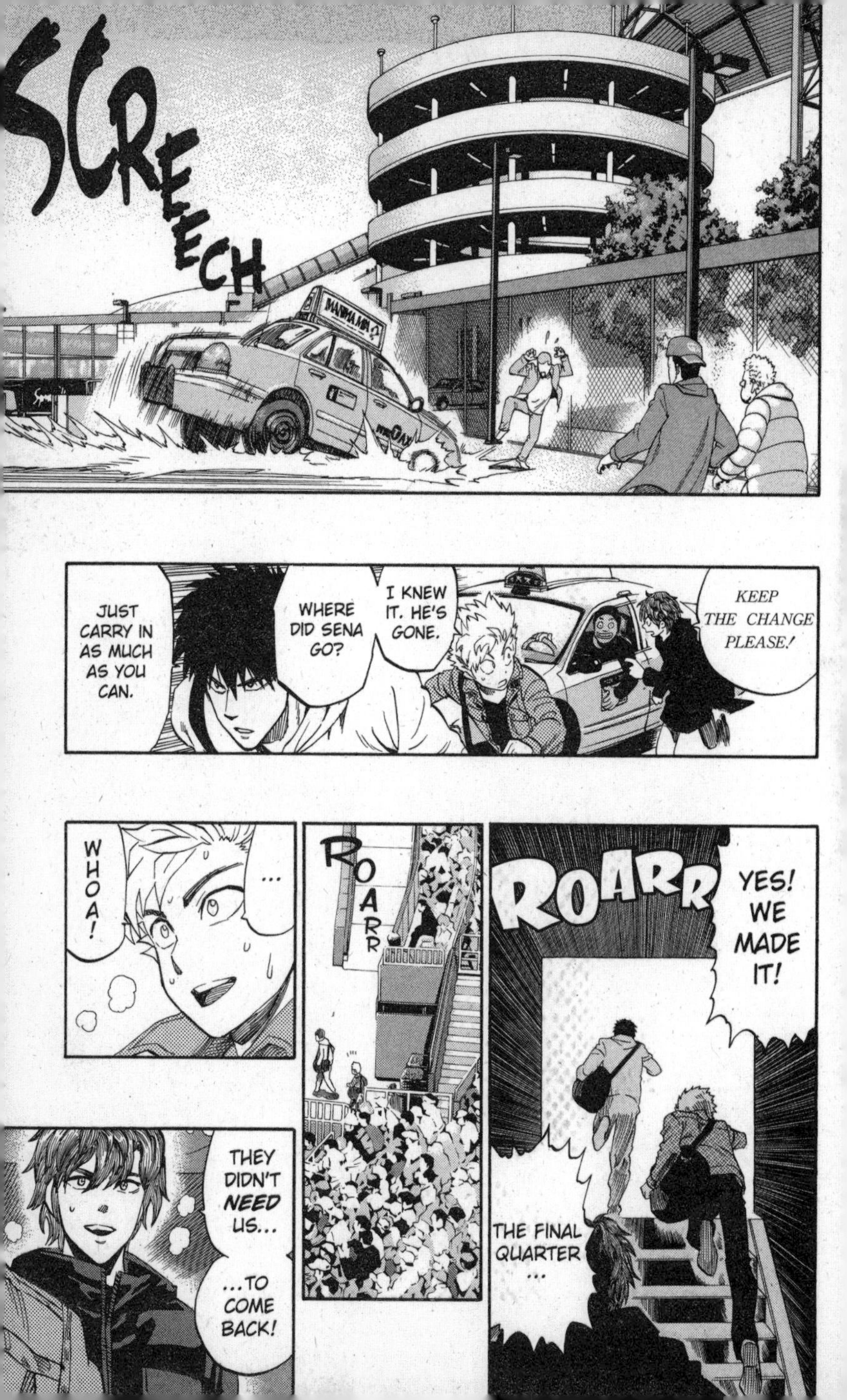
SCREECH
KEEP THE CHANGE PLEASE!
I KNEW IT. HE'S GONE.
WHERE DID SENA GO?
JUST CARRY IN AS MUCH AS YOU CAN.
ROARR
YES! WE MADE IT!
THE FINAL QUARTER...
ROARR
WHOA!
...
THEY DIDN'T NEED US...
...TO COME BACK!

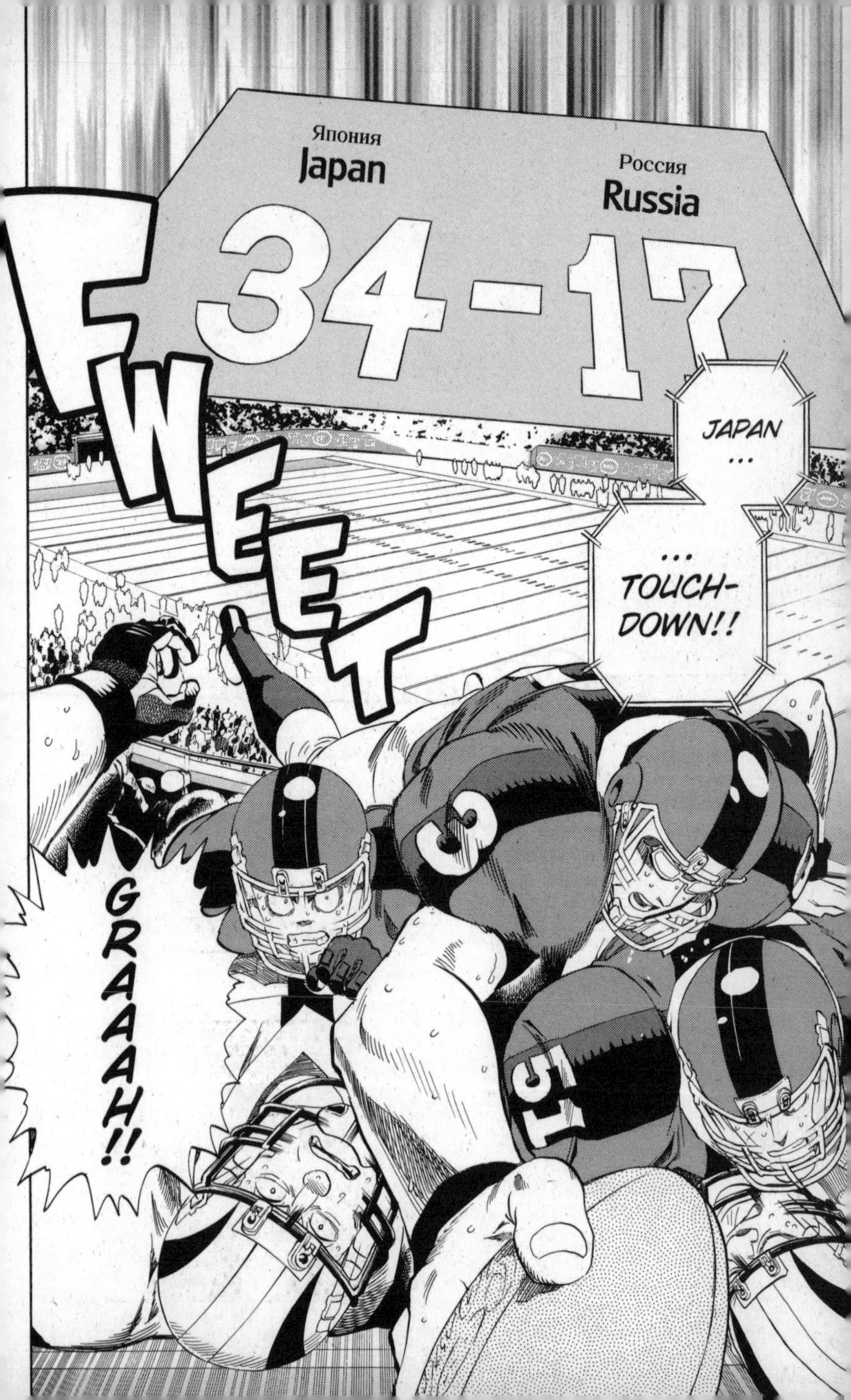
Япония
Japan
Россия
Russia
34-17
FWEEET
JAPAN ...
... TOUCH-DOWN!!
GRAAAAH!!

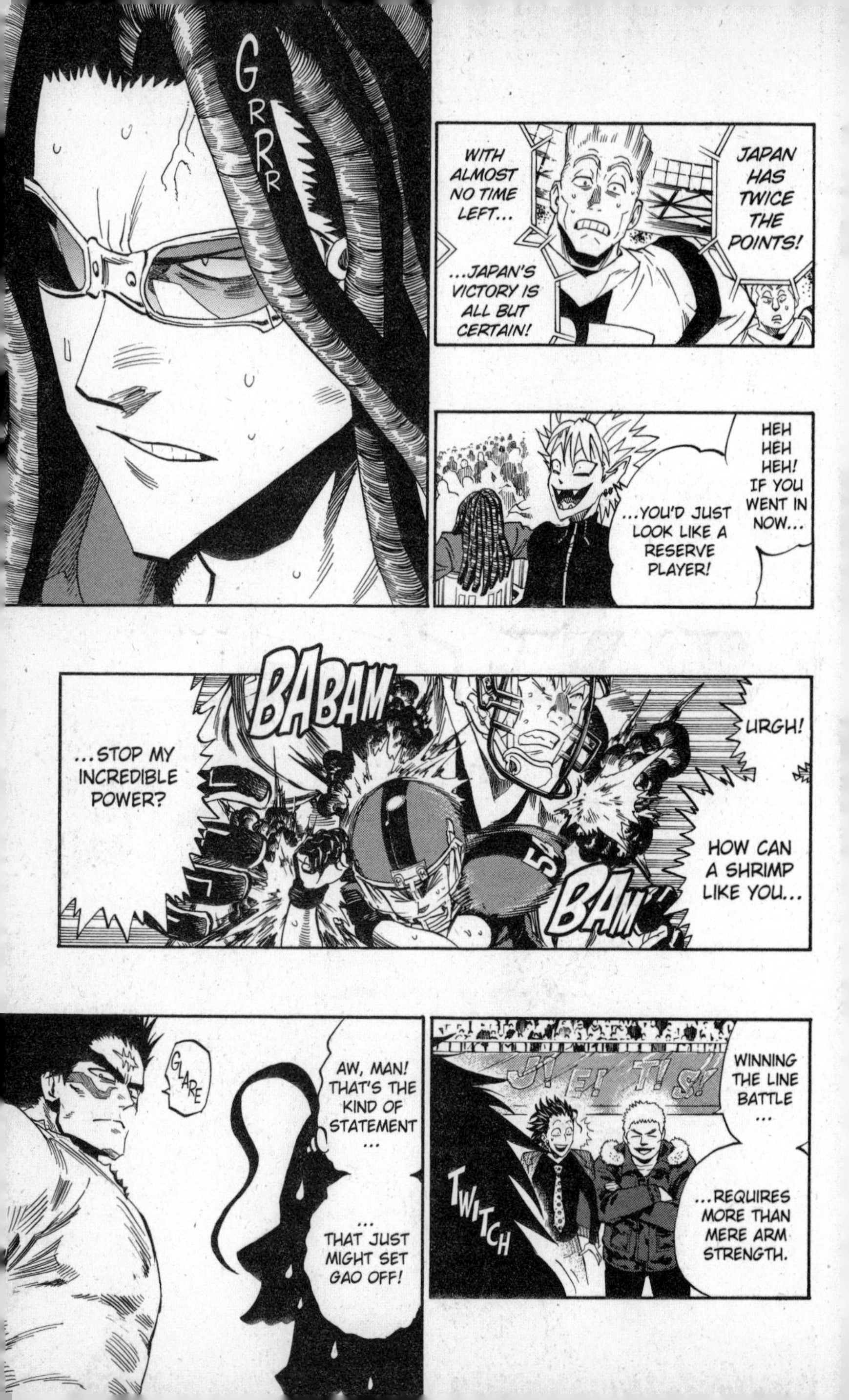
JAPAN HAS TWICE THE POINTS!
WITH ALMOST NO TIME LEFT...
...JAPAN'S VICTORY IS ALL BUT CERTAIN!
HEH HEH HEH! IF YOU WENT IN NOW...
...YOU'D JUST LOOK LIKE A RESERVE PLAYER!
GRRR
URGH!
HOW CAN A SHRIMP LIKE YOU...
BABAM
...STOP MY INCREDIBLE POWER?
BAM
WINNING THE LINE BATTLE...
...REQUIRES MORE THAN MERE ARM STRENGTH.
J! E! T! S!
TWITCH
AW, MAN! THAT'S THE KIND OF STATEMENT...
...THAT JUST MIGHT SET GAO OFF!
GLARE

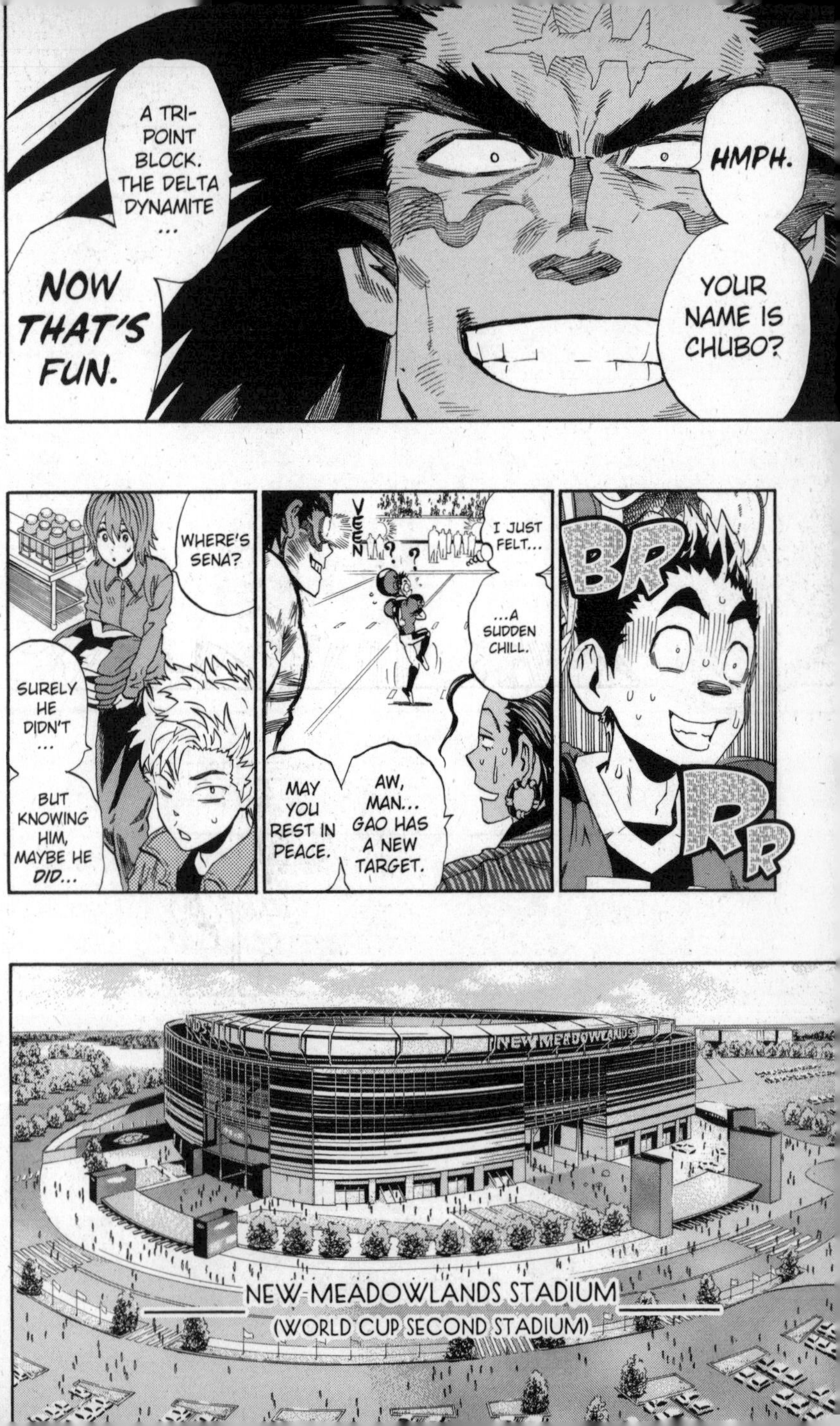
HMPH.
YOUR NAME IS CHUBO?
A TRI-POINT BLOCK. THE DELTA DYNAMITE...
NOW THAT'S FUN.
BRRRR
I JUST FELT...
...A SUDDEN CHILL.
VEEN
?
?
AW, MAN... GAO HAS A NEW TARGET.
MAY YOU REST IN PEACE.
WHERE'S SENA?
SURELY HE DIDN'T...
BUT KNOWING HIM, MAYBE HE *DID*...
NEW MEADOWLANDS
NEW-MEADOWLANDS STADIUM
(WORLD CUP SECOND STADIUM)

ACCKK! I'M AT THE WRONG STADIUM!!

THAT'S WORSE THAN CHUBO...

Japan	
Russia	
Militaria	
Finland	

IF JAPAN WINS... ...WE'LL PLAY THE WINNER.

THIS IS FINLAND ... ...VERSUS MILITARIA.

ROARR

BANG CRUNCH

SUCH WHITE TEETH!

NICE TO MEET YOU!

OH!

THAT'S HÄKKINEN!

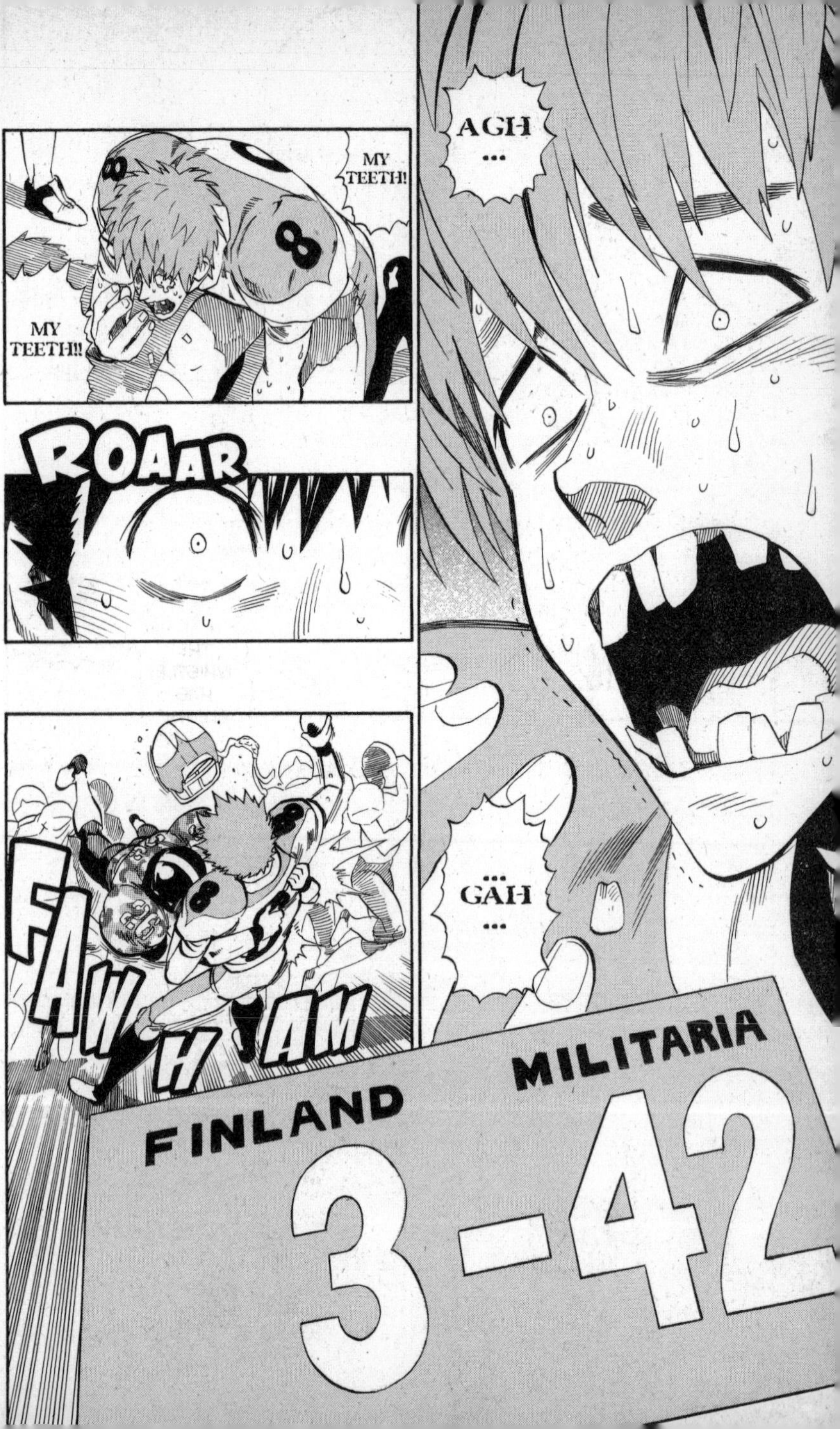
AGH ...
... GÄH ...
MY TEETH!
MY TEETH!!
ROAAR
FAWH AM
FINLAND
3
MILITARIA
42

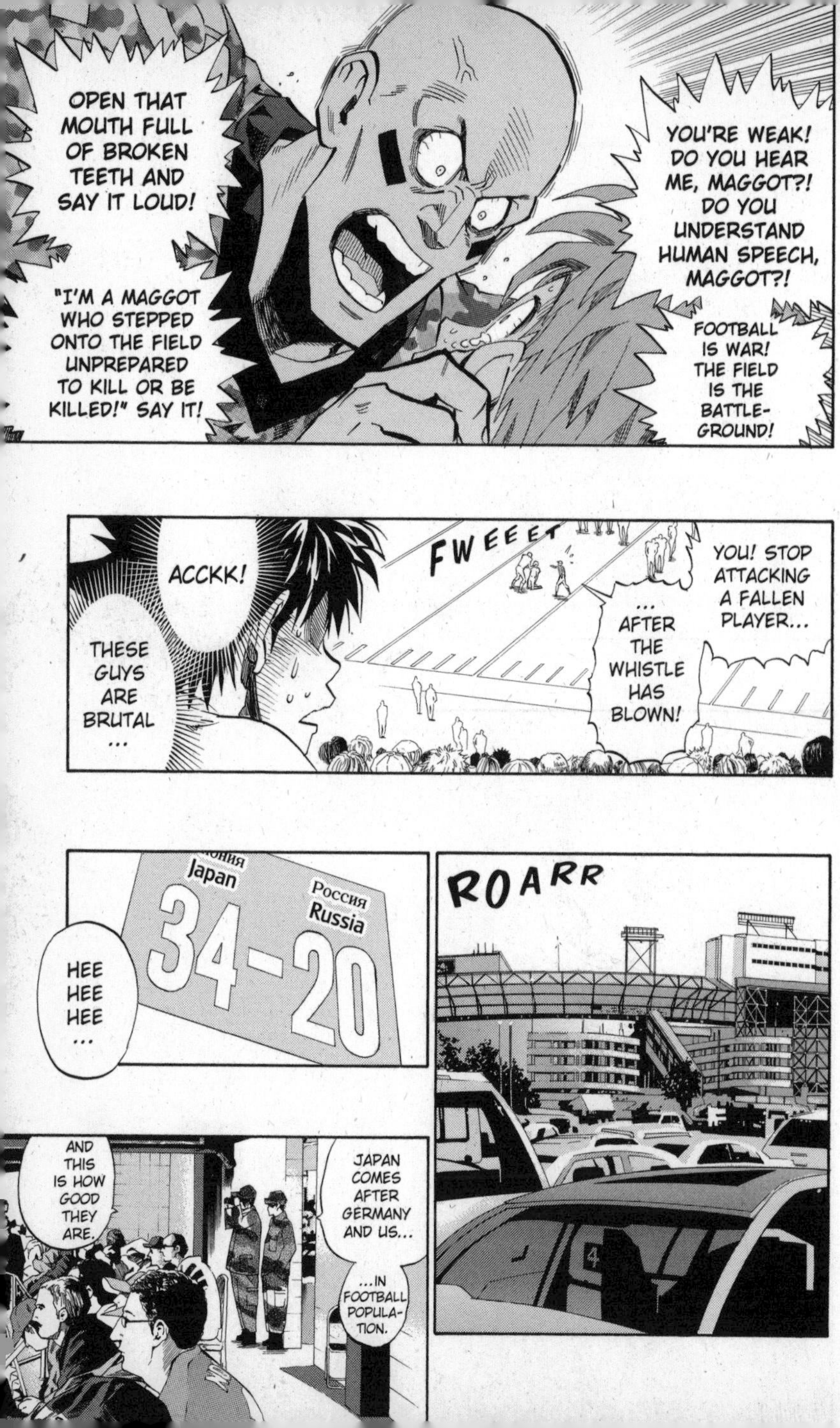
YOU'RE WEAK! DO YOU HEAR ME, MAGGOT?! DO YOU UNDERSTAND HUMAN SPEECH, MAGGOT?!
FOOTBALL IS WAR! THE FIELD IS THE BATTLE-GROUND!
OPEN THAT MOUTH FULL OF BROKEN TEETH AND SAY IT LOUD!
"I'M A MAGGOT WHO STEPPED ONTO THE FIELD UNPREPARED TO KILL OR BE KILLED!" SAY IT!
YOU! STOP ATTACKING A FALLEN PLAYER...
...AFTER THE WHISTLE HAS BLOWN!
FWEEET
ACCKK!
THESE GUYS ARE BRUTAL...
ROARR
Japan
Россия
Russia
34-20
HEE HEE HEE...
JAPAN COMES AFTER GERMANY AND US...
...IN FOOTBALL POPULA-TION.
AND THIS IS HOW GOOD THEY ARE.

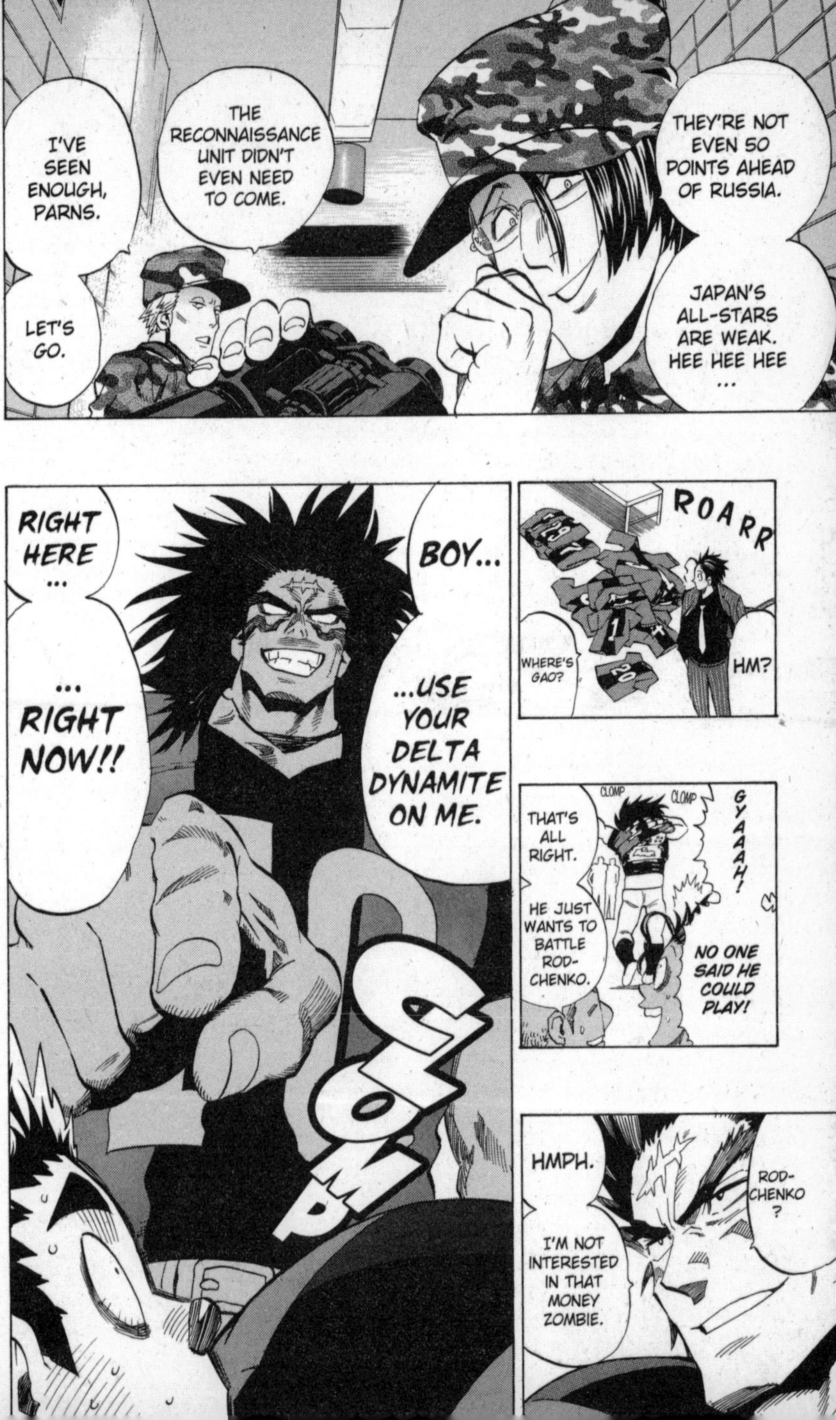
THEY'RE NOT EVEN 50 POINTS AHEAD OF RUSSIA.
JAPAN'S ALL-STARS ARE WEAK. HEE HEE HEE ...
THE RECONNAISSANCE UNIT DIDN'T EVEN NEED TO COME.
I'VE SEEN ENOUGH, PARNS.
LET'S GO.
ROARR
HM?
WHERE'S GAO?
GYAAAH!
CLOMP
CLOMP
NO ONE SAID HE COULD PLAY!
THAT'S ALL RIGHT.
HE JUST WANTS TO BATTLE ROD-CHENKO.
ROD-CHENKO?
HMPH.
I'M NOT INTERESTED IN THAT MONEY ZOMBIE.
BOY...
...USE YOUR DELTA DYNAMITE ON ME.
RIGHT HERE ...
... RIGHT NOW!!
CLOMP

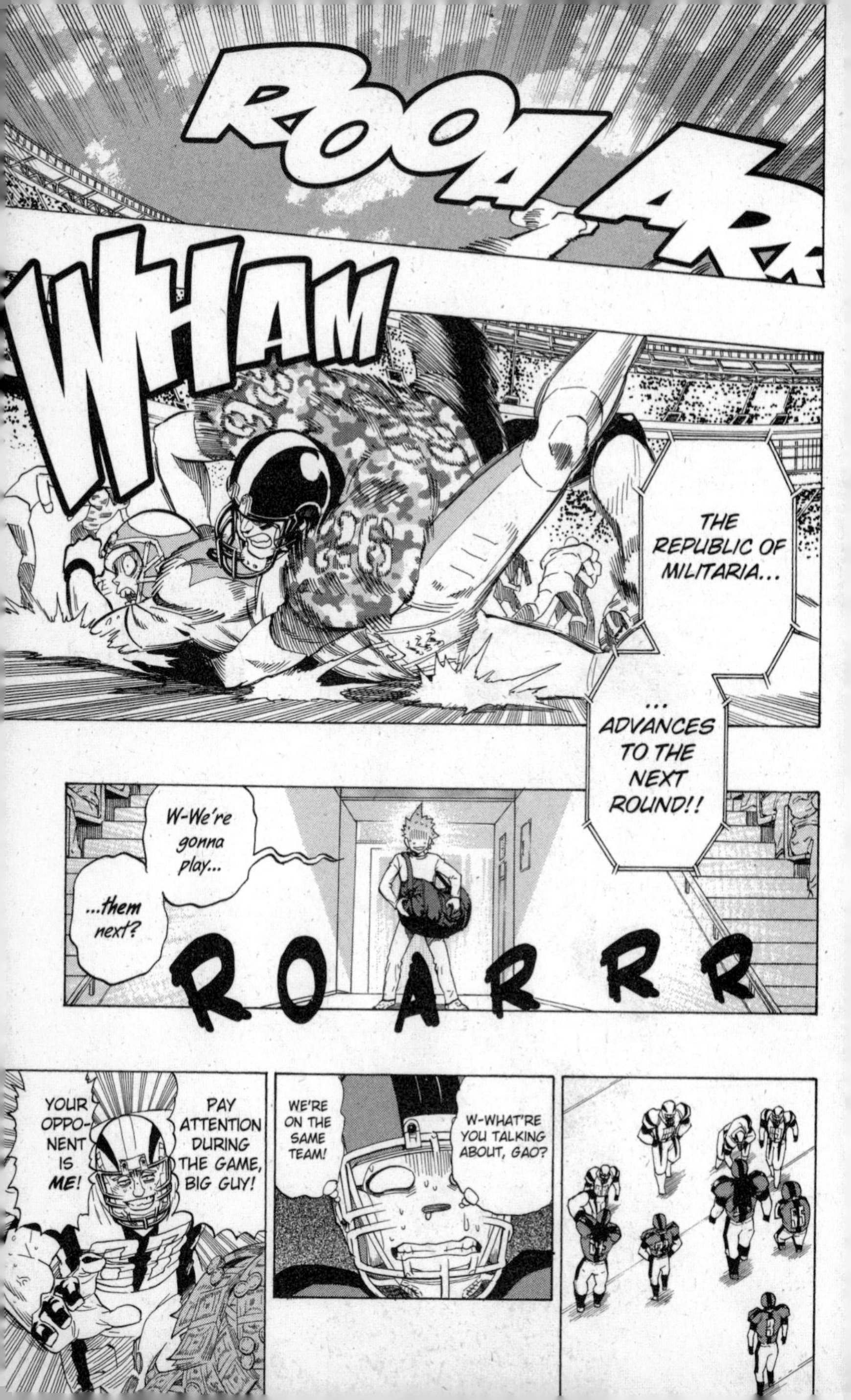
ROOARR
WHAM
THE REPUBLIC OF MILITARIA...
...ADVANCES TO THE NEXT ROUND!!
W-We're gonna play...
...them next?
ROARRR
W-WHAT'RE YOU TALKING ABOUT, GAO?
WE'RE ON THE SAME TEAM!
PAY ATTENTION DURING THE GAME, BIG GUY!
YOUR OPPONENT IS ME!

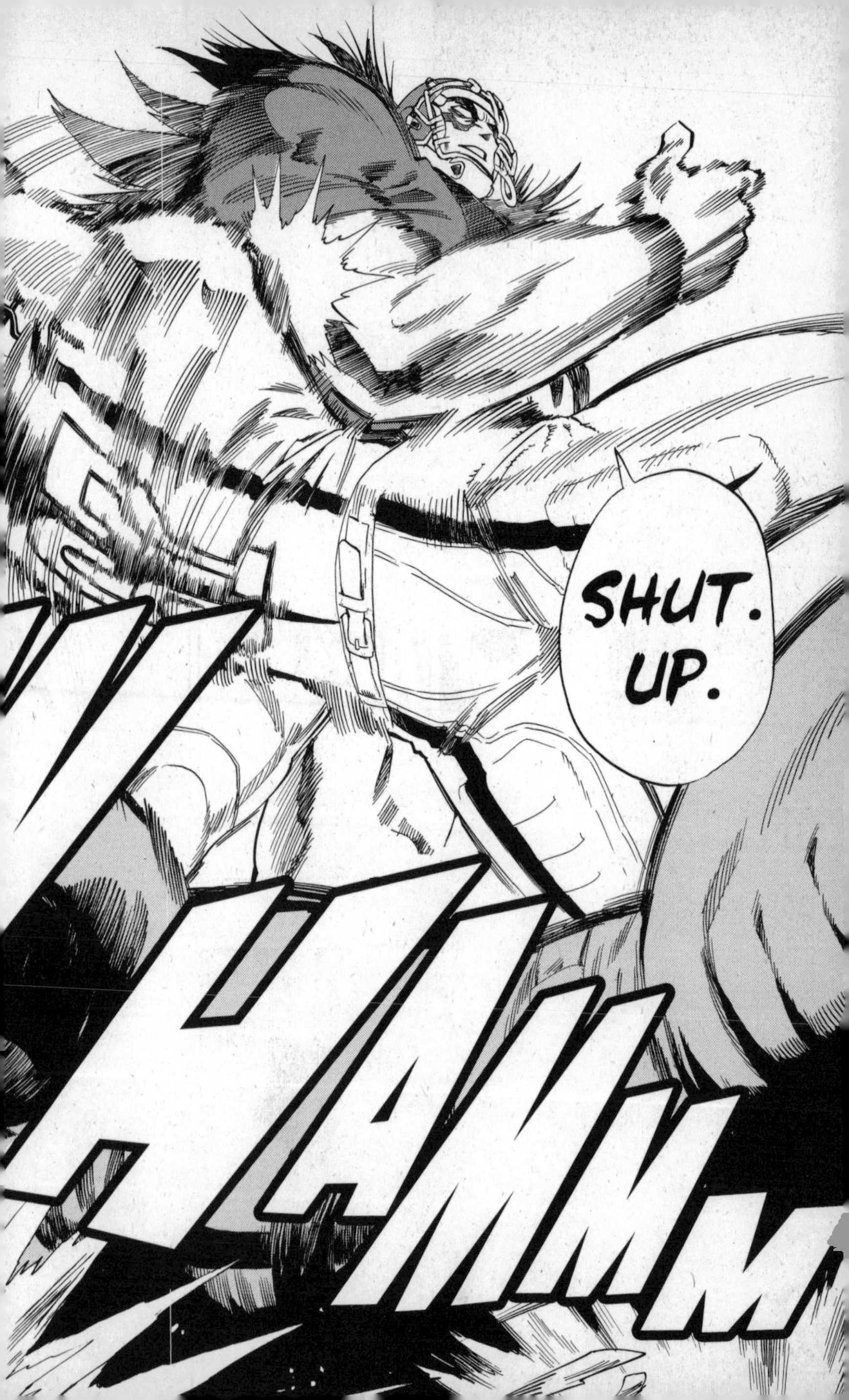
SHUT. UP.

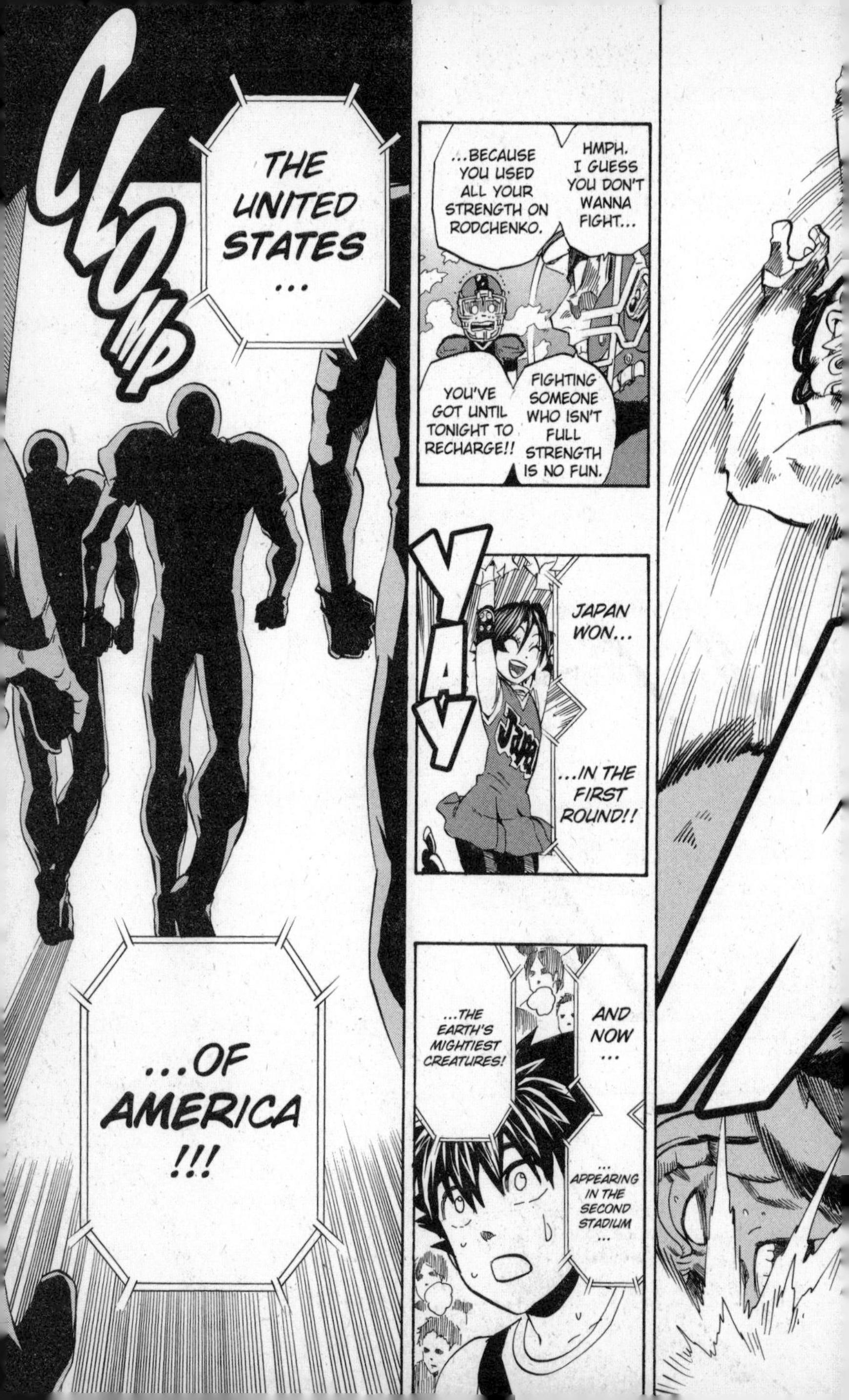
HMPH. I GUESS YOU DON'T WANNA FIGHT...
...BECAUSE YOU USED ALL YOUR STRENGTH ON RODCHENKO.
FIGHTING SOMEONE WHO ISN'T FULL STRENGTH IS NO FUN.
YOU'VE GOT UNTIL TONIGHT TO RECHARGE!!
YAY
JAPAN WON...
...IN THE FIRST ROUND!!
AND NOW...
...THE EARTH'S MIGHTIEST CREATURES!
...APPEARING IN THE SECOND STADIUM...
CLOMP
THE UNITED STATES...
...OF AMERICA!!!

Presenting Teams Playing in the World Cup

Football Population
Approx. 20,000

Running ··· A
Passing ···· B
Line ········ B
Defense ··· A

Overall Rating	A

The militant state of Militaria uses a draft system. All young persons are forced to join the army and train Sparta-style day and night to beef up their bodies!

Those on the football team will be let out of their remaining army time if they win games, so they play as hard as they can!

Key Player

MONTY GOMERY

Age: 18
Hobbies: Picking on
subordinates

Power ·········· A
Speed ·········· A
Technique ······ B

His special move is Ballistic Missile Running. He runs past everyone at top speed across distances of over half the field. The key to this move is the stamina he has built up in the army!

Militaria's
Strong Point

Since they're in the army, they follow orders perfectly! They shave their heads, and if anyone doesn't show proper discipline, they shave off his eyebrows!

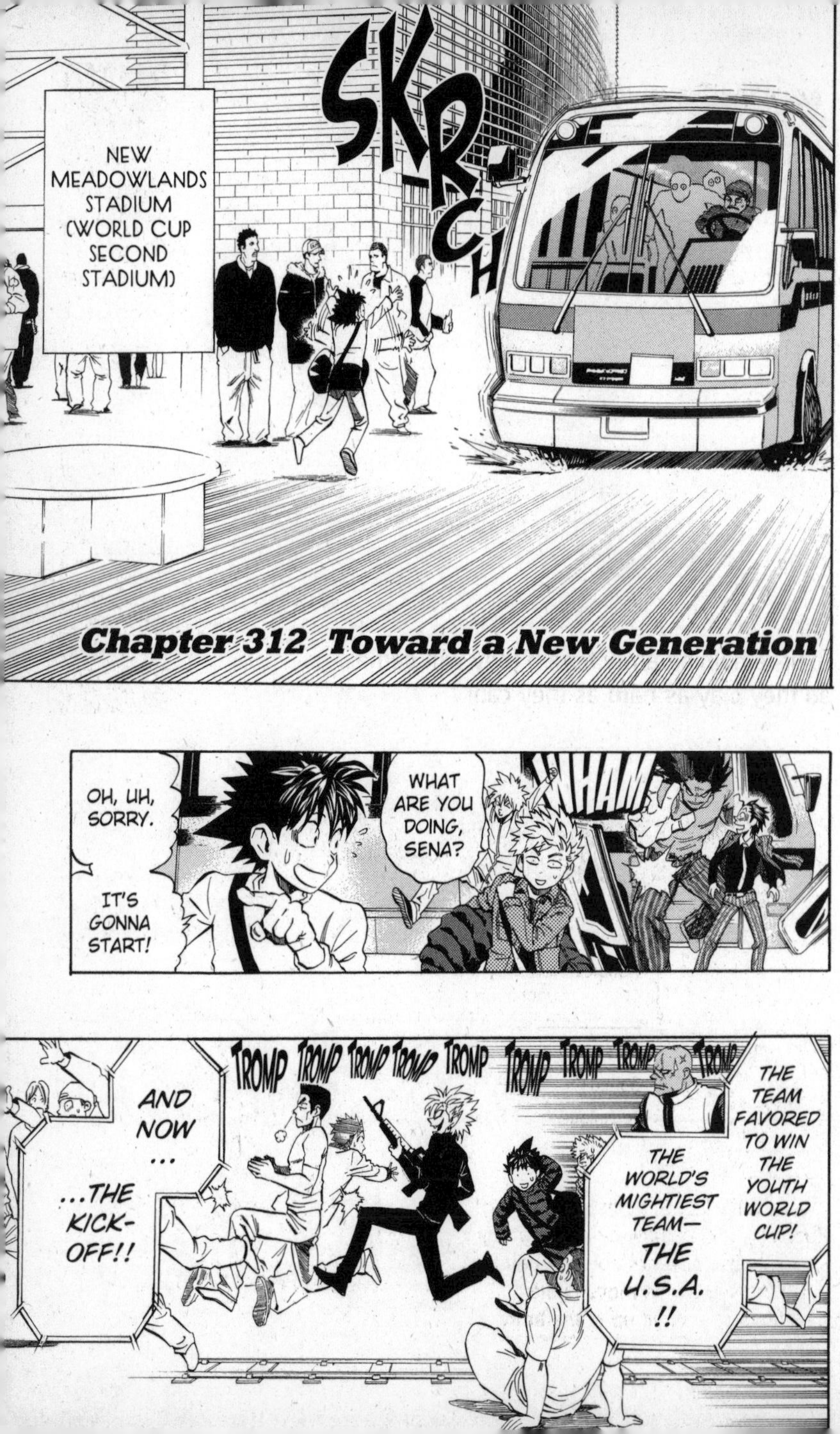
SKRCH
NEW MEADOWLANDS STADIUM (WORLD CUP SECOND STADIUM)
Chapter 312 Toward a New Generation
WHAM
WHAT ARE YOU DOING, SENA?
OH, UH, SORRY.
IT'S GONNA START!
THE TEAM FAVORED TO WIN THE YOUTH WORLD CUP!
THE WORLD'S MIGHTIEST TEAM— THE U.S.A. !!
TROMP TROMP TROMP TROMP TROMP TROMP TROMP TROMP TROMP
AND NOW ...
...THE KICK-OFF!!

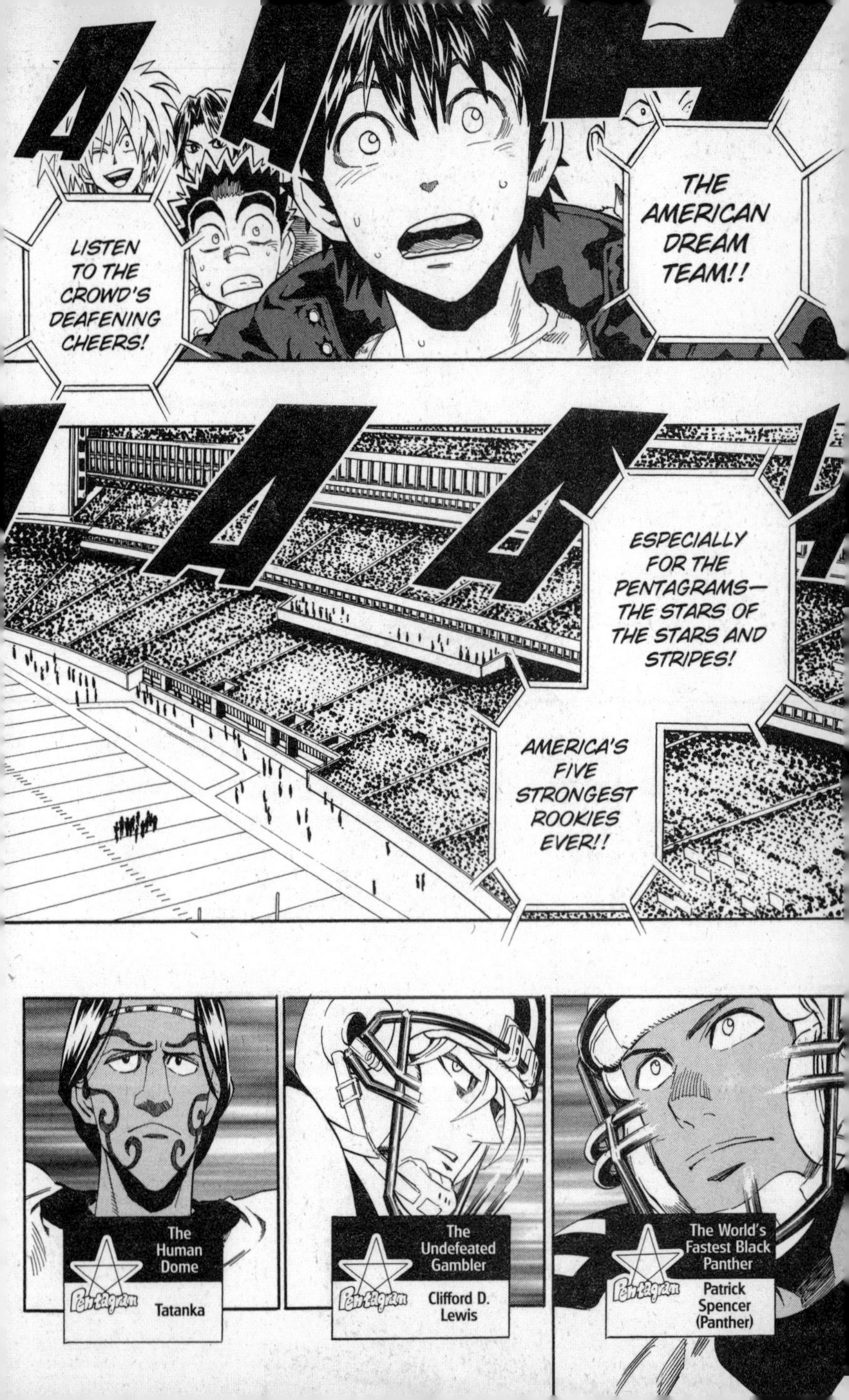
THE AMERICAN DREAM TEAM!!
LISTEN TO THE CROWD'S DEAFENING CHEERS!
ESPECIALLY FOR THE PENTAGRAMS—THE STARS OF THE STARS AND STRIPES!
AMERICA'S FIVE STRONGEST ROOKIES EVER!!
The World's Fastest Black Panther
Pentagram
Patrick Spencer (Panther)
The Undefeated Gambler
Pentagram
Clifford D. Lewis
The Human Dome
Pentagram
Tatanka

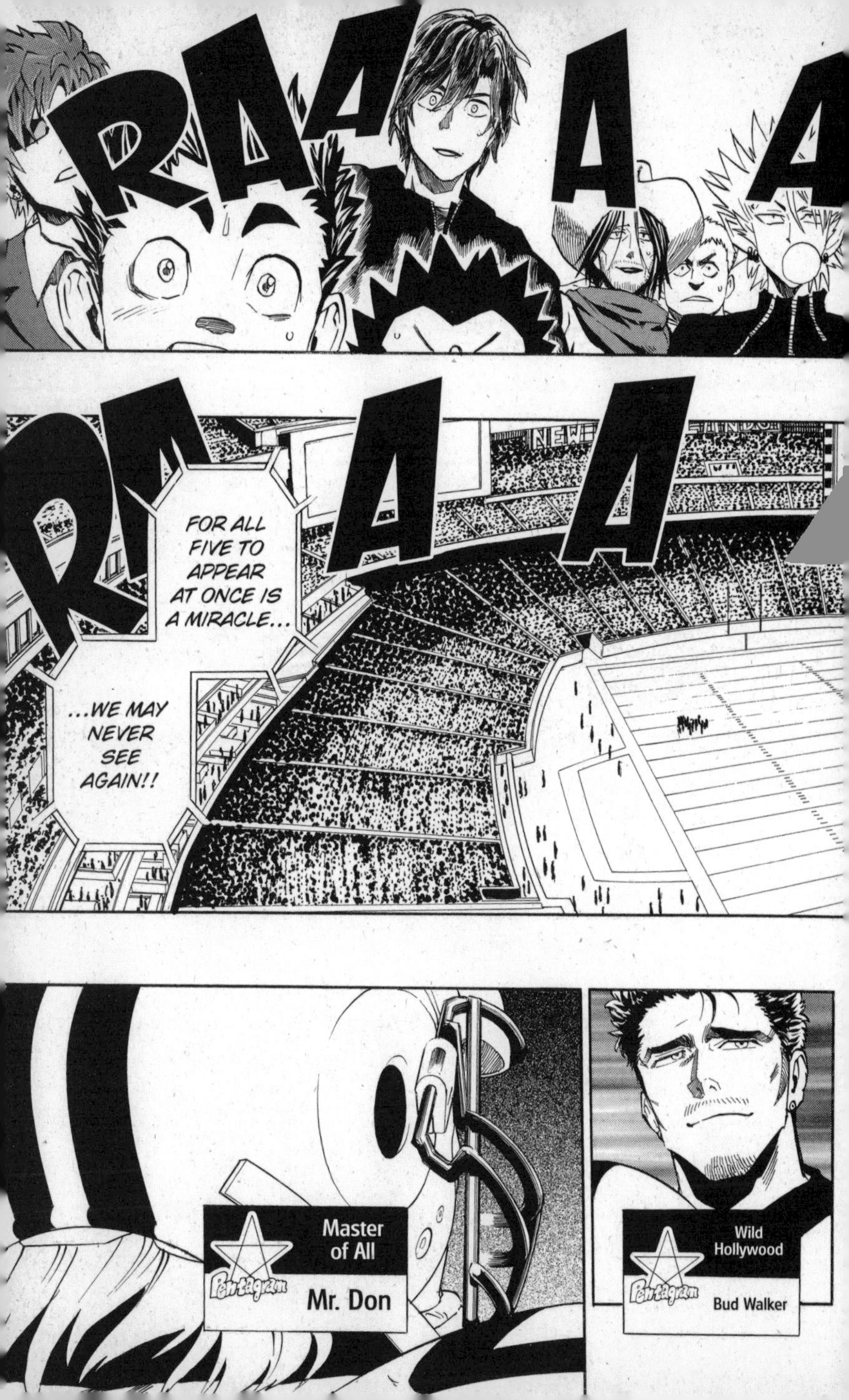
RAAAAA
RAAA
FOR ALL FIVE TO APPEAR AT ONCE IS A MIRACLE...
...WE MAY NEVER SEE AGAIN!!
Wild Hollywood
Pentagram
Bud Walker
Master of All
Pentagram
Mr. Don

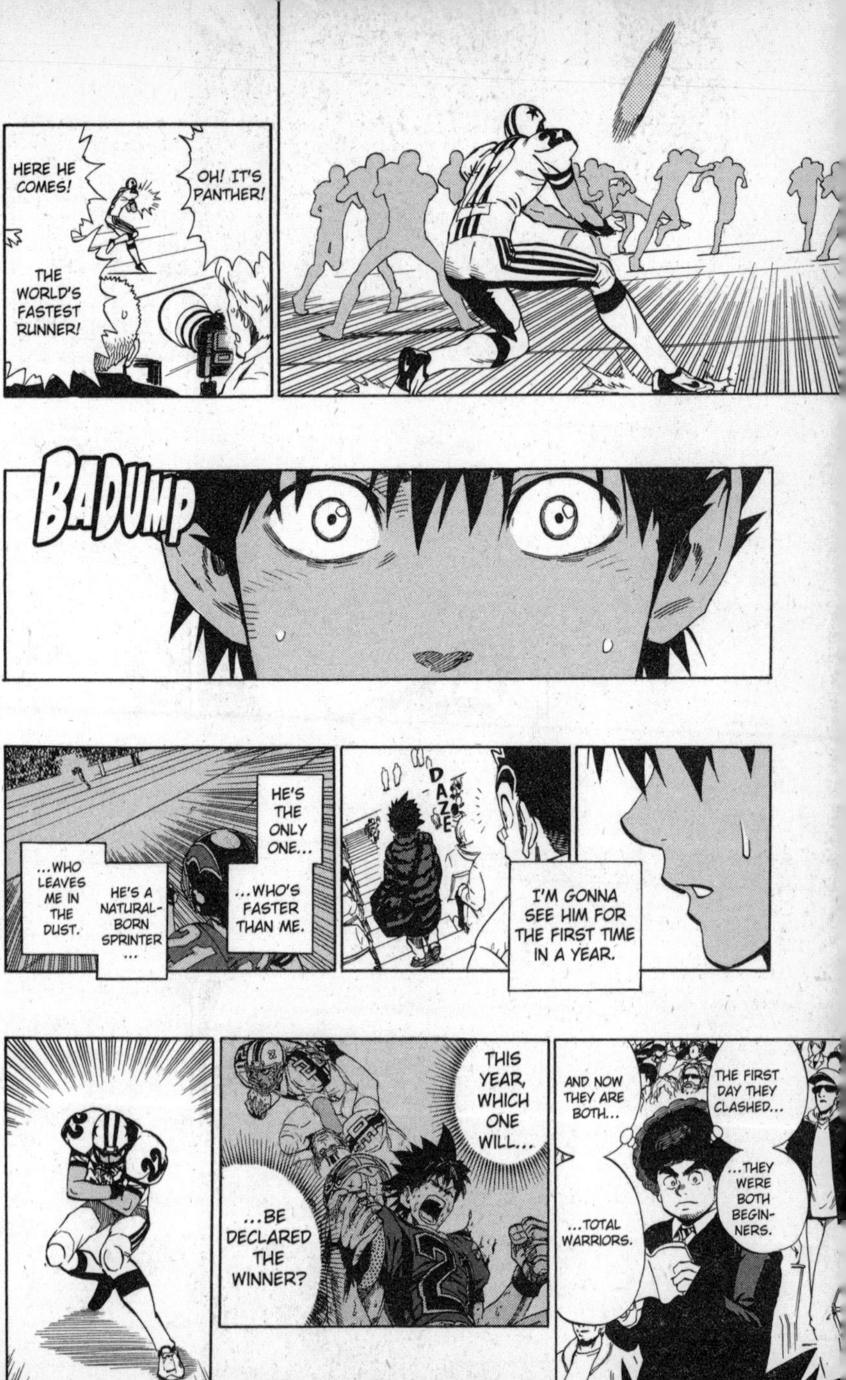
OH! IT'S PANTHER!
HERE HE COMES!
THE WORLD'S FASTEST RUNNER!
BADUMP
DAZE
I'M GONNA SEE HIM FOR THE FIRST TIME IN A YEAR.
HE'S THE ONLY ONE...
...WHO'S FASTER THAN ME.
HE'S A NATURAL-BORN SPRINTER...
...WHO LEAVES ME IN THE DUST.
THE FIRST DAY THEY CLASHED...
...THEY WERE BOTH BEGINNERS.
AND NOW THEY ARE BOTH...
...TOTAL WARRIORS.
THIS YEAR, WHICH ONE WILL...
...BE DECLARED THE WINNER?

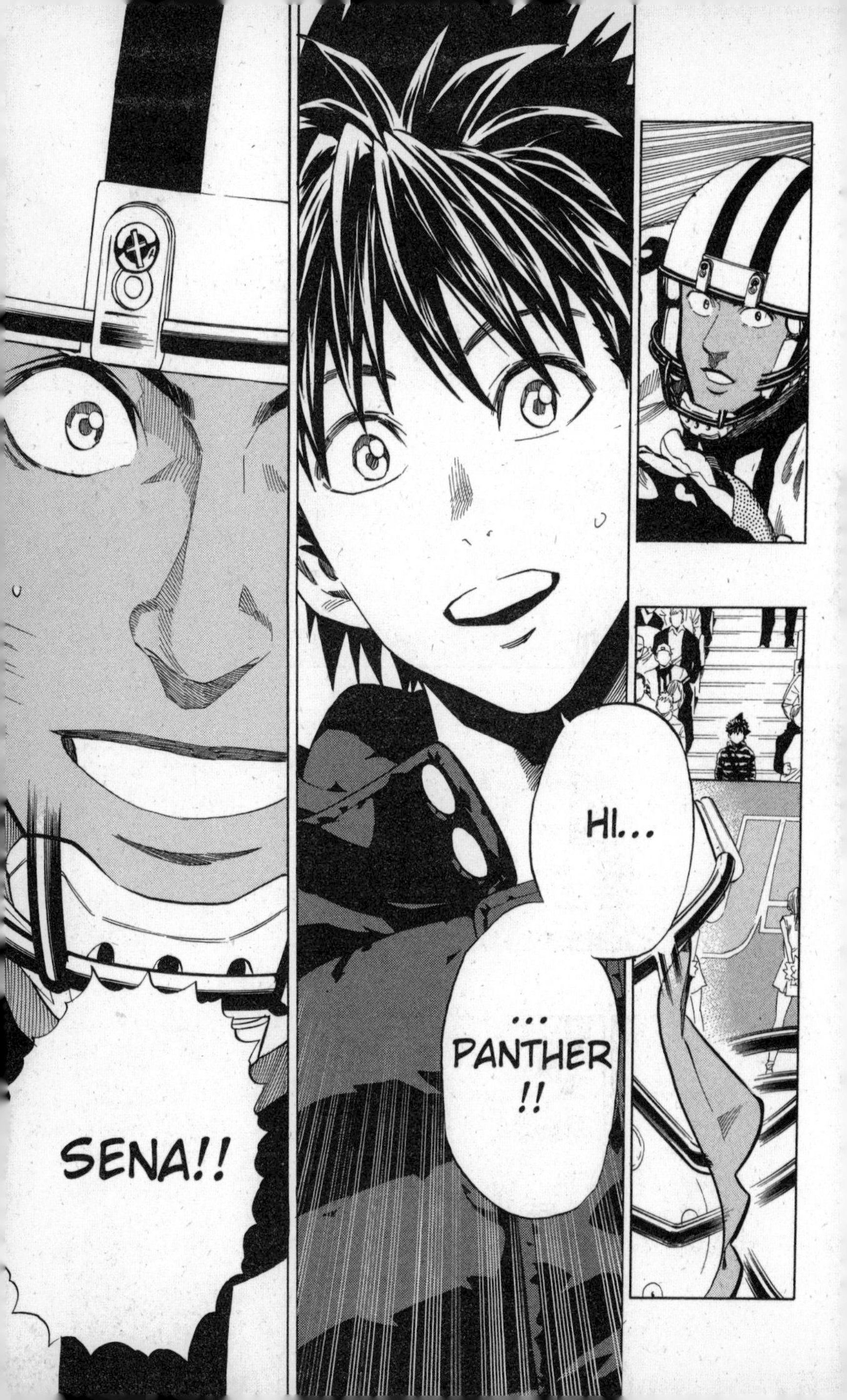
HI...
...PANTHER!!
SENA!!

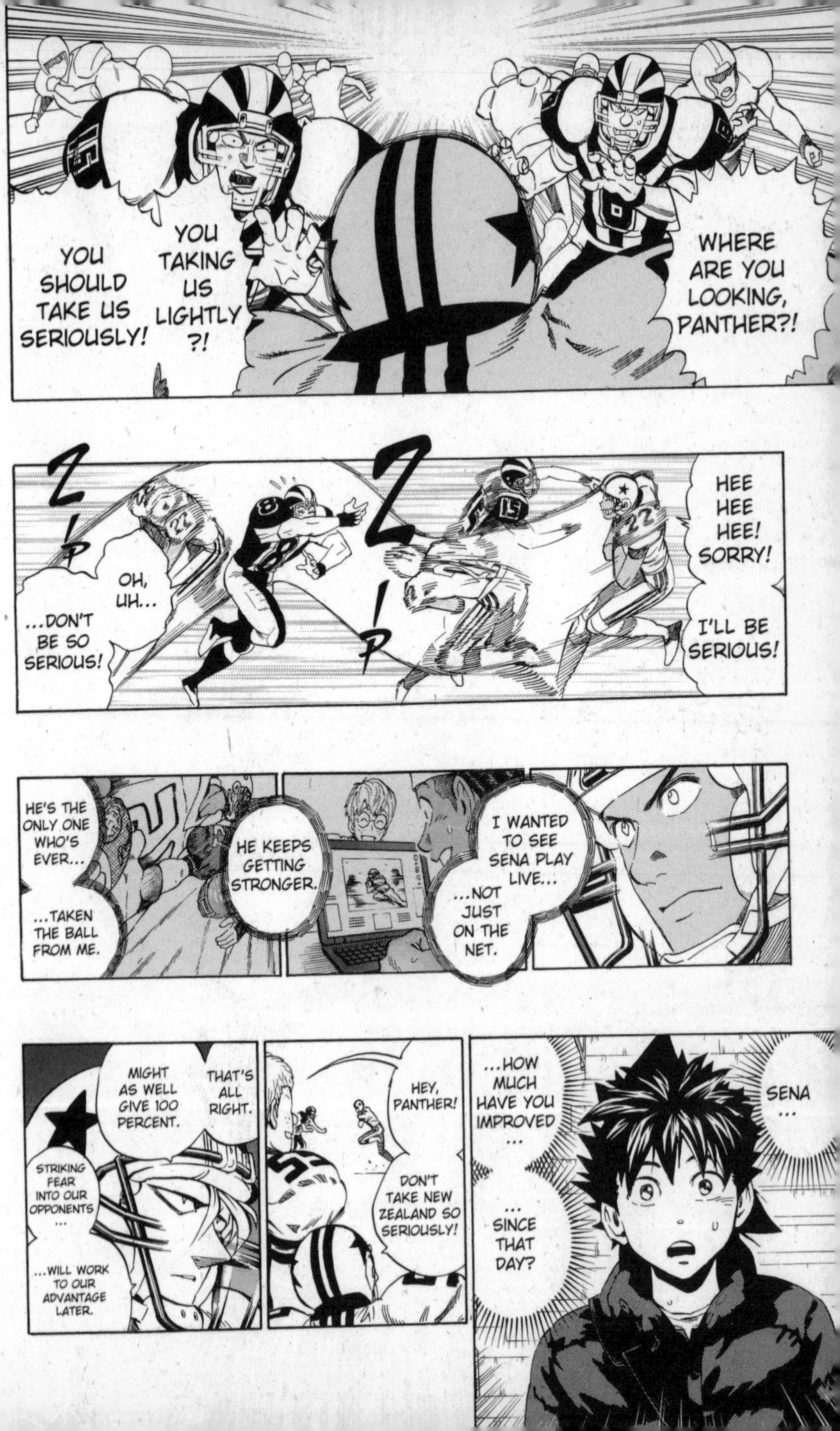
WHERE ARE YOU LOOKING, PANTHER?!
YOU TAKING US LIGHTLY ?!
YOU SHOULD TAKE US SERIOUSLY!
HEE HEE HEE! SORRY!
I'LL BE SERIOUS!
ZIP
OH, UH...
ZIP
...DON'T BE SO SERIOUS!
I WANTED TO SEE SENA PLAY LIVE...
...NOT JUST ON THE NET.
HE KEEPS GETTING STRONGER.
HE'S THE ONLY ONE WHO'S EVER...
...TAKEN THE BALL FROM ME.
SENA...
...HOW MUCH HAVE YOU IMPROVED...
...SINCE THAT DAY?
HEY, PANTHER!
DON'T TAKE NEW ZEALAND SO SERIOUSLY!
THAT'S ALL RIGHT.
MIGHT AS WELL GIVE 100 PERCENT.
STRIKING FEAR INTO OUR OPPONENTS...
...WILL WORK TO OUR ADVANTAGE LATER.

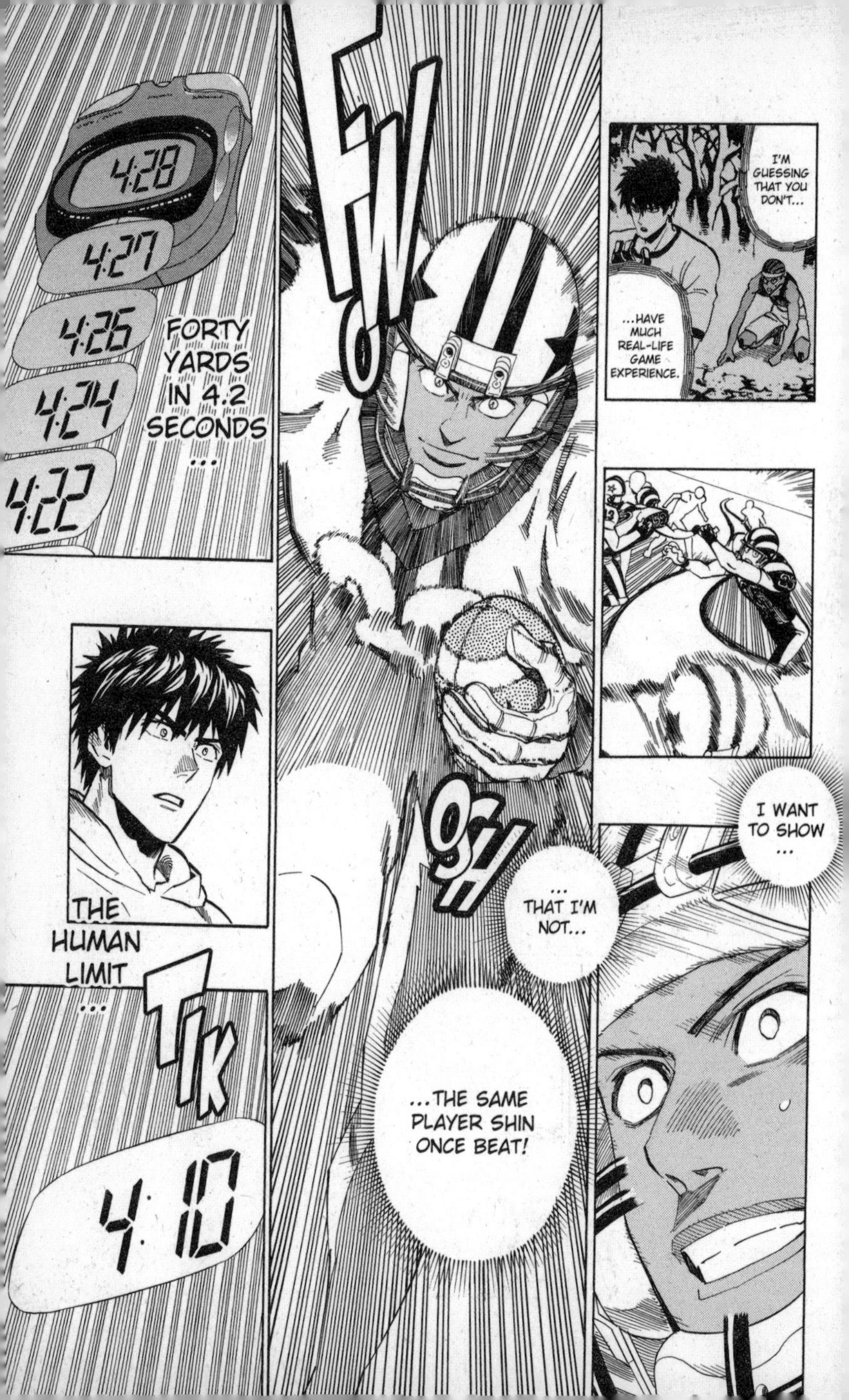
I'M GUESSING THAT YOU DON'T...
...HAVE MUCH REAL-LIFE GAME EXPERIENCE.
I WANT TO SHOW...
...THAT I'M NOT...
...THE SAME PLAYER SHIN ONCE BEAT!
FW
OSH
4:28
4:27
4:26
4:24
4:22
FORTY YARDS IN 4.2 SECONDS...
THE HUMAN LIMIT...
TIK
4:10

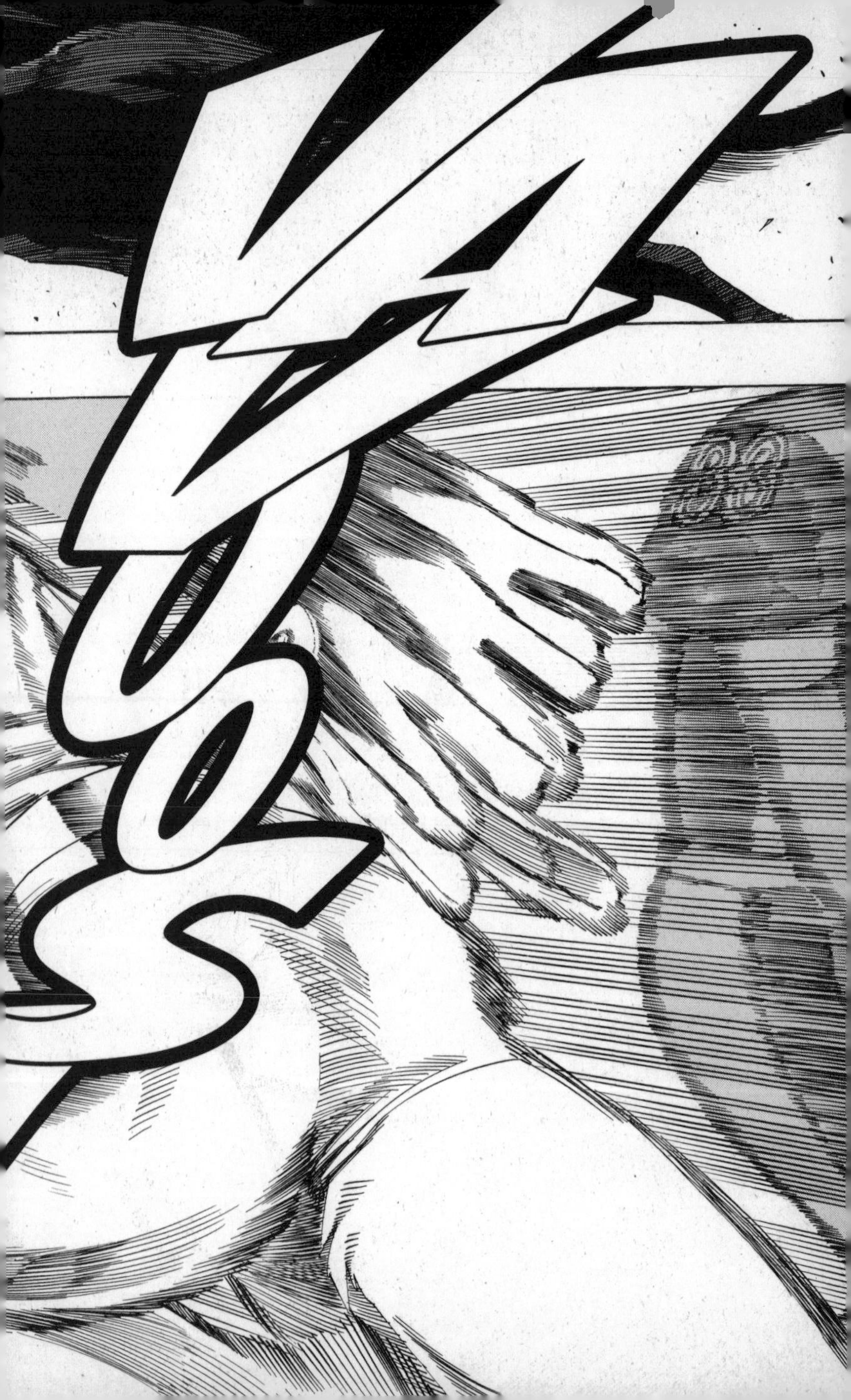
WHOOS

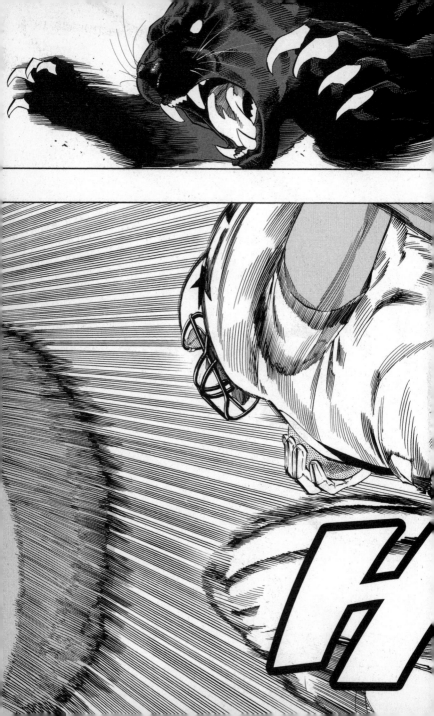

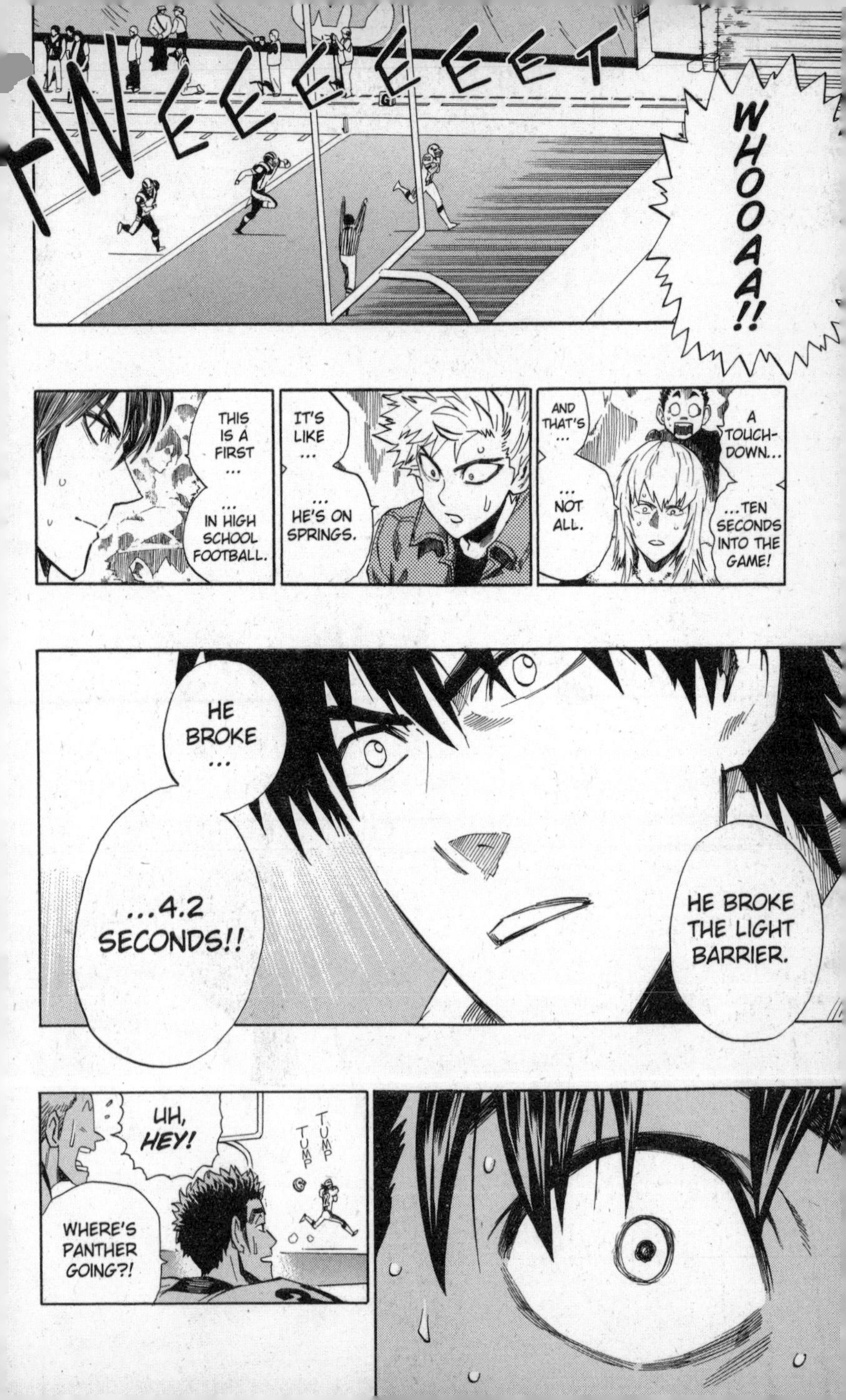
TWEEEEEET
WHOOOAAA!!
A TOUCHDOWN... ...TEN SECONDS INTO THE GAME!
AND THAT'S ... ... NOT ALL.
IT'S LIKE ... ... HE'S ON SPRINGS.
THIS IS A FIRST ... ... IN HIGH SCHOOL FOOTBALL.
HE BROKE ...
...4.2 SECONDS!!
HE BROKE THE LIGHT BARRIER.
UH, HEY!
TUMP TUMP
WHERE'S PANTHER GOING?!

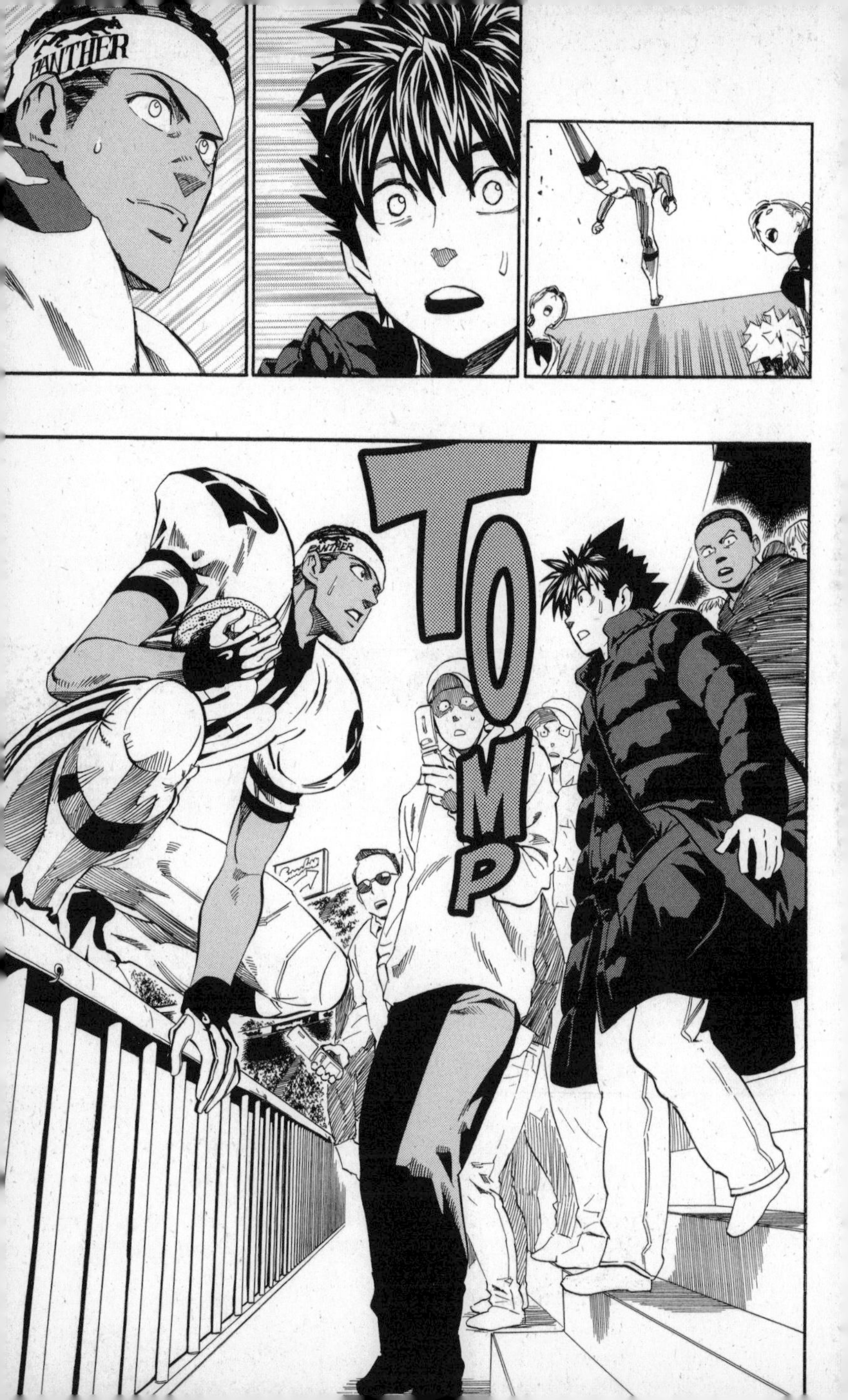
PANTHER
PANTHER
TOMP

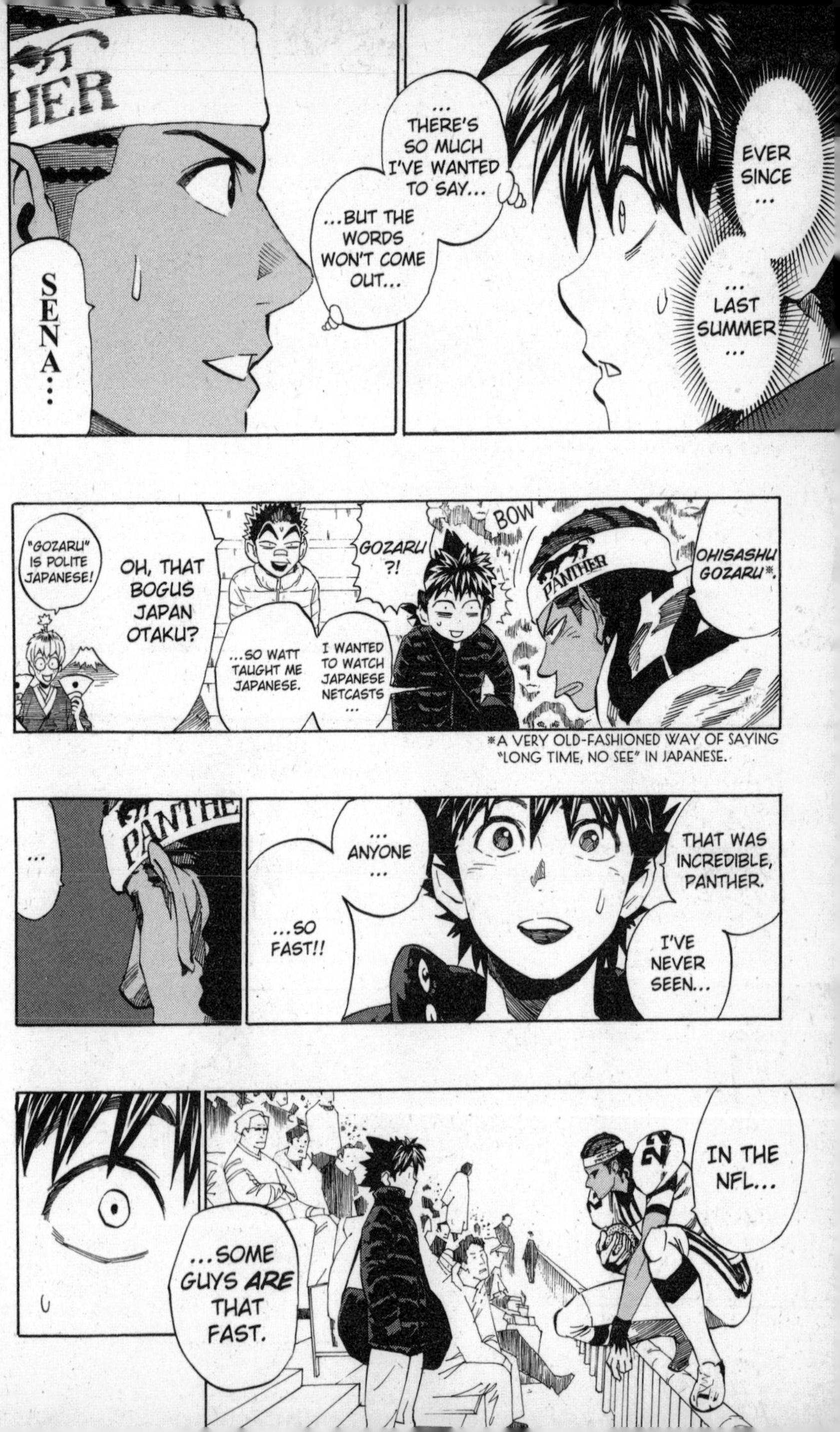
EVER SINCE ...
... LAST SUMMER ...
... THERE'S SO MUCH I'VE WANTED TO SAY...
...BUT THE WORDS WON'T COME OUT...
SENA...
BOW
OHISASHU GOZARU※.
GOZARU ?!
I WANTED TO WATCH JAPANESE NETCASTS ...
...SO WATT TAUGHT ME JAPANESE.
OH, THAT BOGUS JAPAN OTAKU?
"GOZARU" IS POLITE JAPANESE!
PANTHER
THAT WAS INCREDIBLE, PANTHER.
I'VE NEVER SEEN...
... ANYONE ...
...SO FAST!!
...
IN THE NFL...
...SOME GUYS *ARE* THAT FAST.

※A VERY OLD-FASHIONED WAY OF SAYING "LONG TIME, NO SEE" IN JAPANESE.

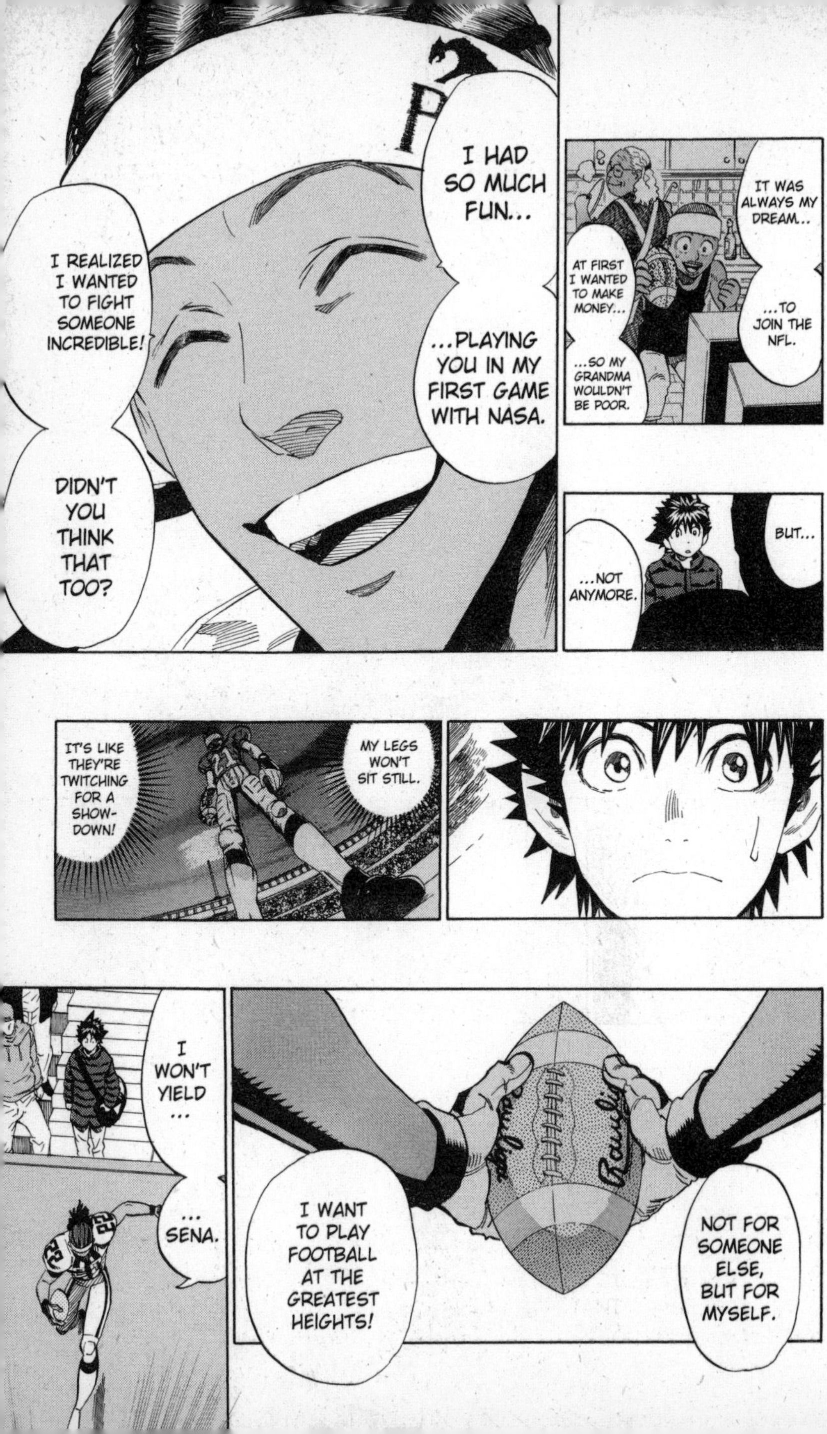
IT WAS ALWAYS MY DREAM...
...TO JOIN THE NFL.
AT FIRST I WANTED TO MAKE MONEY...
...SO MY GRANDMA WOULDN'T BE POOR.
BUT...
...NOT ANYMORE.
I HAD SO MUCH FUN...
...PLAYING YOU IN MY FIRST GAME WITH NASA.
I REALIZED I WANTED TO FIGHT SOMEONE INCREDIBLE!
DIDN'T YOU THINK THAT TOO?
MY LEGS WON'T SIT STILL.
IT'S LIKE THEY'RE TWITCHING FOR A SHOW-DOWN!
NOT FOR SOMEONE ELSE, BUT FOR MYSELF.
I WANT TO PLAY FOOTBALL AT THE GREATEST HEIGHTS!
I WON'T YIELD...
...SENA.

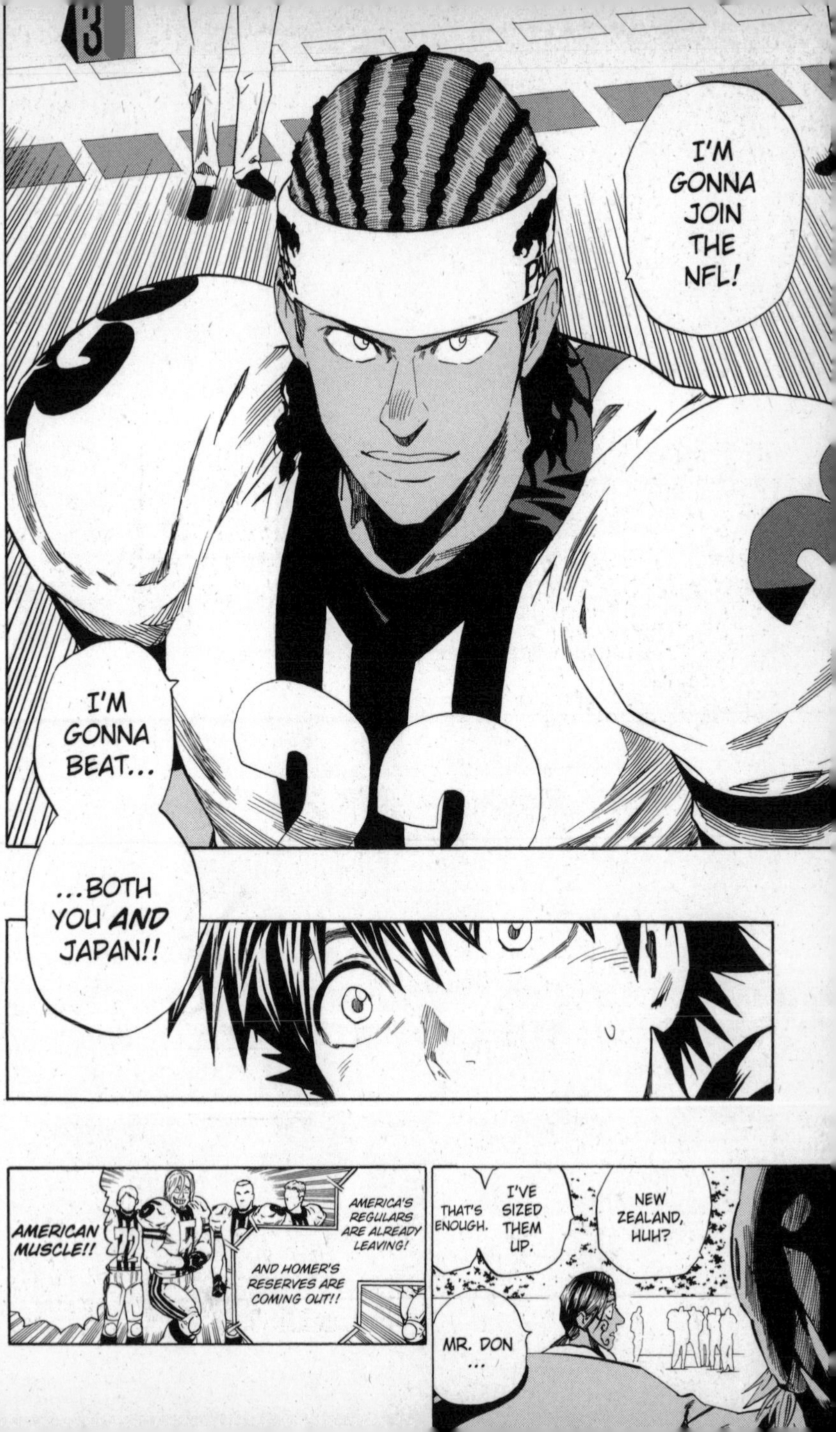

I'M GONNA JOIN THE NFL!
I'M GONNA BEAT...
...BOTH YOU AND JAPAN!!
NEW ZEALAND, HUH?
I'VE SIZED THEM UP.
THAT'S ENOUGH.
MR. DON ...
AMERICA'S REGULARS ARE ALREADY LEAVING!
AMERICAN MUSCLE!!
AND HOMER'S RESERVES ARE COMING OUT!!

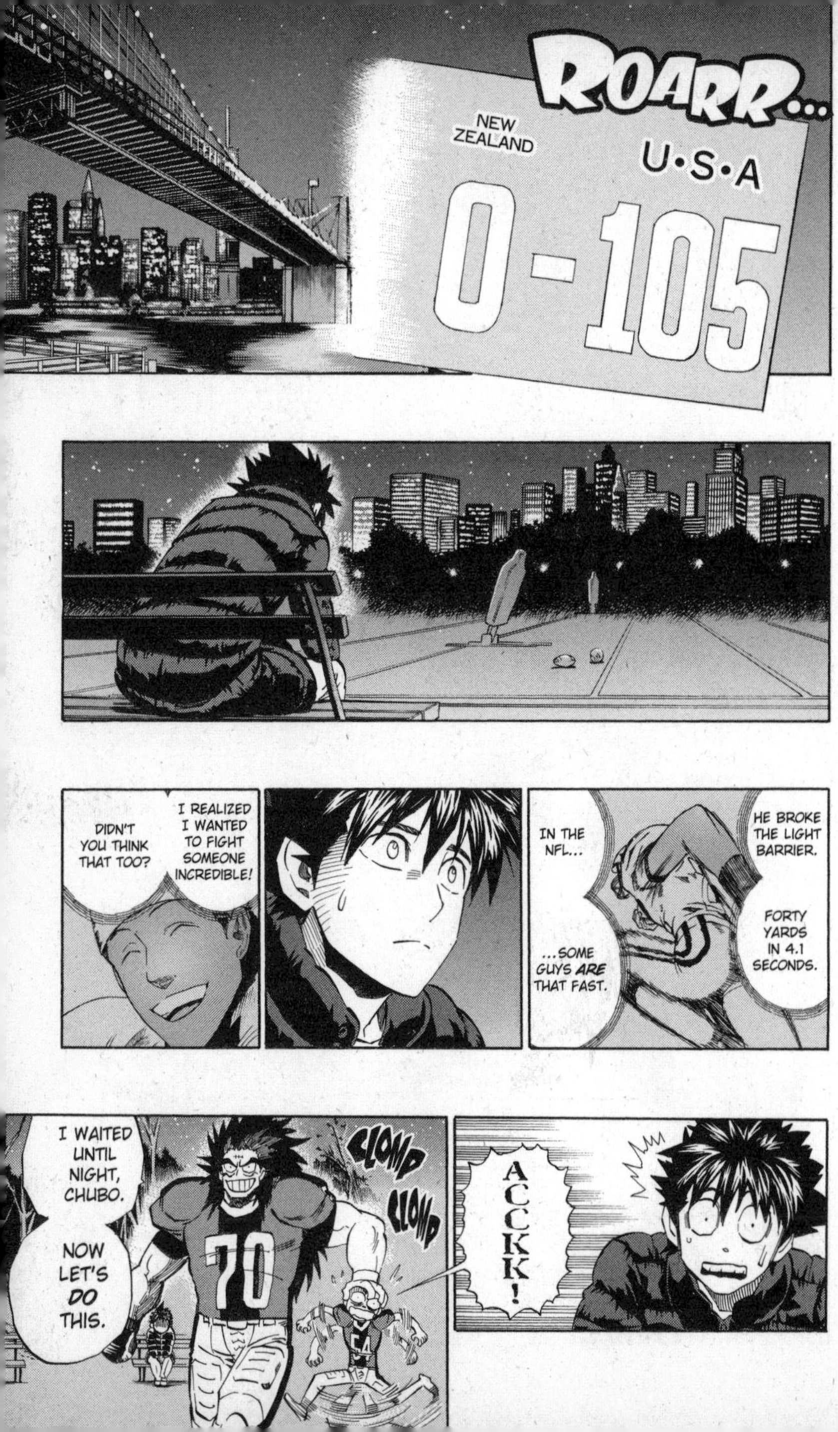
ROARR...
NEW ZEALAND
U·S·A
0-105
HE BROKE THE LIGHT BARRIER.
FORTY YARDS IN 4.1 SECONDS.
IN THE NFL...
...SOME GUYS *ARE* THAT FAST.
I REALIZED I WANTED TO FIGHT SOMEONE INCREDIBLE!
DIDN'T YOU THINK THAT TOO?
ACCKK!
CLOMP
CLOMP
I WAITED UNTIL NIGHT, CHUBO.
NOW LET'S *DO* THIS.

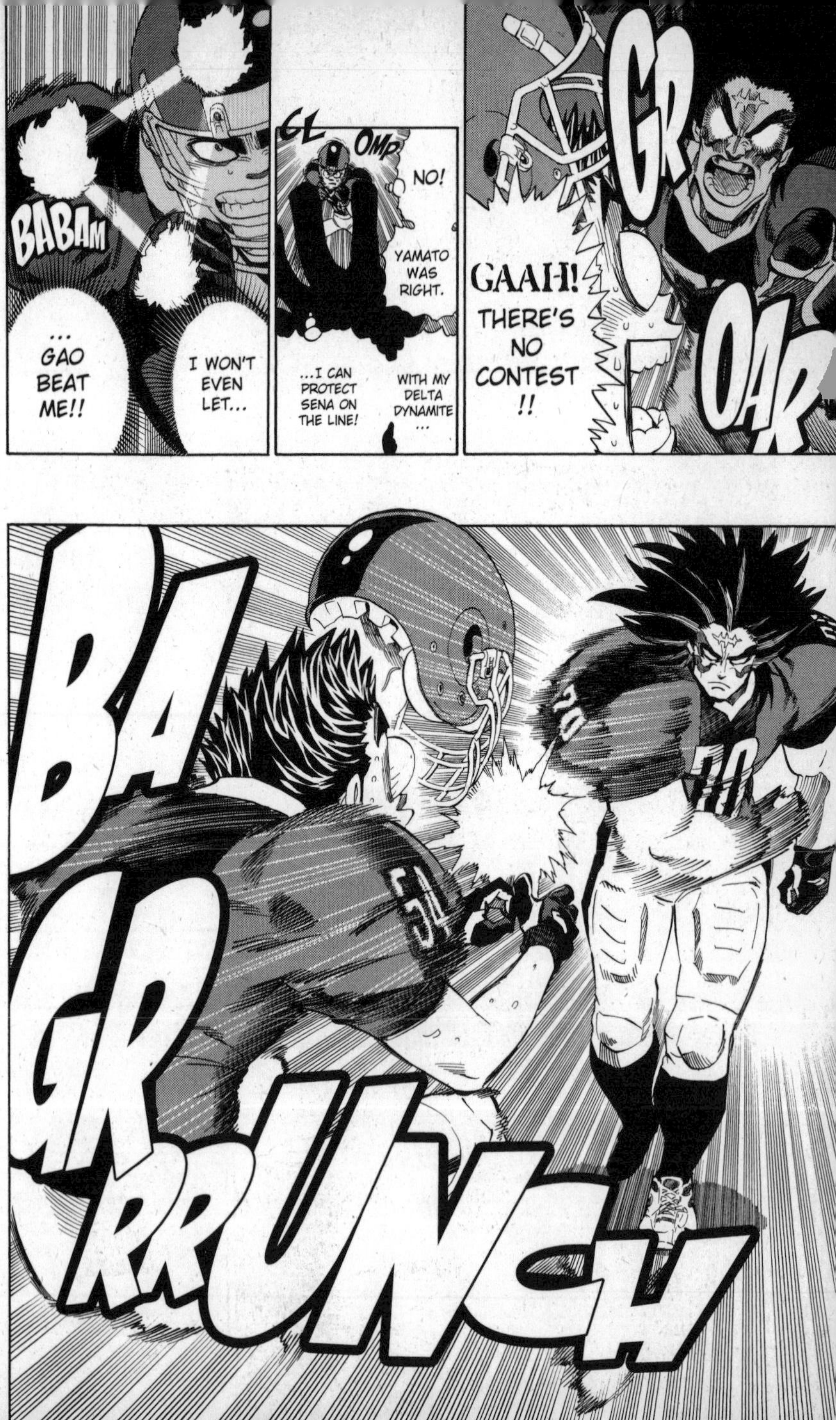
GR
OAR
GAAH! THERE'S NO CONTEST!!
GL OMP
NO!
YAMATO WAS RIGHT.
WITH MY DELTA DYNAMITE...
...I CAN PROTECT SENA ON THE LINE!
BABAM
I WON'T EVEN LET...
...GAO BEAT ME!!
BA
GR
RRUNCH

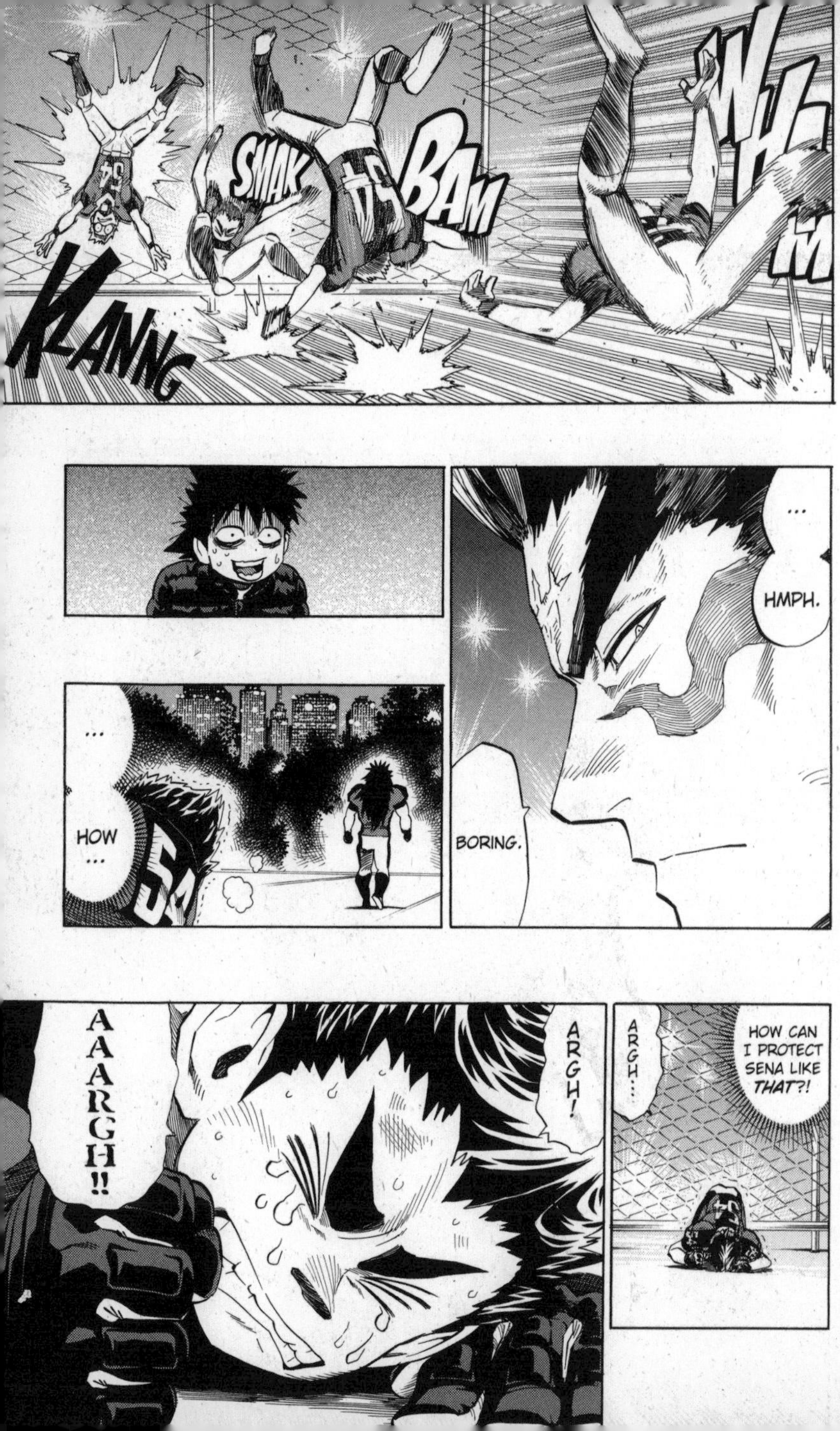
BAM
SMAK
KLANNG
...
HMPH.
BORING.
...
HOW ...
HOW CAN I PROTECT SENA LIKE *THAT*?!
ARGH...
ARGH!
AAAARGH!!

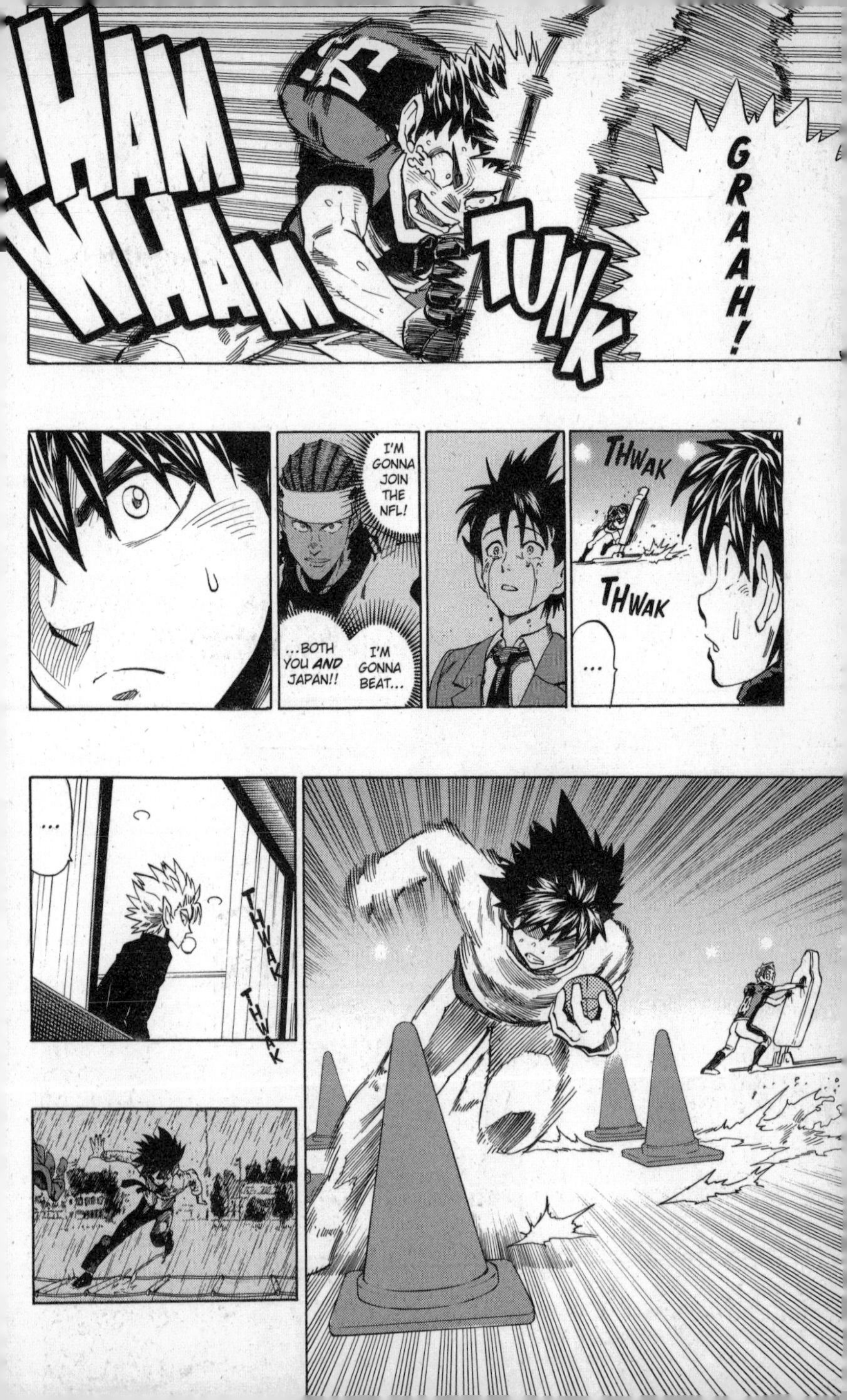
GRAAH!
TUNK
WHAM
WHAM
THWAK
THWAK
...
I'M GONNA JOIN THE NFL!
I'M GONNA BEAT...
...BOTH YOU AND JAPAN!!
...
THWAK
THWAK

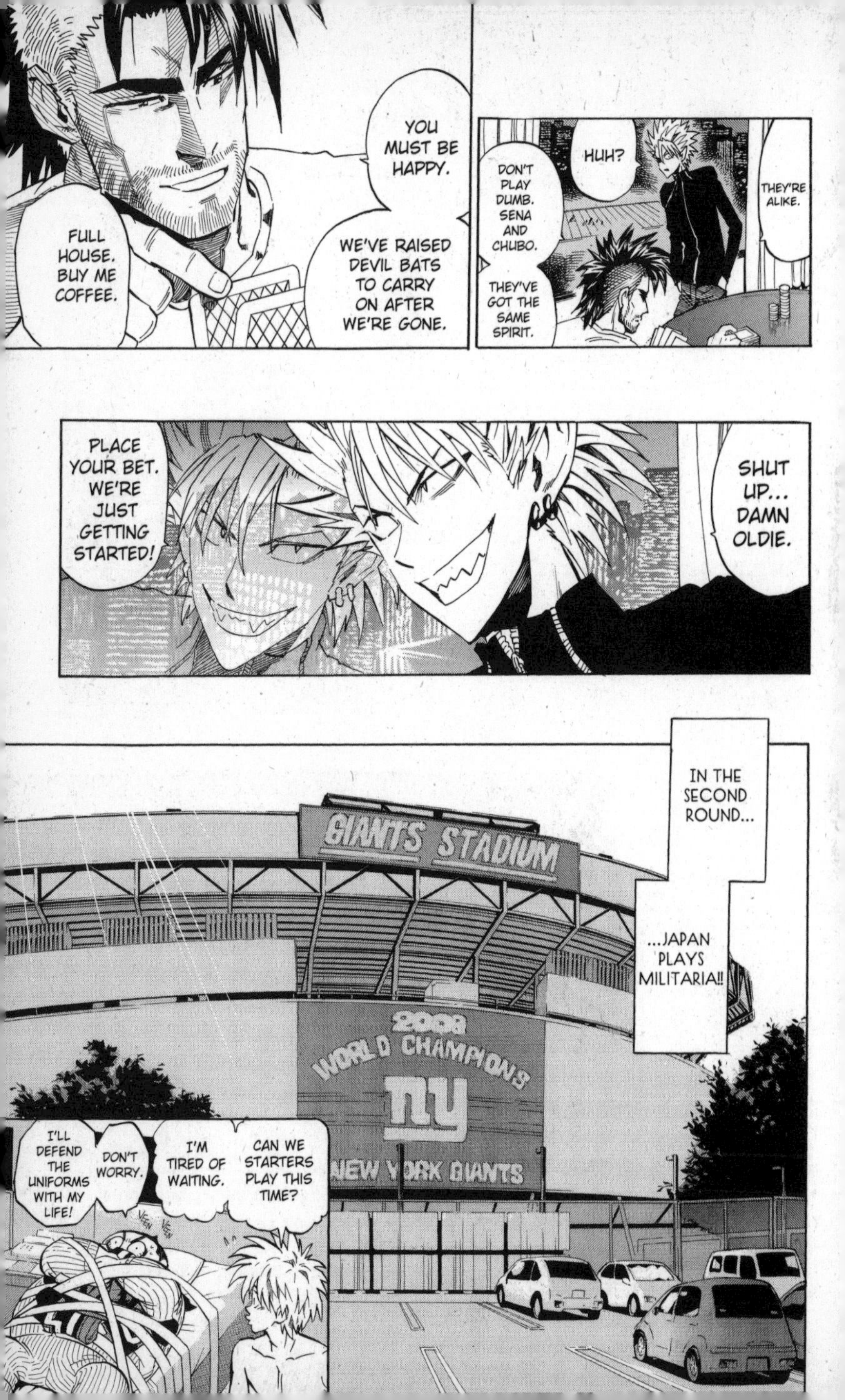
THEY'RE ALIKE.
HUH?
DON'T PLAY DUMB. SENA AND CHUBO.
THEY'VE GOT THE SAME SPIRIT.
YOU MUST BE HAPPY.
WE'VE RAISED DEVIL BATS TO CARRY ON AFTER WE'RE GONE.
FULL HOUSE. BUY ME COFFEE.
SHUT UP... DAMN OLDIE.
PLACE YOUR BET. WE'RE JUST GETTING STARTED!
IN THE SECOND ROUND...
...JAPAN PLAYS MILITARIA!!
GIANTS STADIUM
2008 WORLD CHAMPIONS
NY
NEW YORK GIANTS
CAN WE STARTERS PLAY THIS TIME?
I'M TIRED OF WAITING.
DON'T WORRY.
I'LL DEFEND THE UNIFORMS WITH MY LIFE!

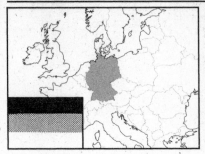

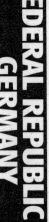

FEDERAL REPUBLIC OF GERMANY

Presenting Teams Playing in the World Cup

Football Population
20,000-30,000

Running··· S
Passing···· A
Line ········· A
Defense··· A

Overall Rating S

The second greatest football superpower after the U.S.A. Germany has five teams in the European pro league and they always rank high in international tournaments.

Rumor has it they're as good or better than Japan. Which team will earn the right to battle America?!

Germany's Strong Point

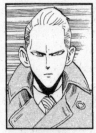

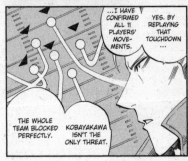

YES. BY REPLAYING THAT TOUCHDOWN ...
...I HAVE CONFIRMED ALL 11 PLAYERS' MOVE-MENTS.
KOBAYAKAWA ISN'T THE ONLY THREAT.
THE WHOLE TEAM BLOCKED PERFECTLY.

They don't evaluate themselves either highly or poorly. Through thorough analysis of data, they try to improve their chances by every percentile point possible!

Key Player

HEINRICH SCHERZ

Age: 18
Hobbies: sudoku

Power ·········· B
Speed ·········· S
Technique ······ A

The fastest man in the European pro league. By replaying football plays in his head with his Ultimate Memory, he can adapt perfectly to his opponents' movements.

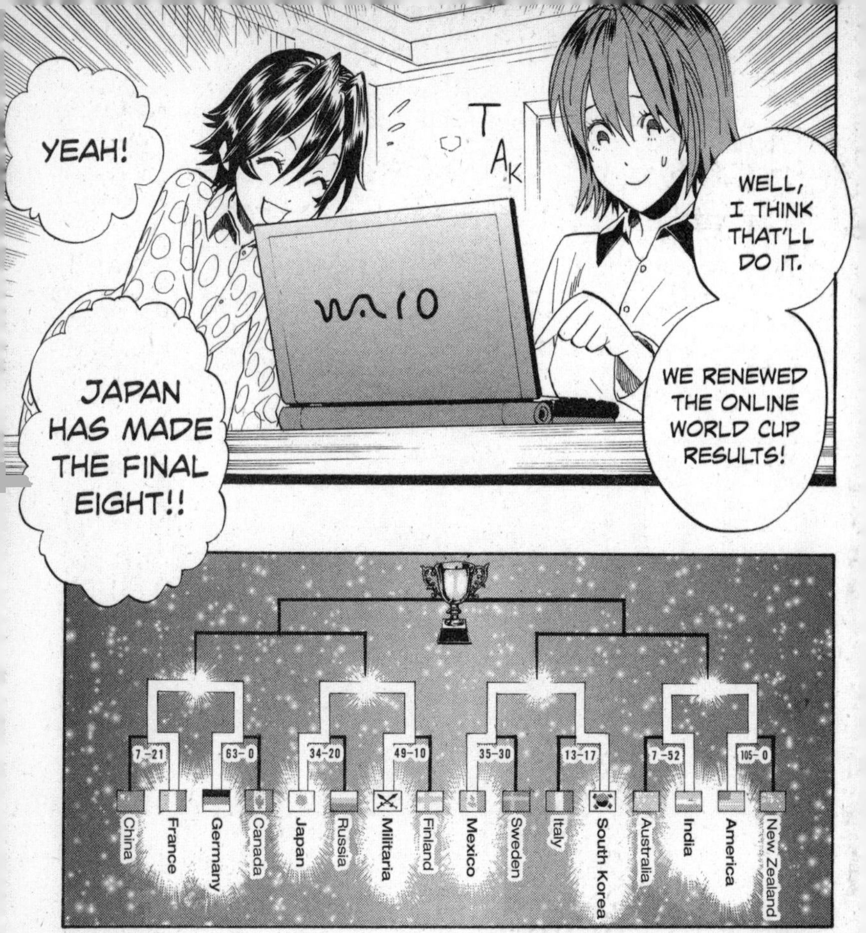
TAK
WELL, I THINK THAT'LL DO IT.
WE RENEWED THE ONLINE WORLD CUP RESULTS!
YEAH!
JAPAN HAS MADE THE FINAL EIGHT!!
7–21
63–0
34–20
49–10
35–30
13–17
7–52
105–0
China
France
Germany
Canada
Japan
Russia
Militaria
Finland
Mexico
Sweden
Italy
South Korea
Australia
India
America
New Zealand

Chapter 313 Ambition

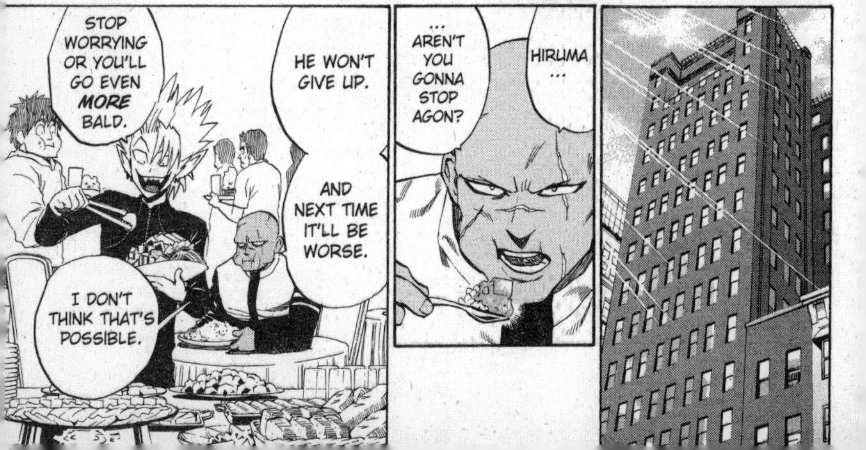
HIRUMA...
...AREN'T YOU GONNA STOP AGON?
HE WON'T GIVE UP.
AND NEXT TIME IT'LL BE WORSE.
STOP WORRYING OR YOU'LL GO EVEN *MORE* BALD.
I DON'T THINK THAT'S POSSIBLE.

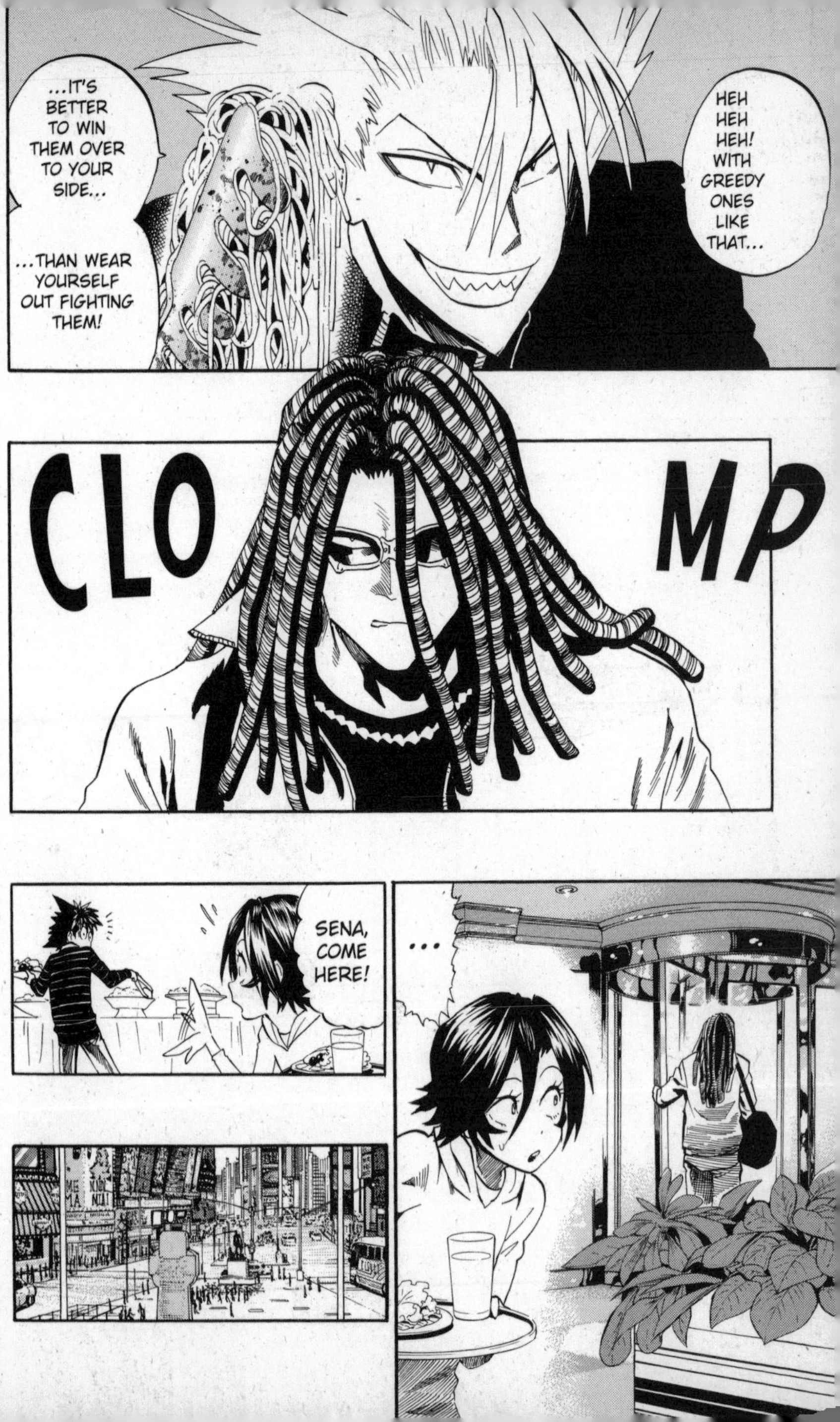
HEH HEH HEH! WITH GREEDY ONES LIKE THAT...
...IT'S BETTER TO WIN THEM OVER TO YOUR SIDE...
...THAN WEAR YOURSELF OUT FIGHTING THEM!
CLOMP
...
SENA, COME HERE!

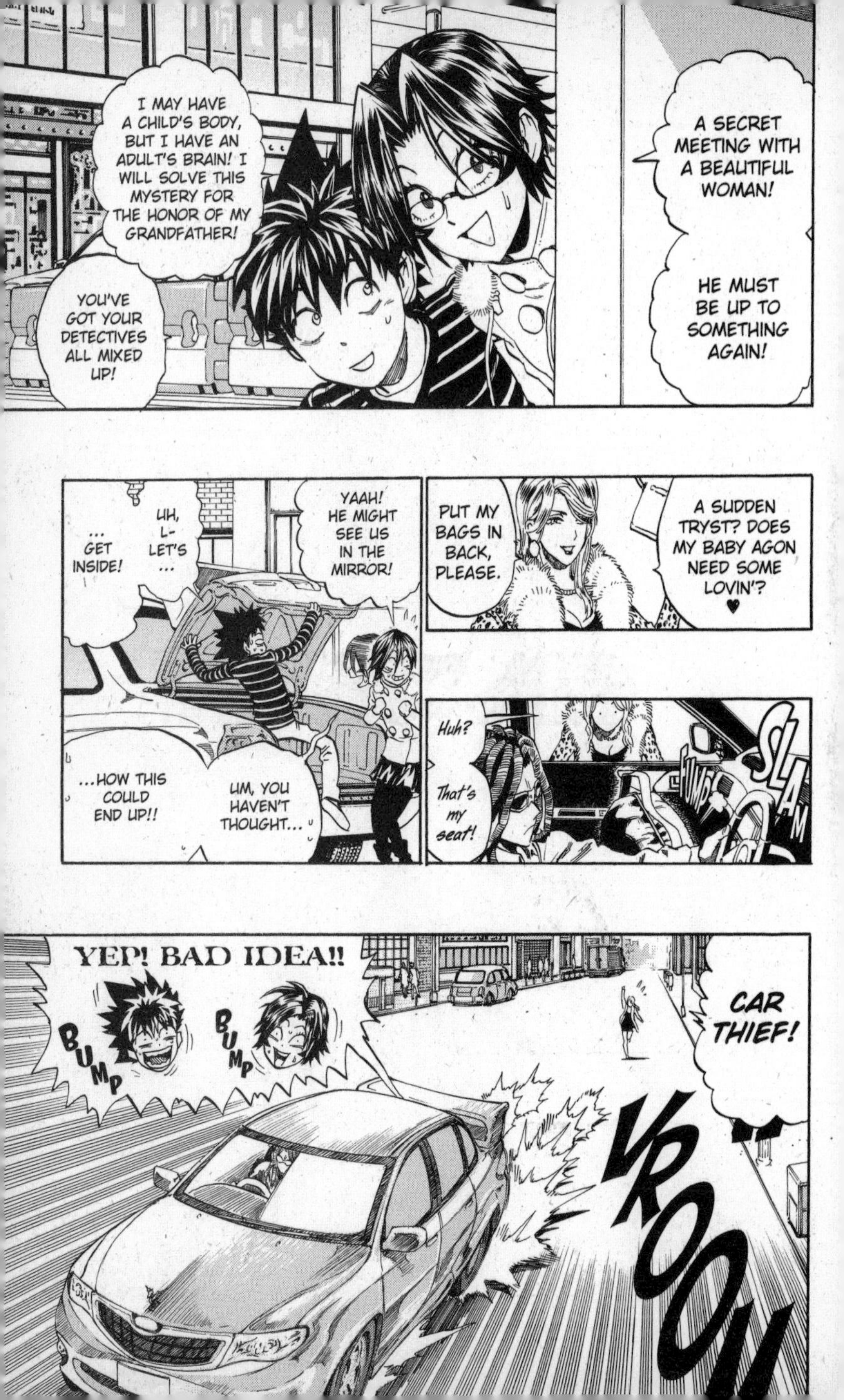
A SECRET MEETING WITH A BEAUTIFUL WOMAN!
HE MUST BE UP TO SOMETHING AGAIN!
I MAY HAVE A CHILD'S BODY, BUT I HAVE AN ADULT'S BRAIN! I WILL SOLVE THIS MYSTERY FOR THE HONOR OF MY GRANDFATHER!
YOU'VE GOT YOUR DETECTIVES ALL MIXED UP!
A SUDDEN TRYST? DOES MY BABY AGON NEED SOME LOVIN'? ♥
PUT MY BAGS IN BACK, PLEASE.
SLAM
Huh?
That's my seat!
YAAH! HE MIGHT SEE US IN THE MIRROR!
UH, L- LET'S ...
... GET INSIDE!
UM, YOU HAVEN'T THOUGHT...
...HOW THIS COULD END UP!!
CAR THIEF!
YEP! BAD IDEA!!
BUMP
BUMP
VROOM

Chapter 313 Ambition

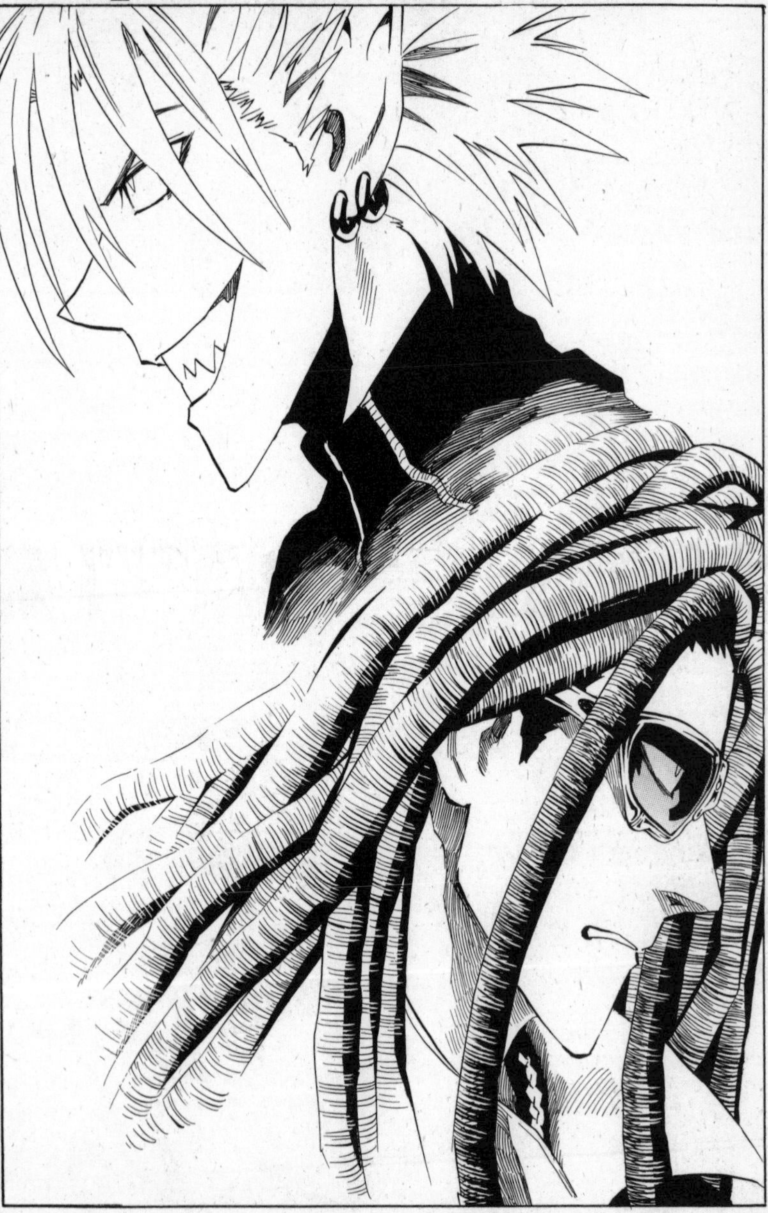

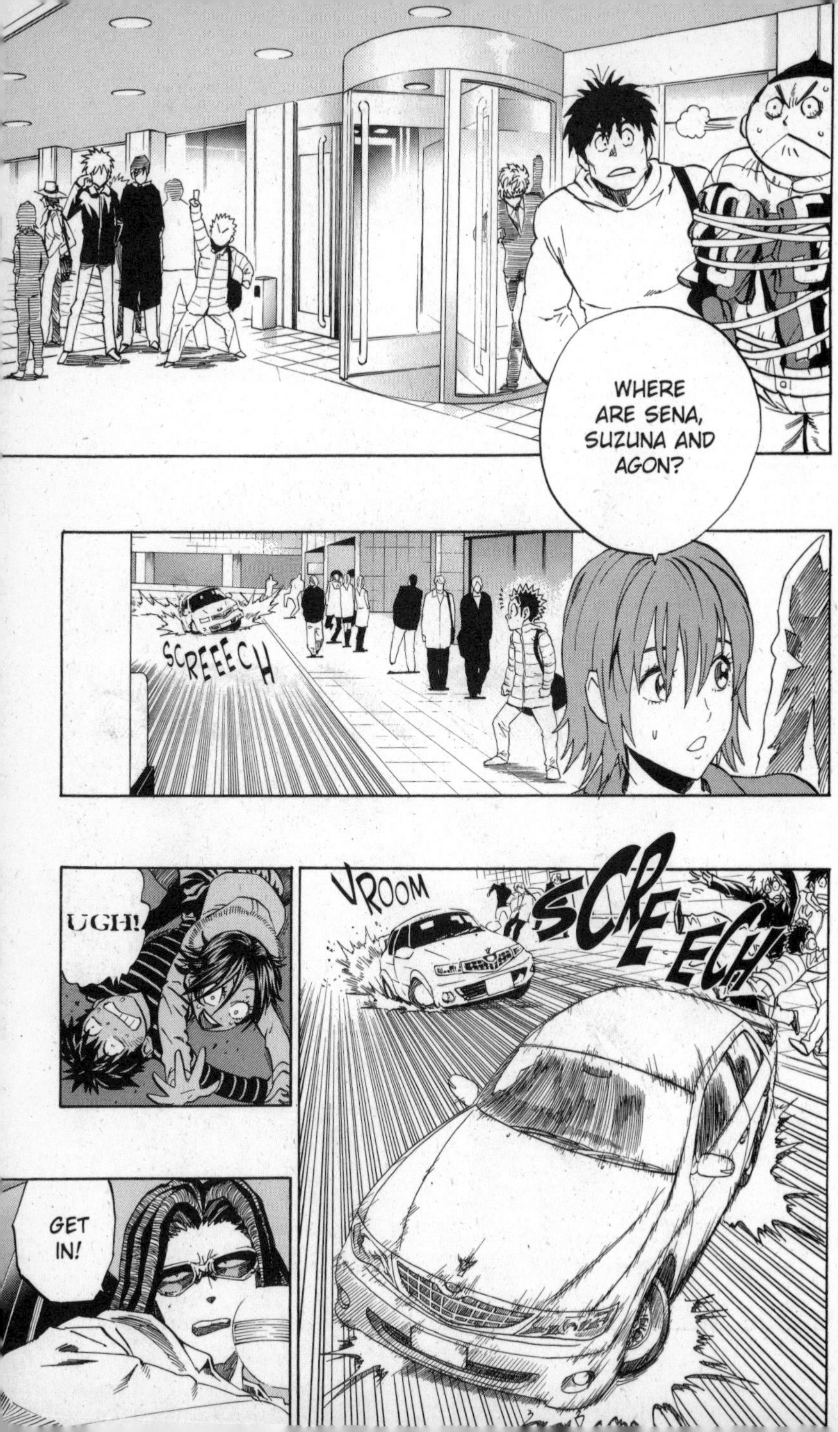
WHERE ARE SENA, SUZUNA AND AGON?
SCREEECH
VROOM
SCREECH
UGH!
GET IN!

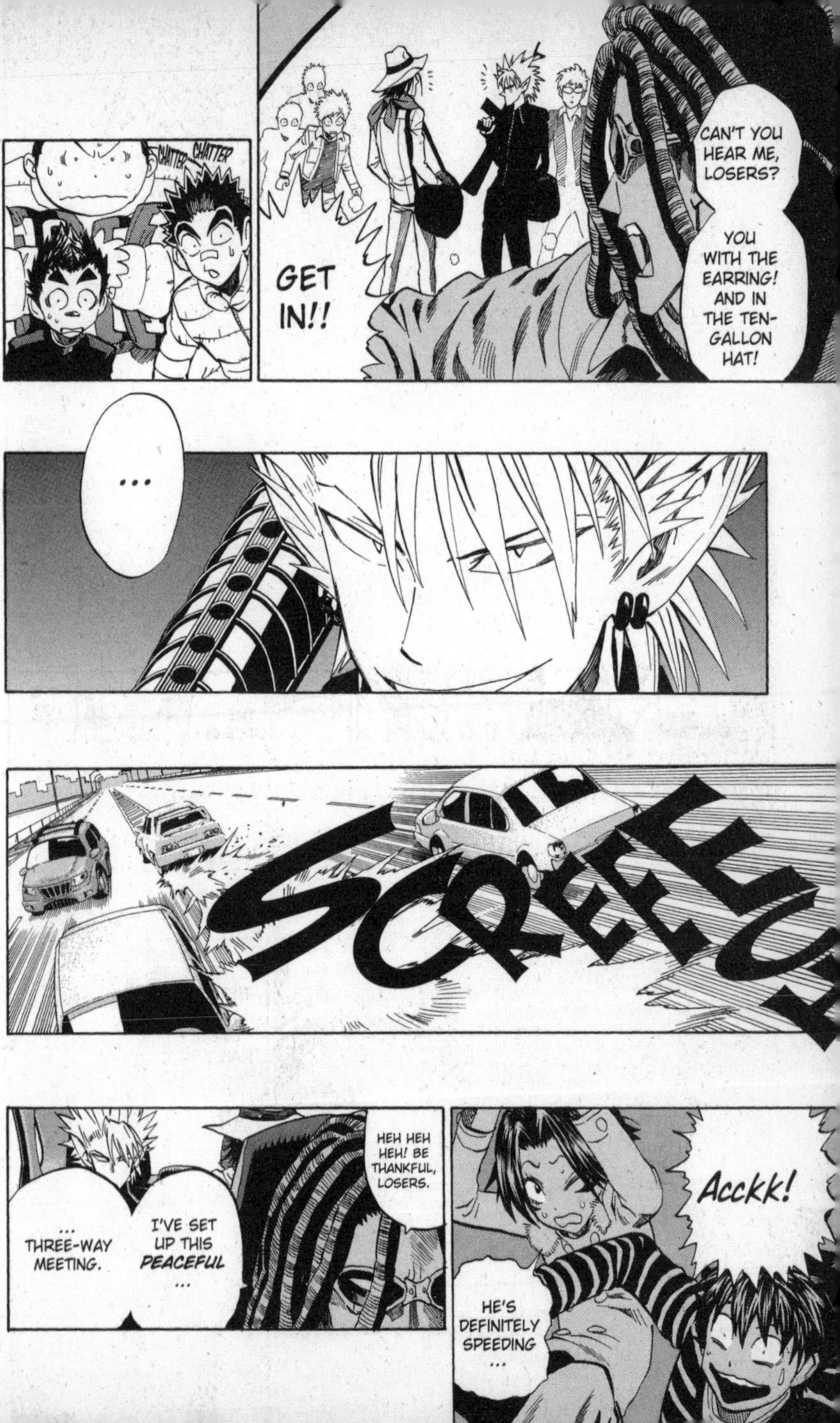
CAN'T YOU HEAR ME, LOSERS?
YOU WITH THE EARRING! AND IN THE TEN-GALLON HAT!
GET IN!!
CHATTER
CHATTER
...
SCREEE
Acckk!
HE'S DEFINITELY SPEEDING ...
HEH HEH HEH! BE THANKFUL, LOSERS.
I'VE SET UP THIS *PEACEFUL* ...
... THREE-WAY MEETING.

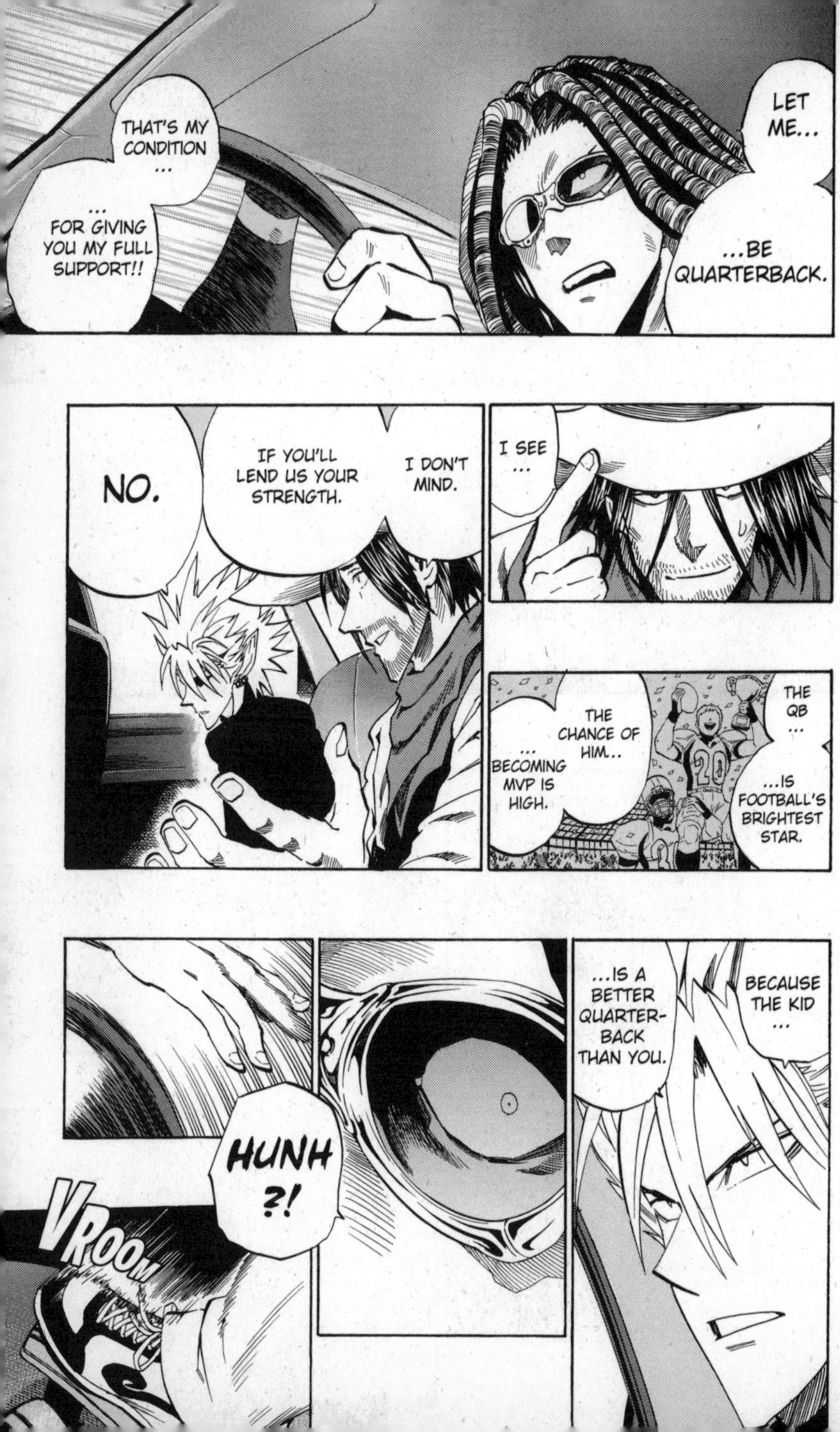
LET ME...
...BE QUARTERBACK.
THAT'S MY CONDITION ...
... FOR GIVING YOU MY FULL SUPPORT!!
I SEE ...
THE QB ...
...IS FOOTBALL'S BRIGHTEST STAR.
THE CHANCE OF HIM...
... BECOMING MVP IS HIGH.
I DON'T MIND.
IF YOU'LL LEND US YOUR STRENGTH.
NO.
BECAUSE THE KID ...
...IS A BETTER QUARTER-BACK THAN YOU.
HUNH ?!
VROOM

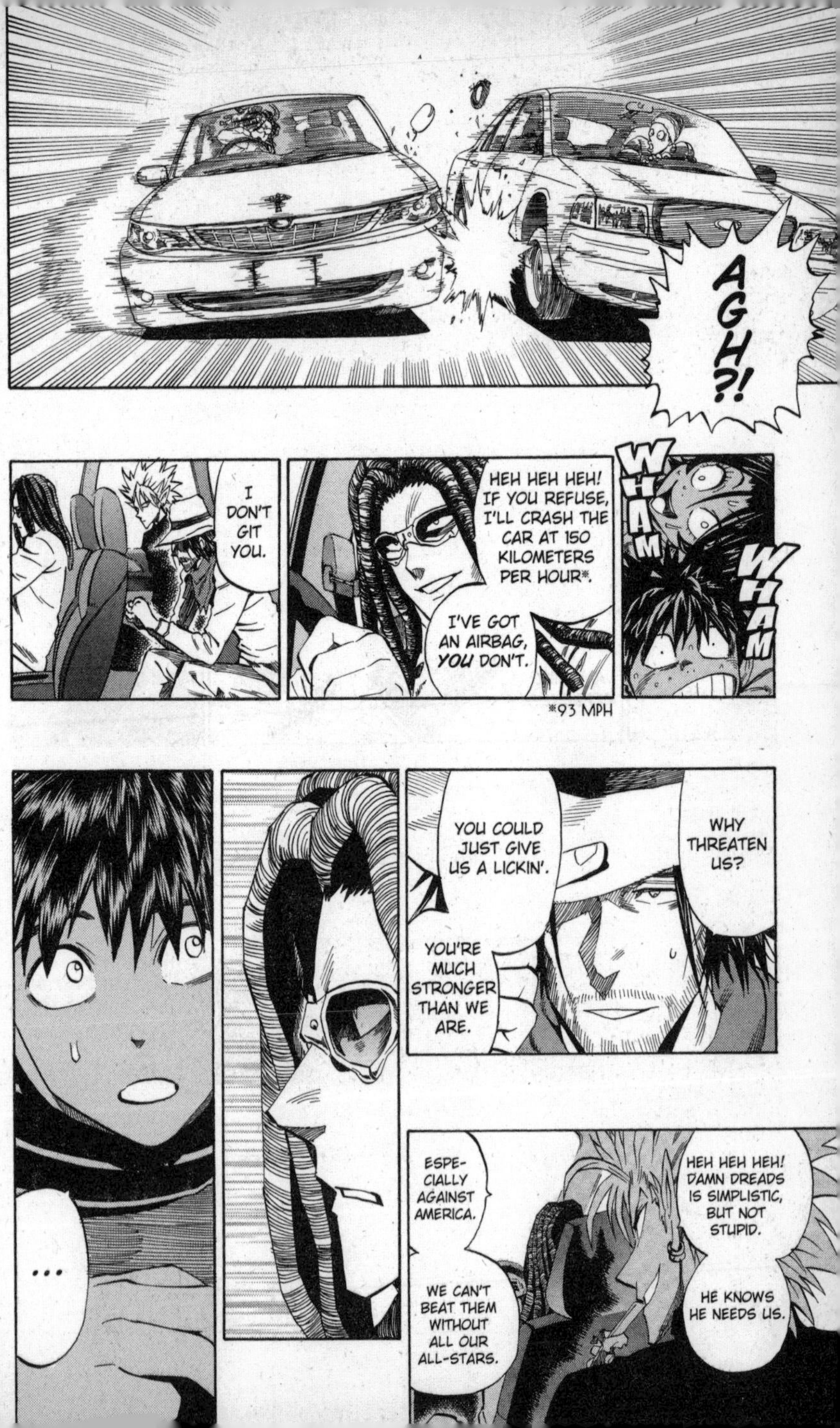
AGH?!
WHAM
WHAM
HEH HEH HEH! IF YOU REFUSE, I'LL CRASH THE CAR AT 150 KILOMETERS PER HOUR*.
I'VE GOT AN AIRBAG, *YOU* DON'T.
I DON'T GIT YOU.
WHY THREATEN US?
YOU COULD JUST GIVE US A LICKIN'.
YOU'RE MUCH STRONGER THAN WE ARE.
HEH HEH HEH! DAMN DREADS IS SIMPLISTIC, BUT NOT STUPID.
HE KNOWS HE NEEDS US.
ESPECIALLY AGAINST AMERICA.
WE CAN'T BEAT THEM WITHOUT ALL OUR ALL-STARS.
...

*93 MPH

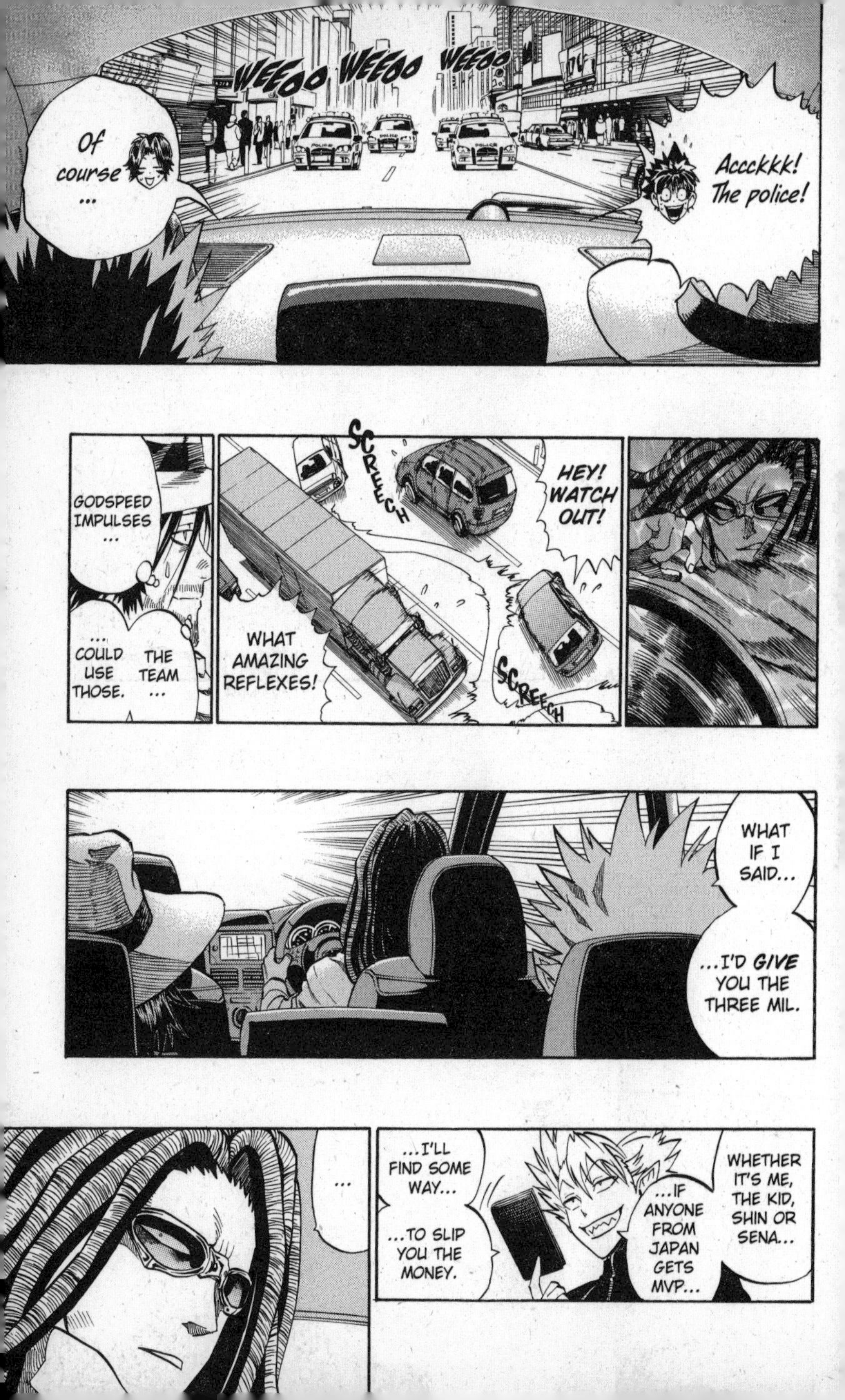
WEEOO WEEOO WEEOO
Accckkk! The police!
Of course ...
HEY! WATCH OUT!
SCREECH
WHAT AMAZING REFLEXES!
SCREECH
GODSPEED IMPULSES ...
THE TEAM ...
... COULD USE THOSE.
WHAT IF I SAID...
...I'D **GIVE** YOU THE THREE MIL.
WHETHER IT'S ME, THE KID, SHIN OR SENA...
...IF ANYONE FROM JAPAN GETS MVP...
...I'LL FIND SOME WAY...
...TO SLIP YOU THE MONEY.
...

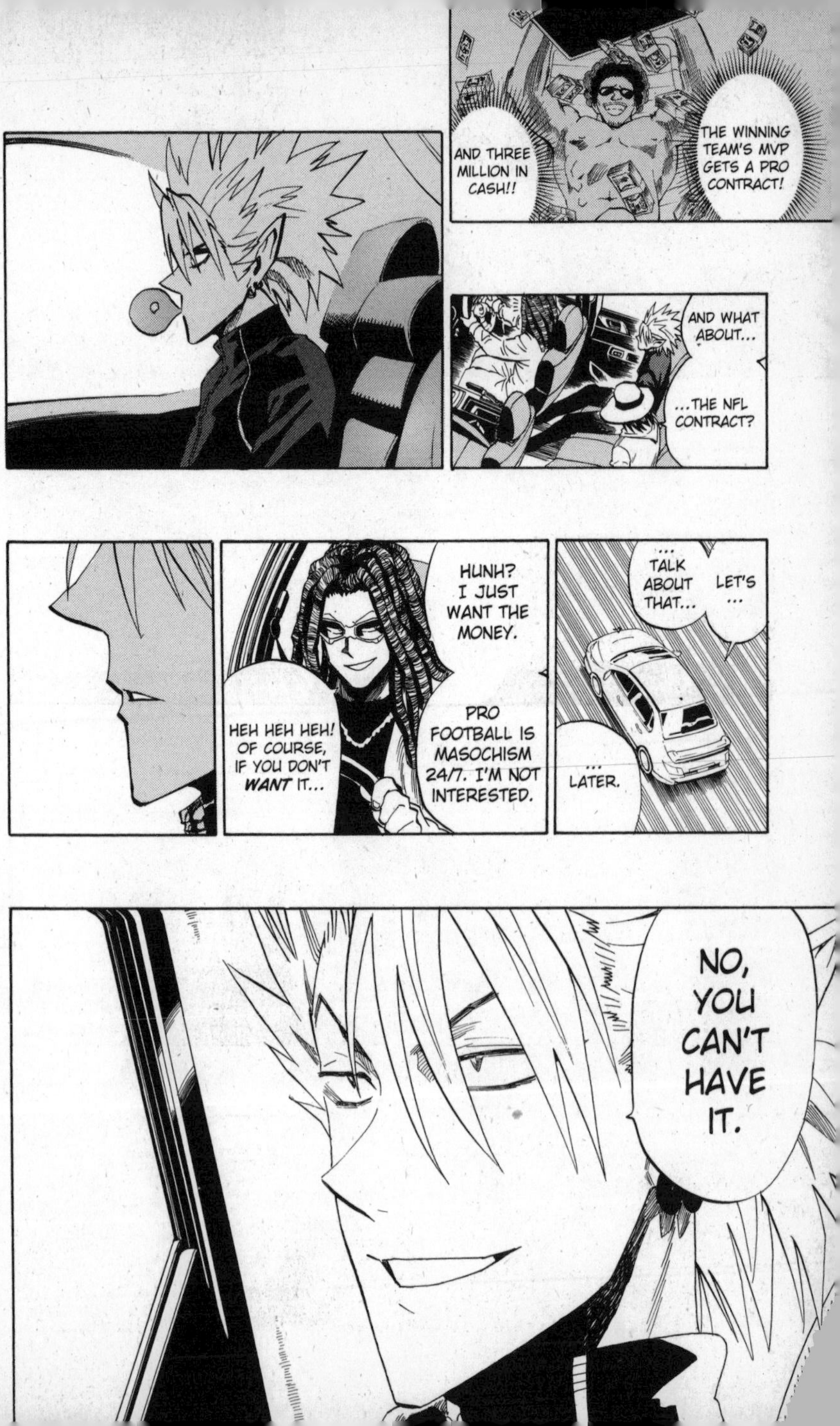
THE WINNING TEAM'S MVP GETS A PRO CONTRACT!
AND THREE MILLION IN CASH!!
AND WHAT ABOUT...
...THE NFL CONTRACT?
LET'S ...
... TALK ABOUT THAT...
... LATER.
HUNH? I JUST WANT THE MONEY.
PRO FOOTBALL IS MASOCHISM 24/7. I'M NOT INTERESTED.
HEH HEH HEH! OF COURSE, IF YOU DON'T *WANT* IT...
NO, YOU CAN'T HAVE IT.

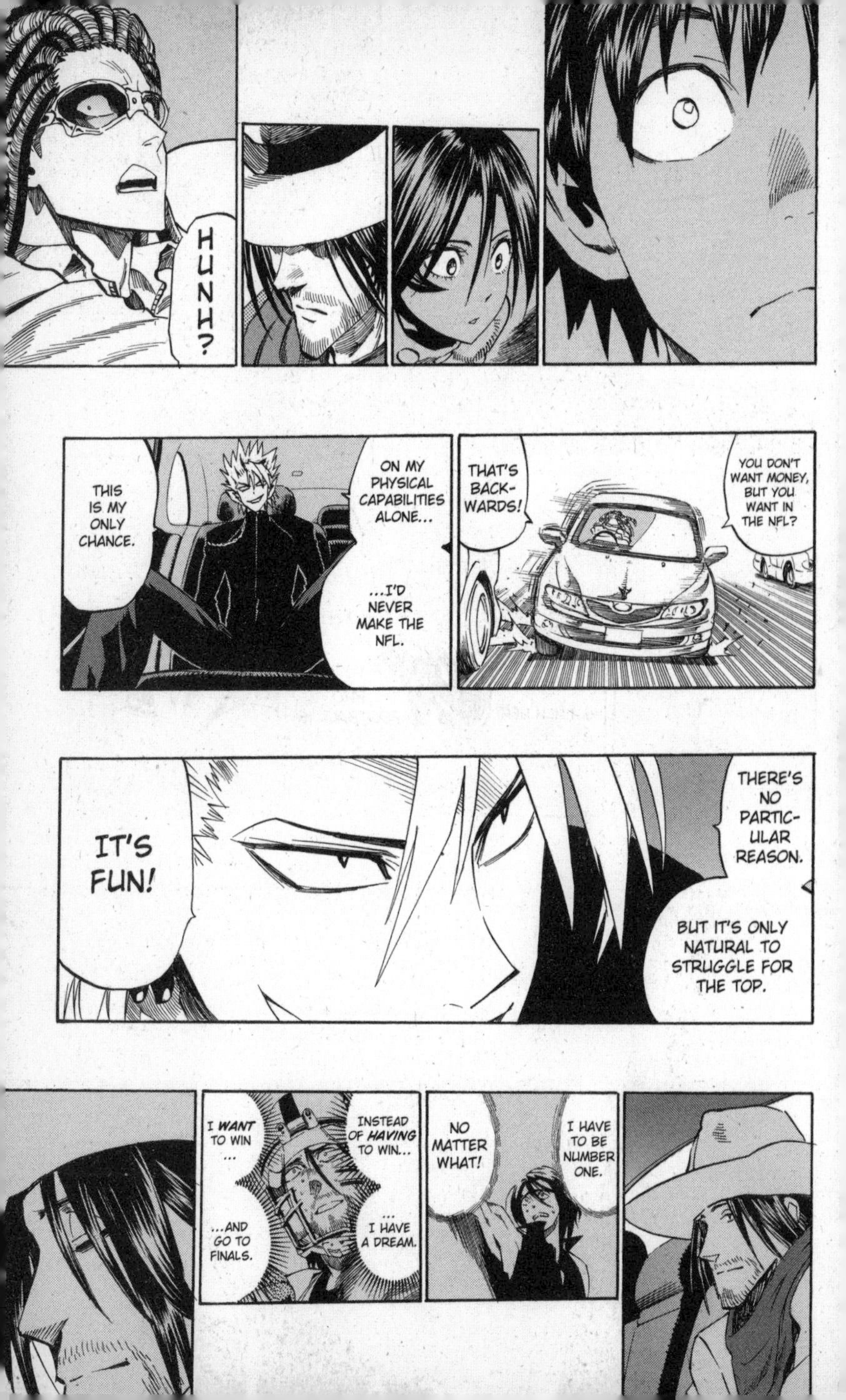
HUNH?
YOU DON'T WANT MONEY, BUT YOU WANT IN THE NFL?
THAT'S BACK-WARDS!
ON MY PHYSICAL CAPABILITIES ALONE...
...I'D NEVER MAKE THE NFL.
THIS IS MY ONLY CHANCE.
THERE'S NO PARTIC-ULAR REASON.
BUT IT'S ONLY NATURAL TO STRUGGLE FOR THE TOP.
IT'S FUN!
I HAVE TO BE NUMBER ONE.
NO MATTER WHAT!
INSTEAD OF *HAVING* TO WIN...
I *WANT* TO WIN ...
... I HAVE A DREAM.
...AND GO TO FINALS.

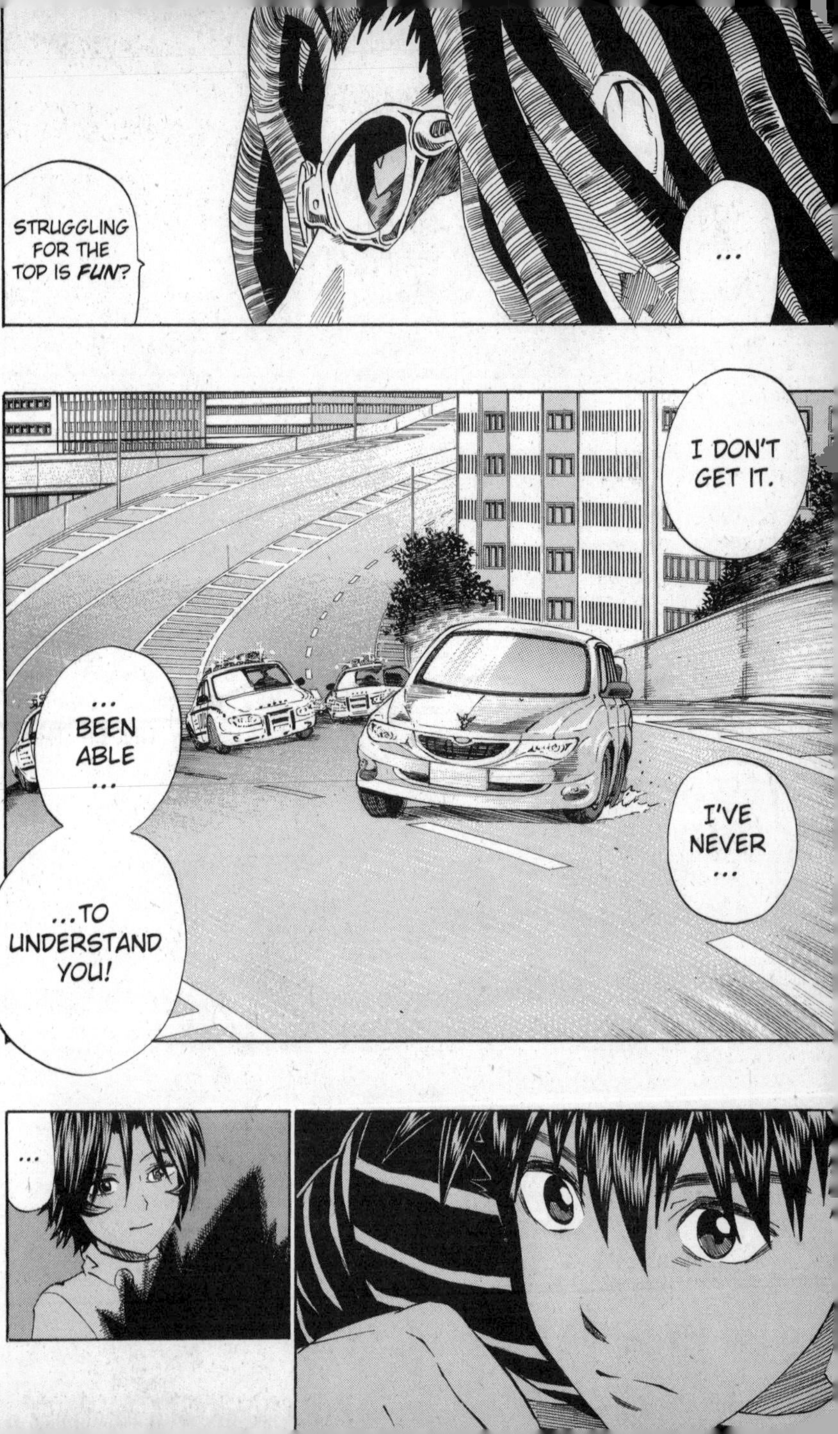
...
STRUGGLING FOR THE TOP IS FUN?
I DON'T GET IT.
I'VE NEVER ...
... BEEN ABLE ...
...TO UNDERSTAND YOU!
...

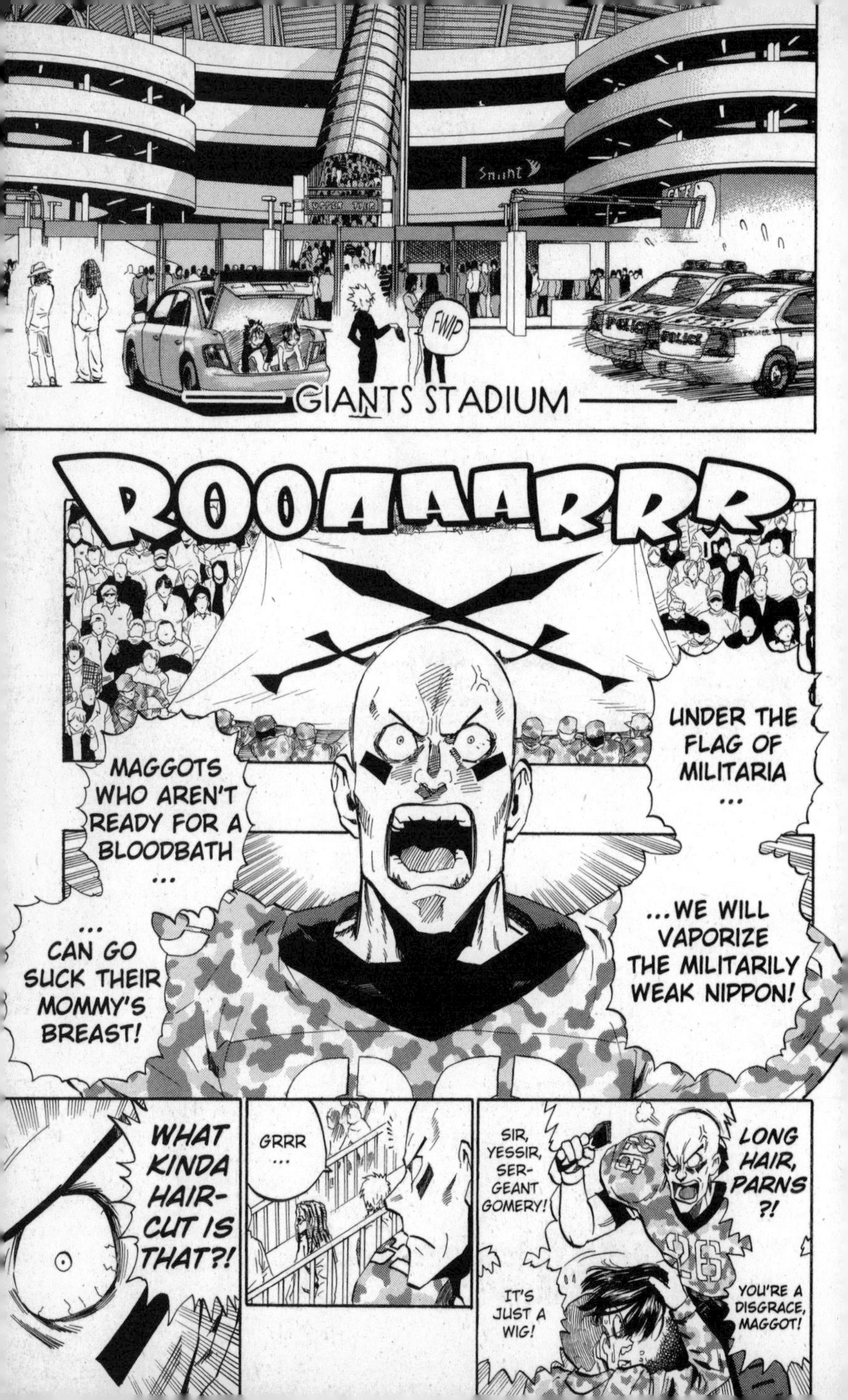
FWIP
POLICE
GIANTS STADIUM
ROOAAARRR
UNDER THE FLAG OF MILITARIA ...
MAGGOTS WHO AREN'T READY FOR A BLOODBATH ...
...WE WILL VAPORIZE THE MILITARILY WEAK NIPPON!
... CAN GO SUCK THEIR MOMMY'S BREAST!
LONG HAIR, PARNS ?!
SIR, YESSIR, SER-GEANT GOMERY!
YOU'RE A DISGRACE, MAGGOT!
IT'S JUST A WIG!
GRRR ...
WHAT KINDA HAIR-CUT IS THAT?!

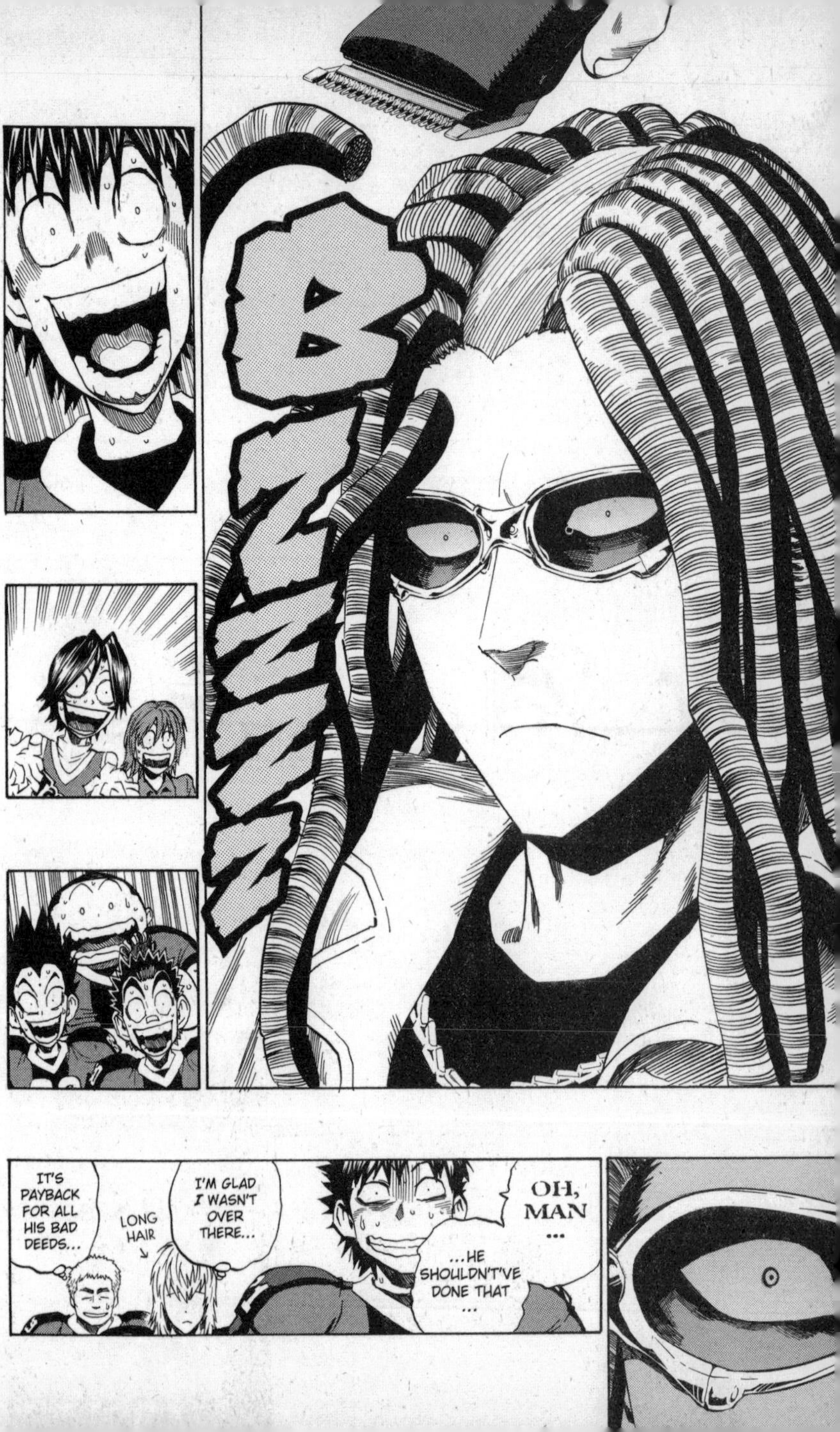
OH, MAN ...
...HE SHOULDN'T'VE DONE THAT ...
I'M GLAD I WASN'T OVER THERE...
LONG HAIR
IT'S PAYBACK FOR ALL HIS BAD DEEDS...

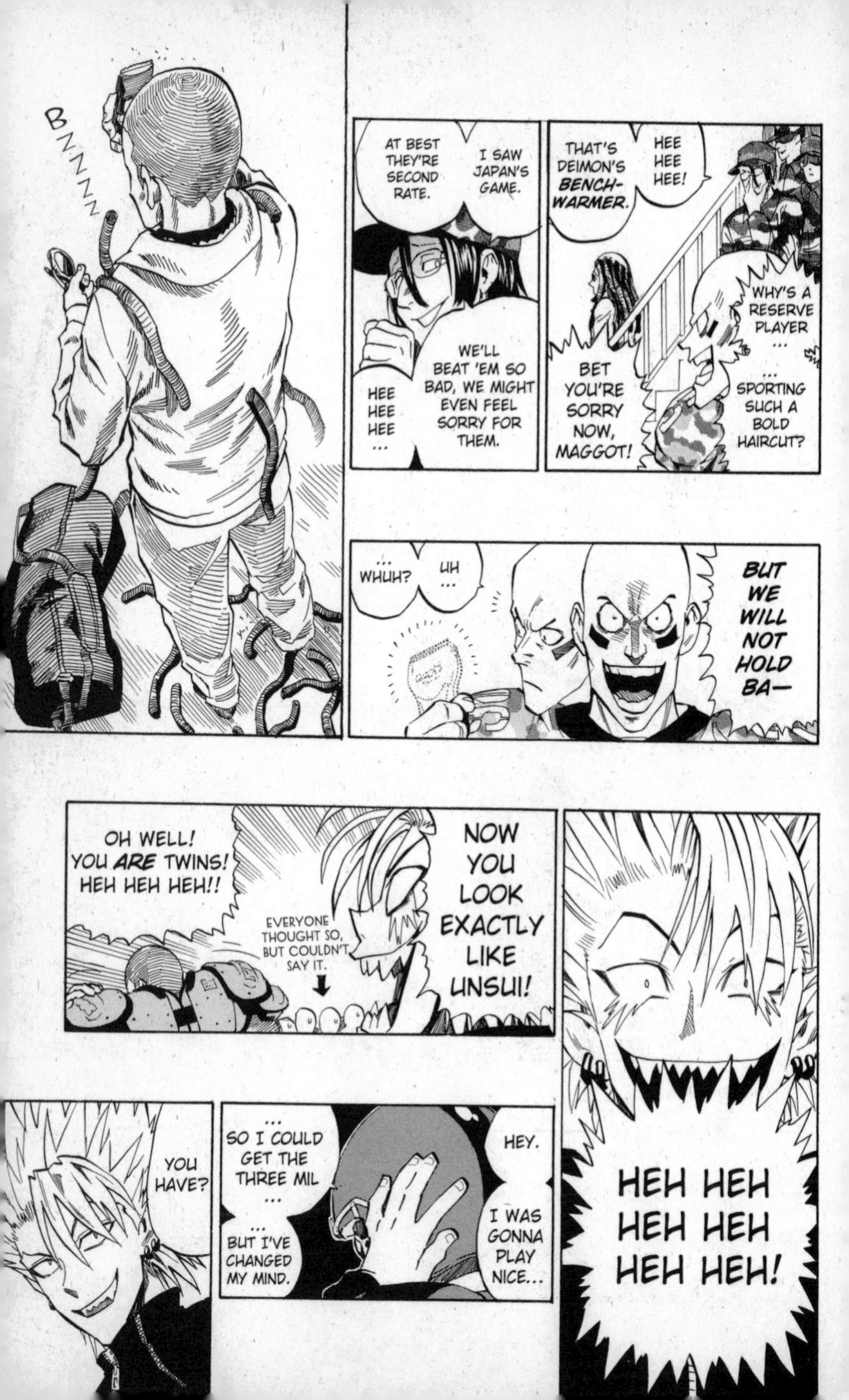
HEE HEE HEE!
THAT'S DEIMON'S BENCH-WARMER.
WHY'S A RESERVE PLAYER ...
... SPORTING SUCH A BOLD HAIRCUT?
BET YOU'RE SORRY NOW, MAGGOT!
I SAW JAPAN'S GAME.
AT BEST THEY'RE SECOND RATE.
WE'LL BEAT 'EM SO BAD, WE MIGHT EVEN FEEL SORRY FOR THEM.
HEE HEE HEE ...
BUT WE WILL NOT HOLD BA—
UH ...
... WHUH?
BZZZZZ
HEH HEH HEH HEH HEH HEH!
NOW YOU LOOK EXACTLY LIKE UNSUI!
OH WELL! YOU ARE TWINS! HEH HEH HEH!!
EVERYONE THOUGHT SO, BUT COULDN'T SAY IT.
HEY.
I WAS GONNA PLAY NICE...
... SO I COULD GET THE THREE MIL ...
... BUT I'VE CHANGED MY MIND.
YOU HAVE?

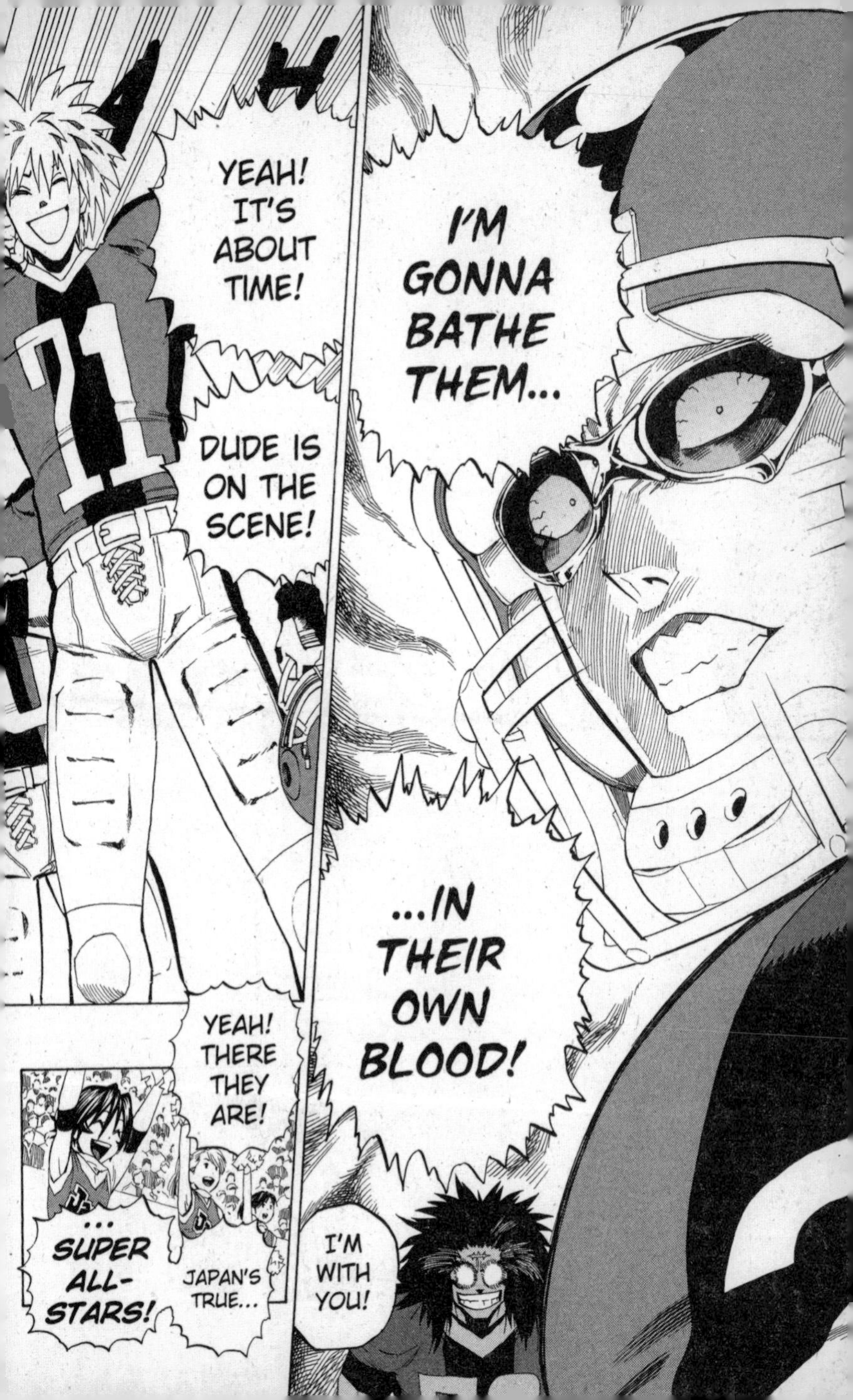

I'M GONNA BATHE THEM...
...IN THEIR OWN BLOOD!
I'M WITH YOU!
AH
YEAH! IT'S ABOUT TIME!
DUDE IS ON THE SCENE!
YEAH! THERE THEY ARE!
JAPAN'S TRUE...
...SUPER ALL-STARS!

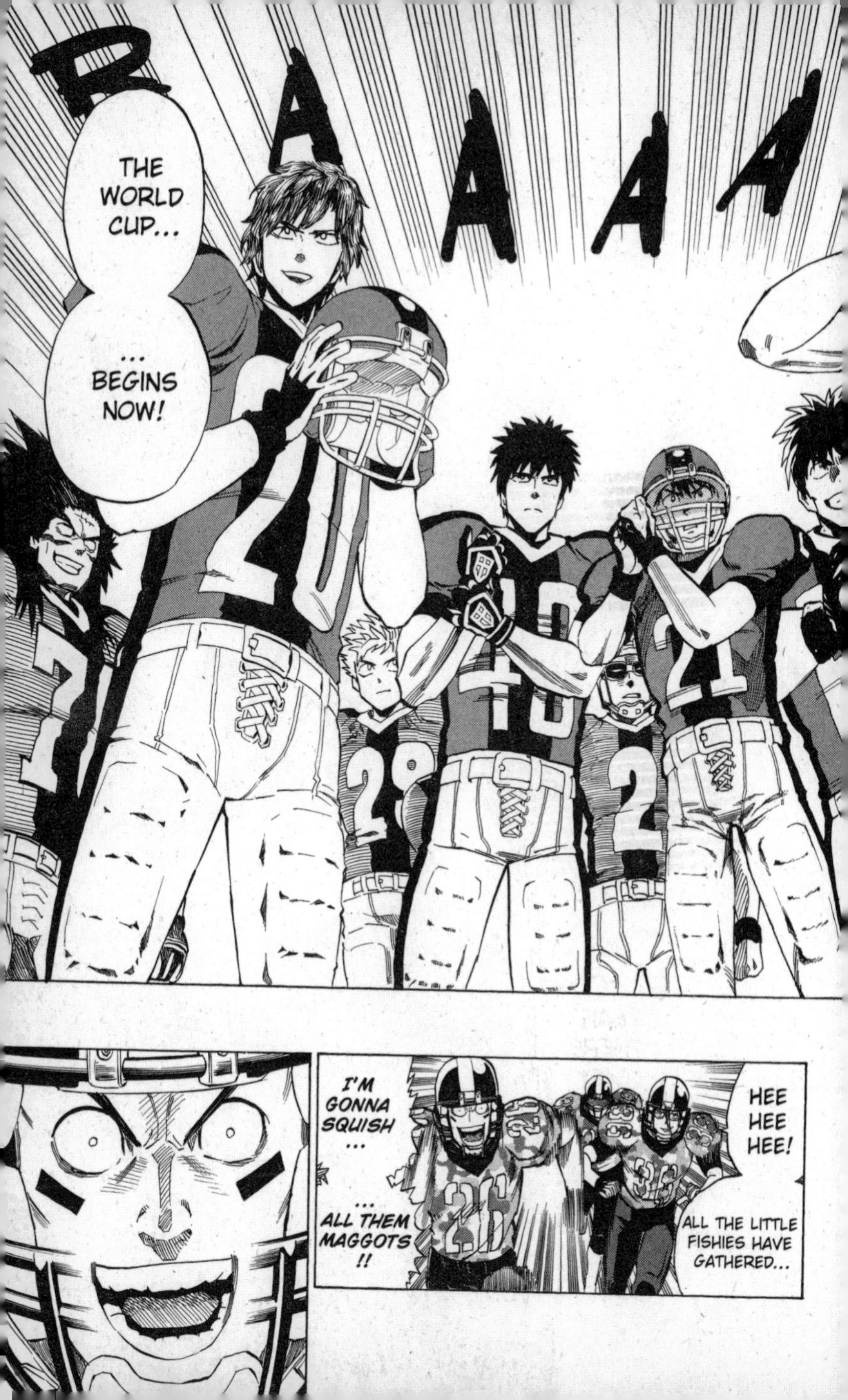
RAAAA
THE WORLD CUP...
...BEGINS NOW!
HEE HEE HEE!
ALL THE LITTLE FISHIES HAVE GATHERED...
I'M GONNA SQUISH...
...ALL THEM MAGGOTS!!

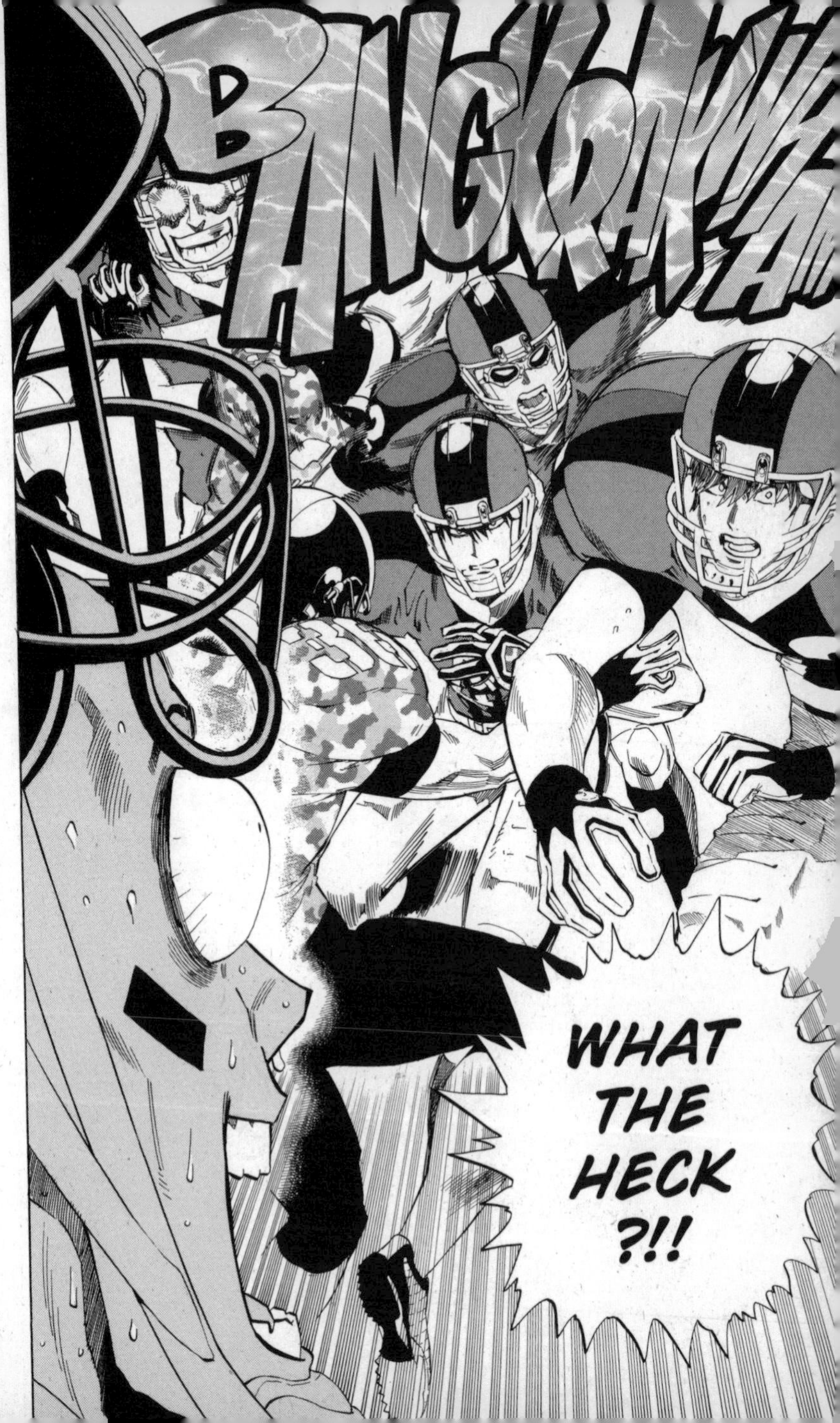
WHAT THE HECK ?!!

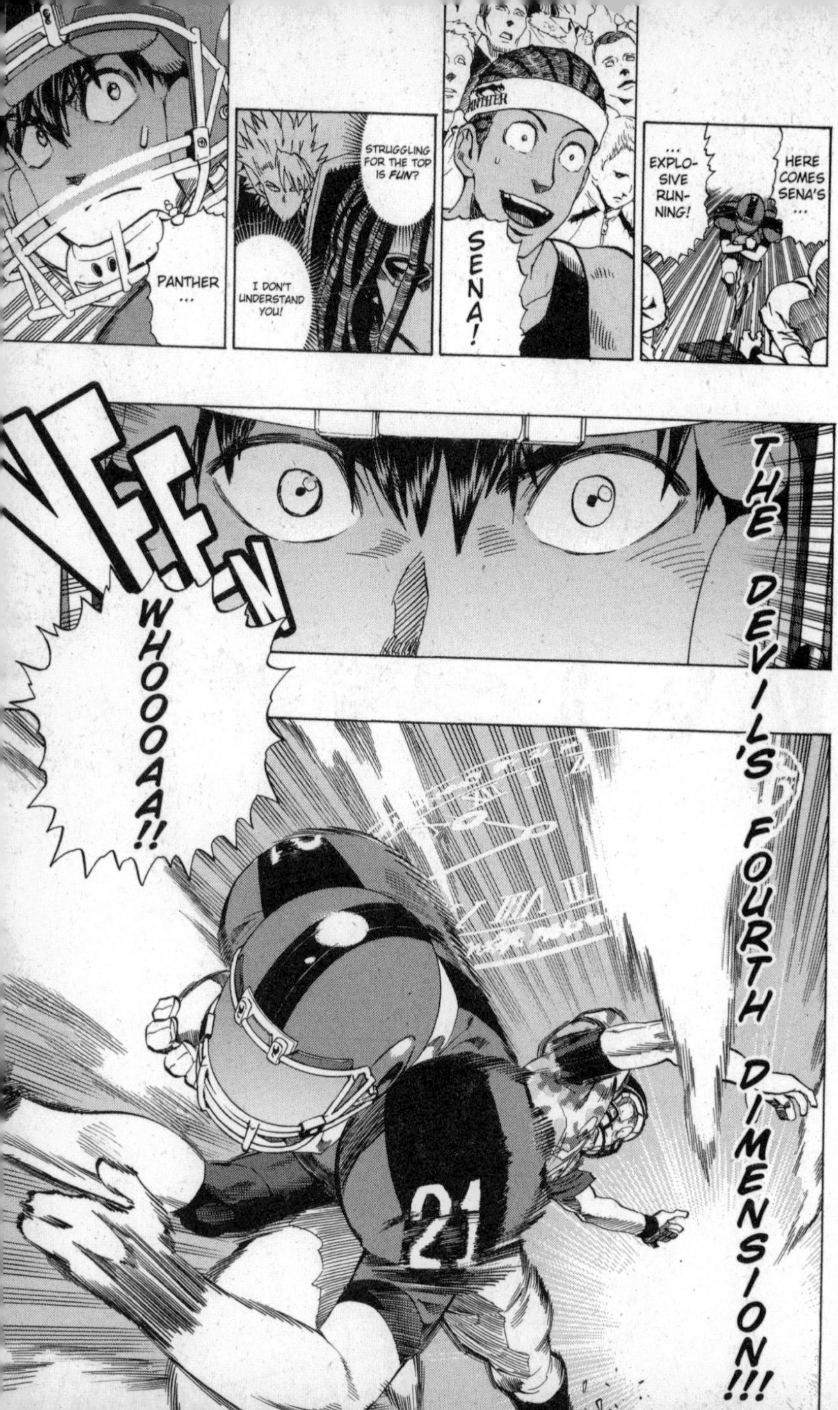
HERE COMES SENA'S ...
... EXPLOSIVE RUNNING!
SENA!
STRUGGLING FOR THE TOP IS FUN?
I DON'T UNDERSTAND YOU!
PANTHER ...
THE DEVIL'S FOURTH DIMENSION!!!
WHOOOOAAA!!

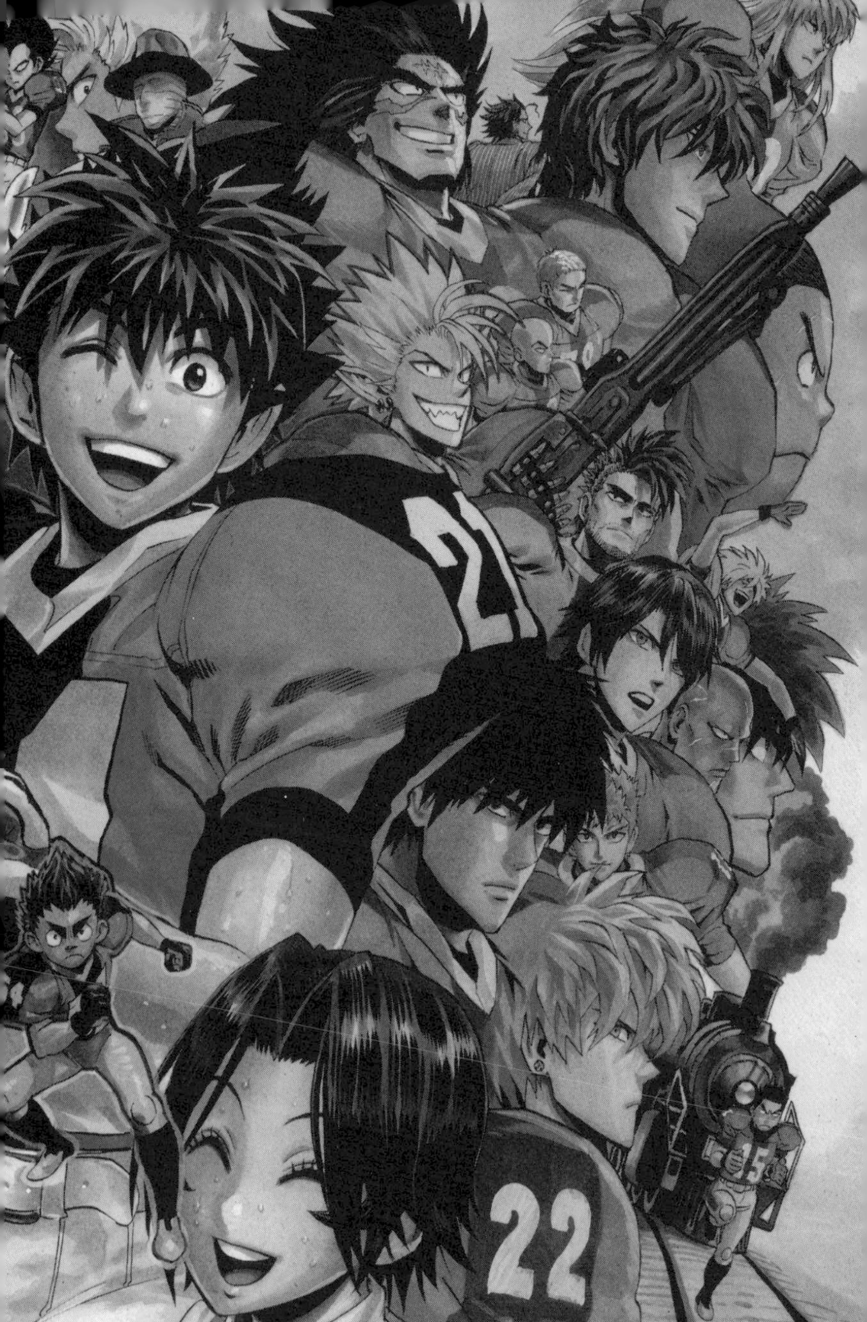

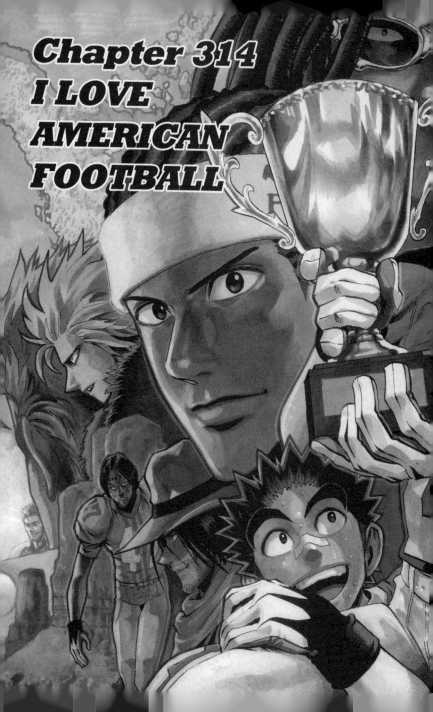

Chapter 314
I LOVE
AMERICAN
FOOTBALL

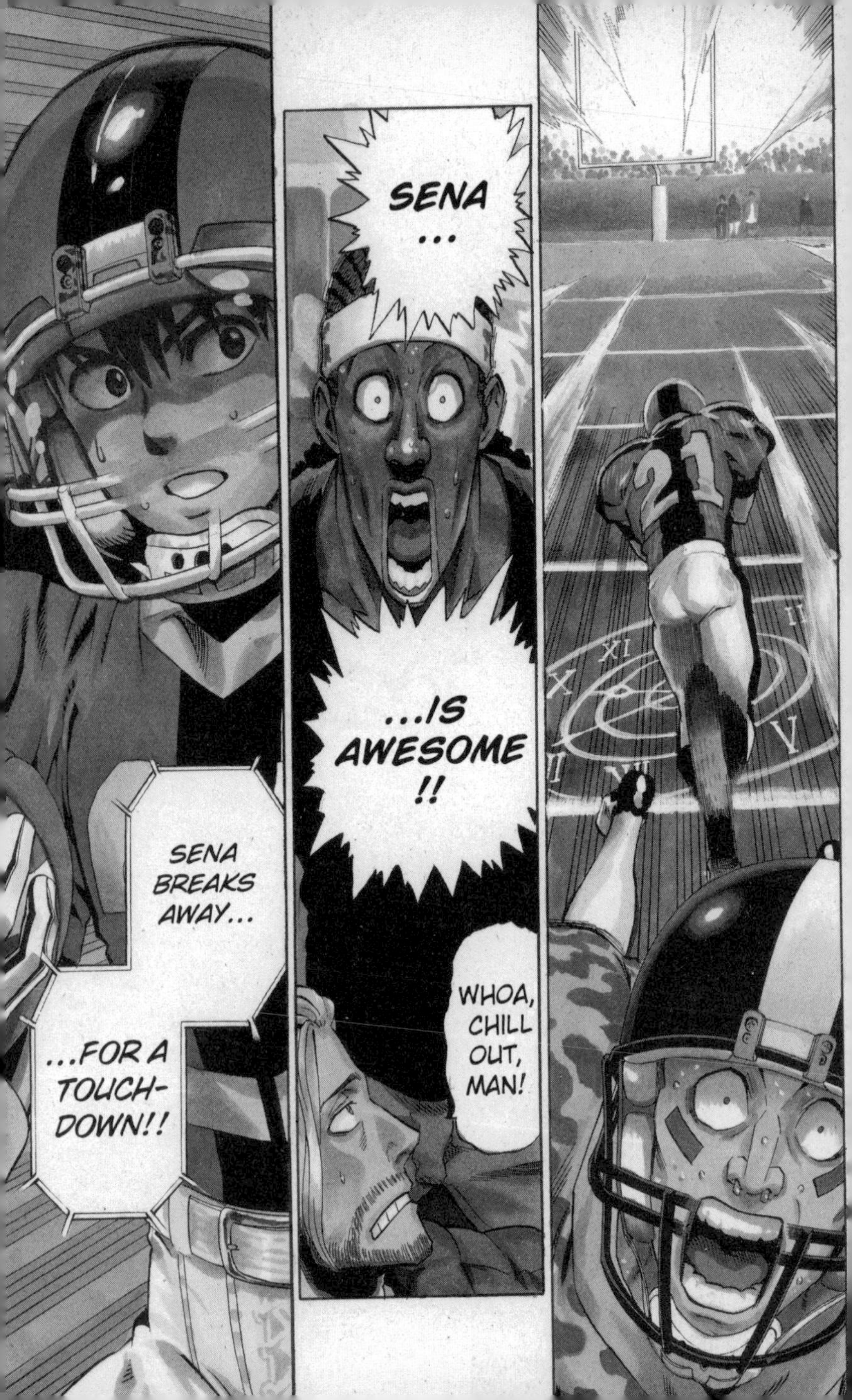
SENA ...
...IS AWESOME !!
WHOA, CHILL OUT, MAN!
SENA BREAKS AWAY...
...FOR A TOUCH-DOWN!!

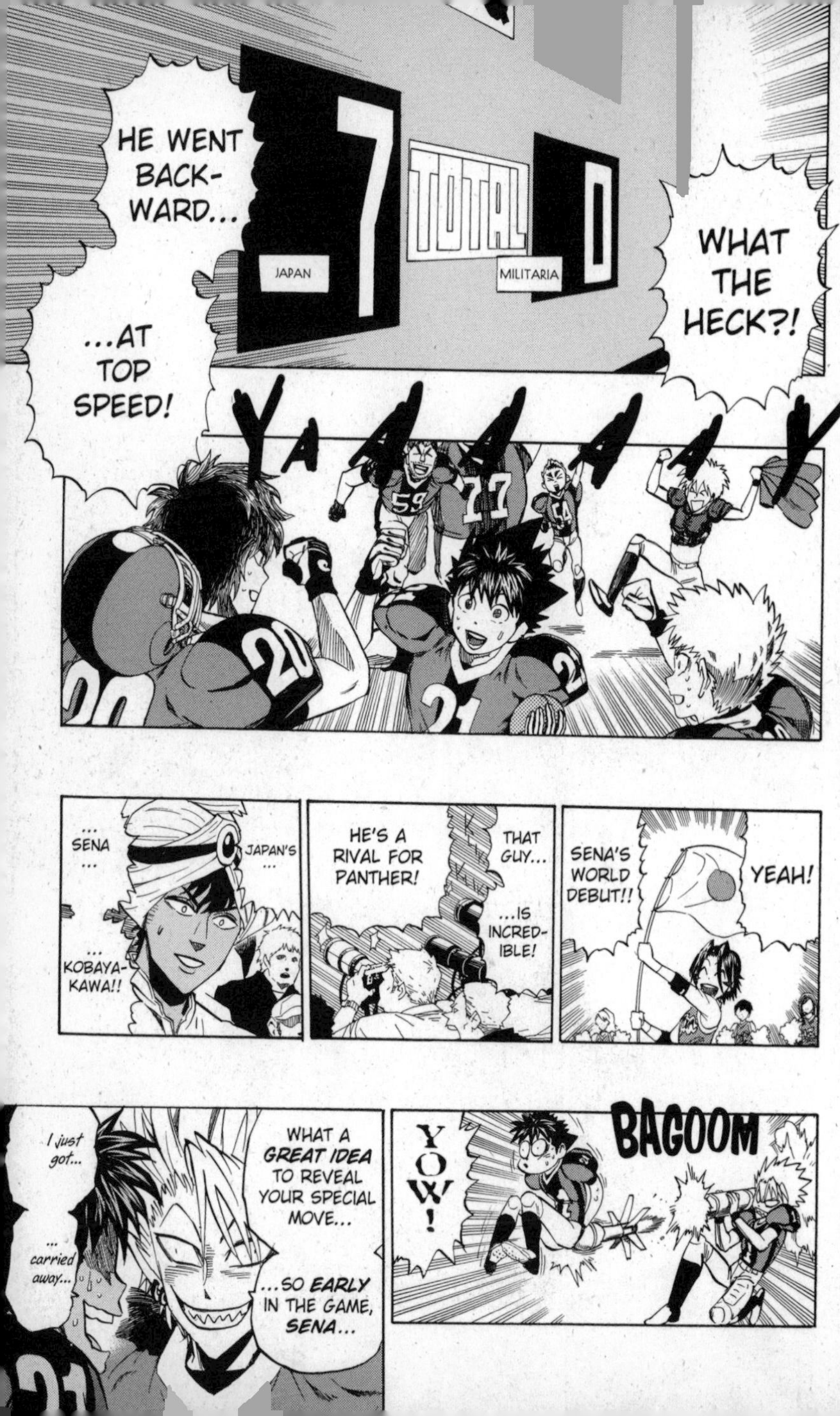
WHAT THE HECK?!
HE WENT BACKWARD...
TOTAL
JAPAN
7
MILITARIA
0
...AT TOP SPEED!
YAAAAAAY
YEAH!
SENA'S WORLD DEBUT!!
THAT GUY...
...IS INCREDIBLE!
HE'S A RIVAL FOR PANTHER!
JAPAN'S...
...SENA...
...KOBAYAKAWA!!
BAGOOM
YOW!
WHAT A GREAT IDEA TO REVEAL YOUR SPECIAL MOVE...
...SO EARLY IN THE GAME, SENA...
I just got...
...carried away...

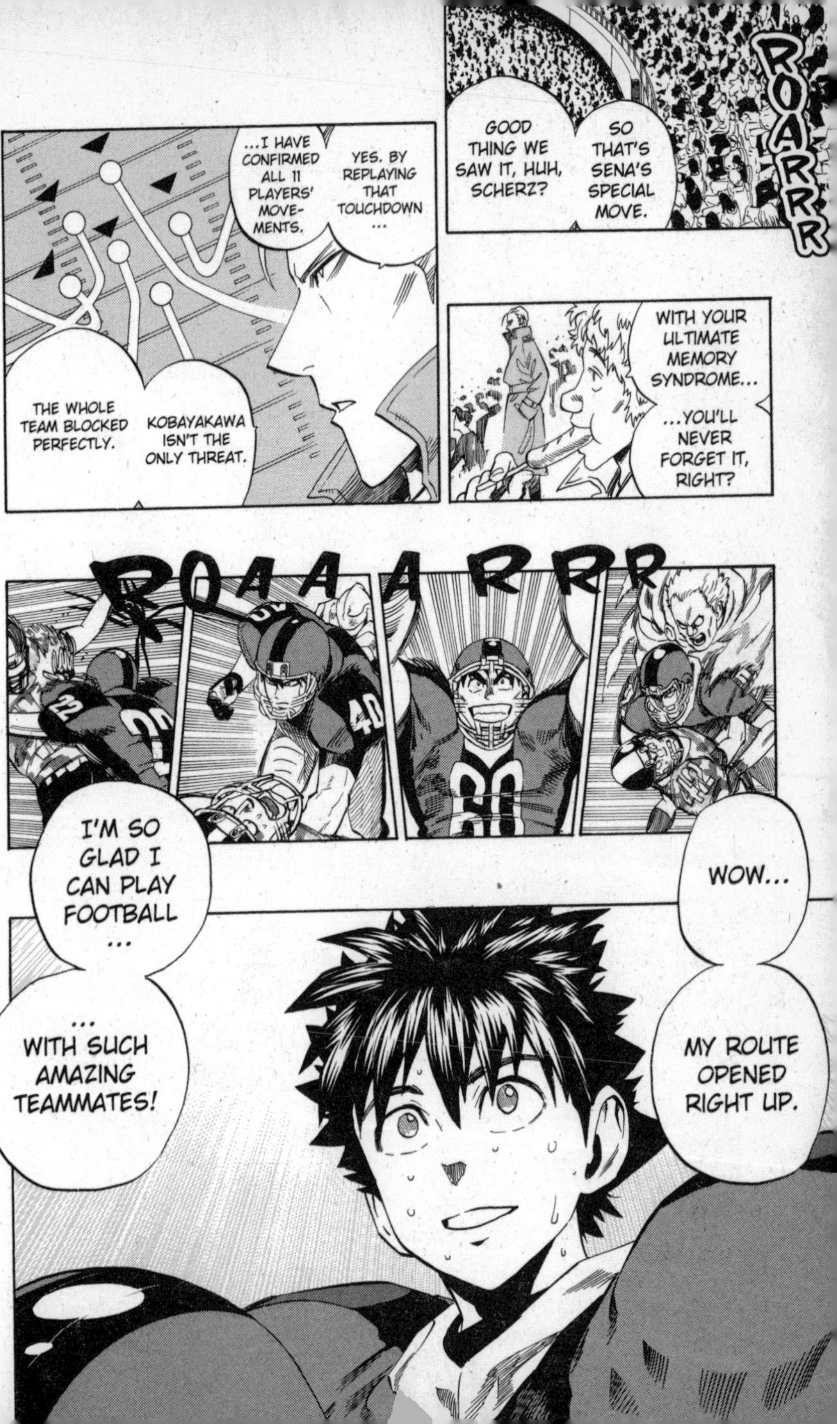
ROARRR
SO THAT'S SENA'S SPECIAL MOVE.
GOOD THING WE SAW IT, HUH, SCHERZ?
WITH YOUR ULTIMATE MEMORY SYNDROME...
...YOU'LL NEVER FORGET IT, RIGHT?
YES. BY REPLAYING THAT TOUCHDOWN...
...I HAVE CONFIRMED ALL 11 PLAYERS' MOVEMENTS.
KOBAYAKAWA ISN'T THE ONLY THREAT.
THE WHOLE TEAM BLOCKED PERFECTLY.
ROAAARRR
WOW...
MY ROUTE OPENED RIGHT UP.
I'M SO GLAD I CAN PLAY FOOTBALL...
...WITH SUCH AMAZING TEAMMATES!

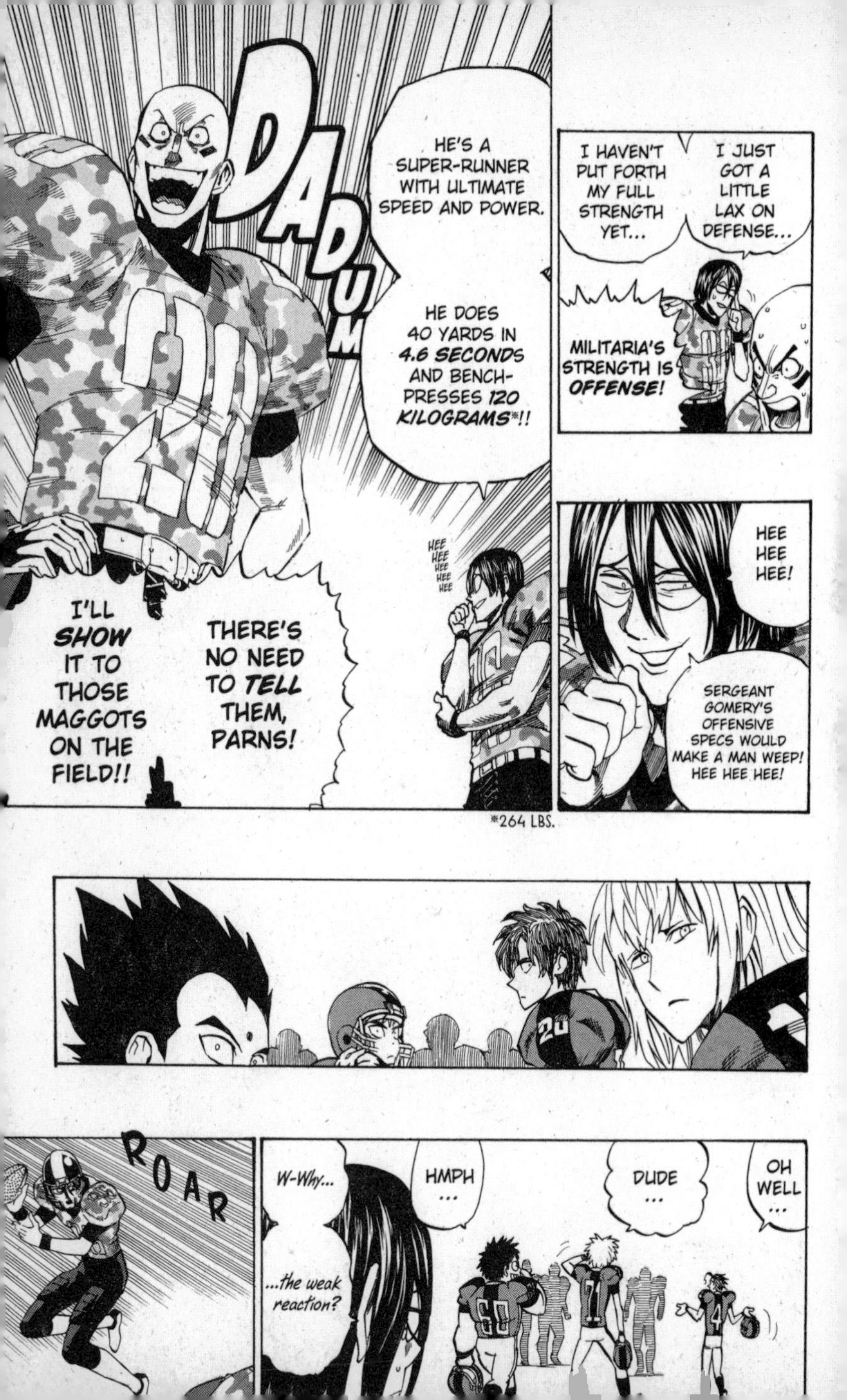
I JUST GOT A LITTLE LAX ON DEFENSE...
I HAVEN'T PUT FORTH MY FULL STRENGTH YET...
MILITARIA'S STRENGTH IS OFFENSE!
HEE HEE HEE!
SERGEANT GOMERY'S OFFENSIVE SPECS WOULD MAKE A MAN WEEP! HEE HEE HEE!
HE'S A SUPER-RUNNER WITH ULTIMATE SPEED AND POWER.
HE DOES 40 YARDS IN 4.6 SECONDS AND BENCH-PRESSES 120 KILOGRAMS*!!
DADUM
HEE HEE HEE HEE HEE
THERE'S NO NEED TO TELL THEM, PARNS!
I'LL SHOW IT TO THOSE MAGGOTS ON THE FIELD!!
*264 LBS.
OH WELL...
DUDE...
HMPH...
W-Why...
...the weak reaction?
ROAR

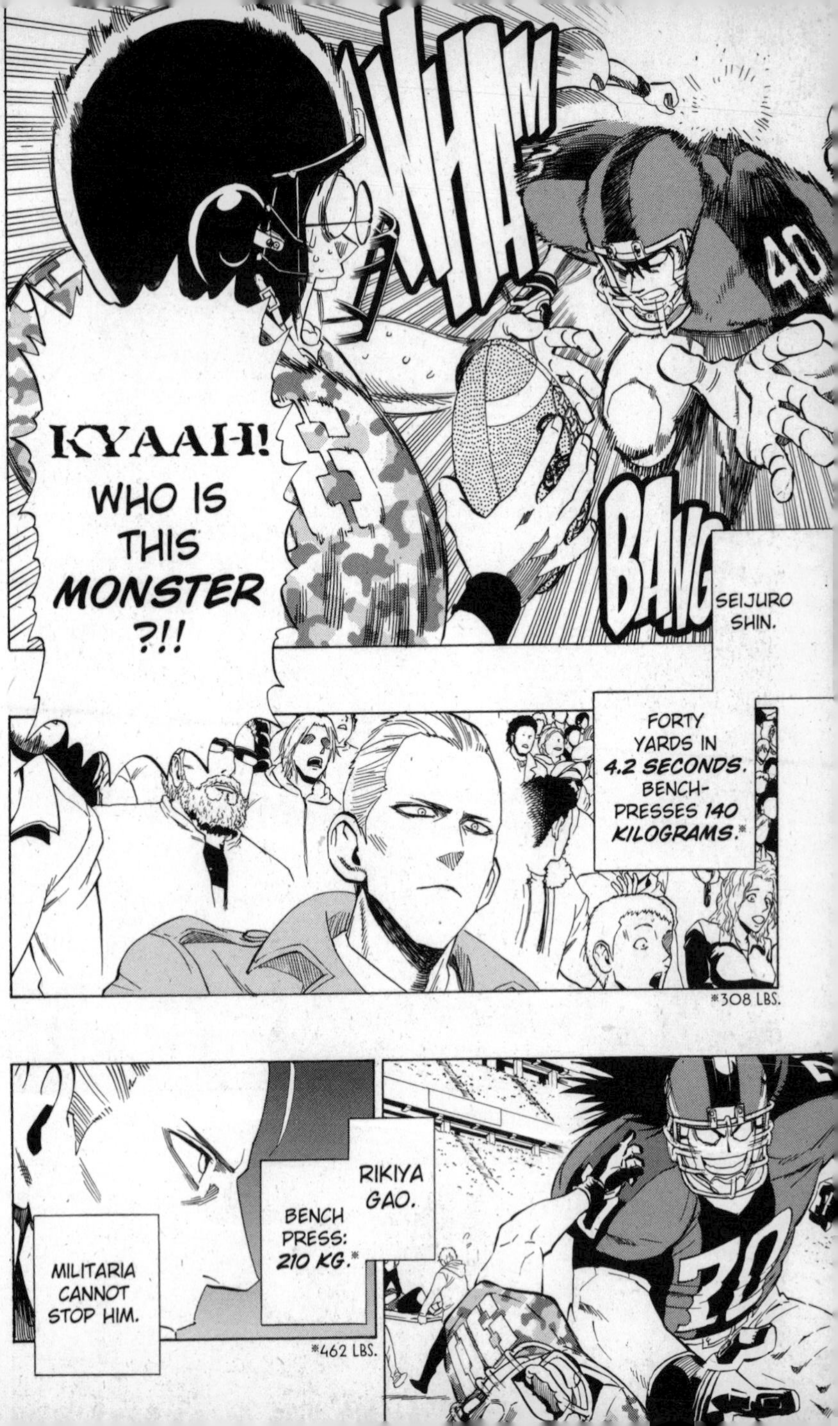

WHAM
BANG
SEIJURO SHIN.
KYAAH! WHO IS THIS MONSTER?!!
FORTY YARDS IN 4.2 SECONDS. BENCH-PRESSES 140 KILOGRAMS.*
*308 LBS.
RIKIYA GAO.
BENCH PRESS: 210 KG.*
MILITARIA CANNOT STOP HIM.
*462 LBS.

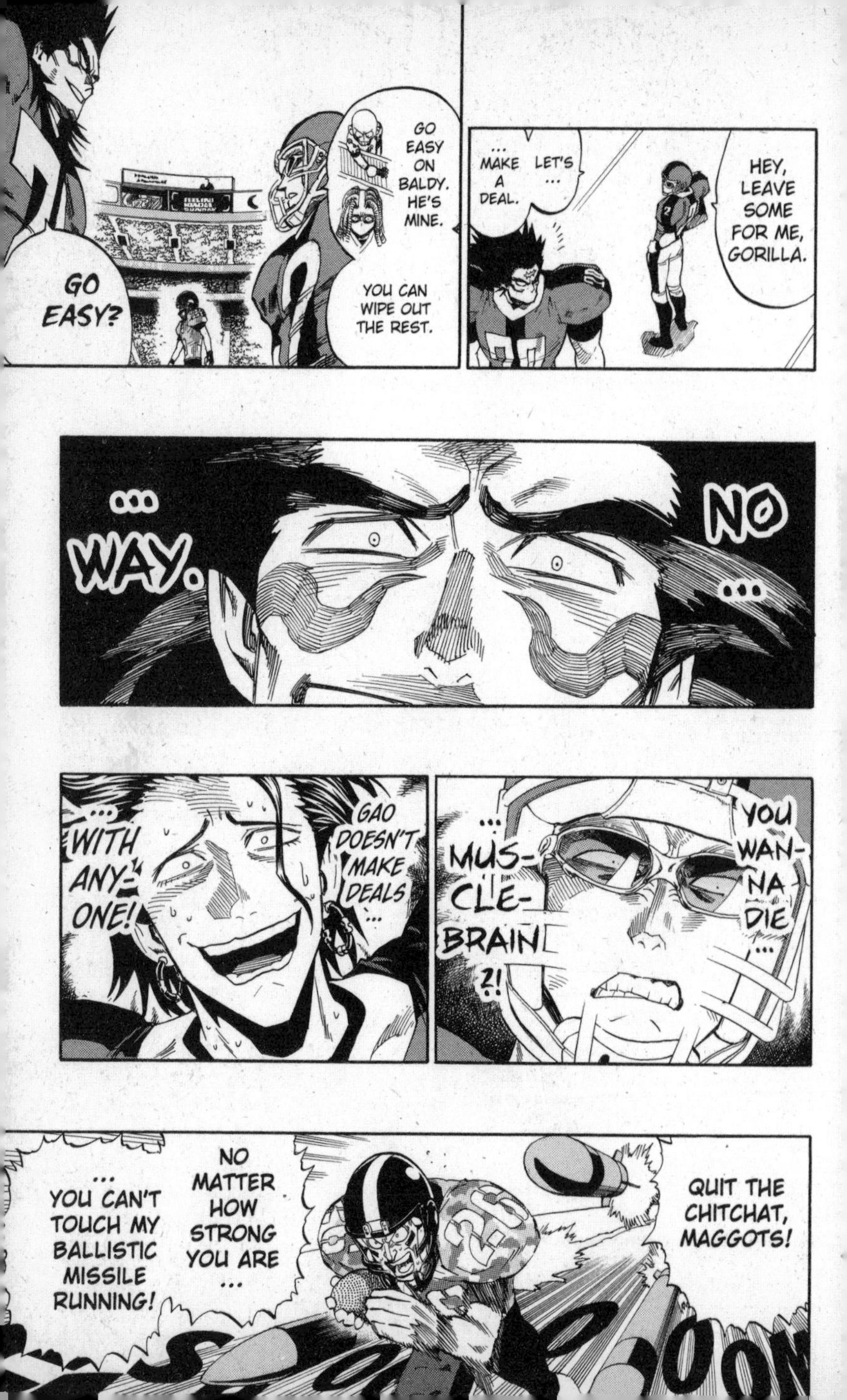
HEY, LEAVE SOME FOR ME, GORILLA.
... LET'S ...
... MAKE A DEAL.
GO EASY ON BALDY. HE'S MINE.
YOU CAN WIPE OUT THE REST.
GO EASY?
NO ...
... WAY.
YOU WAN-NA DIE ...
... MUS-CLE-BRAIN?!
GAO DOESN'T MAKE DEALS ...
... WITH ANY-ONE!
QUIT THE CHITCHAT, MAGGOTS!
NO MATTER HOW STRONG YOU ARE ...
... YOU CAN'T TOUCH MY BALLISTIC MISSILE RUNNING!

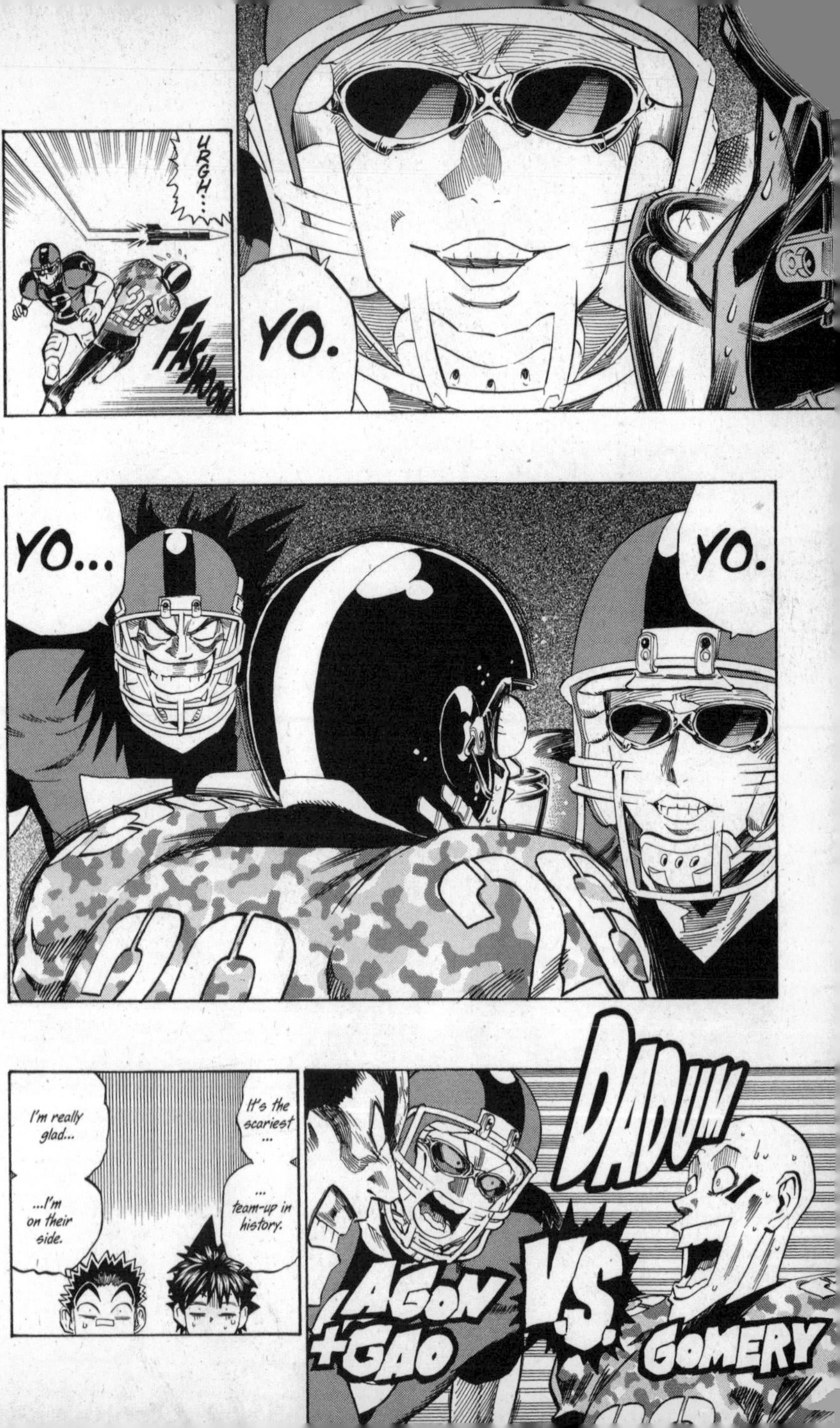
YO.
URGH...
FASHOOM
YO.
YO...
DADUM
AGON
+GAO
VS.
GOMERY
It's the scariest...
...team-up in history.
I'm really glad...
...I'm on their side.

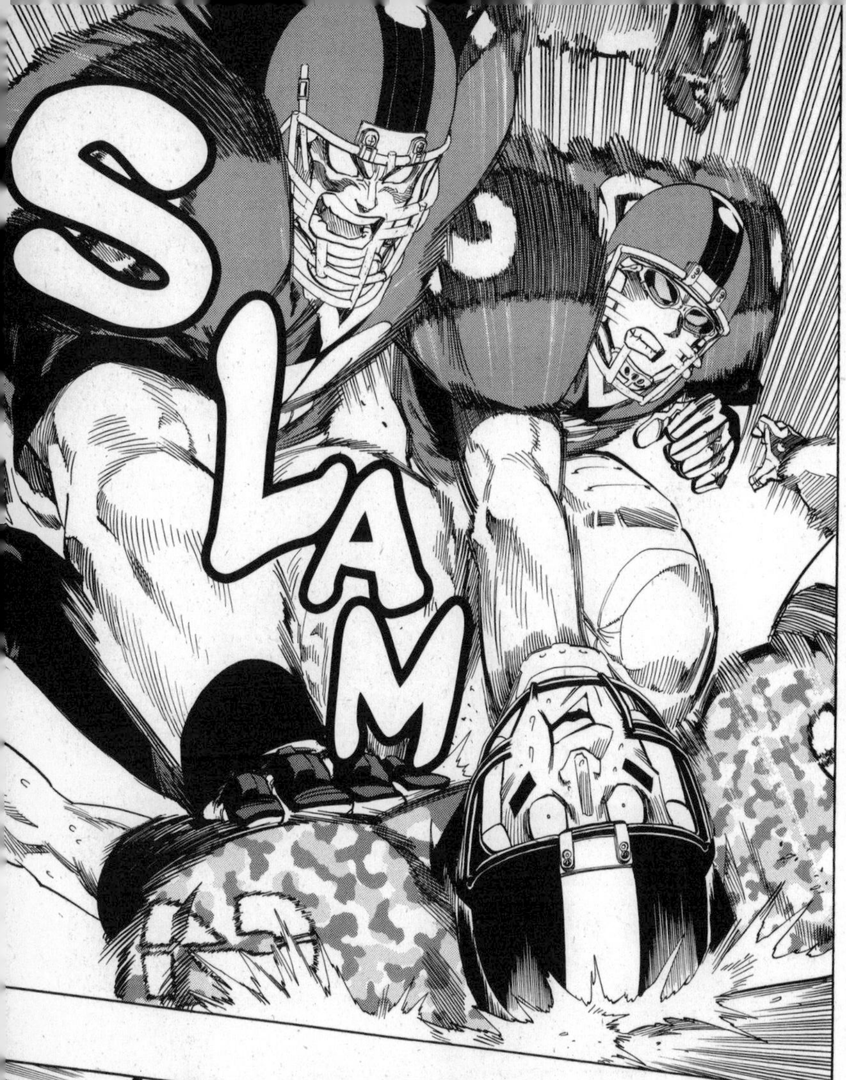
SLAM
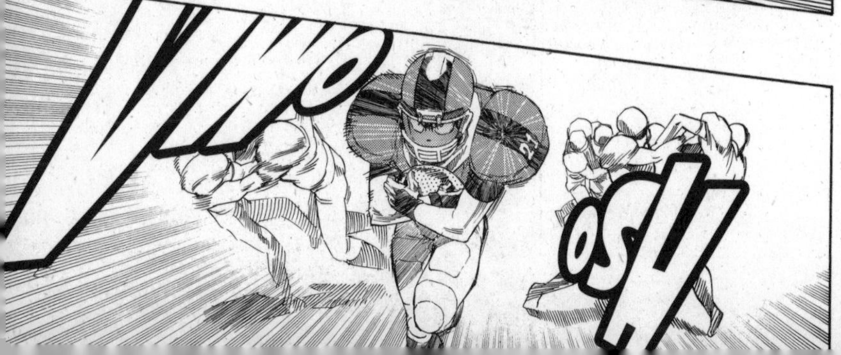
WHOOSH

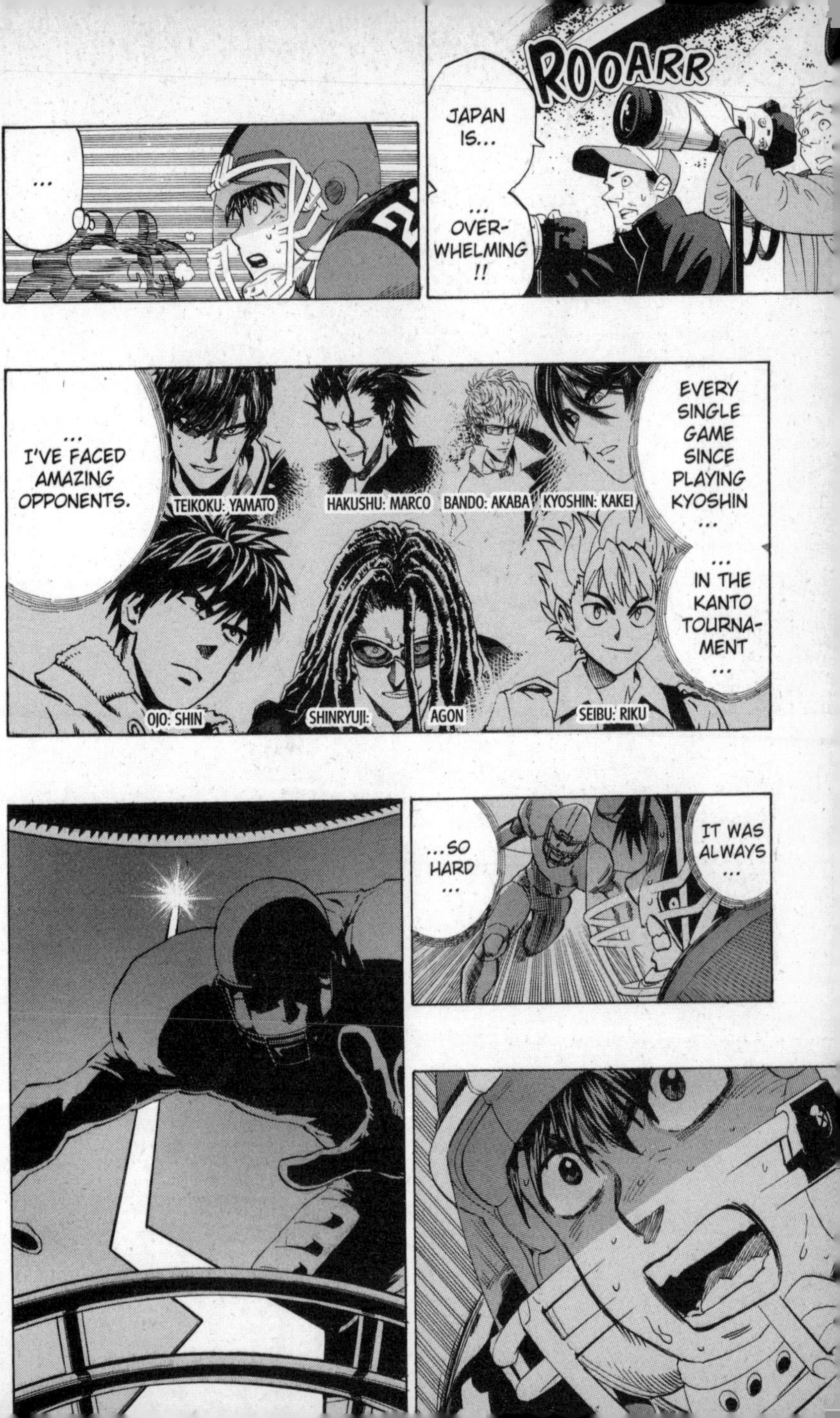
ROOARR
JAPAN IS...
... OVER-WHELMING !!
...
EVERY SINGLE GAME SINCE PLAYING KYOSHIN ...
... IN THE KANTO TOURNAMENT ...
... I'VE FACED AMAZING OPPONENTS.
KYOSHIN: KAKEI
BANDO: AKABA
HAKUSHU: MARCO
TEIKOKU: YAMATO
SEIBU: RIKU
SHINRYUJI: AGON
OJO: SHIN
IT WAS ALWAYS ...
...SO HARD ...

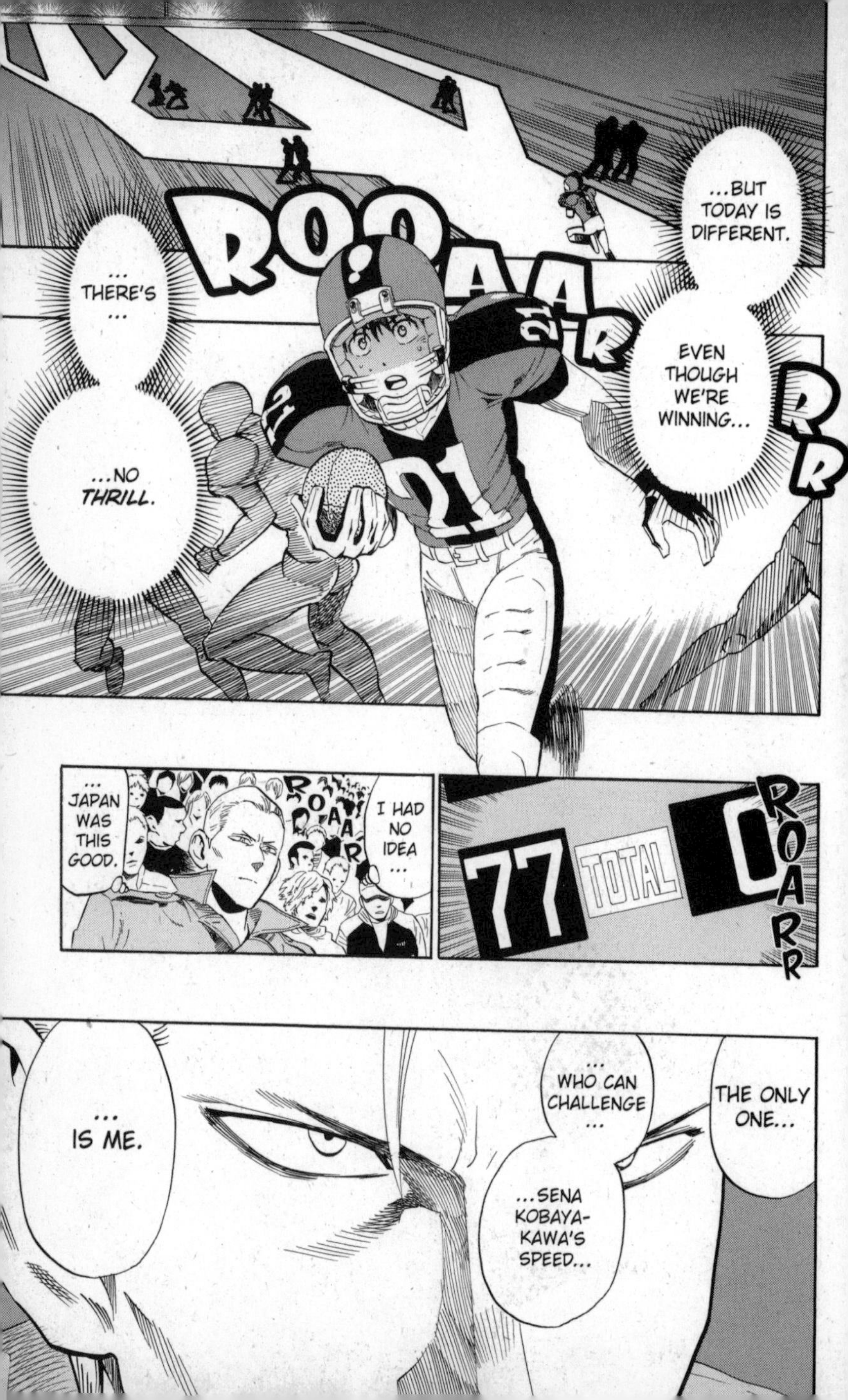
...BUT TODAY IS DIFFERENT.
EVEN THOUGH WE'RE WINNING...
... THERE'S ...
...NO *THRILL*.
ROOAARR
RR
77
TOTAL
0
ROARR
I HAD NO IDEA ...
ROAARR
... JAPAN WAS THIS GOOD.
THE ONLY ONE...
... WHO CAN CHALLENGE ...
...SENA KOBAYA-KAWA'S SPEED...
... IS ME.

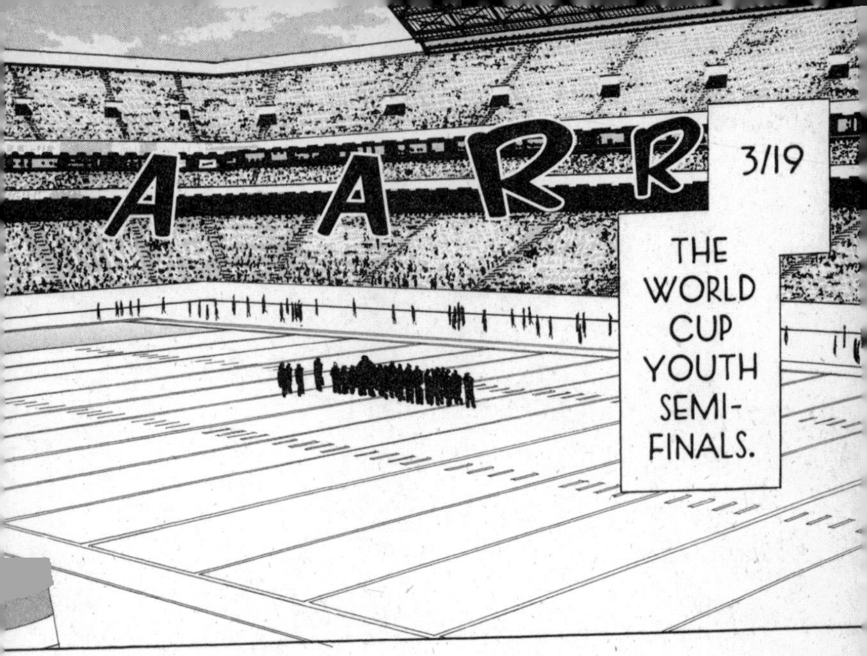
AARR
3/19
THE WORLD CUP YOUTH SEMI-FINALS.

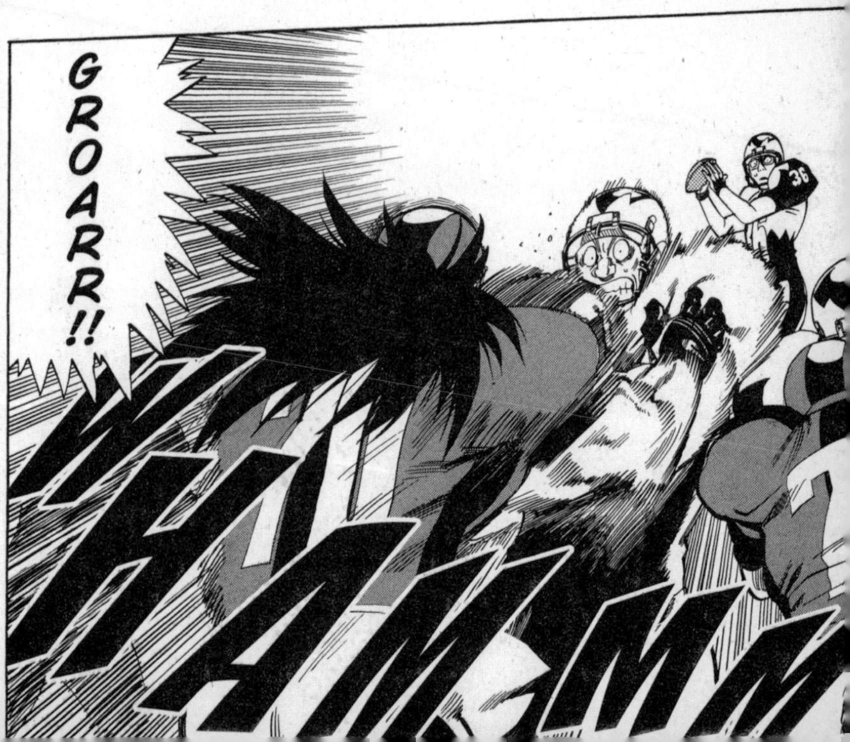
GROARRR!!

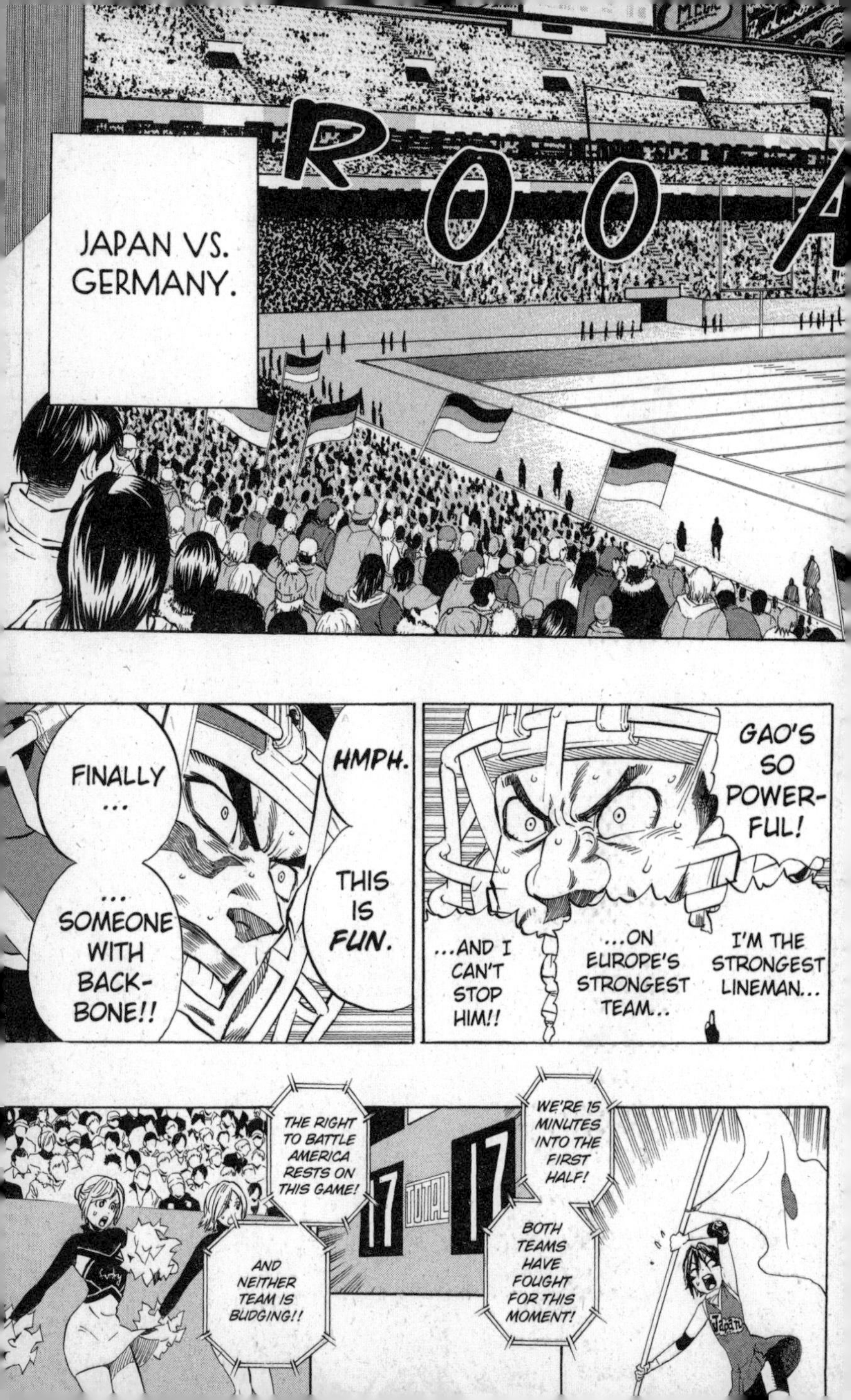
ROOA
JAPAN VS. GERMANY.
GAO'S SO POWERFUL!
I'M THE STRONGEST LINEMAN...
...ON EUROPE'S STRONGEST TEAM...
...AND I CAN'T STOP HIM!!
HMPH.
THIS IS FUN.
FINALLY...
...SOMEONE WITH BACKBONE!!
WE'RE 15 MINUTES INTO THE FIRST HALF!
BOTH TEAMS HAVE FOUGHT FOR THIS MOMENT!
17
TOTAL
17
THE RIGHT TO BATTLE AMERICA RESTS ON THIS GAME!
AND NEITHER TEAM IS BUDGING!!

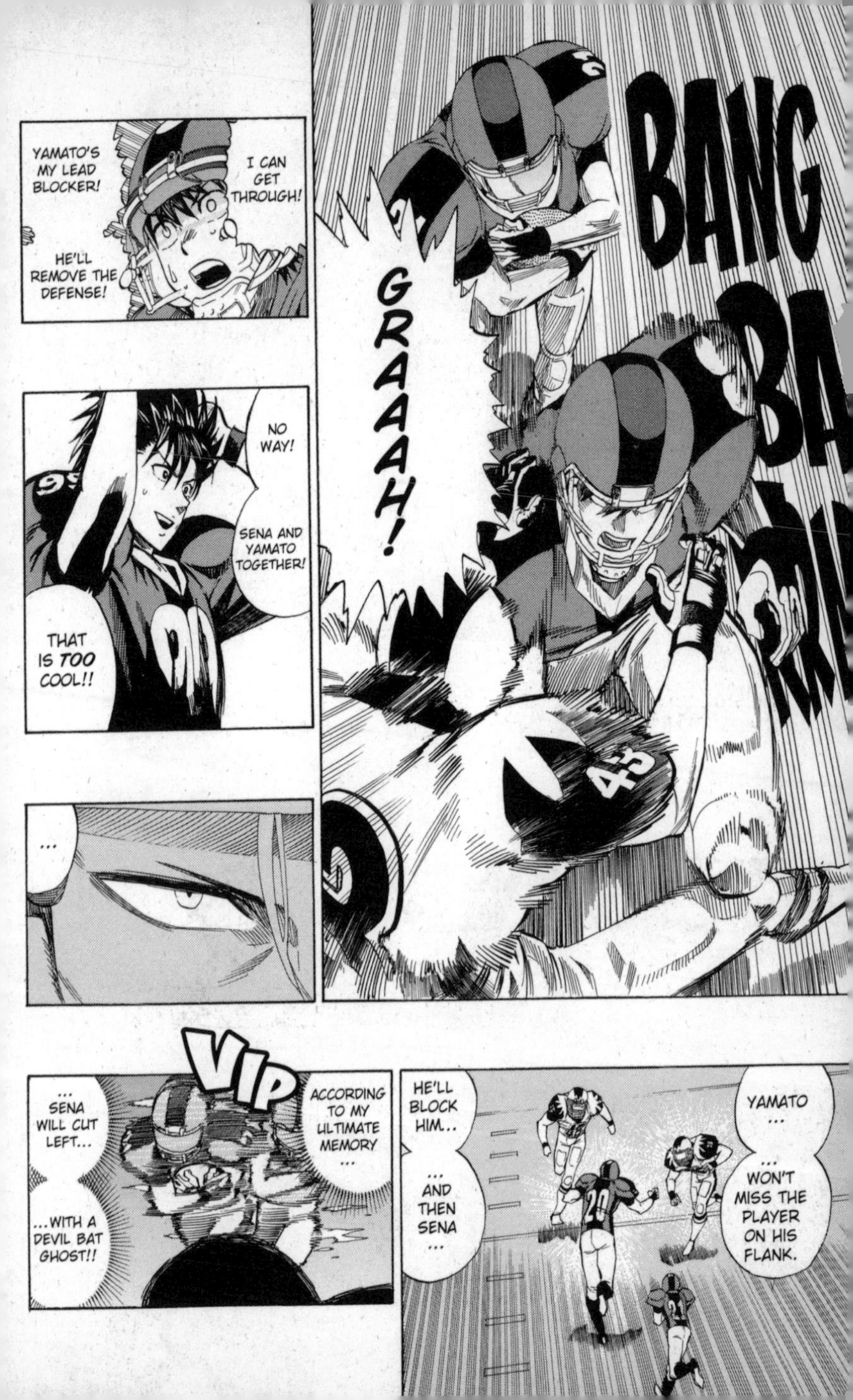
BANG
BA
GRAAAAH!
I CAN GET THROUGH!
YAMATO'S MY LEAD BLOCKER!
HE'LL REMOVE THE DEFENSE!
NO WAY!
SENA AND YAMATO TOGETHER!
THAT IS *TOO* COOL!!
...
YAMATO...
...WON'T MISS THE PLAYER ON HIS FLANK.
HE'LL BLOCK HIM...
...AND THEN SENA...
ACCORDING TO MY ULTIMATE MEMORY...
VIP
...SENA WILL CUT LEFT...
...WITH A DEVIL BAT GHOST!!

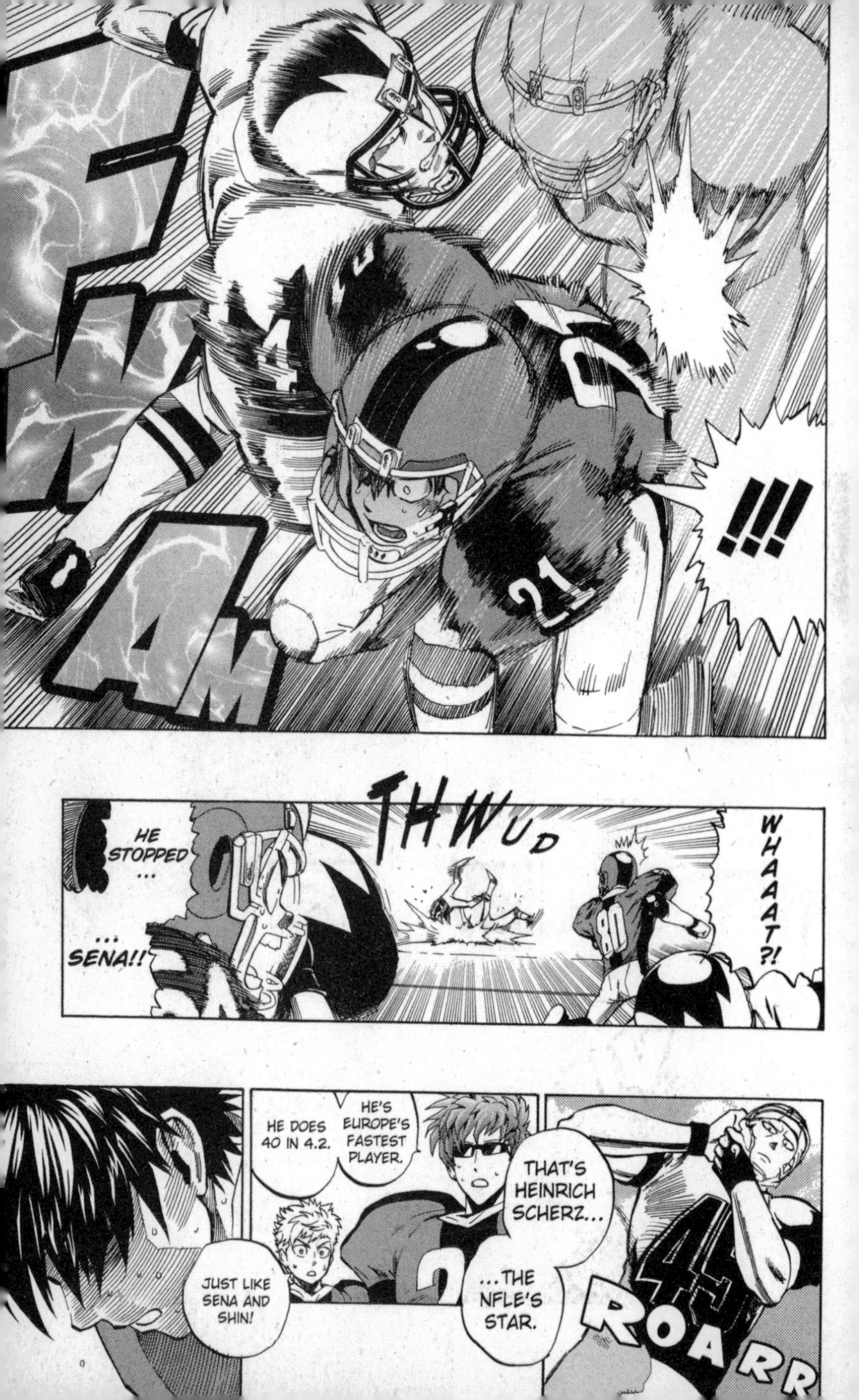
!!!
WHAAAAT?!
THWUD
HE STOPPED...
...SENA!!
ROARR
THAT'S HEINRICH SCHERZ...
HE'S EUROPE'S FASTEST PLAYER.
HE DOES 40 IN 4.2.
...THE NFLE'S STAR.
JUST LIKE SENA AND SHIN!

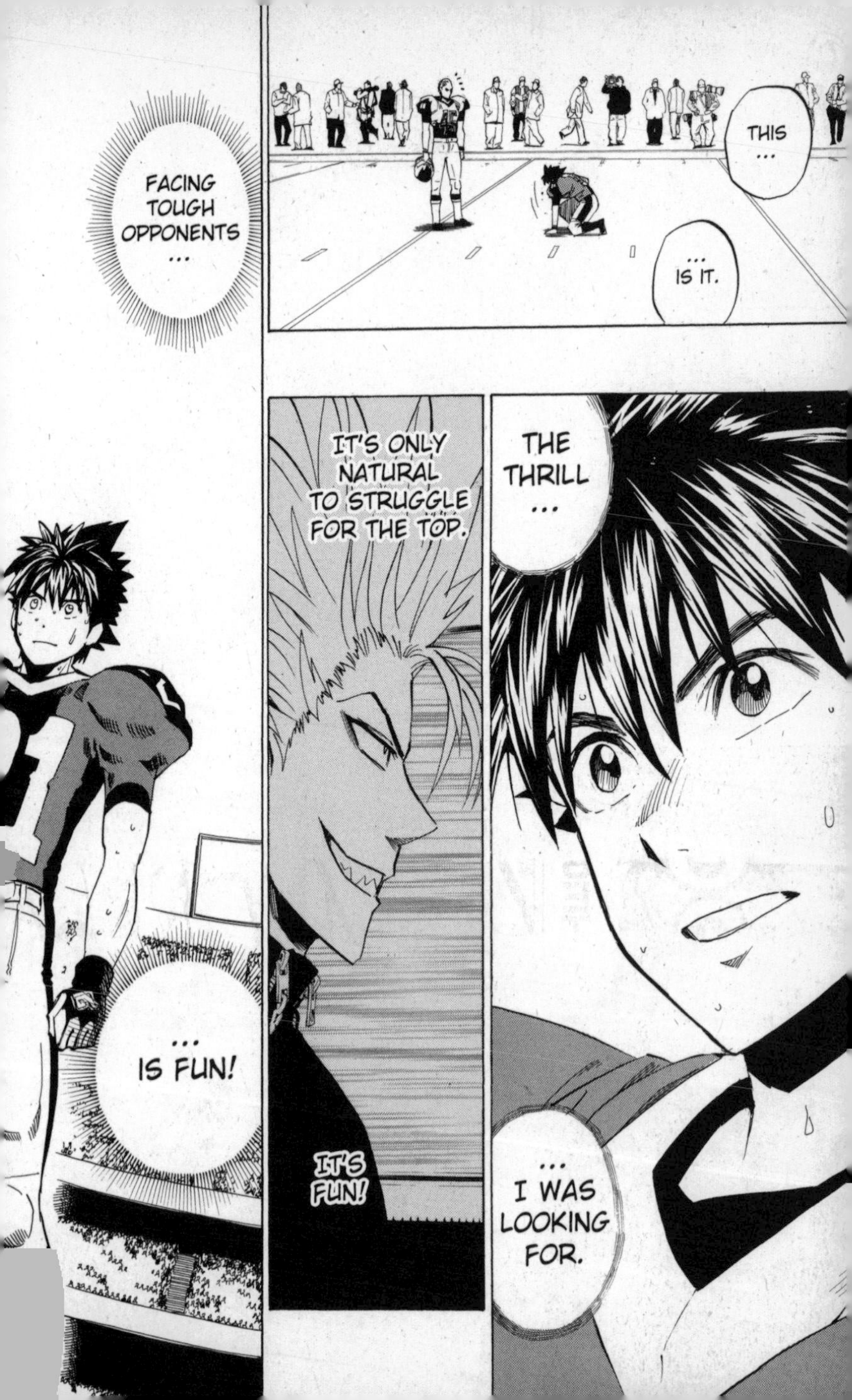
THIS ...
... IS IT.
THE THRILL ...
... I WAS LOOKING FOR.
IT'S ONLY NATURAL TO STRUGGLE FOR THE TOP.
IT'S FUN!
FACING TOUGH OPPONENTS ...
... IS FUN!

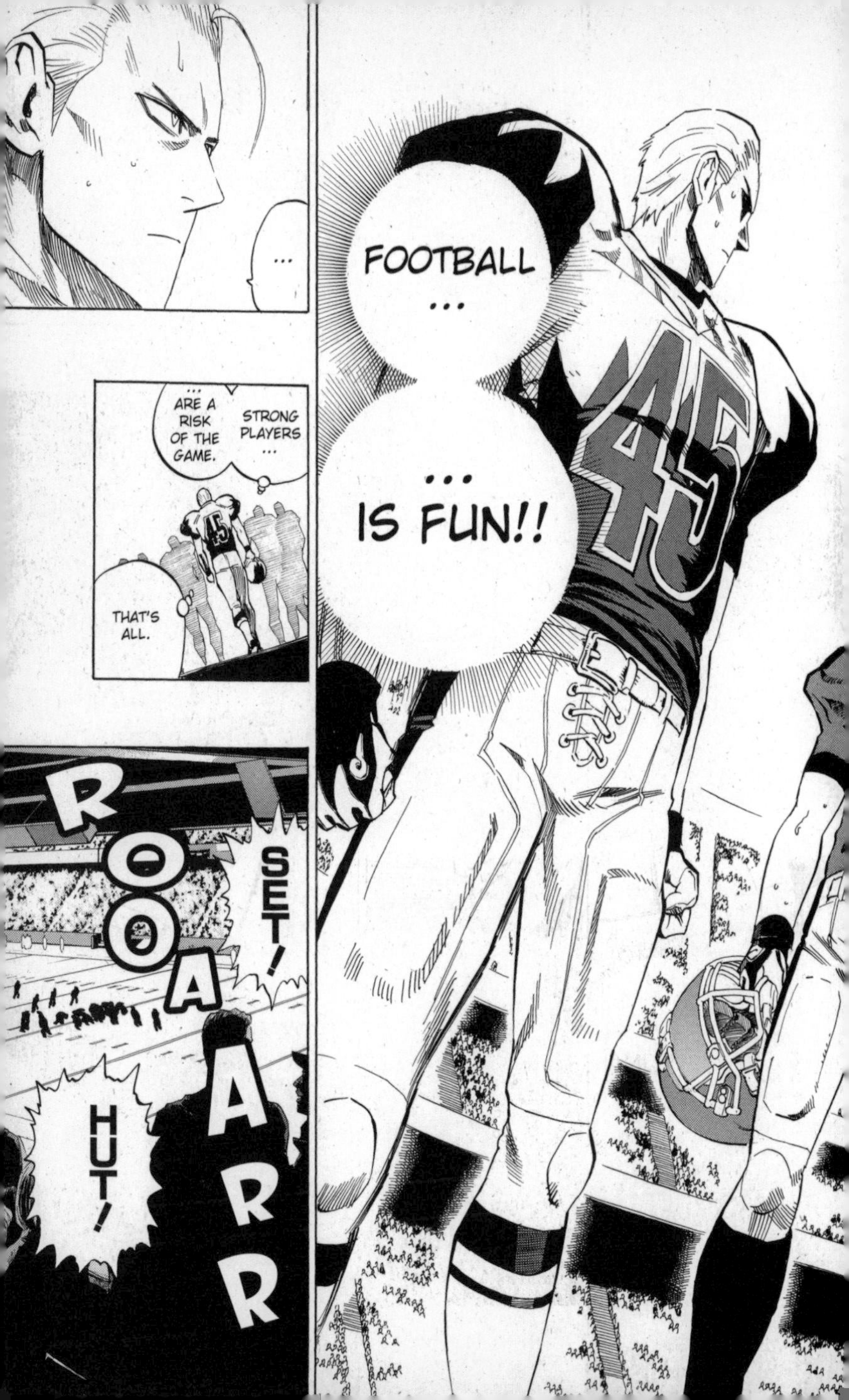
FOOTBALL ...
... IS FUN!!
...
STRONG PLAYERS ...
... ARE A RISK OF THE GAME.
THAT'S ALL.
ROOOAARR
SET!
HUT!

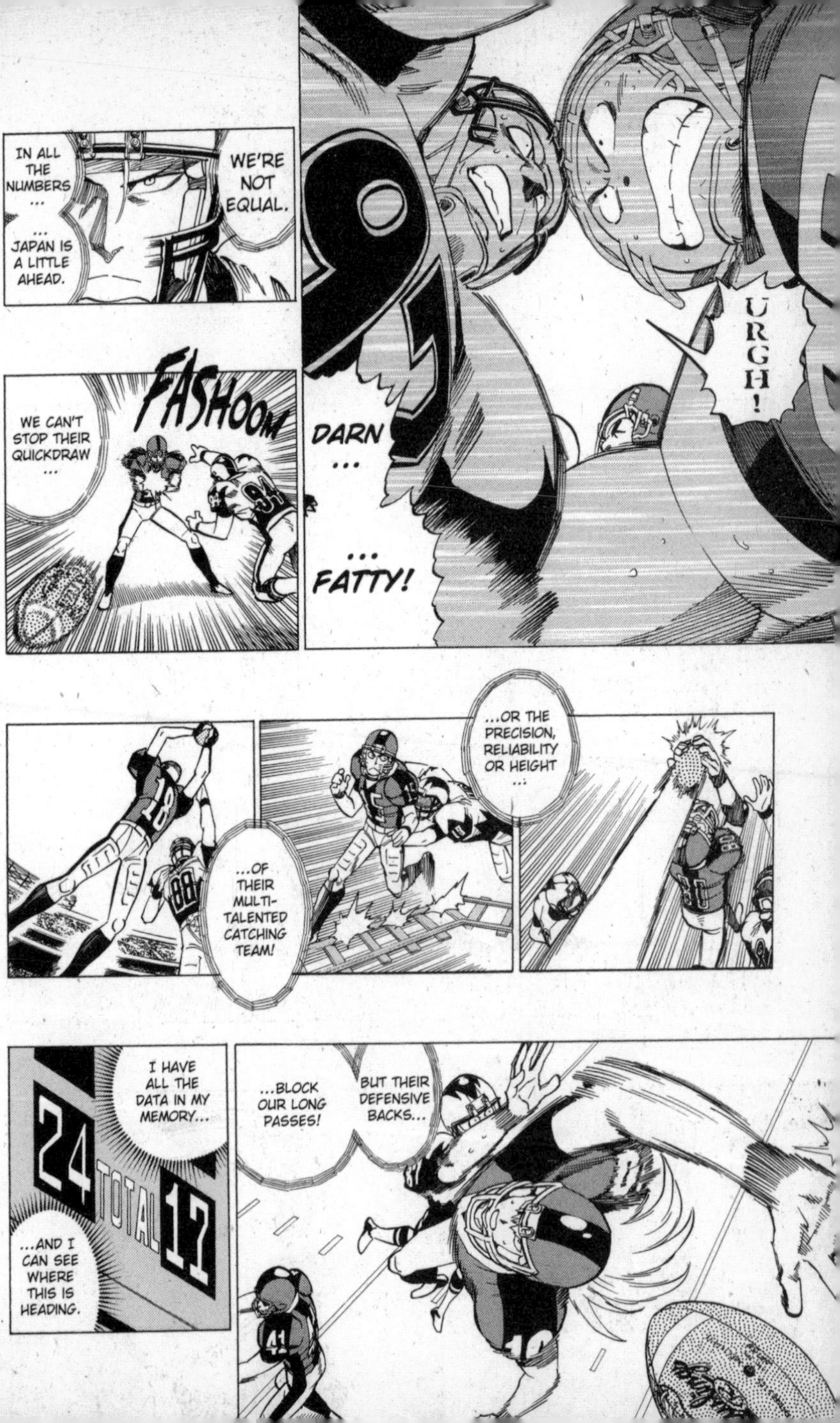
URGH!
DARN ... ... FATTY!
WE'RE NOT EQUAL.
IN ALL THE NUMBERS ... ... JAPAN IS A LITTLE AHEAD.
FASHOOM
WE CAN'T STOP THEIR QUICKDRAW ...
...OR THE PRECISION, RELIABILITY OR HEIGHT ...
...OF THEIR MULTI-TALENTED CATCHING TEAM!
BUT THEIR DEFENSIVE BACKS...
...BLOCK OUR LONG PASSES!
I HAVE ALL THE DATA IN MY MEMORY...
24 TOTAL 17
...AND I CAN SEE WHERE THIS IS HEADING.

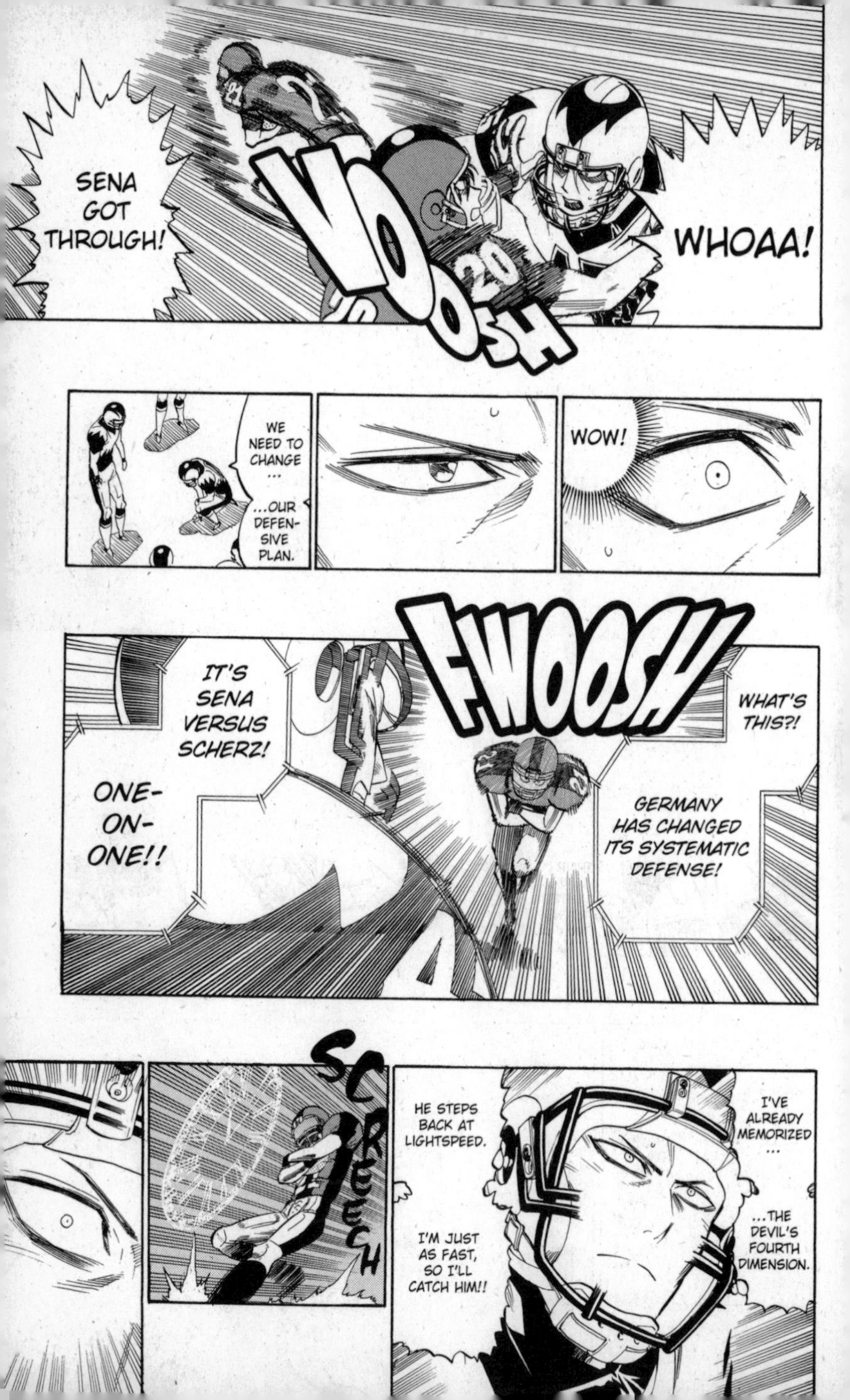
WHOAA!
VOOOSH
SENA GOT THROUGH!
WOW!
WE NEED TO CHANGE...
...OUR DEFEN-SIVE PLAN.
FWOOSH
WHAT'S THIS?!
GERMANY HAS CHANGED ITS SYSTEMATIC DEFENSE!
IT'S SENA VERSUS SCHERZ!
ONE-ON-ONE!!
I'VE ALREADY MEMORIZED...
...THE DEVIL'S FOURTH DIMENSION.
HE STEPS BACK AT LIGHTSPEED.
I'M JUST AS FAST, SO I'LL CATCH HIM!!
SCREECH

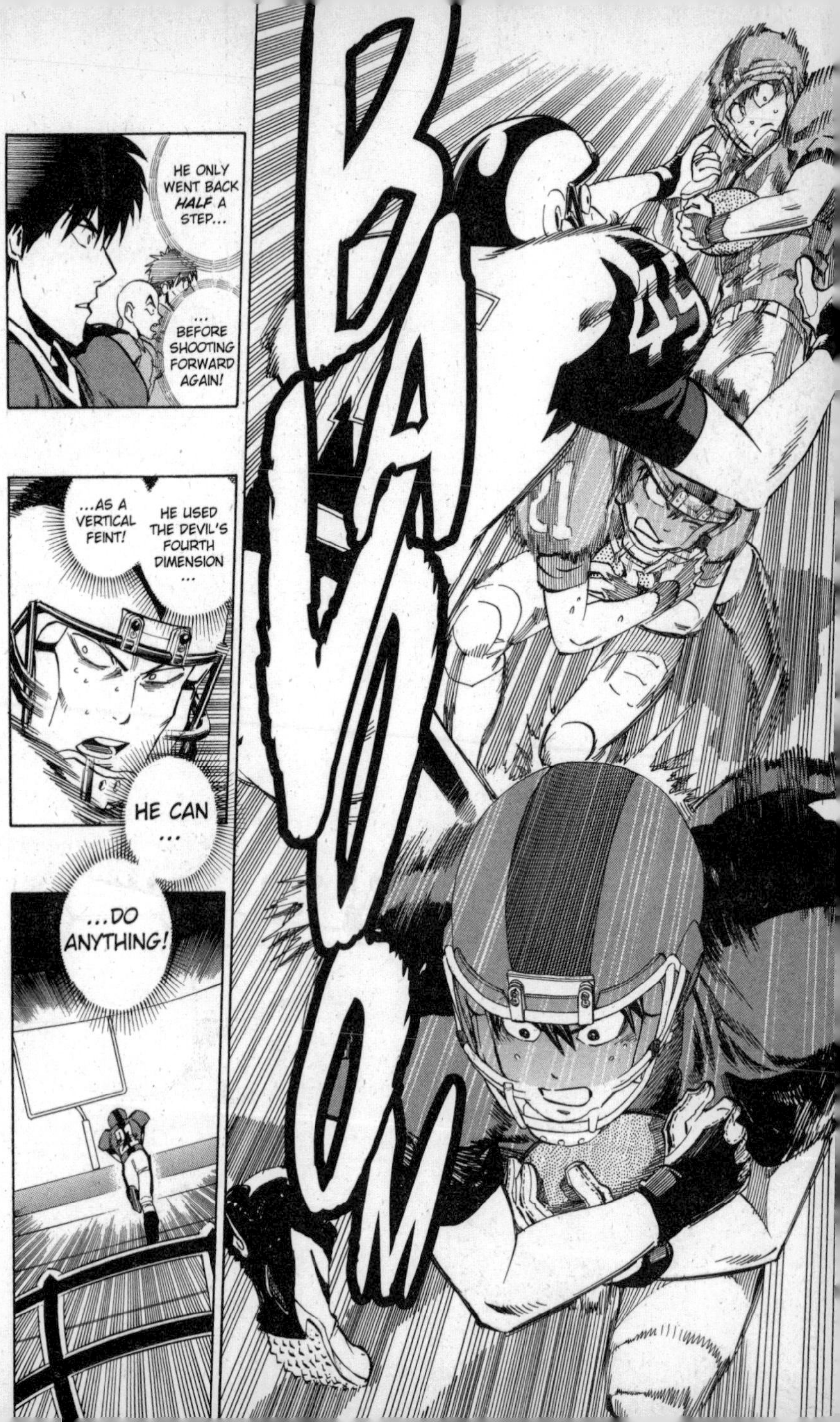
HE ONLY WENT BACK HALF A STEP...
...BEFORE SHOOTING FORWARD AGAIN!
HE USED THE DEVIL'S FOURTH DIMENSION...
...AS A VERTICAL FEINT!
HE CAN...
...DO ANYTHING!

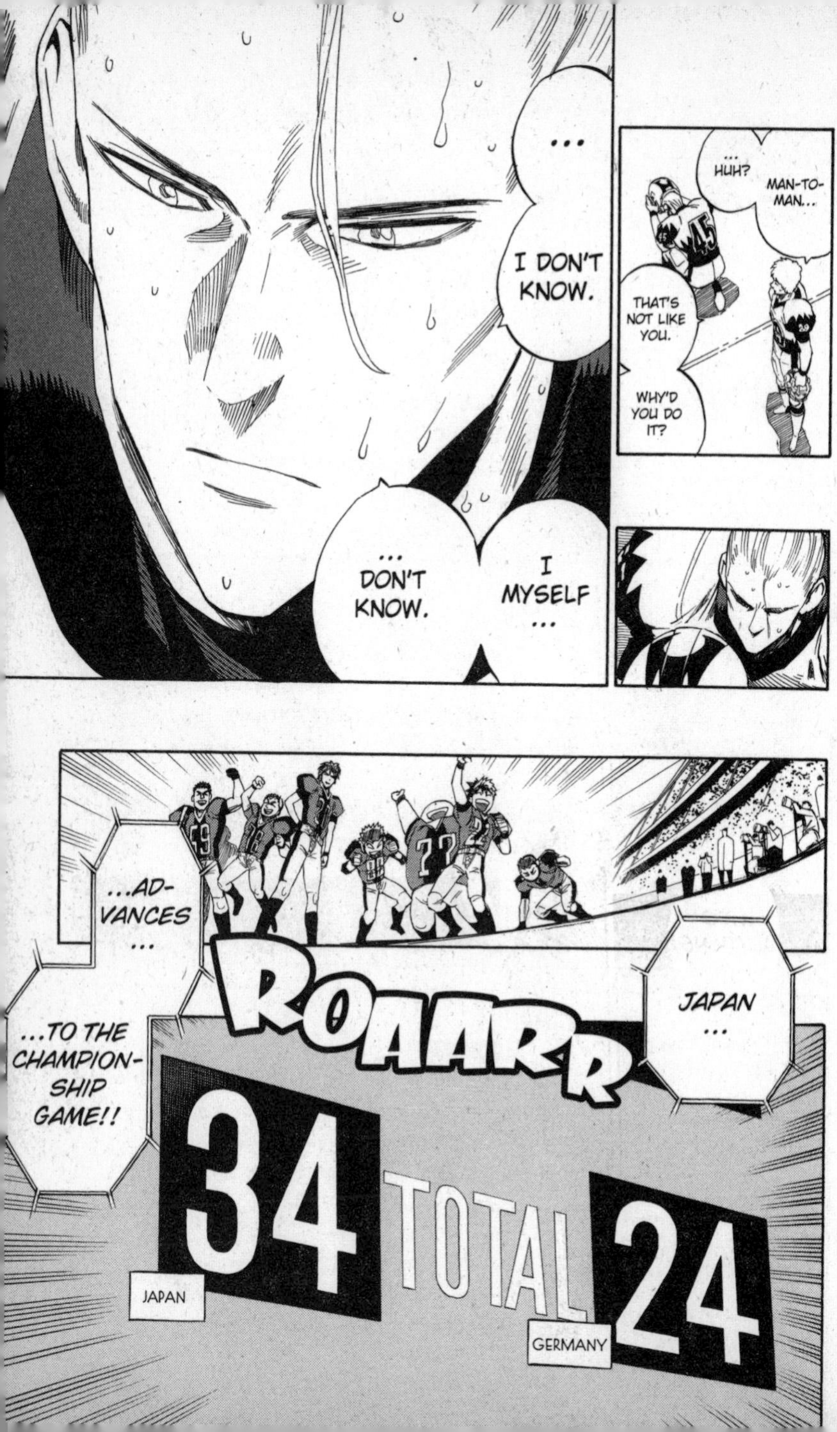
... HUH?
MAN-TO-MAN...
THAT'S NOT LIKE YOU.
WHY'D YOU DO IT?
...
I DON'T KNOW.
I MYSELF ...
... DON'T KNOW.
JAPAN ...
...AD-VANCES ...
...TO THE CHAMPION-SHIP GAME!!
ROAAARR
34
TOTAL
24
JAPAN
GERMANY

Who hardly showed up at all!

Biographies of the World Cup Minor Athletes

Häkkinen

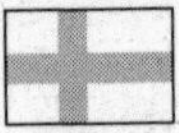

Finland

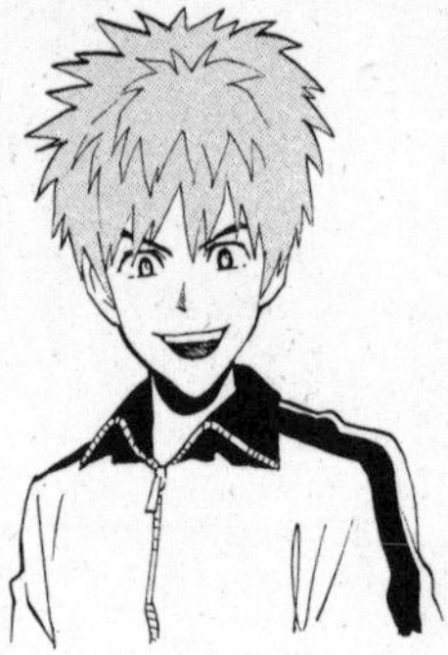

In order to keep his teeth so bright, he has to brush them ***15 times a day***.

Militaria busted all his teeth, but those strong, overpolished chompers were just his ***baby teeth***, so they'll grow back in no time!

Parns

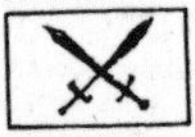

Militaria

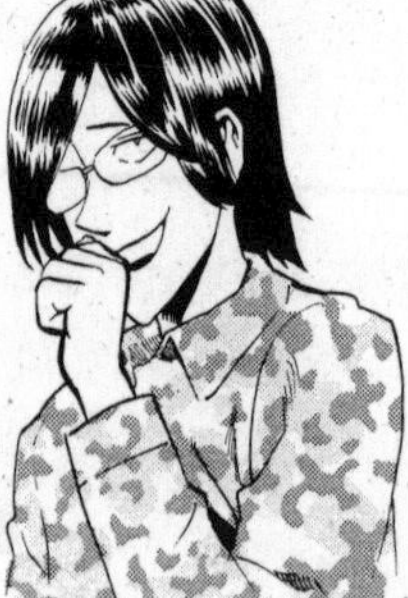

He's hard on others, but soft on himself. He's a specialist at ***making excuses for himself***! He's got over 100 set phrases, such as,

"Huh? I'm not putting forth my full effort..."

"My foot hurts today..."

and

"The ref sucks!"

Gile

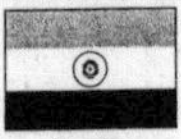

India

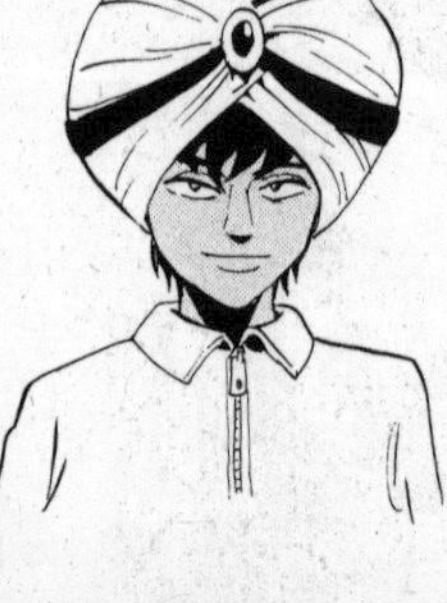

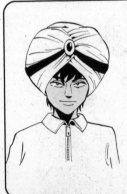

India's energetic captain who thought the World Cup would be a great chance to satisfy everyone's expectations about his country's capabilites.

He wore a ***turban*** for no reason, made all sorts ***of contorted yoga-ish poses***, and suddenly started ***eating curry*** at random times.

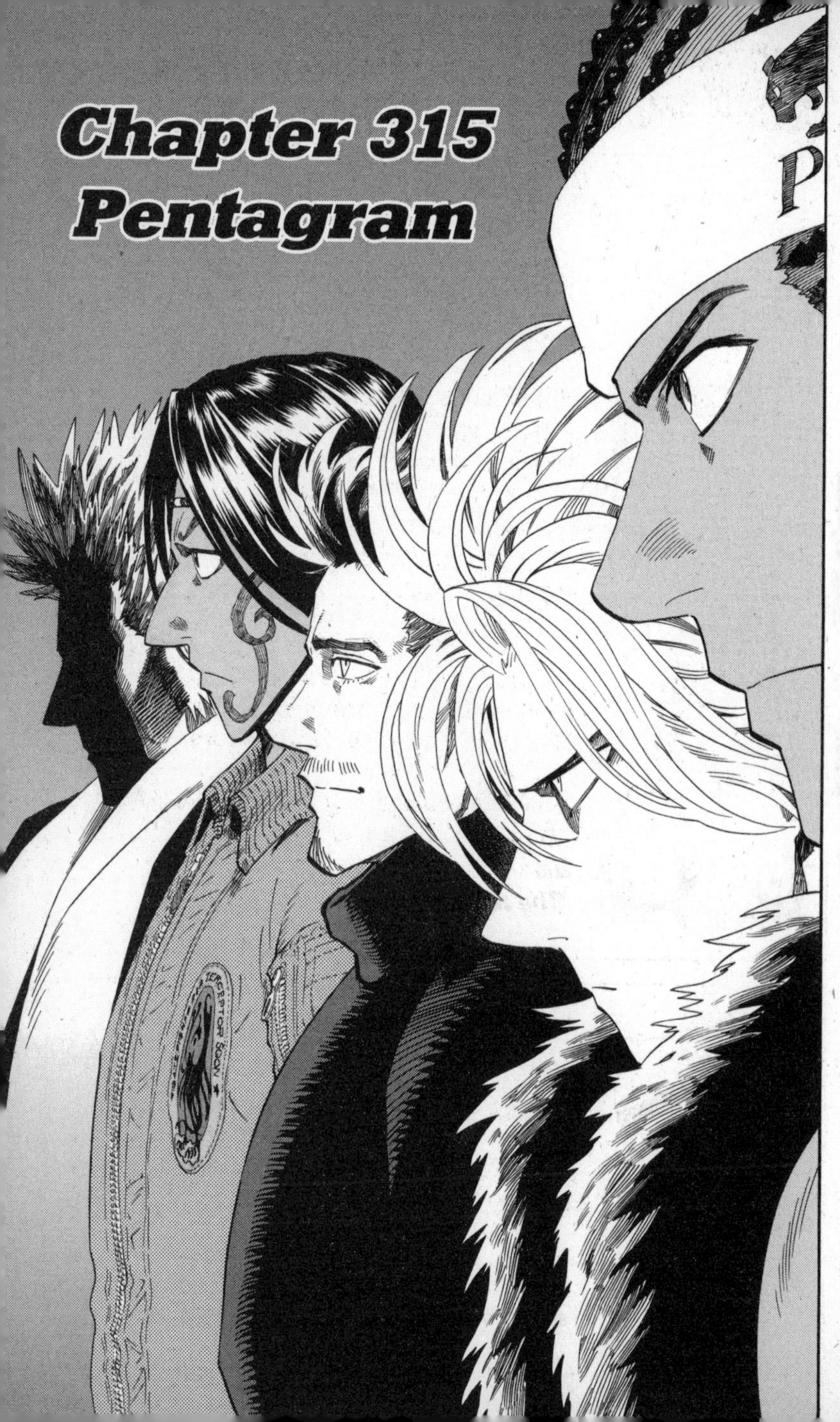
Chapter 315
Pentagram

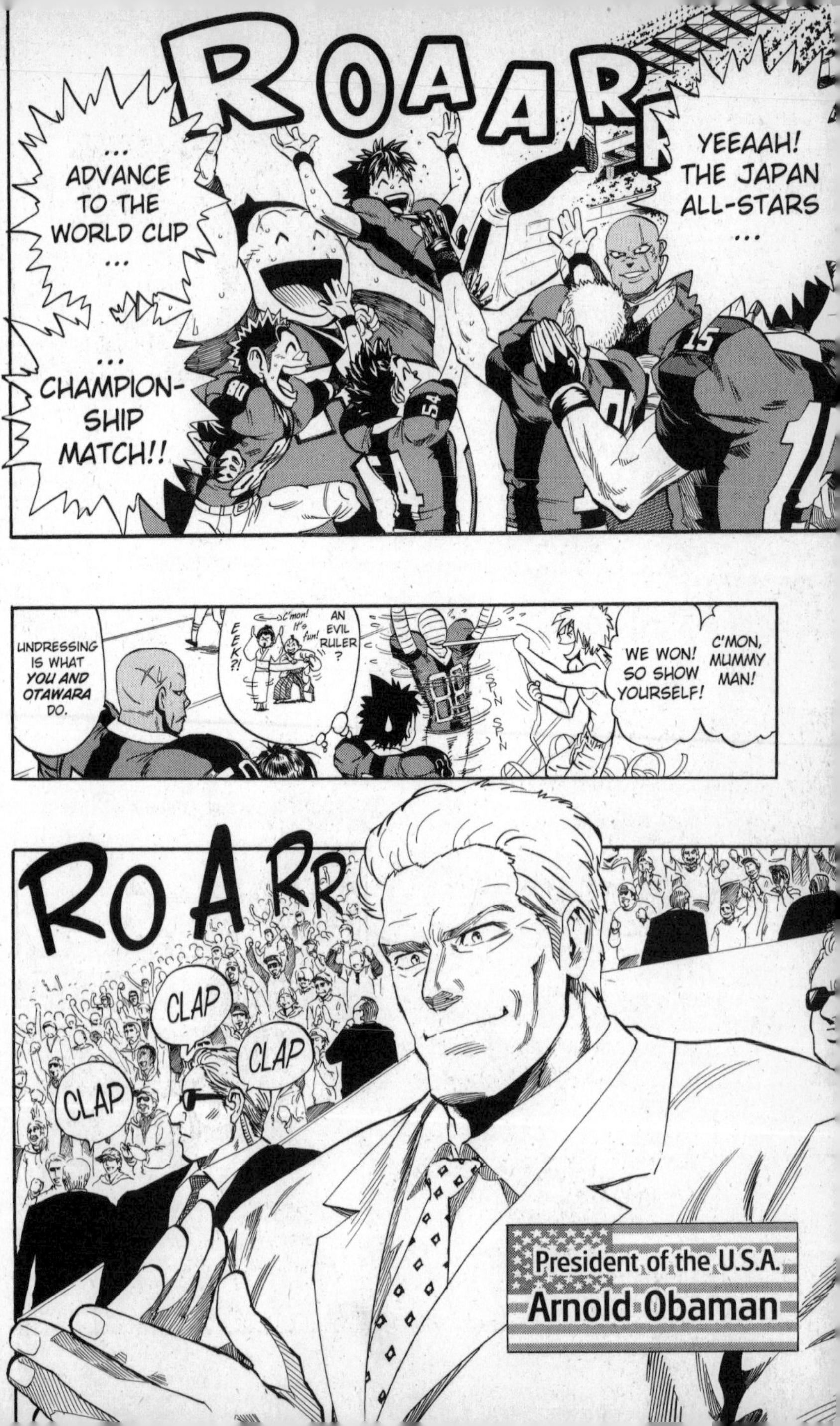
ROAARR
YEEAAH! THE JAPAN ALL-STARS ...
... ADVANCE TO THE WORLD CUP ...
... CHAMPION-SHIP MATCH!!
C'MON, MUMMY MAN!
WE WON! SO SHOW YOURSELF!
SPIN SPIN
AN EVIL RULER ?
C'mon! It's fun!
EEK?!
UNDRESSING IS WHAT *YOU AND OTAWARA* DO.
ROARR
CLAP
CLAP
CLAP
President of the U.S.A.
Arnold Obaman

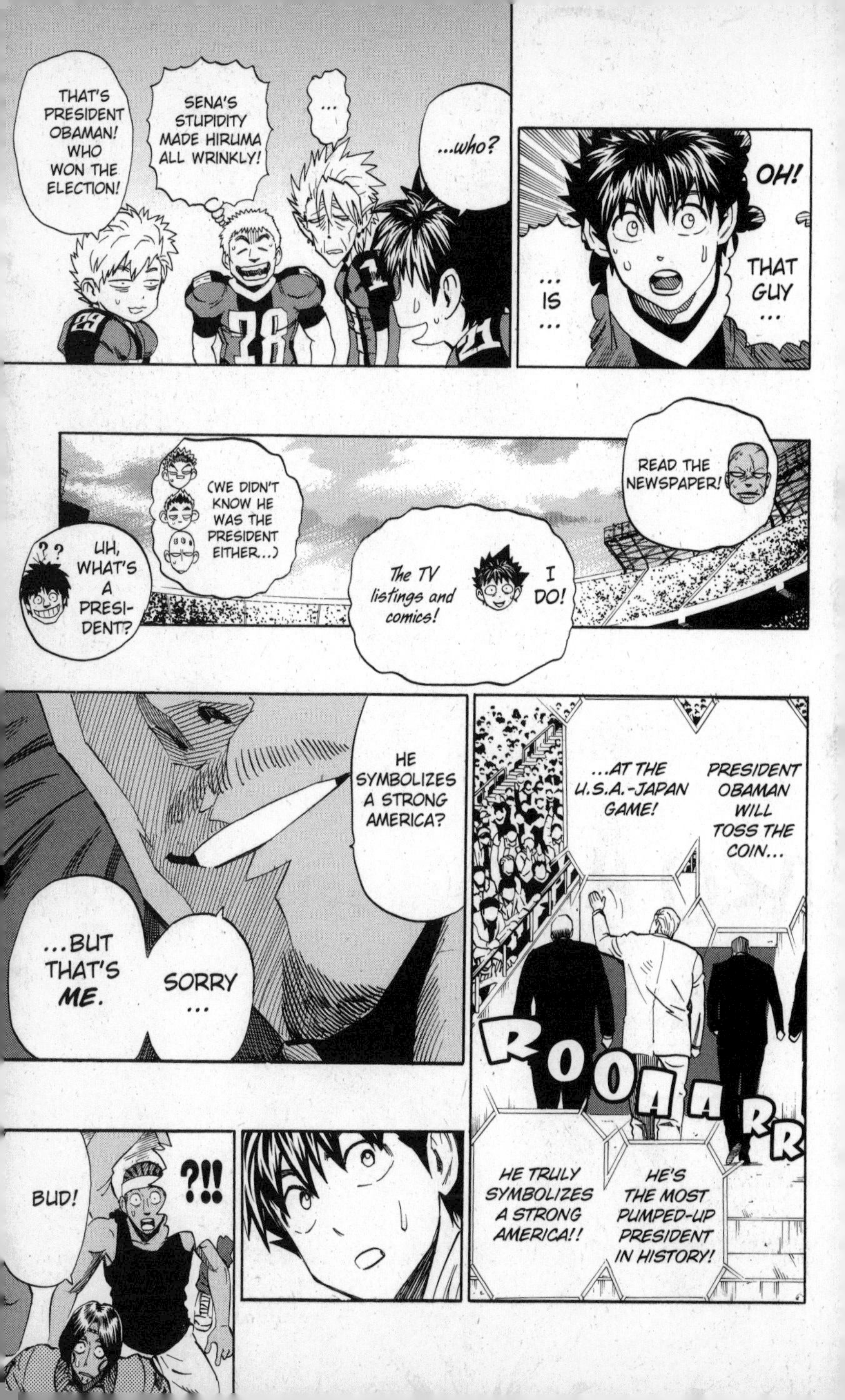
OH!
THAT GUY...
...IS...
...who?
...
SENA'S STUPIDITY MADE HIRUMA ALL WRINKLY!
THAT'S PRESIDENT OBAMAN! WHO WON THE ELECTION!
READ THE NEWSPAPER!
I DO!
The TV listings and comics!
(WE DIDN'T KNOW HE WAS THE PRESIDENT EITHER...)
??
UH, WHAT'S A PRESIDENT?
PRESIDENT OBAMAN WILL TOSS THE COIN...
...AT THE U.S.A.-JAPAN GAME!
ROOAARR
HE'S THE MOST PUMPED-UP PRESIDENT IN HISTORY!
HE TRULY SYMBOLIZES A STRONG AMERICA!!
HE SYMBOLIZES A STRONG AMERICA?
SORRY...
...BUT THAT'S *ME.*
?!!
BUD!

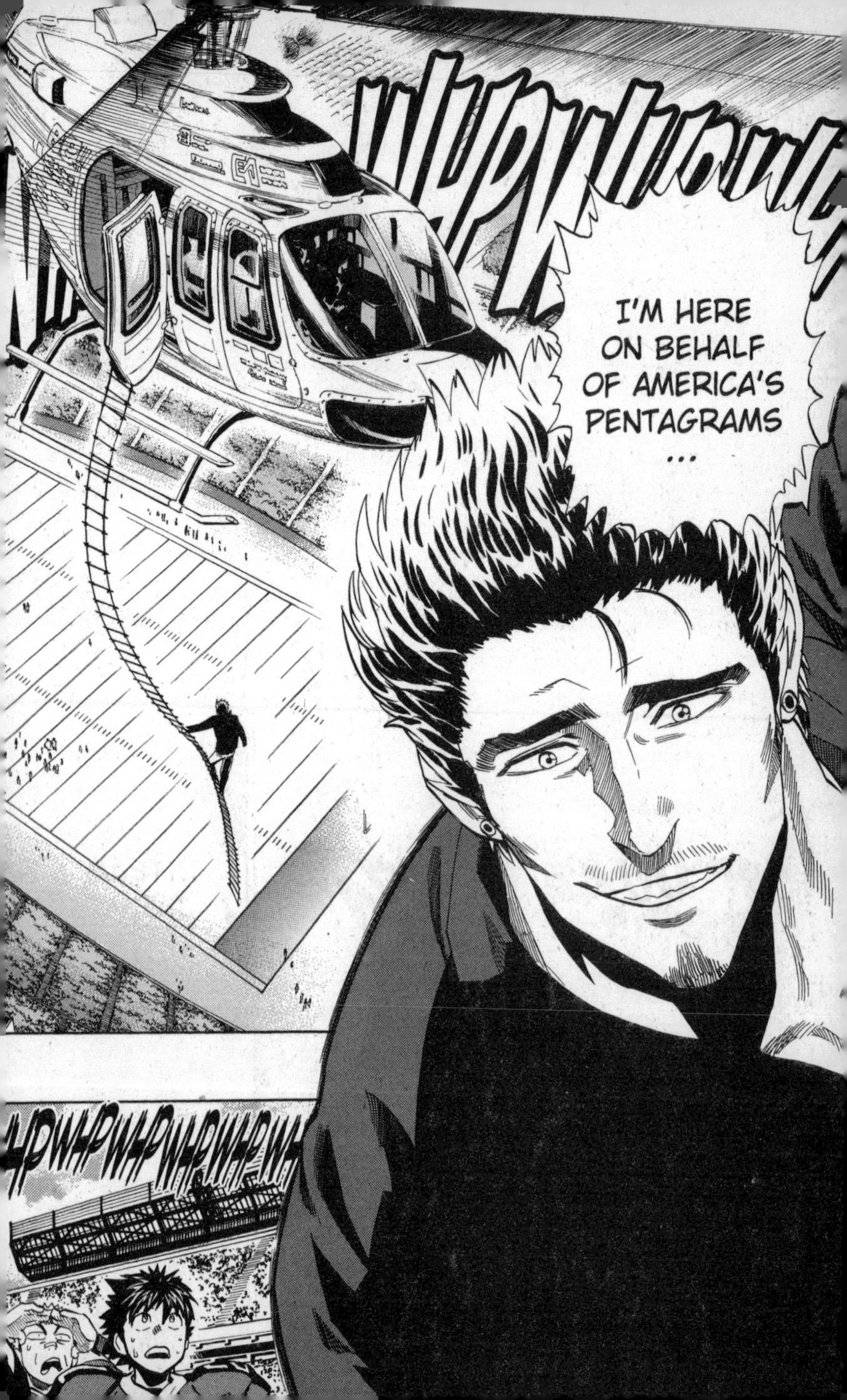
I'M HERE ON BEHALF OF AMERICA'S PENTAGRAMS ...

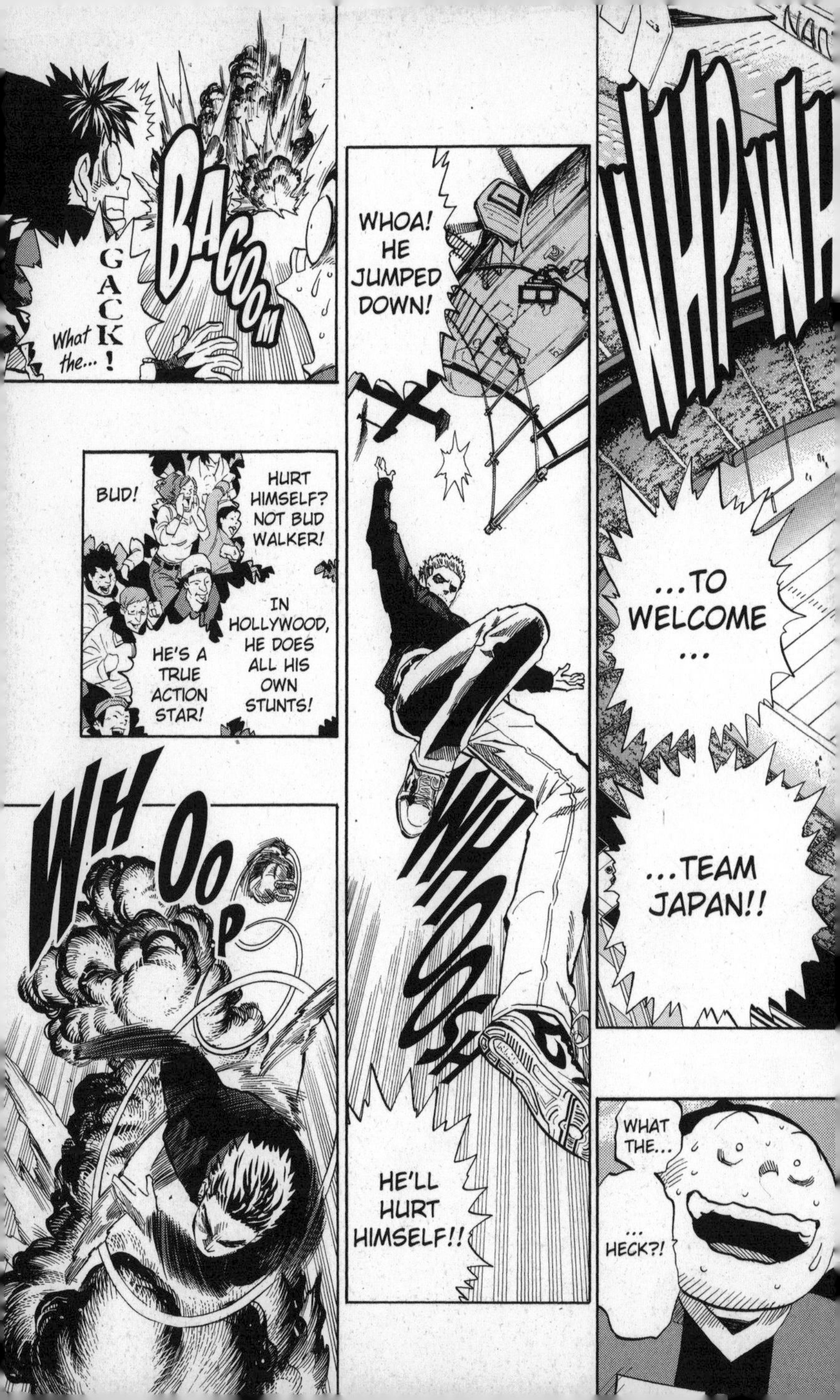
WHAP WHA
...TO WELCOME ...
...TEAM JAPAN!!
WHAT THE...
... HECK?!
WHOA! HE JUMPED DOWN!
WHOOSH
HE'LL HURT HIMSELF!!
BAGOOM
GACK!
What the...
HURT HIMSELF? NOT BUD WALKER!
BUD!
IN HOLLYWOOD, HE DOES ALL HIS OWN STUNTS!
HE'S A TRUE ACTION STAR!
WHOOP

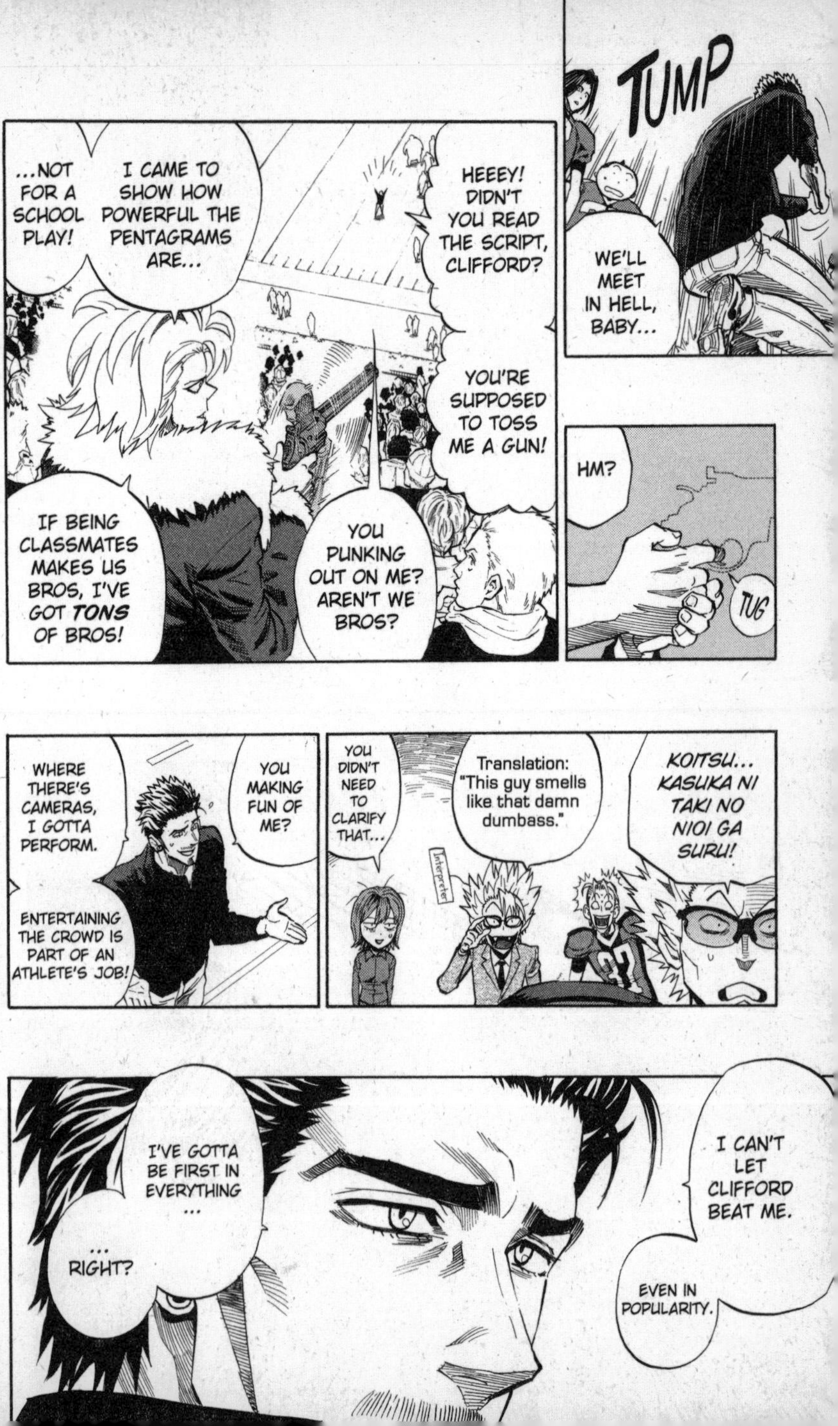
TUMP
WE'LL MEET IN HELL, BABY...
HM?
TUG
HEEEY! DIDN'T YOU READ THE SCRIPT, CLIFFORD?
YOU'RE SUPPOSED TO TOSS ME A GUN!
I CAME TO SHOW HOW POWERFUL THE PENTAGRAMS ARE...
...NOT FOR A SCHOOL PLAY!
YOU PUNKING OUT ON ME? AREN'T WE BROS?
IF BEING CLASSMATES MAKES US BROS, I'VE GOT *TONS* OF BROS!
KOITSU... KASUKA NI TAKI NO NIOI GA SURU!
Translation: "This guy smells like that damn dumbass."
Interpreter
YOU DIDN'T NEED TO CLARIFY THAT...
YOU MAKING FUN OF ME?
WHERE THERE'S CAMERAS, I GOTTA PERFORM.
ENTERTAINING THE CROWD IS PART OF AN ATHLETE'S JOB!
I CAN'T LET CLIFFORD BEAT ME.
EVEN IN POPULARITY.
I'VE GOTTA BE FIRST IN EVERYTHING...
...RIGHT?

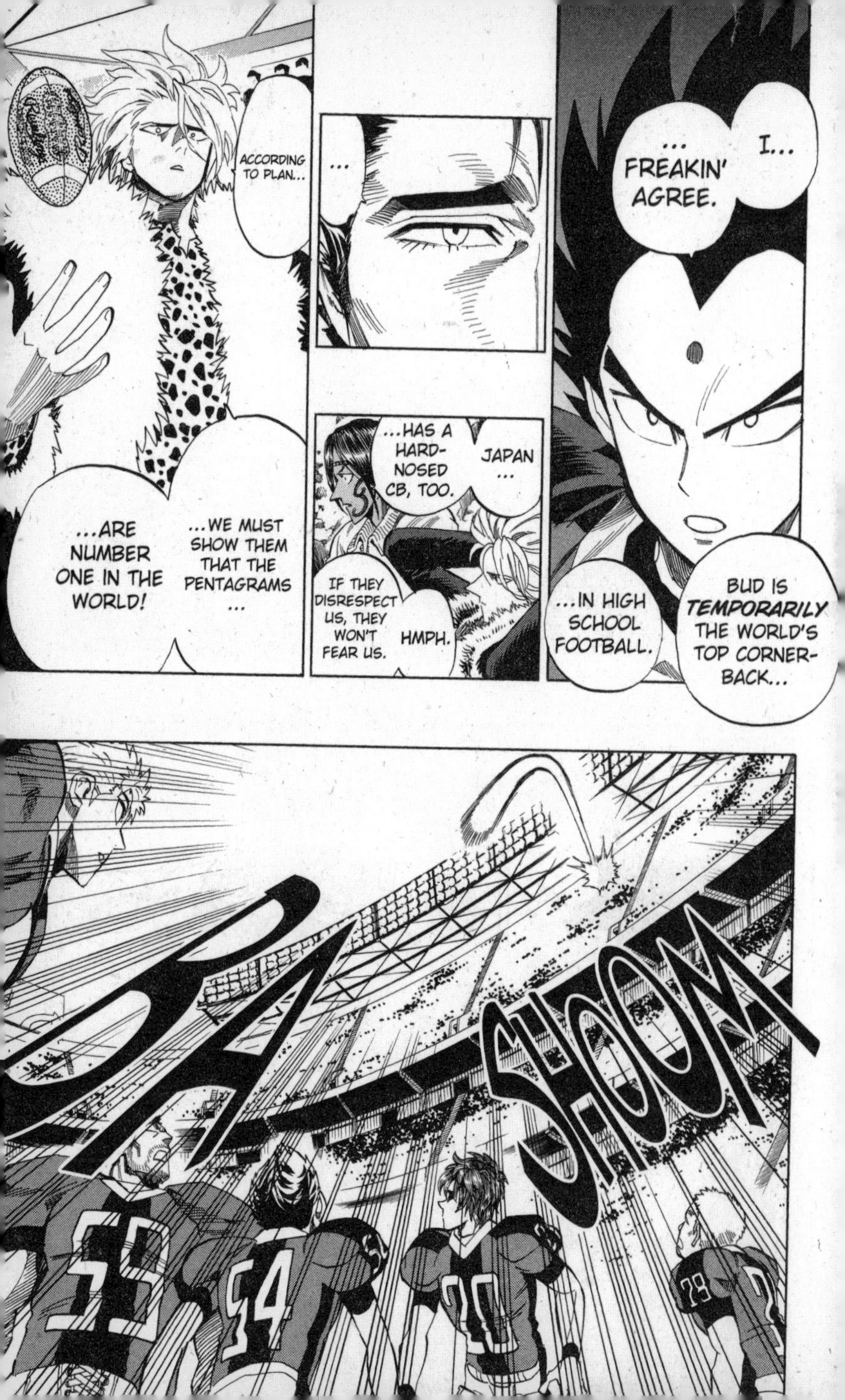
I...
...FREAKIN' AGREE.
BUD IS *TEMPORARILY* THE WORLD'S TOP CORNER-BACK...
...IN HIGH SCHOOL FOOTBALL.
...
JAPAN...
...HAS A HARD-NOSED CB, TOO.
HMPH.
IF THEY DISRESPECT US, THEY WON'T FEAR US.
ACCORDING TO PLAN...
...WE MUST SHOW THEM THAT THE PENTAGRAMS...
...ARE NUMBER ONE IN THE WORLD!
SHOOM

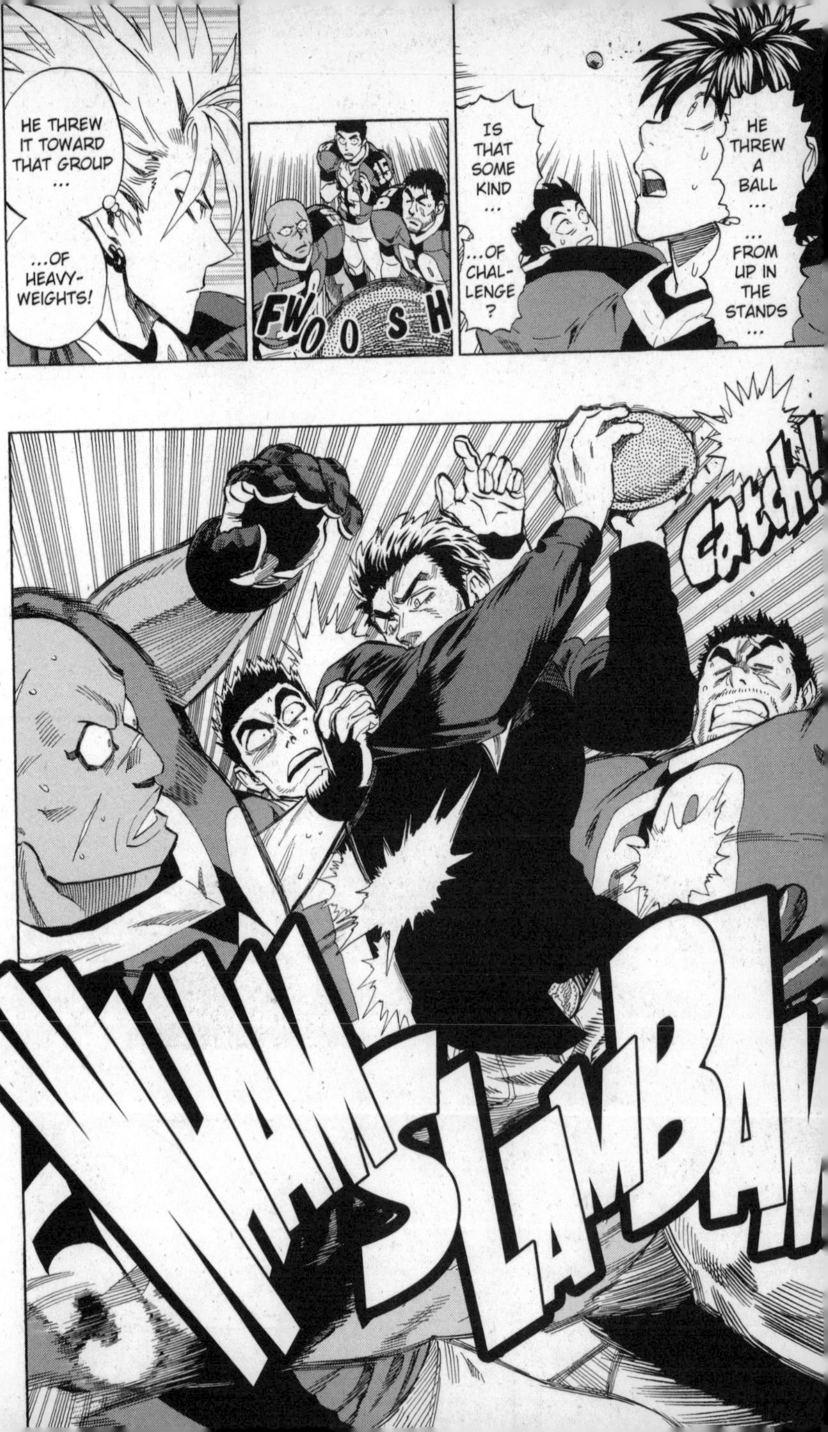
HE THREW A BALL ...
... FROM UP IN THE STANDS ...
IS THAT SOME KIND ...
...OF CHALLENGE?
FWOOSH
HE THREW IT TOWARD THAT GROUP ...
...OF HEAVYWEIGHTS!
Catch!
WHAM
SLAMBAM

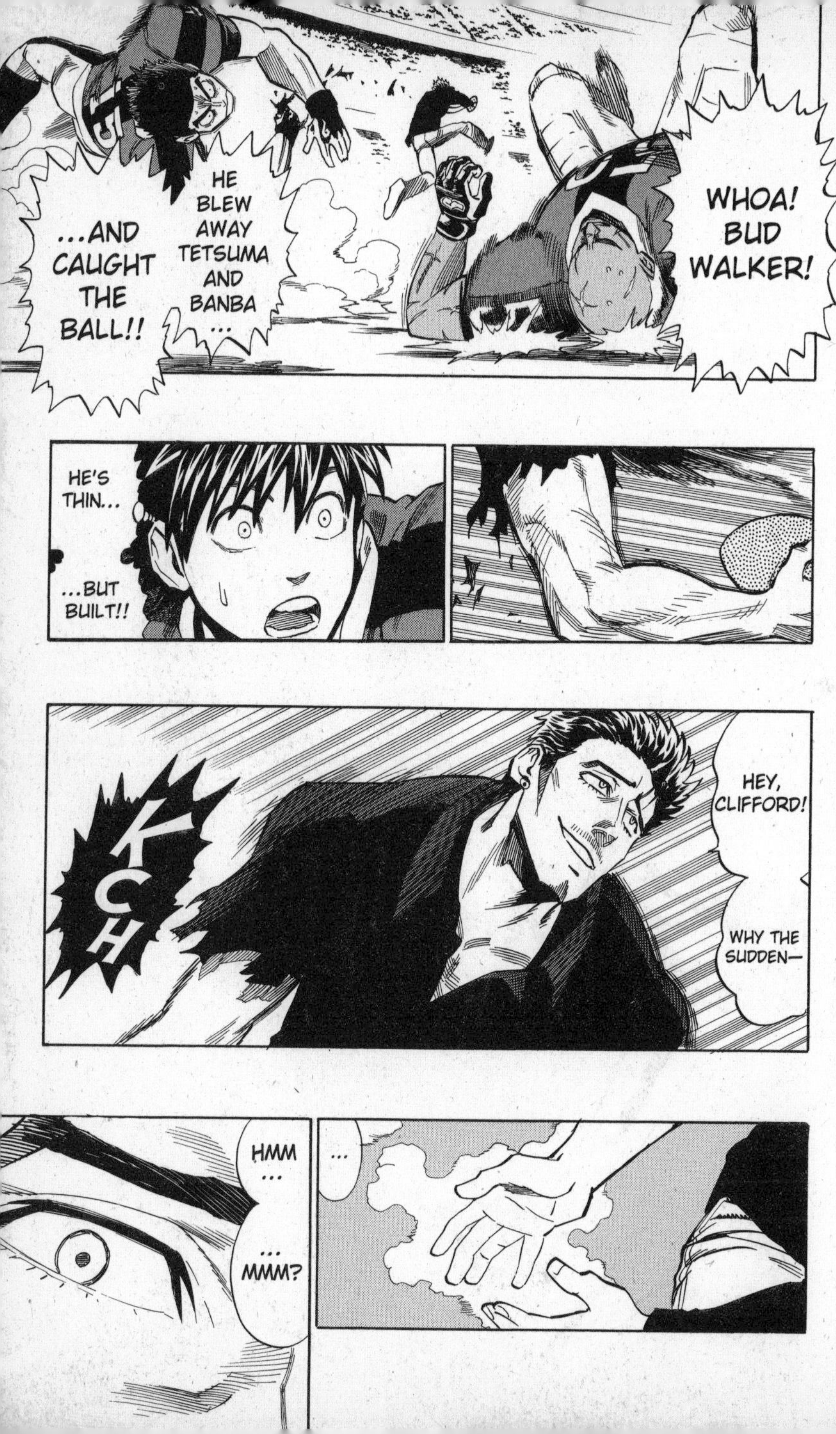
WHOA! BUD WALKER!
HE BLEW AWAY TETSUMA AND BANBA...
...AND CAUGHT THE BALL!!
HE'S THIN...
...BUT BUILT!!
HEY, CLIFFORD!
WHY THE SUDDEN—
KCH
...
HMM...
...MMM?

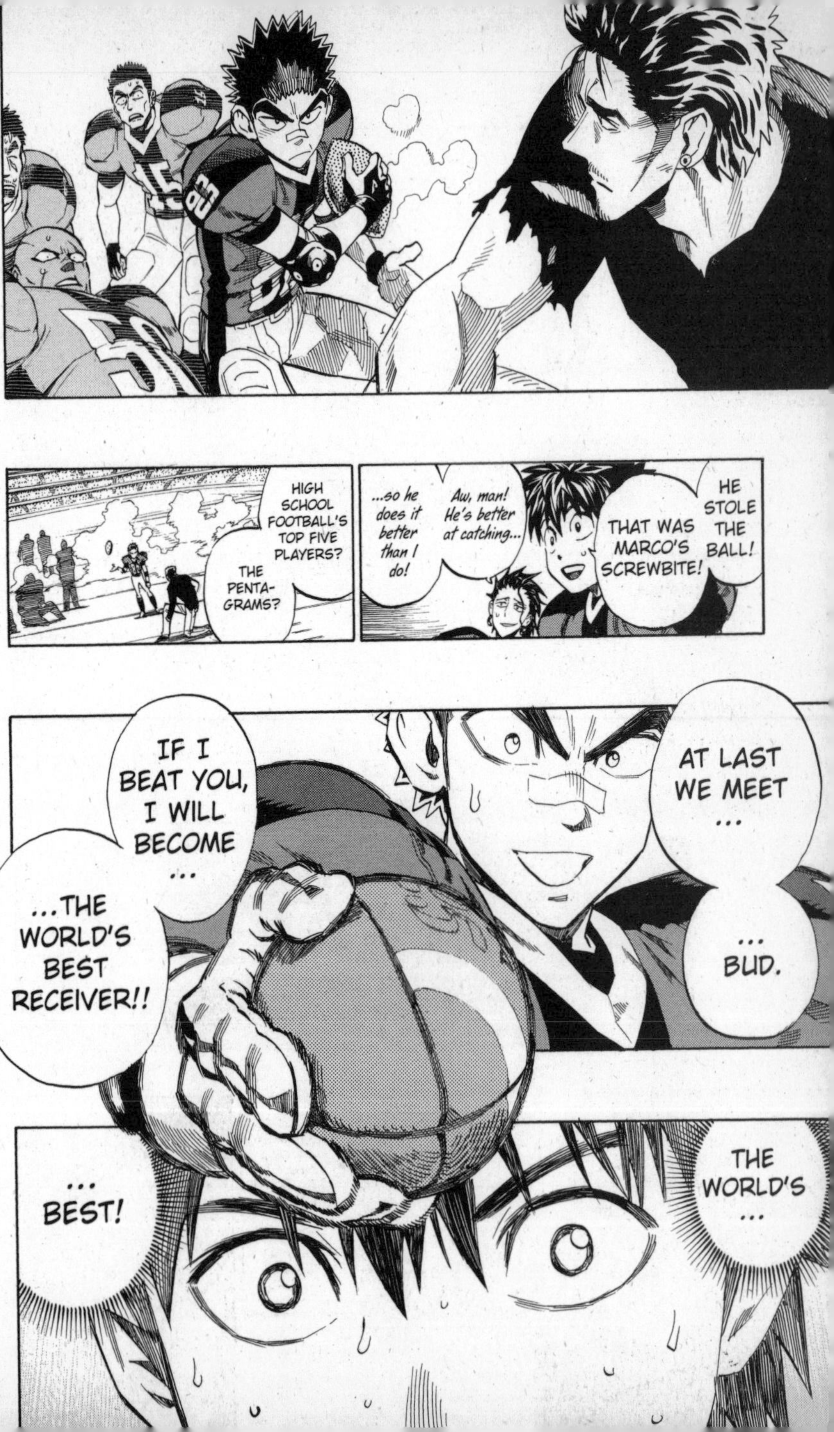
HE STOLE THE BALL!
THAT WAS MARCO'S SCREWBITE!
Aw, man! He's better at catching...
...so he does it better than I do!
HIGH SCHOOL FOOTBALL'S TOP FIVE PLAYERS?
THE PENTA-GRAMS?
AT LAST WE MEET ...
... BUD.
IF I BEAT YOU, I WILL BECOME ...
...THE WORLD'S BEST RECEIVER!!
THE WORLD'S ...
... BEST!

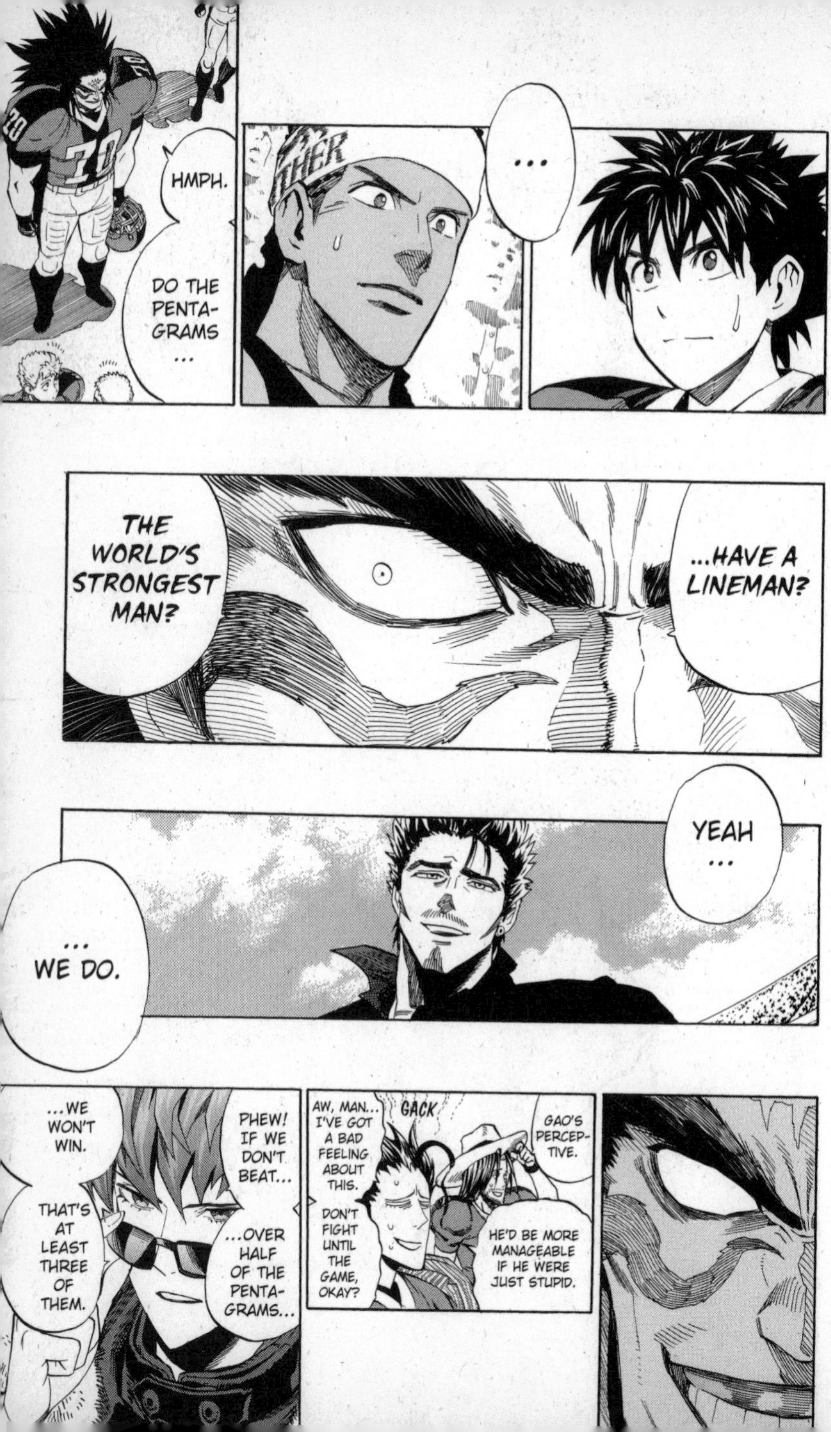
...
HMPH.
DO THE PENTAGRAMS ...
...HAVE A LINEMAN?
THE WORLD'S STRONGEST MAN?
YEAH ...
... WE DO.
GAO'S PERCEPTIVE.
GACK
AW, MAN... I'VE GOT A BAD FEELING ABOUT THIS.
HE'D BE MORE MANAGEABLE IF HE WERE JUST STUPID.
DON'T FIGHT UNTIL THE GAME, OKAY?
PHEW! IF WE DON'T BEAT...
...WE WON'T WIN.
...OVER HALF OF THE PENTAGRAMS...
THAT'S AT LEAST THREE OF THEM.

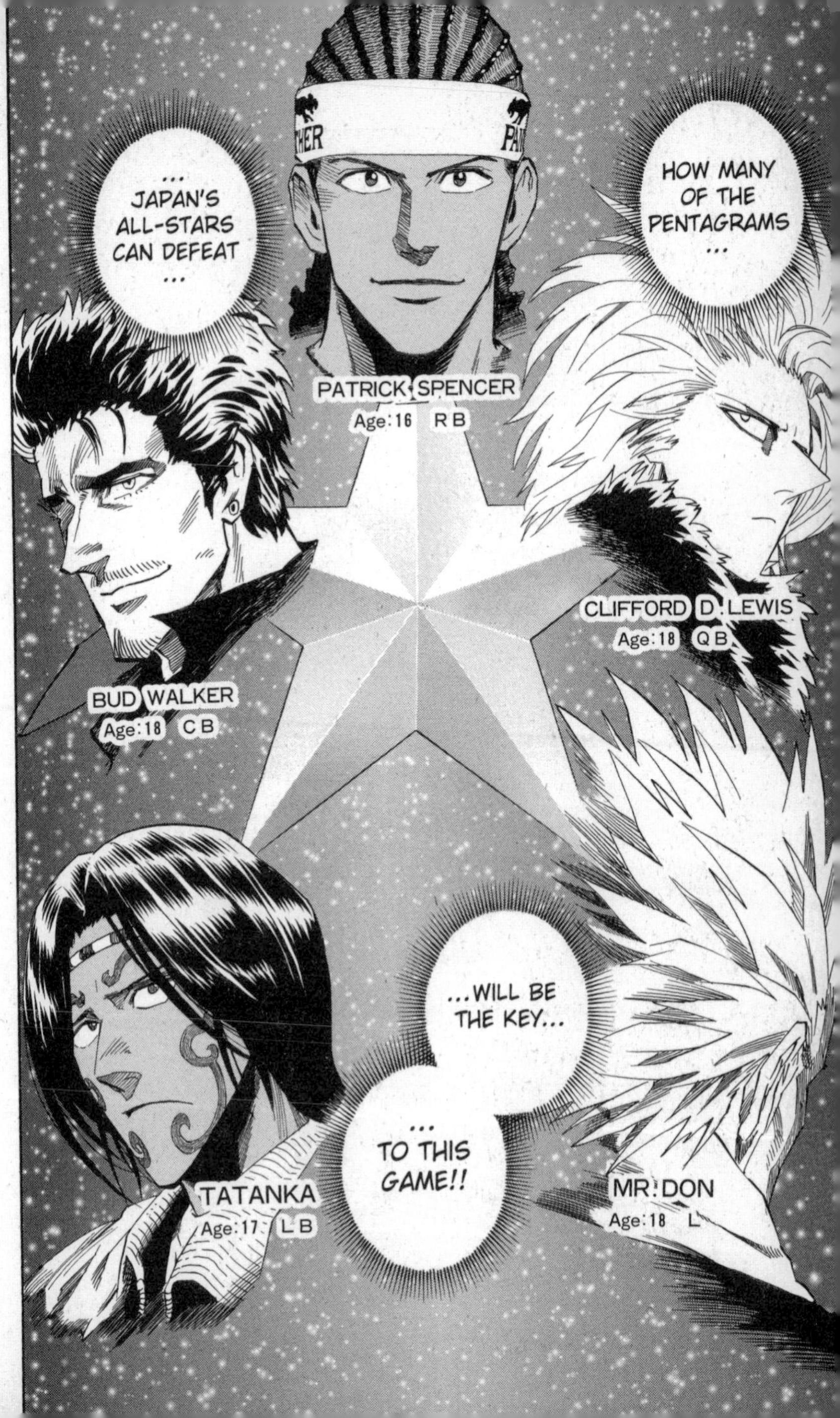

HOW MANY OF THE PENTAGRAMS ...
... JAPAN'S ALL-STARS CAN DEFEAT ...
PATRICK SPENCER
Age:16 RB
CLIFFORD D. LEWIS
Age:18 QB
BUD WALKER
Age:18 CB
...WILL BE THE KEY...
... TO THIS GAME!!
MR. DON
Age:18 L
TATANKA
Age:17 LB

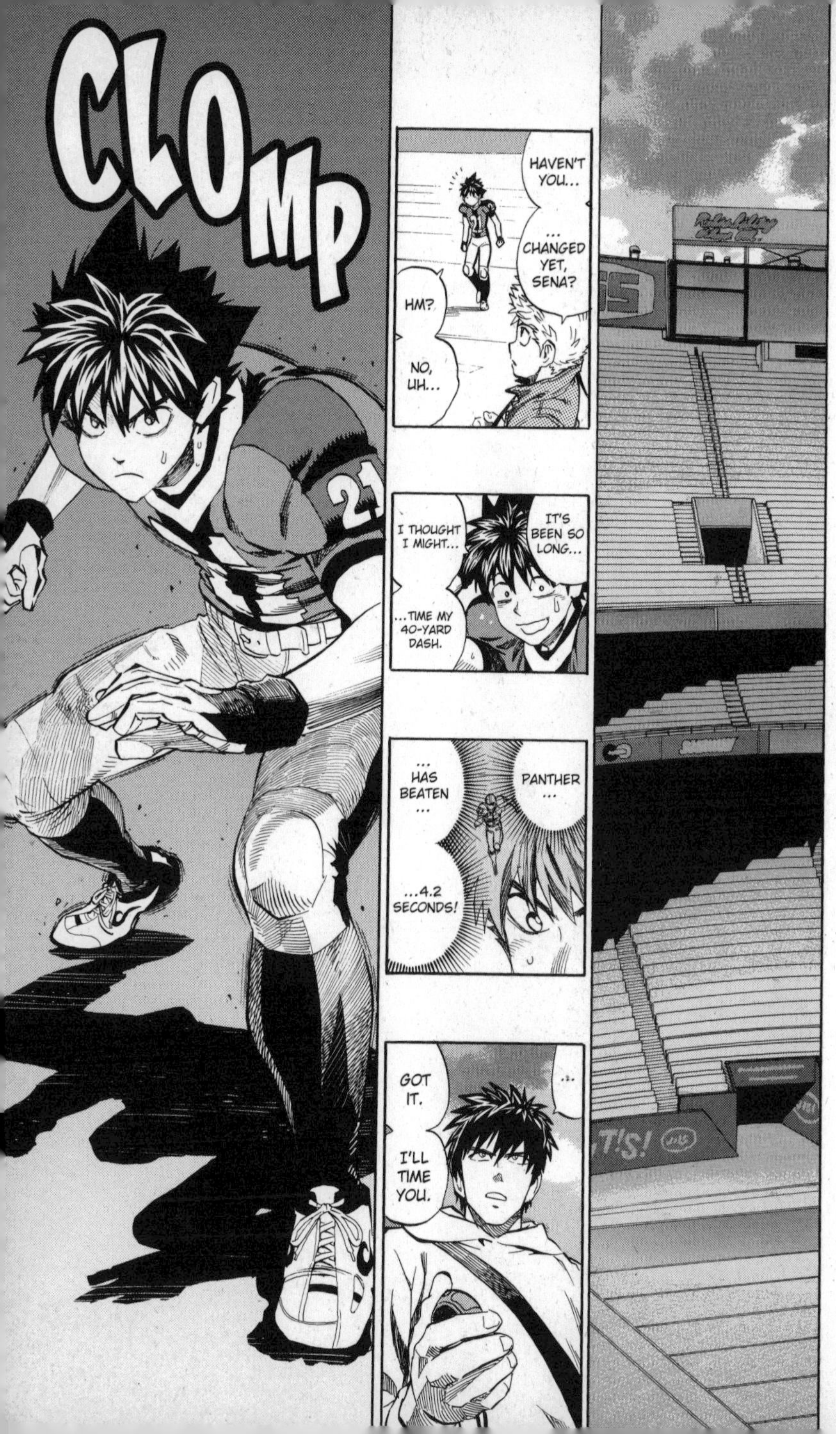
HAVEN'T YOU...
...CHANGED YET, SENA?
HM?
NO, UH...
IT'S BEEN SO LONG...
I THOUGHT I MIGHT...
...TIME MY 40-YARD DASH.
PANTHER...
...HAS BEATEN...
...4.2 SECONDS!
...
GOT IT.
I'LL TIME YOU.
CLOMP

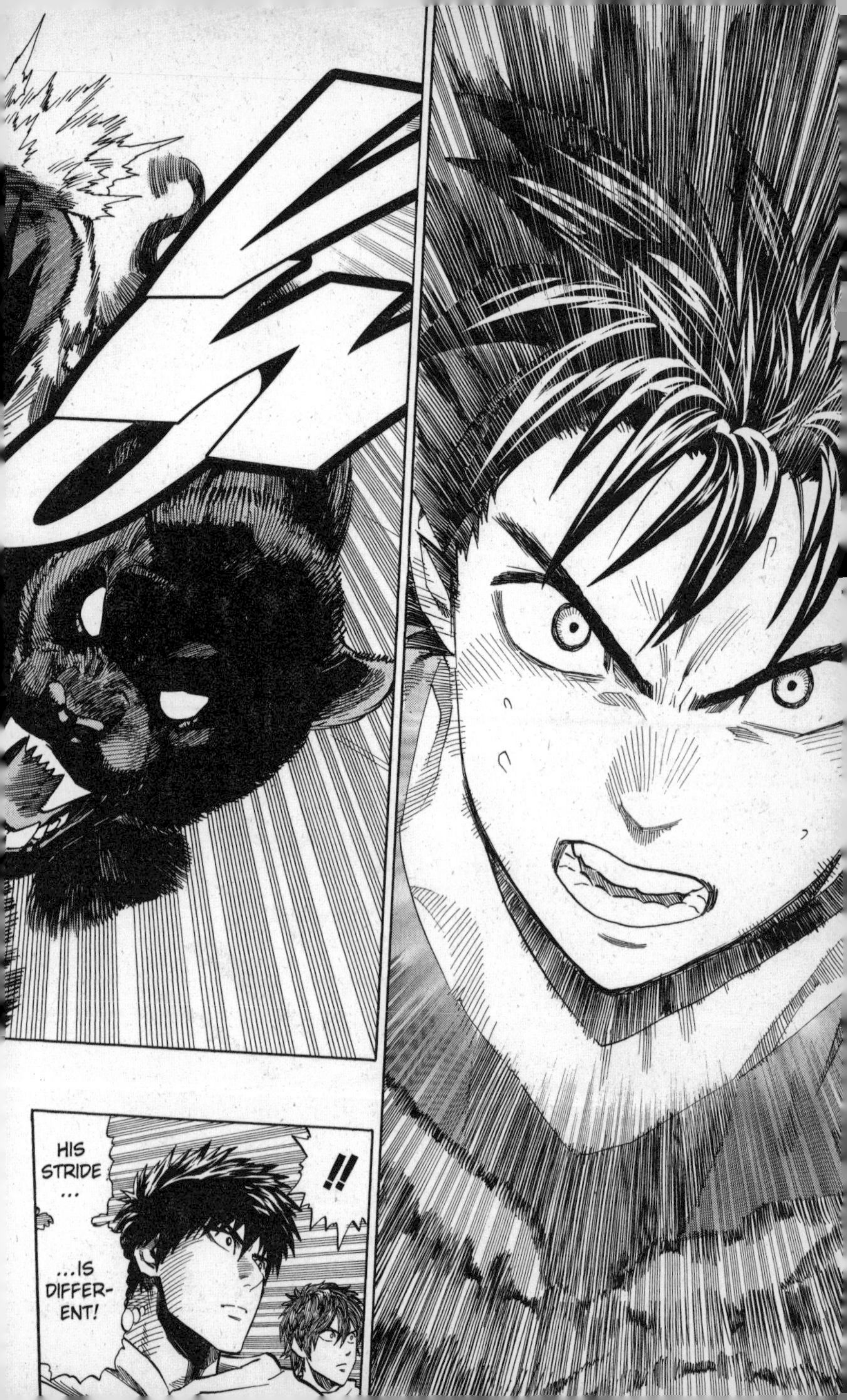
!!
HIS STRIDE...
...IS DIFFERENT!

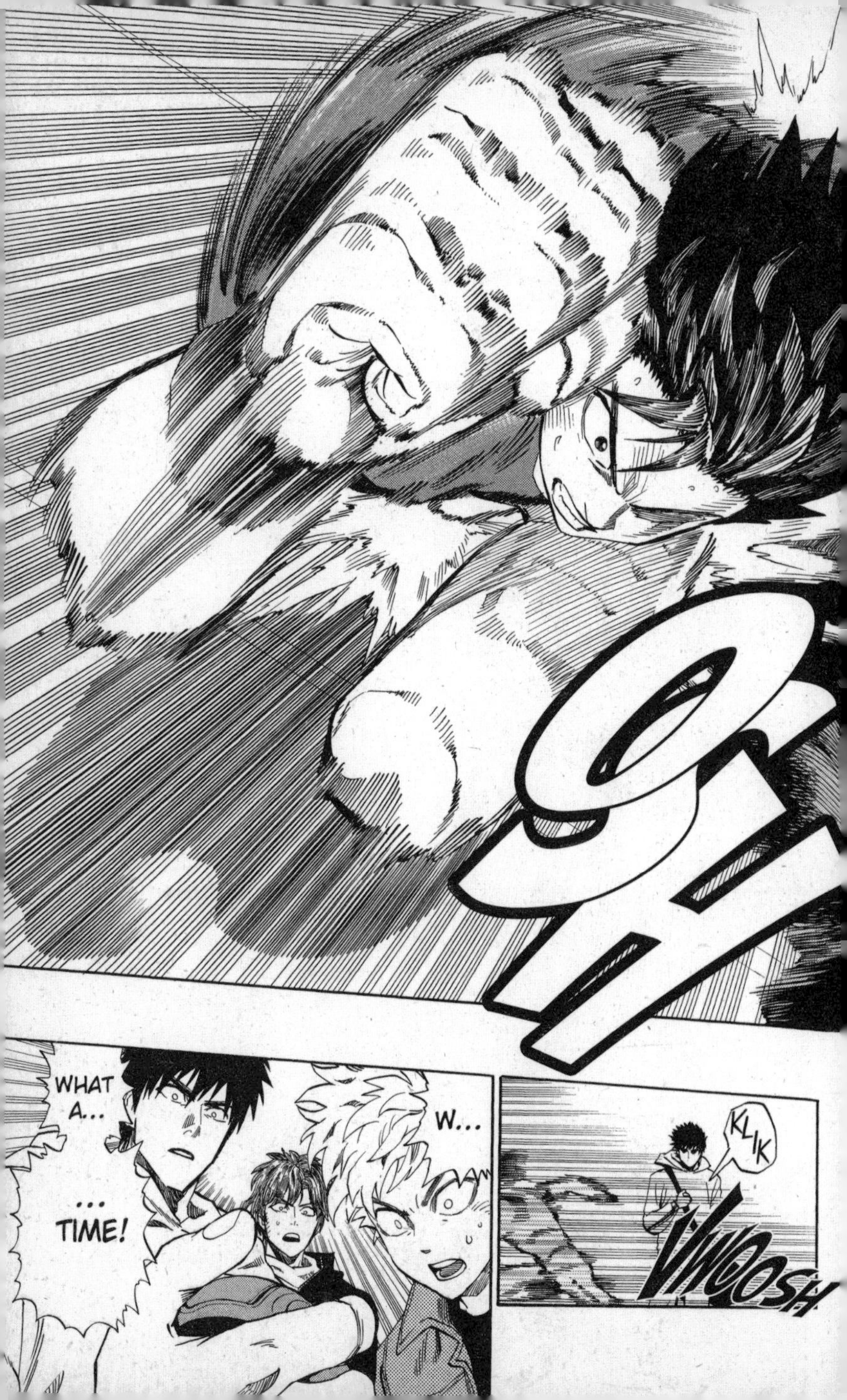
KLIK
VWOOSH
W...
WHAT A...
...TIME!

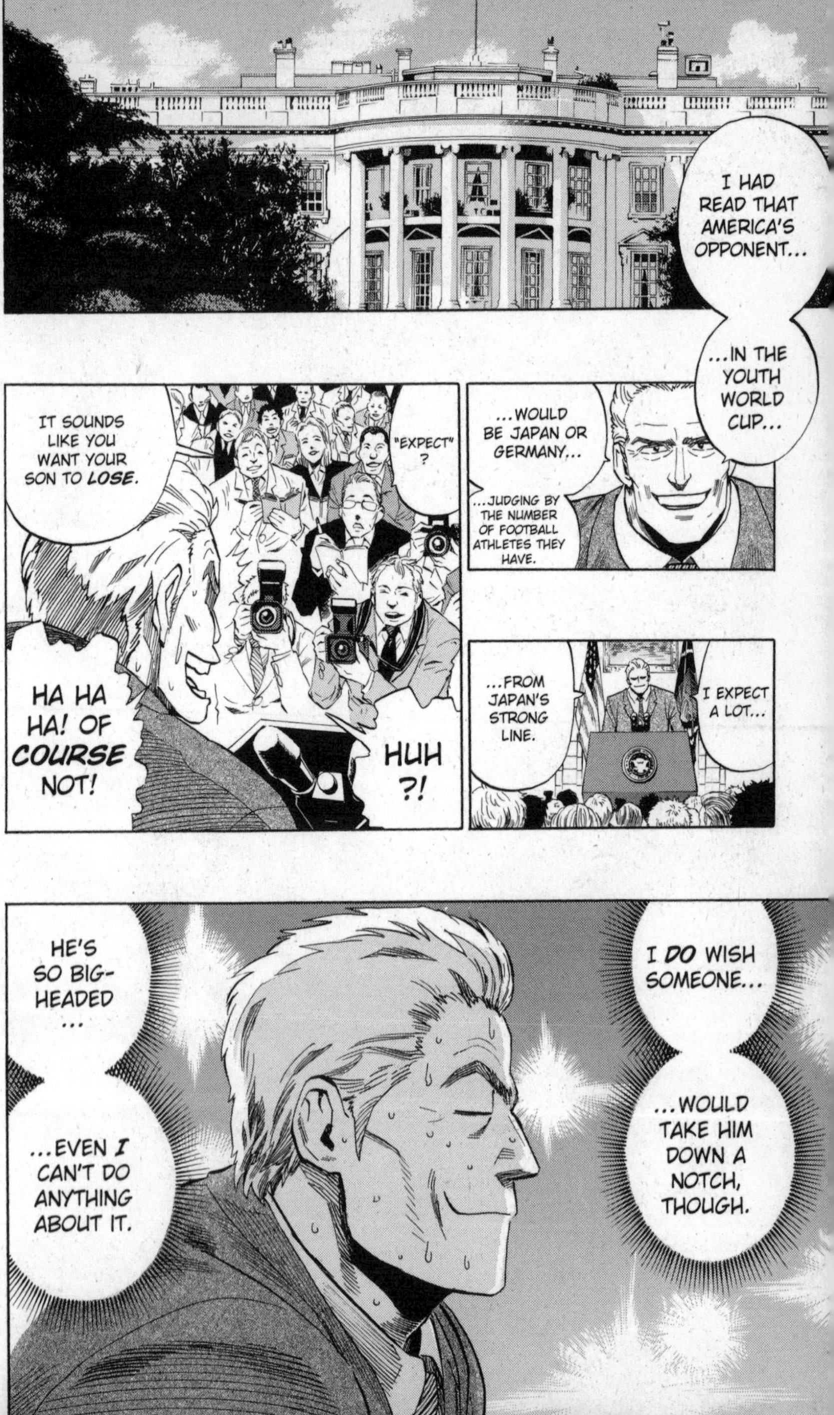
I HAD READ THAT AMERICA'S OPPONENT...
...IN THE YOUTH WORLD CUP...
...WOULD BE JAPAN OR GERMANY...
...JUDGING BY THE NUMBER OF FOOTBALL ATHLETES THEY HAVE.
I EXPECT A LOT...
...FROM JAPAN'S STRONG LINE.
"EXPECT" ?
IT SOUNDS LIKE YOU WANT YOUR SON TO LOSE.
HUH ?!
HA HA HA! OF COURSE NOT!
I DO WISH SOMEONE...
...WOULD TAKE HIM DOWN A NOTCH, THOUGH.
HE'S SO BIG-HEADED...
...EVEN I CAN'T DO ANYTHING ABOUT IT.

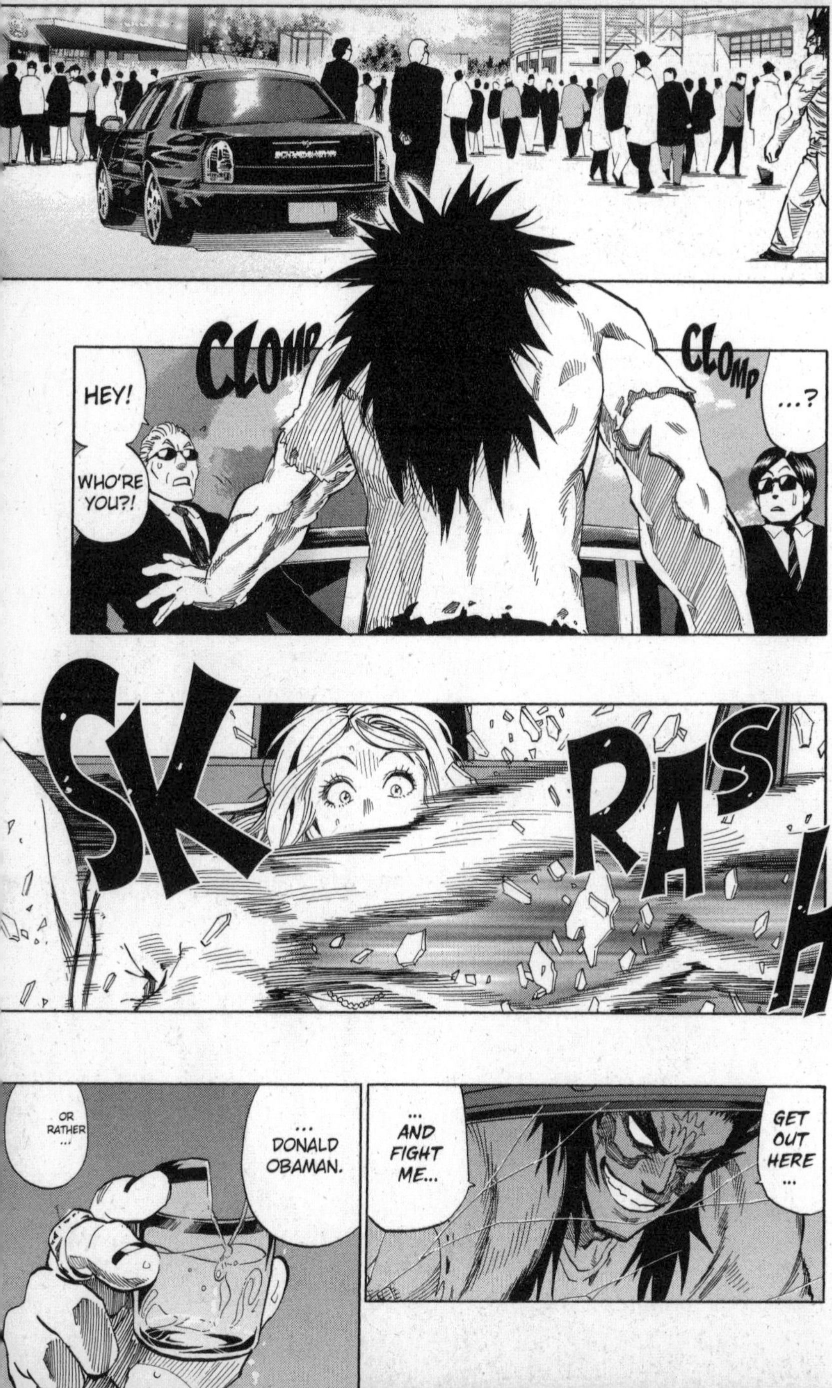
CLOMP
...?
CLOMP
HEY!
WHO'RE YOU?!
SKRASH
GET OUT HERE ...
... AND FIGHT ME...
... DONALD OBAMAN.
OR RATHER ...

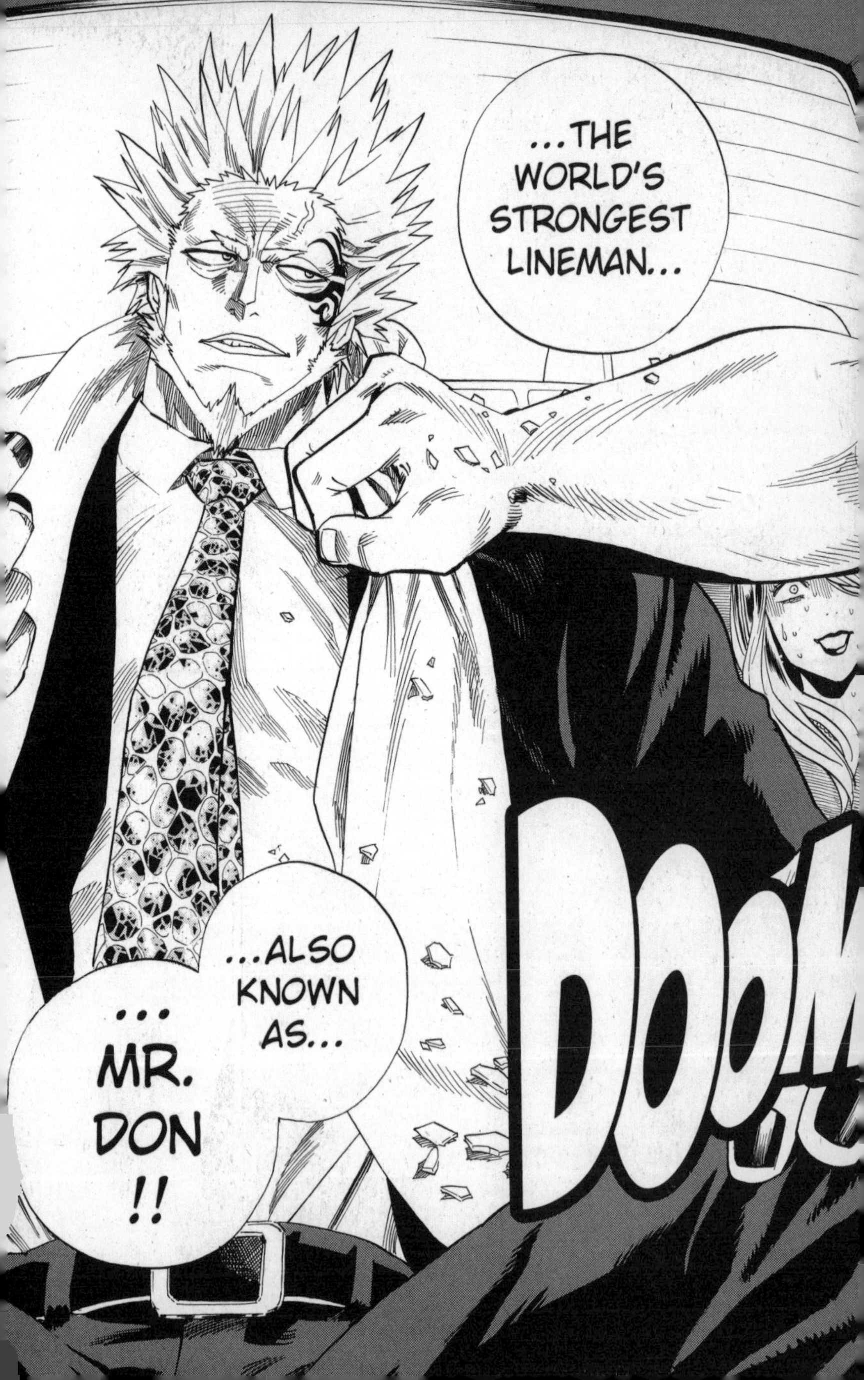
...THE WORLD'S STRONGEST LINEMAN...
DOO
...ALSO KNOWN AS...
... MR. DON !!

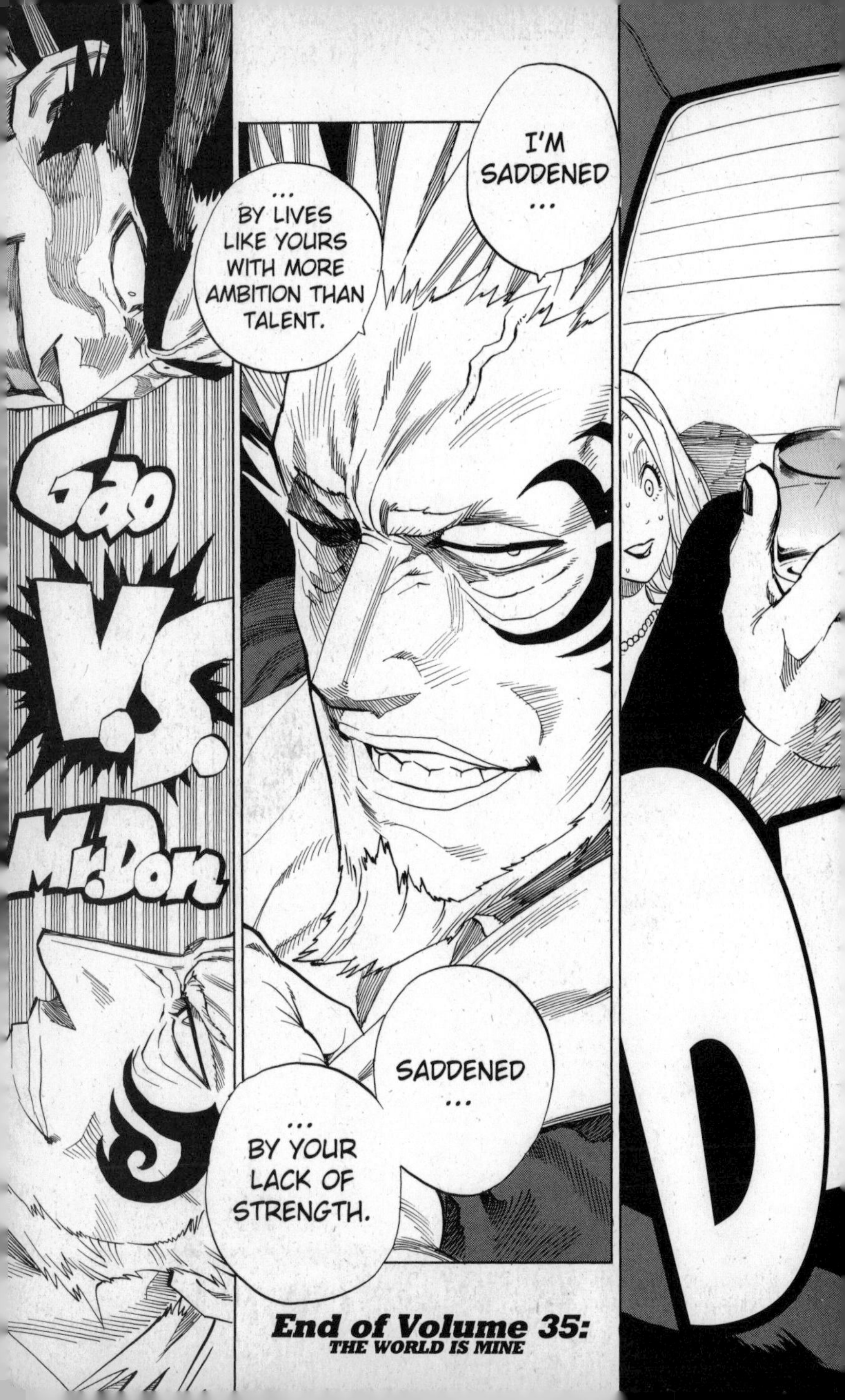
I'M SADDENED ...
... BY LIVES LIKE YOURS WITH MORE AMBITION THAN TALENT.
SADDENED ...
... BY YOUR LACK OF STRENGTH.
GAO
V.
Mr.Don
End of Volume 35:
THE WORLD IS MINE

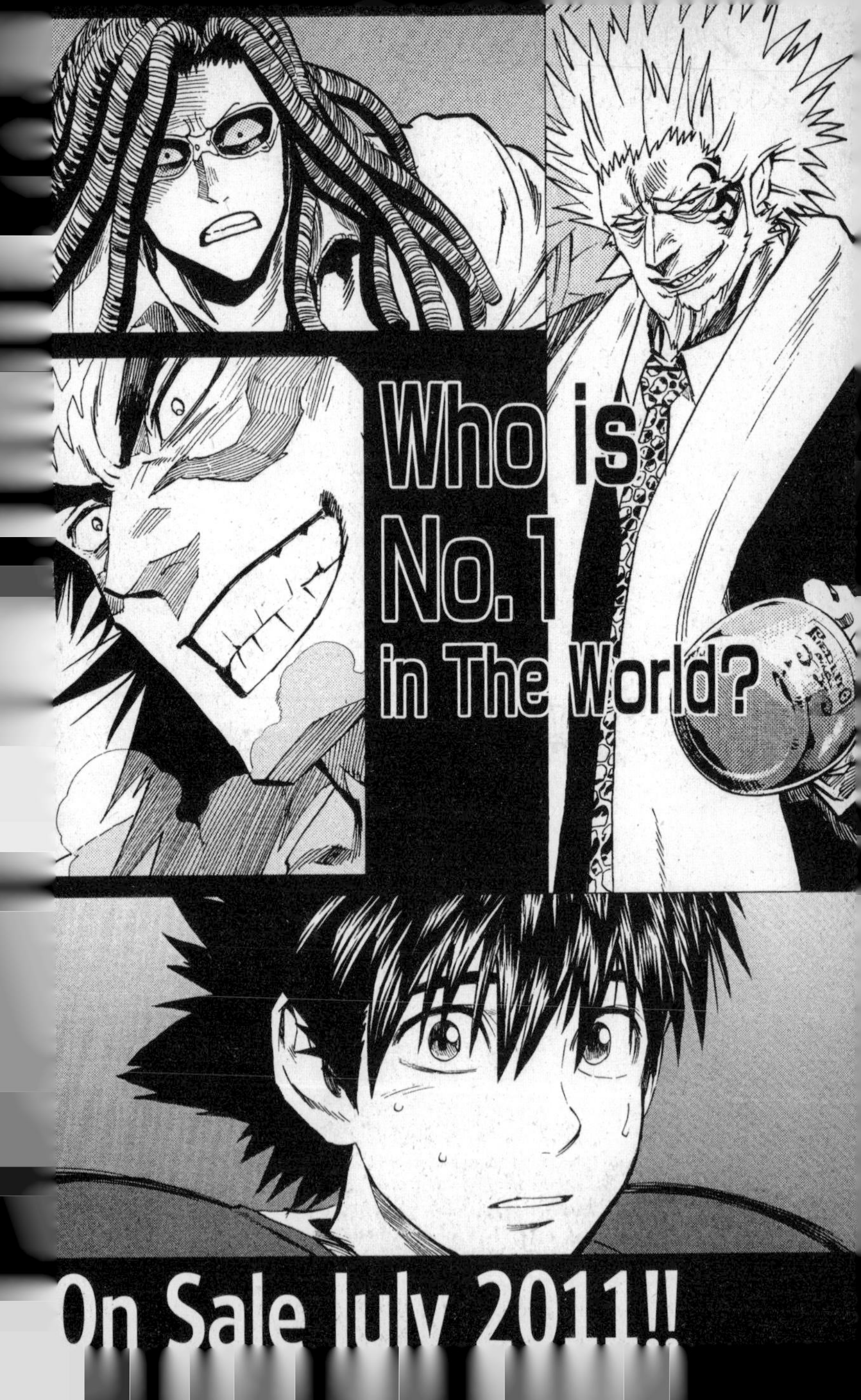
Who is
No. 1
in The World?

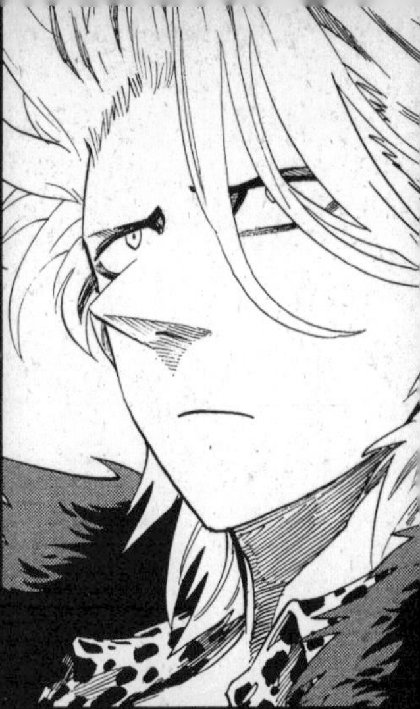

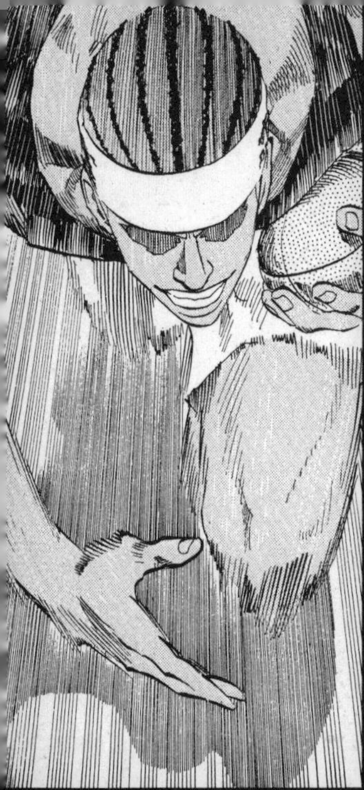

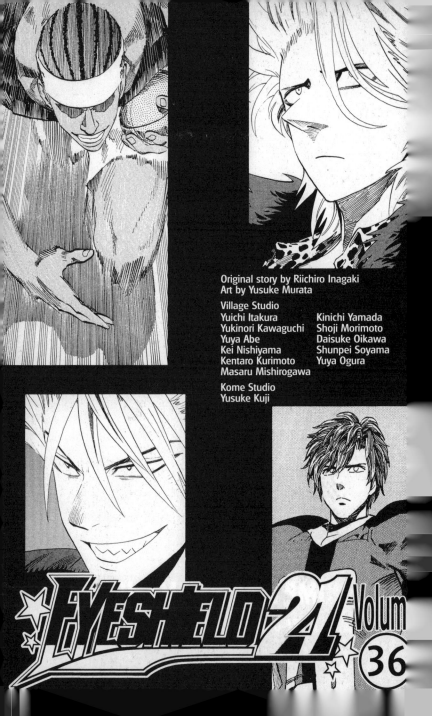

Original story by Riichiro Inagaki
Art by Yusuke Murata

Village Studio

Yuichi Itakura	Kinichi Yamada
Yukinori Kawaguchi	Shoji Morimoto
Yuya Abe	Daisuke Oikawa
Kei Nishiyama	Shunpei Soyama
Kentaro Kurimoto	Yuya Ogura
Masaru Mishirogawa	

Kome Studio
Yusuke Kuji

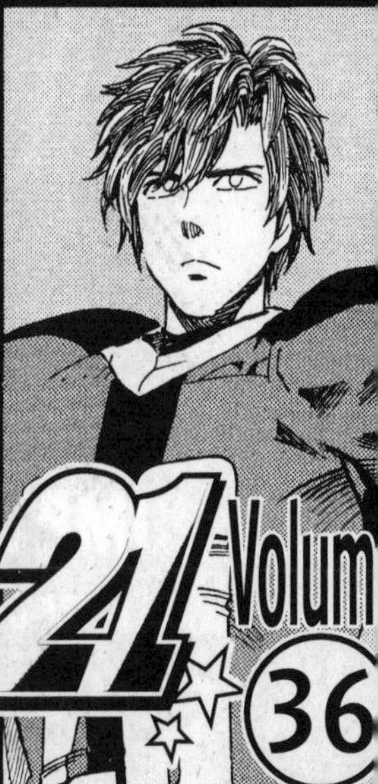

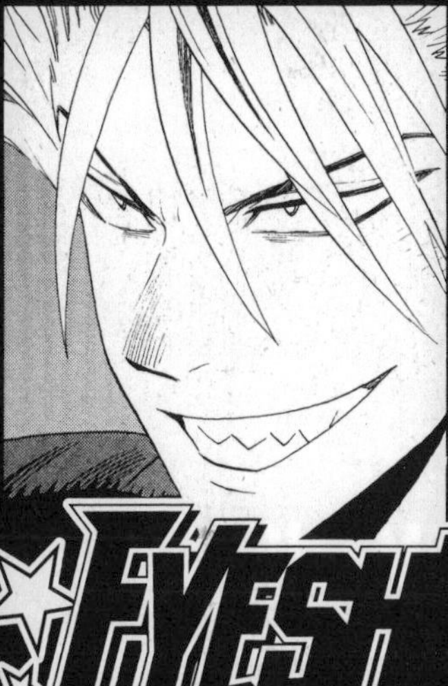

EYESHIELD 21 Volume 36